Musings from an

EX CHRISTIAN

FUNDAMENTALIST

Barbara Symons

Copyright

Dedication

To my sons Ryan, Chris and Keith who support and love me unconditionally.

To my grandchildren Nicolas, Katelyn, Cody, Cooper, Lyla, Ellie and Luci, who are a continual source of inspiration.

To Lyle who helps me find my way home.

Acknowledgements

To my longtime friend and editor **Pam Shudy**, for going above and beyond what was expected. You are a jewel.

To **Nancy Brooke** for your encouragement to write "Musings." This book is proof that a kind and encouraging word can make a difference.

To **Sam**, my formatter, who quit the project after seeing the cover, name and content of ***"Musings from an Ex Christian Fundamentalist."*** Sam, you are teaching me the invaluable lessons of unconditional love, tolerance and acceptance of what is; the foundational message of Jesus Christ. I hope that you, too, will one day step out from fundamentalism and breathe. It is a beautiful world.

Endorsements

"Barbara Symons is a person I refer to as a Divine Conduit - someone who embraces revelation as a gift of Divine Nature.

Through experience, insight, intuition, and instinct she brings clarity to what we have been told is dangerous, sometimes sinful, yet is actually High Truth, the lighted path of our natural heritage, and our direct connection to realizing the Wholeness of I Am. She knocks, undaunted; crosses the threshold of the open door fearlessly.

To label her as a guru or prophet or light-seeker is to limit her abilities to a general box that doesn't allow for the trail-blazing revelations common to ancient mystics in this now postindustrial world.

She relates the mystical, the metaphorical, and the conundrum into common understanding with skill and depth of a master, for the Soul purpose of letting the light of it shine for those willing to view it. She teaches the lessons of the universe, though it is truly the common histories of our own lives — and the truth of our birthright." **Donny Riley**

"As an ex Christian fundamentalist myself, I found it fascinating to read Barbara's first book, "Escaping Christianity, Finding Christ." The title alone impacted me as I was making my way out of a set of beliefs that I had loved and adhered to for more than forty years of my adult life. No-one was more surprised than me to find myself questioning the lifestyle I had been utterly committed to since being saved and born again at age nineteen. Those of a fundamental literalist mindset who experience this dilemma will know the level of inner conflict one endures as you bravely dare to investigate life outside the borders of fundamental evangelicalism. Some way into my personal exodus, I came across Barbara's first book and reading the title, my heart leapt.

Since then I have followed Barbara Symons' writings and musings on social media. There is something wonderful about finding someone else who has experienced similar things to oneself, someone who has already travelled further along that road who offers insight and wisdom and experience. Oh, what comfort, what solace, what encouragement to take heart and continue on the journey despite all its ups and downs! Having already read many of Barbara's musings, I look forward to seeing them compiled into a book at last.

It is an awesome thing to unravel past beliefs or indoctrinations that are no longer healthy for one's well being. As you read Barbara's stories and musings, take time to trust yourself and your own heart. Trust it's wishes and desire to find and search out where it really wants to go. And then, go with what truly resonates within you. "Musings from an Ex Christian Fundamentalist" will certainly have many helpful insights for those embarking on this journey and also for those who have already made their way out of Christian Fundamentalism. Writings and musings such as these are invaluable to the searching heart; I speak as one who knows!" **Janet Bennett**

"I met Barbara Symons through social media several years ago during my own exodus out of Christianity, and the deconstruction that inevitably followed. Her provocative posts and the amazing comments and conversations that followed, revealed that there is a deep awakening happening across the globe. It goes beyond culture, race, religion, age, gender, sexual orientation, economic status or any earthly box we've previously identified with. Humanity is truly awakening to its divinity. We are shedding the old ideas of separation and realizing that we are and always have been one. Barbara is one of those prophetic voices that, like a mirror, is revealing that each of us are (I AM) Christ swaddled or wrapped in a blanket of flesh and blood. His story is our story and our story is Hi-story ... the story of creation ... the story of love. We are that I AM ... infinite awareness manifested." **Dawn Hairston**

"Whether you are an ex-Christian or a practicing Christian, this book gives you a beautiful perspective on the Bible stories many of us grew up with. Did you ever wonder if Jonah was really swallowed up by a whale, or if Mary was really a virgin? I certainly did! Barbara's interpretation of the Bible stories sheds a whole new light on what these stories mean, and what it means to be joined in spirit with our Divine Creator." **Brenda Bender**

"Barbara Symons is a fabulous storyteller, she is able to draw you into the story so well, that you can feel the emotions and become part of the story. She is able to make you feel and understand what she is writing about. I have learned so much from her knowledge and understanding of biblical events. I love listening and reading whatever she writes." **Avis Hall**

"Barbara Symons earnest sharing of her perspectives, before and after her lifetime of experience with Fundamentalist Christianity, is like a big breath of fresh air, to say the least, for those ready to escape the chokehold of fear-based religion. But it's what she says this all leads to afterwards, for a risen co-creative humanity, that is absolutely mind-blowing!" **Joe Danna**, Author, *Reflections of my Higher Self* and *From Smoking and Vaping to Breathing*

"The teachings of Barbara Symons have such beautiful insight into the consciousness of mankind. Non-judgmental views on how we create reality with the concept of all of it having purpose." **Darryl Dement**

"Barbara Symons has the unique ability to take the perplexing metaphors from the scripture, unraveling the mysteries of the universe and the plan of the ages to bring heaven and earth together... not heaven on earth but heaven in earth!" **Edie Chill**

"Barbara's writings are deep, palatable, and have an energetic tuning that make you pause and think to help connect dots and see a bigger picture for the liberation of our freedom and wholeness, not only individually but collectively as well. What she unveils in her teachings and writings are undeniable as it is brought forth with precise clarity of knowing. It is enriching to read her material and brings an expansion to the soul that is needed for such a time as this." **Brenda Ojala**

CONTENTS

THREE

FOUR

FIVE 63

SIX 77

SEVEN 95

EIGHT 111

NINE   125

TEN   149

ELEVEN 169

TWELVE 189

THIRTEEN

207

FOURTEEN

227

FIFTEEN   245

SIXTEEN   265

SEVENTEEN 285

EIGHTEEN 303

NINETEEN   **319**

TWENTY   **339**

TWENTY-ONE   357

TWENTY-TWO   379

TWENTY-THREE   397

TWENTY-FOUR   417

Preface

Over the last several years I have had a lot of false starts trying to write my second book. I would write an article, or the beginning of a chapter and then stop and inevitably post it on social media. I suppose I was pleased with the instant gratification from those who liked what I had to say.

Often, I would wake up in the morning with a thought or a phrase that would not stop running through my head until I sat down at my computer and wrote it down. From there, words would flow, and I would think, "Aha! I have the beginning of a new book!" Well, I had several beginnings, and somewhere along the way I abandoned writing another book in favor of enjoying the inspirational process of just writing whatever was percolating in my head.

There is no unfolding of information here like a typical book, as each entry has its own beginning and end. Each thought that has been written is challenging on its own, and will encourage you to explore your own responses, feelings and ideas that it may provoke. I won't say that this material is channeled, but it certainly came from somewhere other than my conscious mind! Oftentimes, I would re-read what I had just written and be astounded at the implications of the material.

The book flows in the order beginning with what was written several years ago and ends with what was written just a few months ago. I have separated the book into twenty-four sections containing 18 entries in each section. Each section will provide for the reader a smorgasbord of ideas, thoughts and information. Each section is stand alone, and I trust that as my comprehension increased, the reader will, likewise, expand in their spiritual understanding.

I also left in some repetitive concepts. You may find that I speak of "The Word of God" or, the concept of "tithing" more than once. I did this because some concepts need reinforcement; at least they did for me. I learn through repetition.

As for content, I am a recovering Christian fundamentalist. I spent 43 years immersed into the fundamentalist system and had to go through years of deprogramming. I used to think that the Bible was to be taken literally; I now see that it is a book of mysteries that belongs to the world, not just to Christianity. There is content that will challenge the reader to see the mysteries not only within the Bible, but within life. It is hard to describe entirely, because of the diversity of topics; however, I am sure it will be a provocative read!

The book title reveals that I am no longer a Christian fundamentalist and one might ask, what am I now? I don't know the answer to that. I don't think I fit into any religion or belief and I am thankful for that. I used to have so many different beliefs that made me judgmental, arrogant, fearful *and ashamed*. I don't necessarily *believe* this or that, now I *know* this or that. I am happy to be out of the box and free to explore all sorts of ideas about the entity we call "God." I will choose knowing over belief any day.

It is noteworthy to say that Jesus did not start Christianity, and that the term "Christian" was around long before the believed birth of Jesus. Christ was a term for an enlightened person, and many held this "verb" of a title. Christianity has evolved over the centuries and millennia into something that resembles little of the teachings of Jesus.

No matter what your religious affiliation, or lack thereof, there is a lot of information in this book that will help you begin to think new, or for yourself; and more importantly, will most definitely renew your God-given intuitive mind – the mind of Christ. When I say *"think anew,"* processing information from a non-programmed mind will help set the course for new beginnings.

Foreword

For over 25 years we have been on a journey with Barbara Symons that has taken us up to the mountain tops (literally) and deep into the darkness as we asked, searched and knocked for spiritual answers. We first met Barbara in the mid 1990's as our church family began to experience what is called "deliverance." For us, deliverance was helping people gain freedom from oppressive, negative and even demonic influences. Although we lived four hours from Barbara (a stone's throw in Texas terms!) we joined Barbara in this ministry, but along with helping others gain their spiritual freedom, we realized that we were finding our own way out from an oppressive and controlling religious system. Looking back, we wondered how we got into this predicament that left us fearful of a loving God and controlled by fearful men. With retrospect, we now see that we had been indoctrinated.

We began to question amongst ourselves and even questioned the church leadership. That was the beginning of the end of our tenure in church. Eventually the three of us left our respective fellowships and found ourselves on an unfamiliar platform called FEARLESS FREEDOM. This is where we issued a collective sigh of relief and where our hearts have been forever knit in the bond of true friendship.

There is a Johnny Cash song that goes like this:

> *"I hear the train a comin'*
> *It's rolling 'round the bend,*
> *And I ain't seen the sunshine*
> *Since I don't know when..."*

This song verse tells a story that is familiar to many of us who sat on a church pew week after week, often unaware that we hadn't seen the sunshine in a very long time. However, a new day was upon us.

From this platform of freedom and fearlessness we began to seek, ask and knock on as many doors as would appear and suddenly, suddenly this charging locomotive of revelation appeared, and it didn't take much for us to be swept onboard. The three of us spent countless days, weeks and years processing information and it seemed as though we were able to breathe and breathe deeply for the first time. Revelation knowledge and new understanding were our constant companions as each one of us went through years of deprogramming. Then something wonderful happened; we regained our critical thinking.

Which leads us to this book. Barbara has spent the last twenty-five years as a collector of revelation and stories that are both provocative and life changing. This endeavor is going to be a special gift to all who read it, especially those who have been journeying out from organized religion. Every time she put her pen to paper, a new adventure began. Over the last six years, Barbara offers these *seemingly unconnected* social media entries to you in book form, a labor of love as she carries the reader along on her own unfolding path. She yields to a very determined pen, and many will feel the "earth move under their feet" as their understanding shifts out from literalism and into symbolism.

Through this book, Barbara serves us bite-sized pieces ranging to porterhouse portions of "strong meat" to help us expand our understanding of spiritual and scriptural mysteries. You can be assured that the meat has been carefully seasoned with integrity and honesty, marinating with years of soul searching, meditation, contemplation and tears. Many, many tears. We encourage you to chew the information thoroughly, otherwise you may not be able to digest these profound offerings. Take it slow and allow this shift to occur. Oftentimes the shift is palpable. If you are struggling to break free from the overbearing and restrictive nature that religion brings, this book will help you reestablish secure footing on your spiritual quest. If you are a spiritual sojourner not fettered by religion, this book will enhance the internal landscape that you are already fostering.

Barbara's path has not been an easy stroll; rather, this journey has come at a high personal price, especially the loss of friends still within the church system. We know our friend Barbara, and the integrity of her search, and we are so glad that she was willing to pay the price. The book you now hold, hold it dearly and understand what was given to drive her pen to paper.

Several times at the end of a verse in the book of Psalms we see the word "Selah." Selah is a word that admonishes us to pause and reflect upon what has just been read. We say to all of you embarking on this adventure – SELAH!

Pat Gilder and Evie Ritchie

SECTION ONE

ONE

1:1 The Coat of Many Colors

You are but one twelfth of what makes up YOU.

Because you are highly focused in being physical, you cannot perceive that there are other aspects to you. All of your physical senses are set to a frequency that only perceives this physical world. To compare, much in the same way this "one" of you has three aspects – physical body, soul or mind, and eternal spirit – you are actually a part of a system that has twelve aspects that are set to a frequency above what is typical here.

You operate within a very limited bandwidth, sentencing you to perceive, with your five senses, this physical world alone, with very few exceptions.

There are twelve others that surround YOU like a great cloud of witnesses. These twelve others are spoken of in some cultural and Biblical stories of the twelve disciples that the Christ finds, develops and gathers about itself. The Christ is the oversoul that joins you in your physical experience.

The part of you that is physical is the part that has descended into mortality, as in BAPTISM under the waters of a physical body.

This descending process has allowed for a slowing down of your vibration so that your congealed form may function in the atmosphere of time. Your clump of cells functions within the construct of celestial movement, having been born into the midst of the material universe. As you traveled through the matrix, the physical dimension opened, and you were pushed out of the womb as the flood of waters broke and welcomed you, as you drew your first breath.

This physical experience affords you great opportunity to be separate and unaware of your multidimensional nature so that you may experience being physical. You greatly desired this! It is sort of like leaving your family to attend a university in another country. You have extended yourself into the physical and material world while remaining in proximity to the other eleven.

As Joseph was cast out and away from his eleven brothers, left to die (to become mortal in time), so have you been birthed out of your celestial family. Joseph was given a coat of many colors by his father – this coat represented all of the aspects of his multidimensional self. It was this coat that was covered in the blood of a slaughtered animal to feign his death and was returned to his father as proof of his death journey.

Joseph was indeed left for dead in the hole of the Earth and covered in the blood of being human. He was captured and sold into slavery, where he would remain until the time to receive again his brothers and, indeed, all of his family, as they sojourned to him to escape the drought.

We are sold into the aspect of mortality, a slave to time and mortality … until.

My feeling is that, as we raise our personal vibration (with unconditional love, forgiveness and non-judgment), these other aspects organically join us as our frequency rises to become compatible with theirs.

1:2 Just Don't Do It

If you want to incorporate unconditional love into your spiritual practices, if you want to be inclusive in your understanding and offer forgiveness unabashedly …

then do not turn to any religion to practice these things.

Look within, to the God that has always been there. Do not look to a religion that coaxes you into submission with casual threats of separation.

Do not follow a God that is in an epic battle with Satan.

Do not follow a God that teaches you to separate yourselves from others.

Do not follow a God that involves himself in political debates.

Do not follow a God that takes sides.

Do not follow a God that will shut the door on you for eternity and burn your flesh with fire … forever.

Do not follow a God that withholds eternity from you because you did not get sprinkled with water.

Do not follow a God that says you must babble in other tongues.

Do not follow a God that institutionalizes himself for money.

Do not follow a God that requires you to pay a tithe to a building.

Just don't do it.

1:3 Mental Health and Spiritual Warfare

I was flipping through the channels yesterday afternoon, when I saw a *Dr. Phil* promo about their upcoming guest. She was homeless, with a lot of debt, living off of her enabling children, who had been increasingly concerned about their mother's mental health. In short, she is a fundamentalist Christian deeply involved in spiritual warfare against the Devil. She fancies herself an advisor of sorts to Trump and Putin, giving them advice on her Facebook page; everything from who to fire in Trump's administration to launching attacks against perceived foes. Putin is in love with her, she says, and he communicates with her through the sort of ties that he wears with his suits. She says that the Lord told her that she and Putin would marry and that she would bear him a child.

As the show progresses, Dr. Phil reveals that the woman had been the victim of several rapes, as a young teen, that left her traumatized, and that she was showing classic signs of Erotomania; a disorder where a person believes – with strong delusion – that someone else is in love with them. He offers her counseling.

This struck a little close to home. Back in the early 1990s, I was deeply involved in spiritual warfare. As we convened to pray, we compared notes to see how our efforts might be influencing world events. We were amazed at how dark the world was, with Satan pulling strings behind the scenes, and how fortunate and favored we were to be able to see the truth of the matter.

I remember, with great detail, one time where a friend found a stray dog and took her in. My friend showed me satanic markings on the dog's belly that had been tattooed in place, identifying this dog as a "watcher" where local Satanists would, through astral projection into the dog, be able see into our intercessory prayer times (if the dog was in the room with us), in order to counter our strategic prayer. She had performed an exorcism on the dog.

It seemed a little far-fetched, but I thought they must know something I didn't. I have since learned that when a female dog is spayed, they will tattoo the lower abdomen, letting future animal care folks know that she had already had the surgical procedure done.

I can name a few accounts where females within our group were delusional, having the same issues with Erotomania. There are so many hurting people out there who run to the church to find a cure for their traumatic histories. I ministered to hundreds of souls for over a decade, where they exchanged one form of mental illness for another – fundamentalism.

Escaping Christianity ~ Finding Christ is my book about my journey out of Christianity and my return to critical thinking. It brings into focus the sector of Christianity called "fundamentalism" that believes in the literal and rigid interpretation of the Bible and that embraces doctrines and dogma (unquestioned beliefs) that endorse control, intolerance, division and judgment. There are millions of souls who have been hurt, and even damaged by this system. It is to those individuals within this system, who have been held captive spiritually and emotionally, that I seek to bring light and understanding.

1:4 What Kind of Person Are You?

What kind of person are you, that experiences intolerance and then practices it yourself?

Do you hate tailgaters and then tailgate someone?

I remember, back in the very late 1980s, when the AIDS "epidemic" was the hot topic on news stories, and gay people were targeted as the Devil. During that time, gay people faced an incredible amount of intolerance and, in some respects, seen as justifiably so – after all, wouldn't they threaten the "normal" definition of relationships, and couldn't they, if left unchecked, infect the population with an incurable disease?

Remember all that hype???

And now, all the polarization that comes with politics ... there seems to be no end in this.

And, of course, those now labeled as "anti-vaxers" – those not wanting to vaccinate their children – are feeling the same intolerance as gay people in the late 1980s because of the fear-based threat of spreading worldwide disease.

There are opportunities for intolerance out there, and there are remedies abundant. If you have been shown intolerance, isn't it love to practice tolerance rather than intolerance? Remember the Golden Rule???

One such remedy is to choose LOVE, above all.

Intolerance is about as ugly a word as there is. This eleven-letter word is responsible for all the hate in the world. It separates family from family, friends from friends, and neighbors from neighbors.

To whom have you shown intolerance? Who have you judged because they think differently than you?

1:5 Anatomy of Forgiveness

Yesterday, I was talking to someone who told me that she has made the decision to forgive daily, a situation that hurts her daily, as the situation is ongoing and has been for seven years. She cannot change the situation, so she extends her heart every day and forgives every day, so that she may continue to LOVE every day.

I told her of my choice to likewise, forgive daily. If I don't forgive, I build a wall between me and the ability to love and to receive love, and not just from the person who causes me pain.

Unforgiveness is like focusing on an object that is close in range for an extended period of time, and when I finally take my eyes off of it, everything in the distance is a little fuzzy. My eyes must get used to focusing outward.

When we remain focused on our pain (in-looking), it prohibits us from having a healthy outlook. When all we can see is the object that is closest to us – our pain point – it prohibits us from seeing and perceiving the love that is in and out there for us.

When we don't forgive, it does something detrimental to our energetic body – it closes doors in the fragile human energetic exchange with others and allows all kinds of dysfunction to set up residence in our minds, and even in our bodies' health. When we shut down to love, a door closes us off to receiving love from others. Eventually, that vital human energetic exchange intrinsically knows NOT TO SEND LOVE TO A CLOSED RECEPTACLE. It will simply go around you.

This act of forgiveness does not change the person causing us pain; it changes us. It allows us to walk through life and affords us the choice to experience the contrasting hues of being human.
Forgiveness means that you keep your heart open to all of what life has to offer – even heartache. Forgiveness allows you to FEEL your way through life. Herein lies our ultimate purpose.

1:6 Act of Death

This is a mystery.
Forgiveness is an act of death.
As we abandon our right to be right,
We recognize that we are not victims, but rather, participants,
Forgiveness is an act of awakening,
Something only the ego can do,
For it is the unjust steward that retains debt, and thereby "squanders wealth"
Rather than to let it go.
Forgiveness is an invaluable resource that must be spent
In this life.
Forgiveness signifies that we are going to the cross
To die to this life,

And to apprehend the resurrection that is promised.
It is a trifold death as the thieves that have stolen from us
The body, the soul – the aspects that allow us to experience pain
That have robbed us of our peace, our joy, our dignity
Dies with us as self intersects Divinity.
Your need to be justified fades in the light of a new day.
Yes, go to your cross, go quickly
And remember, there is life after this death.
Remember …

1:7 I Had to Chuckle

I had to chuckle the other day when I read a message that encouraged people not to read various books out there, but to read the Bible instead. I laughed because I had said the same thing back when I was "churched". I felt that people would be deceived if they read too much.

I understand the thinking to warn people because I was there, in the same position, wielding the same fear. After all, new information might undermine my dogma. Christians need consensus to feel safe. Without consensus there is fear. The Bible talks about reading too many books, that there is no end to it, which is true. But that same passage does not recommend reading only the Bible, as the Bible was not in the form of a book back then.

We are encouraged, however, to turn within to hear the still small voice of the Divine. We are living epistles, are we not?

Once the voice of the Divine is heard, there is no end to the revelation found within this church of flesh and blood constructed with bone and sinew. The ecclesia is commonly referred to as the "called out ones" and is actually a reference to those who will trumpet the words heard from within – to "call them out" to the masses. This is the true form of evangelism and is what caused Jesus to change Simon's name to Peter – the ability to hear, receive and to trumpet out Divine messages from within the walls of the biological church. Messages from the source of all; the Father. It is on this "rock" that we will be built into the habitation of the Most High.

The Divine does not dwell in structures made by man – the church did not exist in its present form back then, and neither did the Bible. I choose to read the Bible and other books, and I will not fear those who say that there is deception out there. Any voice that incites fear is not speaking with the voice of perfect love, for perfect love casts out and away ALL FEAR.

1:8 Worshipping Jesus

Speaking from my experience within Christianity, it is the norm to worship Jesus. However, I can see no instruction from Jesus to worship him. There are scriptures that say, "Every knee will bow, every tongue confess that Jesus Christ is Lord." However, I see this mystically in that I must humble myself (the ego within) so that I might recognize that my Divine nature is master of my body. I yield to my higher self, that of Divinity, the Father (progenitor) within, so that I might become the helpmate Divinity desires.

Jesus compared himself to the serpent on the pole, and if this is accurate, then we must realize from the scriptural account, that when the people in the wilderness began to worship the snake on the pole rather than "look" to it, it was destroyed by an edict of God. Christianity is in a state of implosion with 6 million people leaving the fundamentalist structure each year. We must awaken to see the patterns so beautifully expressed in scripture rather than to follow winds of doctrine that are not in keeping with the truth.

It should be said also that the Old Testament (old consciousness) pattern was to carry the presence of God on their shoulders in the Ark of the Covenant, so worship to an external force is a pattern. But in the New Testament (new consciousness) Jesus told us that God does not dwell is man-made structures, but rather dwells within us. So, we see with the Old and the New Testaments that our human consciousness is migrating; it is on the move. We err when we try to pull patterns past their season of relevance.

True worship is becoming the object of your admiration.

1:9 Animal Sacrifice or Emotional Sacrifice?

Concerning the practice of animal sacrifice in the Old Testament and other spiritual texts, animals are representative of human emotions, and how they play a central role in our conscious evolution.

Could it be that this ritual, when viewed metaphorically, is actually our willful act to leave behind old, outdated, and irrelevant consciousness, forsaking it so that we may move forward in our own evolutionary process? Not the death of an animal, but rather the death of an aspect of our humanity whose life's blood must be shed.

1:10 Who?

> *"He who will not eat of my body and drink of my blood, so that he will be made one with me and I with him, the same shall not know salvation."*
>
> Mithras
> (Dated from 76 BC, along with other
> messiah myths, amalgamated from
> other myths dating back as far as 4500
> BC.)

> *"Unless you eat of the flesh of the Son of Man and drink his blood, you have not life in yourselves. Whoever eats my flesh and drinks my blood will live in me and I in him."*
> Jesus

Think for yourself.

1:11 It is Wonderful to Behold Our Corporeal Unfolding

It is wonderful to behold our corporeal unfolding as we all come to the same conclusion; that is, Christ in us! Transition is such a key word this hour. As we view the scriptures, we see that it is all about migration, navigation and pioneering to the next place in our human consciousness journey that we are to apprehend. All of our experiences are useful in their order.

They failed to see the pattern behind the story of the serpent on the pole in the wilderness, worshipping it instead when they were told only to "look to it." We, too, will perish in the wilderness until the next generation is birthed; the ones who will grasp the pattern and intent of the story. We will remain in milk when we see scripture literally, worshipping external forces outside of ourselves and never coming to maturity.

True worship is an act of becoming and comes with the willingness to migrate out of old constructs of thinking. The rest is up to this fledgling seed of Christ, the pearl of great price found within the husk of the human shell, to lead and guide us out of these wilderness places.

1:12 The Tithe of Meat

According to Malachi 3, we rob God when we exploit wage earners, widows and orphans and in so doing we rob God. (Where is God? In the wage earner, the widow and the orphan).

When the system seeks money from people to sustain itself, IT IS ROBBING GOD.

"How have we robbed you" the system asks, and God replies, "In tithes and offerings."

The tithe is to come into a storage house where EVERYONE WILL HAVE MEAT, MEAT, MEAT in season. NO ONE GOES HUNGRY. The tithe is not for million-dollar buildings and six figure salaries, light bills etc.

The tithe is to feed people.

THE TITHE IS TO FEED PEOPLE.

We rob God (in people) when we use the money extracted from wage earners for anything other than to FEED PEOPLE.

How many times were we taught this scripture in a twisted and distorted way?

Now for the metaphoric interpretation: MEAT is the teaching that comes from Melchizedek …

The tithe is the Melchizedek order given through the loins of Abraham to Melchizedek. It is seed given over to the priesthood so that, in time, roughly 10% of the population of the Earth (from Abraham's seed) will hold within their frame a higher order of energy sufficient to bridge the gap between dimensional boundaries. They are the flesh and blood bodies that have been given to this order of priests – priests who stand as mediators between this age and the next.

> *Though he were a Son, yet learned he obedience by the things which he suffered; And being made perfect, he became the author of eternal salvation unto all them that obey him; Called of God a high priest after the order of Melchizedek, of whom we have many things to say, and hard to be uttered, seeing ye are dull of hearing. For when for the time ye ought to be teachers, ye have need that one teach you again which be the first principles of the oracles of God; and are become such as have need of milk, and not of strong meat. For every one that uses milk is unskillful in the word of righteousness: for he is a babe. But strong meat belongs to them that are of full age, even those who by reason of use have their senses exercised to discern both good and evil.* (Hebrews 5:8-14)
>
> *Therefore, leaving the principles of the doctrine of Christ, let us go on unto perfection.* (Hebrews 6:1)

This MEAT is strong indeed, and there is enough for all through the tithe.

Are you one of them?

1:13 The Journey of Spiritual Awakening

Everyone must make the journey of spiritual awakening alone. It is a solitary path that requires intuitive advantage – and that, unlike intellect, cannot be borrowed from another.

1:14 The Ego Crucified

We may always state what it is that we want from another human being, but their giving or withholding of our request should not influence our well-being – otherwise. our happiness is dependent on another person. If we are affected by their negligence to honor our request, we have engaged in present-age technologies, knowing good from evil, right from wrong, pleasure from pain, receiving from withholding.

The knowing of these things, and the judgment between them, is the mechanism that maintains and sustains this present age; for what we focus upon and give our emotional currency toward, we create. Therefore, if we focus upon the gift being withheld and feel the emotions of lack, we create more situations that create the same feelings as lack – in fact, we create MORE LACK.

Fifth dimensional technology (or kingdom mentality) is this: Finding joy, peace and contentment, regardless of our interaction with others – this is the next step in our evolutionary process, as enlightened beings.

It is also the first step in crucifying the egocentric self, which is the mystical understanding and underlying message of the cross.

The cross is not for one man, but for all.

1:15 Linear vs. Cyclical

How is it that people we consider ancient had more knowledge of sophisticated celestial movements? And that these same ancient souls left for us clues within ancient stone structures that mapped, charted and calculated these celestial movements that occur within mammoth swaths of time?

How can it be, if we – being the most advanced – are reduced by those that lived thousands and thousands of years ago?

We have a problem, because we think in terms of linear time – a straight line, where things that happened a long time ago reflected barbaric men, barbaric tools and barbaric cultures. We fail to discern that time occurs within CYCLES, and that the planetary hosts experience golden ages and dark ages.

We have had times when things were golden, and human beings lived for centuries and centuries before their bodies gave out. It is those people who left the future human race clues (in megalithic structures) to these giant swaths of time, so that we, too, upon awakening from the dark plunge into baseness, would see the truth of our planet and that of the galaxy, and indeed, the universe around us.

This plunge is seen in the figurative interpretation of BAPTISM. Baptism is NOT ABOUT GETTING WET. According to the world premiere expert on interpreting myths from all cultures and religions, water represents human consciousness. Within the ritual, then, the being is submerged under the waters of human consciousness, where the divine breath is held until the time of awakening.

The same can be said about taking the last supper or communion. The bread is "broken," which symbolizes the divine laying aside its immortal essence, "breaking" it, so that it may be swallowed up within human consciousness for a time. The same symbolism is hidden within the story of Jonah and the great fish.

We are not so sophisticated when we refuse to see the figurative, and instead, embrace the literal interpretation of such things. This failure will keep us right where we are – forever seeking a savior outside of ourselves, and failing to see that the Christ is internal, and awakening only when summoned by the human ego that has willingly been crucified and resurrected.

Jesus continually stated that we should "lift our eyes" to understand, and spoke in rich, figurative language called "parables."

History vs. mystery, and the consideration of which is the call to awaken.

1:16 These Two are Necessary

There is no substitute beyond radical acceptance of the way things are and absolute forgiveness of the way things were. These two are necessary steppingstones that lead to the bridge of the age to come.

1:17 Writing from the Heart

There is a stronghold of misconception in this country – that we are a nation founded on Judeo-Christian principles – Where does it say that? It is my understanding that this nation was founded on freedom, especially spiritual freedom; principles that allow the expression of faith in any form. This, however, seems to have been forgotten when we decided to construct the infrastructure of this great nation on the backs of slaves and to separate ourselves from those who believed differently than we. We are a nation of schism; religiously, politically and socio-economically. Back in 2006, I was told that, for this reason, America was under restriction, much like a child is under its parents' rule and supervision. We are spiritually immature. There is a scripture that says this:

> *1What I am saying is that as long as an heir is underage, he is no different from a slave, although he owns the whole estate. 2The heir is subject to guardians and trustees until the time set by his father. 3So also, when we were underage, we were in slavery under the elemental spiritual forces of the world. 4But when the set time had fully come, God sent his Son, born of a woman, born under the law, 5to redeem those under the law, that we might receive adoption to sonship.* Galatians 4

Because we have stripped an entire race of their freedom to build our own fiefdoms, we ourselves have become slaves and are no better than children under tutelage. We propagate a broken and delusional society that cannot foster vision from within, ever looking outward to our governors. We are babes that need milk and that cannot suffer to chew on the meat of higher understanding. We are mortals under the elemental forces of the world.

Time to grow up and to lay aside those things of adolescence. America, stop listening to those overseers that seek to control your thought. You are free. You are free. Move on! You are an heir to ALL THINGS.

1:18 No Mistakes

I don't know about you, but I find all of my terminology changing. Former terms bring my mind to former things. Some say the terms sound "new-agey" and they are! It is a new age!

Language helps in the creative processes. At some level, words create even when there is not thought or emotion to propel them. I have noticed our terminology changing en masse for about a decade (or more) and I feel that this change in language is helping us to remember who we are and why we are here.

No – Hell – for – you – ya! (Hallelujah) and Namaste (No mistakes)

SECTION TWO

TWO

2:19 Be Perfect

"BE PERFECT, even as my father in Heaven is perfect" … yet, we seem to think that this is unattainable.

Where is this elusive Heaven? Jesus tells us that the kingdom is within, yet we continually look outside of ourselves to find it. Jesus warned them that many would come and say that they are THE Christ and warned them not to believe them. This is because we will not be looking to any ONE man, because this appearing is within all men if they believe.

> *The kingdom does not come with observation… The kingdom of God cometh not with observation: 21Neither shall they say, lo here! or, lo there! for, behold, the kingdom of God is within you.* Luke 17:21

Jesus came to display openly to us that He and the Father are ONE. As he is, so are we in this world. This is a mystery....

> *By this is love perfected with us, so that we may have confidence for the day of judgment, because as he is so also are we in this world.* John 4:17

> *Verily, verily, I say unto you, He that believeth on me, the works that I do shall he do also; and greater works than these shall he do; because I go unto my Father.* John 14:12

The Christ (in you) goes to the Father (in you). Therefore, greater things shall you do…!

Are we God? Yes. Are we men? Yes. Jesus set the pattern of the God-man, the Emmanuel. If we continually look externally, we will miss his appearing. Christ in you, the hope of Glory. This is why we are asked to believe IN HIM…IN YOU.

Perfection means CONSUMMATE, which means to come together, as in marriage or union. How will we ever apprehend this understanding if we continually believe we are separate and not good enough? Again, the Old Testament patterns are of the old consciousness, or the frame of mind that men had during that timeframe before the advent of the coming of the Christ. We must shed the old and obtain the new. We must believe. We must KNOW.

You are perfect. You are whole. You are COMPLETE.

2:20 A Private Message from a Fundamentalist

Keep in mind, I have never spoken with this person of spiritual things. He doesn't understand that I accept ALL and appreciate ALL. His message is below:

> *"I hold what you believe in utter contempt. What you have written are damnable lies. (But your heart may be hardened to that type of talk, so you will not hear it often from me). Your inability to suffer any criticism is predictable, your intolerance of opposing viewpoints is its own indictment of your so-called tolerance. And your friends are worse."*

Nice, huh? So much for the love of Christ. When things like this happen, it pushes me further into the arms of the Father that I know loves me and accepts me no matter what.

2:21 Cultivating Intuition

Intention is everything. Once we make the choice to be more "intuitive", we will be! I know this sounds simple, but it is the truth.

Also, we must recognize that there is a difference between logic and intuition.

For problem solving, when we enlist our left brain, we are accessing logic, history, learned behavior or facts. When we enlist our right brain, we are electing to search for "possibilities" to be revealed to us.

When we ponder possibilities, we are enlisting our intuitive mind, which does not have its basis in linear thought as in accessing logic, history, learned behavior or facts. Rather, our "possibilities" are endless as we enlist our Divine nature to help us. Oftentimes, our intuition does not make rational sense to our logical mind.

One thing that has helped me immensely is to ponder symbolism. Symbolism is only accessed by the intuitive mind. So, I might look at the "floating ax head" in scripture and wonder what it could possibly mean symbolically. This exercises our intuitive muscle.

When faced with a dilemma, oftentimes instead of reacting I will stop and try to access that other part of me that "knows all things." I will wait and see what pops up from that "wealth of knowing" and act based on what appears.

This is the bride communicating with the groom. The groom (masculine) provides the "seed" and the bride (feminine) provides the womb to bring the idea to birth. Without the seed, there is no force. Without the womb, there is no forming.

2:22 Every Babe Needs the Womb

Every babe needs the womb, this soft watery environment serving as its primary source of nourishment, like the church was for me.

But soon, this environment became too small and it became impossible to move within it. My nice, soft place became a compression chamber that forcefully expelled me when I had become too "big".

And through the narrow way I traveled; the restrictive nature of the chamber forced the old consciousness from my little lungs, ushering me, helping me move into a new way of breathing.

This constriction surrounded me in many forms, as friends and colleagues pushed me "out", bidding me "good riddance" as I ventured further and further away.

Can I despise the form that gave me birth? No. Like the woman who gives birth to the man-child in Revelation 12 and is forced into the wilderness where God nourishes her until her time, too, comes, these within the church system have served you and me. They deserve honor, as does anyone else who seizes the role of a servant.

It is in reflection and retrospect that I can appreciate the role of this mother. Birth is never easy. I must remain in a state of appreciation for my beginnings, my small beginnings, and know that the same love that I feel from All That Is, is surrounding them, getting them ready for their own time within the chamber. We will anxiously await their arrival and help to swaddle them in this new way of being.

2:23 Worthy is the Lamb

Worthy is the lamb…

> *"Saying with a loud voice, Worthy is the Lamb that was slain to receive power, and riches, and wisdom, and strength, and honor, and glory, and blessing."*
>
> Revelation 5:12

For some background here, Christianity worships Jesus, when in actuality nowhere in scripture did Jesus ask for this, nor are we told to do it. Christianity has elevated this Christ to a position outside of ourselves; it sees him as a literal Messiah that was born, was slain and was resurrected. Even if we are told to worship (worship's true meaning is to revere), so must we "give place" to this Christ within. Paul said that he labored to bring to birth this Christ, IN US.

If we are to see the mystery of these events, then we see that the Christ is being birthed in us, living through us, helping us bring the life of self (the ego) to a place of death and ultimately to bring the same to resurrection. Herein is the coming of Christ, that is, human consciousness that has submitted, as in marriage, to the Divine within, becoming ONE.

Should we be asking if Jesus should be elevated? Through the figurative interpretation of scripture, we are being exhorted to give place (the throne) of this Christ (the union of God and man within our body/being/consciousness). Remember, Christ is not a last name – it is a title for an enlightened being. This term was in existence long before the coming of the man we call Jesus. Also, the letter "J" was not even in use until the 1500s.

Was this man, Jesus, a representative, as you ask? He was the "way". Whether we take this story literally or figuratively, this "way" is unconditional love, non-judgment and an obvious aversion to religious systems that seek to control the masses through rituals and fear.

So, is this lamb worthy to receive power, riches (not what we think), wisdom and strength?

Absolutely. And this "lamb" is within you.

2:24 Pain and Suffering

Pain and suffering. It is really important to the Divine within to feel human pain, and it is equally important for the human part of us to experience it.

Why?

Most always ask, "Why? Shouldn't we be joyful and buoyant beings?" YES. So why must we experience suffering?

Divinity desired baptism into the waters of human consciousness to experience ALL things.

Why?

Early on, in 2005, I begged God not to make me go through "it". I didn't know what "it" was, but I knew something was coming. Then, in November 2005, my middle son, Christian, had his wreck and lost two limbs.

> *Now I rejoice in my sufferings for your sake and fill up on my part that which is lacking of the afflictions of Christ in my flesh.* (Colossians 1:24)

Why did Paul rejoice in his sufferings FOR THEIR SAKE?

Why did the body of CHRIST lack affliction?

How can Paul's suffering help us, help the body of Christ?

Paul understood the purpose in suffering and recognized that the corporeal body (the body of Christ) must "fill up" where the valuable experience of affliction is lacking. Remember the scripture that says the, "He learned obedience from the things He suffered." Hebrews 5:8. The afflictions of "Christ" are the experiences that the Divine experiences, along with its human counterpart, us, that are necessary to become adept at the movement and distribution of our emotions – our emotional currency. Emotions are the creative juice that accompanies thought. The body of Christ (collective humanity) must experience all things good and evil. After all, if emotions are likened to a color palette, we can't create a beautiful painting with just one color.

Emotions are a type of currency.

> *I will give you the treasures of darkness, riches stored in secret places.*
> (Isaiah 45:3)

The "secret places" is the vault within that stores valuable emotional currency.

There is divine purpose in dualism, as it teaches us how to manage our emotions. Emotions accrue a powerful energetic currency that we must learn to spend wisely. If we never come to an awakened state, then we suffer the dream to continue. This is the karmic cycle of life and death, life and death, life and death. That is Hell – never entering into the imperishable life that is promised.

Like the saying, "Don't throw good money after bad," disengagement means to stop throwing your valuable emotional currency at the bad circumstances of life. Judgment is absolutely creative. When the human imbued with Divinity judges a thing as good or evil, it reinforces the nature of the thing being judged and sustains reality, as we know it.

When we judge something, we are spending a type of vibrational currency in the form of emotional energy. This emotional current is dispensed like payment from our energy body to create the fabric of our lives. The typical human creates by default; not realizing its ability to create reality using focused thought and emotion.

The world of dualism produces an energy spectrum every time someone judges between good and evil, dispensing valuable emotional currency into the environment. As we continue with the awakening process, the range of vibration on the planet rises along with us. It is like changing the environment within a terrarium, when the energy changes, the growth within the terrarium changes as well.

In short, our mortal bodies are experiencing a sort of transmutation process as we migrate into the next age in consciousness. We are experiencing a type of Divine Alchemy.

Each level of consciousness produces an atmosphere. and the level we presently occupy is where the human learns through and about the currency of emotions by discerning and judging events. Unfortunately, we are most adept at learning through the events that bring about pain and suffering.

> *Though he were a Son, yet learned he obedience by the things which he suffered; And being made perfect, he became the author of eternal salvation unto all them that obey him; Called of God an high priest after the order of Melchizedek.* (Hebrews 5:8-10)

2:25 Birthed Out of Divinity?

This question above was asked, and I thought I would reply:

> *Another great question!!! My friend Lynn Hayes (and others) teaches that the word "dust" in Genesis actually has connotations of "stardust." I believe the part of us that is Divinity always "is." It, like Melchizedek, has no mother or father, and was not birthed from an egg and sperm.*
>
> *The part of us that is physical/biological was the product of the egg and sperm and has an earthly mother and father and a unique identity through which Divinity may partner (as in marriage) so that it, along with its helpmate, may experience the physical universes.*
>
> *Divinity courts this helpmate, its intended spouse until "she" (feminine energy – the "womb" man) willingly submits (our human will) to marriage.*
>
> *It is then that she is an equal partner with creating, establishing and filling the multiverses with a glory that surpasses our present understanding.*

2:26 Hungry Minds

The Spirit delights in hungry minds. It is through hunger that the Spirit of truth manifests. The rigid adherence to religion is what upset Jesus enough to call the religious folk "whitewashed tombs filled with dead men's bones" and "a brood of vipers."

I am in favor of reading and studying the Bible, but not from a Christian standpoint. Jesus was not a Christian, and much of the Old and New Testaments were borrowed from the Egyptian *Book of the Dead*. Gives one something to think about, doesn't it?

Christianity is fading quickly. People will no longer subject themselves to a controlling and manipulative religion that uses fear to captivate the mind. There comes a time when we must overturn the tables (platforms for money exchange!) of religious systems that have been dragged past their season of relevance.

The Christ will forever have zeal for the "father's house" – You.

2:27 Seek

I am a tireless seeker of truth. I can't help myself. I am probably not unlike many of you. I can remember the first time I read the gospel of Thomas verses 1&2:

> *(1) And he said: He who shall find the interpretation of the words shall not taste of death.*

> *(2) Jesus said: He who seeks, let him not cease seeking until he finds; and when he finds he will be troubled, and if he is troubled, he will be amazed, and he will reign over the All.*

I am troubled, disturbed, perplexed and amazed.

I have read many spiritual books and investigated the thinking that Jesus was a myth. When I first heard this, I was really uncomfortable. Was Jesus history or mystery? Was he an historical figure or was he an allegory that patterns our very own story?

The evidence is OVERWHELMING that the character we have come to know as Jesus was not a historical character, but rather the story was pulled from many cultural myths; myths that have the same general message in common: a virgin birth, the temptation with evil, overcoming evil, gathering disciples, a baptism, a death and resurrection. Many are coming to understand the Bible as a figurative book, much to the dismay of those who take it literally.

If taken figuratively, it is wrought with potent mysteries that contain the nature of our personal and spiritual evolution. Why would this be kept hidden from the masses? Why would the early Catholic Church hide these other sacred and ancient documents that tell of this myth of the God-man?

There is a grand cycle of time we participate in that takes us through the 12 signs of the zodiac, two thousand years each, totaling 24,000 years. Many say that the twelve signs are the disciples that follow the Sun/son.

Each sign or constellation, if you will, expresses a quality/vibration/nature that helps mankind evolve. Many mistake this progression to be linear – it is not. Our progression is circular – by that, I mean that during this great cycle of time, we begin in high culture – we are immortals that have been clothed with humanity; having agreed to be immersed (baptized) into flesh and blood, we submit ourselves to death and enter into mortality. This is symbolized by the Last Supper, communion. The broken bread (Jesus said, "I am the bread from Heaven") willingly breaks its immortal status and becomes human and mortal, having descended through the portal of death (symbolism of the throat in *Romans 3:13*) and rests in the belly of the Earth (the story of Jonah being swallowed up in the belly of the great fish – most likely in the age of Pisces). We eat from the "tree" of duality, knowing good from evil. Our lifelines are at first very long, living almost one thousand years, but slowly, over time, we eventually enter the "dark ages" where lifespan is approximately 23 years long. The books of the ancients are all but destroyed and our intuitive faculties extremely compromised.

Enter the Catholic Church. Men were savage, having digressed from their God-like status over millennia. The creature had been made subject to futility, not willingly (our divinity chose this process), but by the one who subjected it in hope. The Church exercised its power to control the masses and concocted the story of Hell, the Devil and, of course, Jesus. It took the numerous stories of the myth, which showed up in the centuries prior to the dark ages, to remind humanity of its beginning and ultimate return to the golden ages, and made it historical; happening to one man, rather than to ALL men. "Believe and be saved," it said.

So, I ask your thoughts on this today. History or mystery?

For those interested in this great cycle of time, there is a fantastic book and DVD – The book is titled, *The Lost Star* and the DVD is *The Great Year* both by Walter Cruttenden and both are EXCEPTIONAL. This great cycle of time is said to occur because of our Sun being in a gravitational relationship with another star very far away. Its gravitational relationship pulls us through an ellipsis that brings us through all twelve of the influential zodiac signs. This is not the first 24,000-year cycle we are in. I believe this is the 6th 24,000-year cycle – 6 x 24K = 144,000 years. We are nearing the "rest" or the "Sabbath" that scripture eludes to, where the Earth is dormant for a millennium while it is purified from our excesses. Only the things hewn from stone will remain.

2:28 Neural Pathways

This journey is to diverge from the neural pathways in consciousness that have been forged throughout our life. It can be most disconcerting to "move" out from group think and from the conditioning set by our family, friends and humanity in general. We must begin to listen to the still, small voice; that compass within that says, "This is the way, walk in it!"

This is when we must become the "observer." We must ask ourselves, "Why do I think this way?" or "Why did I react that way?" When we observe, we step into our Divine mind (Christ) and are able to see things from an elevated position in consciousness. He meets us in the "upper room" and we begin to see our programming and conditioning set with stakes of fear.

We must pull up those stakes and allow the networking of fear to dissolve. We are multidimensional pioneers charting the path out from limitation and into the infinite mind.

2:29 The Cross

The cross is where the two parts of us (Divinity and humanity) intersect.

It is where we have our Garden of Gethsemane experience as well – "nevertheless not my will, but thy will be done."

What is the will of Divinity? From the pattern, we see that Jesus "listened to His Father" and did nothing he did not see or hear his father say or do.

This "father" is within and is the creative component; the source of all creation and creating; the father/source we cannot reach unless we apprehend it by Christ – not Jesus. (I am the way… no one comes to the Father but by me…)

Christ is the amalgamation of the Divine and man in synergy or union.

Christ is what we are when we surrender our egocentric operating system for that of the Divine. Hearing the Father is within – it is that still, small voice that speaks when the ego is silent and waiting.

Seeing is in the mind's eye; what we "see" when the vision of duality becomes single.

So, we understand that this powerful creative power/source is within but cannot be accessed without "Christ;" that is, your human will in submission to that of the Divine source, within.

2:30 I AM the Way...

I AM the Way... no one comes to the Father but by me ....

This Father, this potential, this unprecedented creative source of all, is within.

We cannot access it when we remain in contrast; that is, judging between good and evil.

In order to tap into that potent source, we must follow the "Way!" And that "Way" is Christ.

Christ is the marriage between the human and Divinity.

Christ is the human in submission to the Divine.

Christ is what is formulated/created once the human ceases to cooperate with the M.O. of this present world.

Christ is the amalgamation between God and man.

Christ is birthed in you, in your human frame, when the ego willingly steps aside and dies, surrendering its life force to the grave; its right to judge and to discern differences; light and dark; good and evil.

Christ then has access to the treasure trove of the SOURCE.

This source is the progenitor (father) where all substance is formed.

This source is not shared with egocentric humanity, lest it will create unlimitedly and MORTALLY.

This access is granted to a Christed being, one that has died the death in the Garden of Gethsemane (the olive press) and has said, "Nevertheless, NOT MY WILL, but THY WILL..." Not human will, but the will of our great counterpart, Divinity.

2:31 Pay Your Tithe?

That is, offer yourselves as living sacrifices.

There is a "tithe" in the Earth that will be the forerunner of this present age. This tithe is a people group that will bridge the gap between dimensional boundaries.

They house, within their bodies, a greater frequency/sound/vibration; one that is able to mediate between ever-present dimensional gaps.

This tithe must experience an exchange of power within – they must move from an egocentric mind into the mind of Christ. The ego (the Son of Perdition) must surrender its throne.

It is my understanding that when the "tithe" experiences this transition of power (yields its throne to Divinity), we will be building a "bridge" out from mortality into immortality.

But it will take the tithe (10% of humanity) to surrender egocentricity so that a different frequency breaks forth into consciousness, causing an upgrade.

When this 10% hums and buzzes with this higher frequency, THEN we will begin to see dramatic changes in our world scape.

This higher frequency will bust consciousness loose from the grip of fear and enable us to apprehend the "promised land."

We will then be navigating across this vibrational bridge, experiencing transfiguration as we go.

The world, as we know it, will break down, much like a rotting tree, and begin again, having been purified by the fire of transfiguration.

There will be a new Heaven (consciousness) and a new Earth (our body).

This 10% is the Melchizedek Priesthood. This "priest" is what bridges the gap between mortality and immortality.

There is that time when our physical is cocooned and breaks down, but reforms into a new creation within. This encompasses the cataclysmic events outlined in Matthew 24 as our "earth" (body) experiences transfiguration.

2:32 You Are WONDER FULL

I hear comments from people all the time about the speed at which we are becoming enlightened. There is so much at our fingertips – so much truth to comprehend. At times it staggers me.

For those who have made phone appointments with me (there are a lot of you out there – Thanks!), you know the depth of the information that I give out – sometimes without the asking (and I might need to apologize for that!). I have never had a good "governor" on my speed petal and I often dispense too much. My husband says it is like offering a drink of water to someone using a firehose :/.

I guess what I am trying to say (feebly) is that it is time to throw off the restraints and embrace the new, the new wineskin and the new wine. New wine is defined by one word: VOLATILE. New wine has yet to go through the fermentation process, and so once it is within the new wineskin of your consciousness, its only movement is EXPANSION. You will be STRETCHED!!!

I am continually amazed at the depth of the waters the intuitive mind is allowed to swim in. Some waters are preexistent, some are futuristic, and some are created by your thoughtful imagination and intent. None are dismissible – all consciousness is valuable!

So Jacob, lay your head upon the rock of revealed knowledge and apprehend the divine essence that encapsulates your identity – it is then you will see messengers ascending and descending within you, within your DNA, bringing messages for you to discover, to ponder and to CREATE.

Now is your time. You need just ask to see and to be tucked into the cleft of the rock to see the transfiguration of the Son of Man, that man that you are, that is I AM.

Throw the shackles of fear off of you, for they are only as real as you imagine them to be. God is not mad at you for utilizing what he gave you – A MIND THAT IS FILLED WITH WONDER.

You are WONDER FULL.

2:33 Truth, at Its Core, is LOVE

Truth, at its core, is LOVE and is tolerant of all human learning through experience.

Intolerance is the fodder of religions that seek to "hem God in" with human attributes.

Christianity prescribes to a Jehovic God in nature and, as such, has human attributes – Jehovah loved and hated, rewarded and punished, incited war, rape and pillaging, murder and the like.

The father that the Christ spoke of had none of these attributes.

Christ taught us that we could be one with his Father, a union that Christianity reserves for those who believe in raising a hand, walking an aisle and professing the sinner's prayer – none of which Jesus told us to do.

Jesus said, "I AM THE WAY, the truth and the life and no one comes to the Father but by me." This simply means that to reach the creative source/power/love WITHIN, one must be Christ-like. This example is to love unconditionally, to practice non-judgment and to be "self"-sacrificing.

2:34 Kind and Loving Christian People

I know many wonderful, kind and loving Christian people and I do not want to diminish their character or dedication. It is hard for them to come to terms with the books that I write, as I severely challenge their system and their doctrine. I see them in the store and out in my community and feel their dis-ease with me. I seek to help those who are likewise questioning the system and bring into question areas of fundamentalism that are not in keeping with the teachings of Jesus Christ.

Christianity must come to terms with its flawed foundational doctrines based on fear and confront its own creeds and teachings of Hell and separation. It must seek to understand that the tyrant Jehovah of the Old Testament is not the Father that Jesus spoke of in the New Testament, if it desires to progress in spiritual areas. But most of all, it must let go of its rigid adherence to a literal translation of the Bible, foregoing it for rich and expansive figurative prose.

One does not have to look far to find exhaustive research into the flawed historical branding of scripture and the insurmountable evidence offered up supporting the metaphorical, allegorical and figurative interpretation. Furthermore, Christians must stop turning their heads away from the proof that the teachings of Jesus and much of the Old Testament has been found in other cultural stories that far predate Old and New Testament timetables.

There must be a willingness to look beyond what has been accepted, to challenge the status quo, and most of all to look within to allow the teaching and guidance of their innate identity; CHRIST. Christ in you, the hope of glory.

2:35 Like the Shutter of a Camera

Our eyes are opening, like the shutter of a camera, allowing incremental light in as we can bear it.

I see you as perfect because you are.

I am.

We are exactly where we should be in this moment.

Nothing is in vain, no pain, and war may be necessary to bring us where we need to be.

All is purposeful, all things work together. Light and dark is the same to "thee."

Our process of unfolding is as unique as our fingerprint. All serves.

All enlightens.

All is beauty.

2:36 Old and New

There will be conflict between the old order and the approaching age. The old resists the new, and always has. We don't have to dislike the process, but rather, appreciate it for what it is … birth. It is hard on the babe and mother, but necessary if we are to transition through the narrow way.

There are those who stagger in that in-between bridge-like place that are asking for clarity so that they may discern where they belong. When my first child was born, the staff needed to use forceps, because he was too big and became "stuck" in the birth canal; a forceful entry into the new world, indeed.

Those called to migrate into this "age to come", as Jesus put it, are in a precarious position because we have not walked this way before. There are those pioneers who will trumpet the new sound like a beacon so that those entering may find their way. This beacon sound comes from non-judgment, unconditional love, unity and peacefulness.

Anything opposing this new sound is exposed by the Christ, just as Jesus did when he identified the Pharisees as "whitewashed tombs filled with dead men's bones." That is not a particular people group; metaphorically and figuratively, it is the egocentric nature within all of humanity.

SECTION THREE

THREE

3:37 A Southern Baptist Minister ...

She said:

> *About two months ago I had a talk with my father, a Southern Baptist Minister. I asked him, "Dad, did you know that after the Council of Nicaea, Constantine (the founder of Christianity in whom the entire religion entrusted the compilation of the Bible with) went straight home and murdered his family?"*
>
> *You know what he told me? "Yes, I knew."*
>
> *Then I asked him, "Okay, so did you also know that the Bible was virtually plagiarized from the Egyptian Book of the Dead?"*
>
> *His answer, again, was, "Yes, I knew that also."*
>
> *As it turns out, he's known these shocking things for YEARS, but he was taught in seminary NOT TO QUESTION.*

Isn't it interesting that the Jews, when faced with the possibility of annihilation, went willingly into the boxcars, finding it hard to believe that they would ultimately be exterminated?

Denial, and wanting to believe something regardless of the evidence, is a form of hypnotism referred to as cognitive dissonance.

Belief in dogmatism (the tendency to lay down principles as incontrovertibly true, without consideration of evidence or the opinions of others), of any kind, is cognitively dissonant. Some choose to believe, regardless of the evidence.

The good news is that these folks will come to the point of awakening. They have to; it is their destiny as human beings. We will all bloom like springtime flowers, with the chirping of the birds and the buzzing of the bees. It is time for the Earth to yield its harvest to the Moon, to the sickle of separation; that is, the ego in decline.

No more will we separate from one another when we are gathered into the barn. We will be threshed and that which does not serve will be removed. All the doctrines of hate and intolerance, separation and division will fade with the brilliance of the coming Son.

3:38 Jehovah is Not the Father of Jesus

"My point, once again, is not that those ancient people told literal stories and we are now smart enough to take them symbolically, but that they told them symbolically and we are now dumb enough to take them literally."

From John Dominic Crossan, *Who is Jesus?*

The following message is from a letter to a friend who asked me my take on the wars and bloodshed in scripture, as opposed to the all-loving Father we are told to believe in:

It is impossible to reconcile the two Gods that we are presented within the Old and New Testament. Therefore, I have come to these conclusions:

The Bible is not an historically accurate book. When it happens to be accurate (on rare occasions), "it is by accident." (Tom Harpur)

Therefore, the Bible is not a history book.

The Bible is a mystical account of the conscious evolution of mankind.

Jehovah is not the same as the Father of Jesus.

Jehovah shows up in Genesis 2, after mankind "eats" from the tree that produces death.

Jehovah is a representative of how we view God as external and separate - one that rewards and punishes; just like man. Once we began eating from the tree of duality, we needed to see duality – good and evil, light and dark, reward and punishment, life and death.

The Old Testament is reflective of very young or immature consciousness, migrating through the wilderness, fighting serpents (ego), and eventually reaching the promised land, but not taking it fully. All of the wars and such are archetypical and express man's struggle down through the ages. They are not literal. And, even if some are, when we view the Bible literally, we must remember: the letter (literalism) kills, but the spirit (mystical) brings life.

*Jesus shows up to set men free from the tyranny of the law –
reward and punishment – dualism.*

*The New Testament is a transitional view of consciousness as it
migrates out from dualism and into LOVE*

*Revelation is the completely transformed human; it is not a
book about external and futuristic events.*

*The seven churches, scrolls and seals are the human chakra
system; the trumpets are, as well, as the chakras emit a tone or
frequency.*

I began to see that the Bible is a roadmap of our journey as human beings learning
and practicing our God-hood. Jesus is archetypical of all humans imbued with the
Divine spark – birthed within humanity and growing up within the garden of man's
consciousness.

It is up to us to "finish" the story by taking the promised land that is "immortality."

3:39 The Pearl of Great Price

Where is this pearl of great price that the master seeks after? What is within you is
precious beyond earthly value. You house the Christ. It is intrinsic in your nature,
there amongst the salt and fleshy parts of your biology. It hides. It waits. Harvest the
pearl. Let it shine.

3:40 No Longer Believe in a Punitive God

Our concepts of Heaven and Hell are changing.

We are no longer subjecting ourselves to fear or fear-based dogmas.

We no longer believe in a punitive God.

As such, our prayer practices have changed dramatically.

I receive messages from people from all over the world who no longer "know" how
to pray.

Prayer used to be something that we learned from other people. We would watch and
model our system of prayer after them.

Now, because we no longer view God as punitive and external or apart from us, where we have to get "his" attention somehow and say enough of the right and emotionally charged prayers…
Now we enter a place of knowing.

Prayer is not intellectually based, derived from knowing good and evil…

Prayer is now "knowing" that all things work together; that every human experience is valuable. Now, we enter into peace, because our warfare has ended.

Warfare is striving against some force when we judge it to be wrong, evil, hurtful and damaging in some way.

This is a hard concept for those of us still judging between the two polarities – good and evil.

There must be a people group that disengages from the judging criteria; a people at rest, a people at peace. We are becoming a people that recognizes that striving against some form of devil or evil outside of ourselves only serves to maintain this present age of darkened consciousness.

This people group will see the duality in our world and not contribute to it by focusing upon it.

They will, however, focus on what it is they want to see in the world, and thereby create it.

3:41 One God

Did you know that there is one who is the savior of mankind

That is God incarnate

Born in a cave on December 25th

A star appeared at his birth

Is visited by the Magi of the East

Turns water into wine at a wedding

Heals the sick

Casts out demons

Performs many miracles

Is transfigured before his disciples

Rides a donkey into a city

Is betrayed for 30 pieces of silver

Celebrates with his disciples with bread and wine

Is put to death on a cross

Descends into Hell

Is resurrected on the third day

Dies to redeem the world's sins

Ascends into Heaven and is seated beside God as the divine judge…

Who is this man?

Osiris-Dionysus

ONE STORY

ONE GOD

ONE OUTCOME

You have been sent into the world not to condemn (through your judgment) but to save it from the egocentric domination (SIN). Your task is to cultivate a helpmate, a human vessel to inhabit, to partner with. This human vessel will need to surrender to (death), it must die to its own will, yielding to its Divine counterpart as a co-inhabitant of its own flesh that had been born within humanity.

You are then to raise the body from its death state (mortality).

Are you up to it?

It's our story. It's your story. It's you! Awake, oh sleeper!

3:42 The Bible is Not the WORD of GOD

The Bible is NOT THE WORD OF GOD.

There.

The WORD OF GOD is YOUR VIBRATIONAL SIGNATURE that is emitted through THOUGHT, WORD and DEED from YOU. YOU ARE A GOD-MAN. THIS SCRIPTURE IS ELUDING TO YOU!!!

This "WORD" DOES NOT RETURN VOID, or rather, does not RETURN TO YOU WITHOUT FULFILLING THE REQUEST THAT WAS MADE BY YOU, THROUGH YOUR VIBRATIONAL OFFERING.

Therefore, be careful what you think, and be careful what you say, for a new increment of glory is upon you. What you say (through the vibrational offering that comes out of your body while you think, feel and say) WILL CREATE that which you INTEND!!!

Wake up you GOD-MEN, AWAKE!

Joy to the world, the LORD is come, let Earth receive her KING!

3:43 A Message to a Friend, Regarding Demons

I think that what we call demons are just lower, dense, negative energy. I describe this energy like "ballast" in a ship's hull to keep it buoyant in the waters of human consciousness; necessary, until it isn't.

Such negativity lends to us gravity, equal to the task of weighting us down effectively in our human experiences, in our human world. Such energy keeps us focused on external and selfish circumstances, thereby creating and sustaining our environment.

But we are called to transition the age by being in the world, but not of the world. And so, we are challenged to heed the call to think on things that are pure and lovely, thereby raising the frequency of our existence. This will cause a shift upward in our buoyancy so that we may ascend beyond the waters of darkened consciousness.

3:44 Demons Correlate (Co-Relate)

Demons correlate (co-relate) to one's belief system. Eating from the "Tree of the Knowledge of Good and Evil", one sees evil and good, angels and demons. I should know this from my decade spent as an exorcist.

Eating from the "Tree of Life," one sees the correlation of all life as they see things from a vibrational basis and, therefore, sees confluence of all things.

The literal interpretation of scripture produces a belief system based on fear if you do not believe it in literally. So, one must believe in talking snakes, donkeys, a boat that fit every living creature in it, and that the Earth is only 6,000 years old.

These things in the scripture are written in such a way that the immature and fledgling mind/consciousness of humankind would have a PATTERN to intuit by once the conscious had developed enough to see things metaphorically, figuratively and allegorically.

We may live and move and have our being in the literal interpretation, and it is like living in the city where Jim Carrey's character lived in the movie, "*The Truman Show*." His environment appeared very real until he began to challenge the boundaries of his own MIND.

The metaphorical interpretation of scripture opens the vista of interpretation to include endless landscapes for the intuitive mind to embrace. This is impossible for the mind that has been shackled by "beliefs."

The intellectual mind *believes*. The intuitive mind *knows*.

3:45 Take a Good, Long Look in the Mirror

Yes, you are lovely in all of your humanness. Look how your eyes give testimony of a life well lived. Even those times that were so hard, see; they have added a subtle beauty to you.

It is time you know the truth of who you are. You are me. Yes, Divinity is what peers out through your eyes to meet the world. I have been wrapped in the wonderment of your body – it is glorious and remarkably perfect. I want you, for one moment, to see how loved you are, the kind of love that is bereft of anything compromising or shallow. Feel, for a moment, the way I feel about you, being inside of you, living life through you. You have not made one false step – yes, everything has had purpose – great purpose, even though this is difficult for you to fathom. No regrets, oh love of mine! No regrets.

You are experiencing your morning stretch as you awaken from your dream. We are ready to take on this world, to dismantle the norm of judgment and emotions run amok. We will conquer fear and death together – you are highly endowed, unlike any other creation – oh, my human love! Together we will eclipse the age dawning new as we shed the conscious containment of the past. Only you and I together can do this – for in union, there is power.

See for a moment, will you, what I see in you. Your beauty overcomes me! I love you, my tender dove, and I always will.

3:46 The WORD of God is Not the Bible …

I struggled for a long time with this issue regarding the Bible being THE WORD of God. Then I realized that this, too, is a fabrication without foundation in scripture. The WORD is FLESH. That's Christ in you, the hope of glory.

3:47 Jesus is a Portal

> *"I am the way, the truth and the life; no one comes to the Father but through me. If you had known me, you would have known my Father also; from now on you know Him and have seen Him."* John 14

Through these words, we see many things;

Jesus is a portal, or door, through which one must pass to gain access to the Father; that is, the progenitor, the source of all life.
Therefore, we must look at Jesus, his life and pattern, to discern what this "way" is.

Jesus displayed unconditional love, non-judgment and a history of benevolence. The exception to this behavior was in his conflict with the ruling religious order of his day that sought to pull the irrelevant system of the law into his sphere of influence, which was the very antitheses of his message.

He was not moved by human urgency or need but moved by a mandate from within (what his Father said to do).

Jesus did not tell us to walk an aisle, raise a hand to accept him into our heart as our personal Lord and Savior. He said we must believe in him, his actions and teaching, which included inclusiveness for all people and self-sacrifice. He did not say that we must follow and believe in the doctrines and dogma of the Christian Church as they define the means to salvation or getting saved.

To apprehend salvation does not mean we go to Heaven and escape Hell. Jesus never taught about Hell (as Christianity defines it) and Christian dogma does and was instituted by the church system in the first few centuries after his ascension as a means to control the renegade masses as the Earth was being plunged into the dark ages. Furthermore, Christians equate this way to the "Father" as their "Get Out of Jail Free" card. Such nonsense. If they would just seek the truth for themselves and ask, the truth would be given. All too often, they lean upon their programming from youth and replay the tapes of dogma they are so used to.

By following the path and pattern of selflessness, benevolence, non-judgment and inclusion, ANYONE from ANY CULTURE AND BELIEF has ACCESS to the FATHER. The Father does not discriminate and is not HEBREW. The Father that Jesus spoke and taught of is not JEHOVAH.

"If you had known me, you would have seen my Father also ..." They did not know Jesus, and yet he tells them that, "From now on you know him (the Father!) and have seen him." So, this apprehending of the Father is simple. Jesus did not say that they would have to follow the dictates of any religious Christian order (or otherwise) to know the Father.

Money, pride, arrogance and FEAR (of going to Hell) are the underlying threads of most Christian organizations. These very human and egocentric traits are the fabric beneath some very benevolent, well-meaning and well-intentioned people. It is only a matter of time before we begin to see a great new awakening already upon us, carrying us through to the age to come.

Furthermore, believing in Jesus, the pattern, means that you believe in your own Divinity.

Wake up humanity. Your Divinity awaits you.

> *"To them God has chosen to make known amongst the Gentiles the glorious riches of this mystery, which is Christ in you, the hope of glory."* Colossians 1:27

3:48 What Does Moses Symbolize to You?

Metaphorical account of Moses and the Red Sea:

Egypt and Pharaoh represent an environment dominated by the "taskmaster" of our own internal ego-driven life. We see that the whole nation of Israel (representing Divinity within all humankind) must leave their homeland (spiritual wholeness) and enter into slavery and egocentric bondage in Egypt, a necessary experience for the collective whole as it leaves its immortal status and continually eats from the tree of the knowledge of good and evil that produces duality and mortality.

Moses, an archetype of a deliverer, while immersed in humanity (during a time where the male children are being slaughtered) was given to another mother to be raised. This is a metaphor of our deliverer, the ego that yields to Divinity within man, given over to an egocentric (fear-based) environment in which to grow and learn and to eventually overcome it, just as Jesus modeled for us. Moses lived to be 120 years old, a number that represents the limit one may live as a mortal (see Genesis 6:3).

Moses was hidden in symbolic baseness, a straw basket (limited humanity), floating down the Nile (water = human consciousness), and was found by Pharaoh's daughter (egocentric environment), who raised him. Entering adulthood, Moses awakened to the knowledge that he would serve as a deliverer of his people and lead them out of slavery to Egypt. Metaphorically, this is what occurs within the human being when it consciously awakens and realizes its true identity as a partner to Divinity and its task to overcome egocentric domination (slavery to ego). We are all charged with being the savior of our body and to seize the promised land of immortality.

Pharaoh/Egypt (the egocentric domination) was reluctant to release Moses and the slaves (Divinity imbued humanity held captive by the ego) and subsequently received many plagues as a result of this stubborn determination. The plagues all represent various conditions of humanity (sickness, dis-ease, baseness, etc.) as it remains in an egocentric state of consciousness.

The last plague was death of the firstborn son (this firstborn son is representative of our mortal condition brought about by the egocentric domination). The firstborn represents our condition as being born first as a human (secondly as Divinity awakening within humanity). In other words, the symbolism of Passover is that the firstborn, our mortal flesh and blood, does not have to die.

The slaves were instructed to place the blood of a slaughtered lamb (Christ consciousness; gentle as a lamb; the Christ being delivered up to death; we willingly bring our egocentric life into death to experience union with the Divine) on the doorpost so that when the angel of death passed by, the firstborn would be spared. This is called the Passover. Pharaoh did no such thing and his firstborn died, and in his grief, he relented and let the slaves go free.

The blood on the doorpost (portal) is a metaphor for the act of union when the virginal hymen breaks and blood is shed and coats the portal – the union between Divinity and man, the bride and groom, etc. The portal here represents the Vesica Pisces, a symbol of the birth portal or metaphoric and/or cosmic vagina, and also representing the Age of Pisces where the Christ seed would penetrate the human frame.

Therefore, metaphorically we can see that in this union in consciousness with the Divine, the slain lamb (the human in willful submission to Divinity) is essential for mankind to be released from egocentric domination. As the Israelites headed for the Promised Land, Pharaoh's armies chased them to the brink of the Red Sea (human consciousness). While leading the slaves, Moses used his staff to touch the water, thereby parting it so that they could pass over (Passover) to the other side.

As Pharaoh's armies chased them, the Israelites arrived safely on the other side, and the waters of the parted Red Sea collapsed in on the Egyptians. This account of the parted Red Sea is a perfect metaphor for man's dual and divided consciousness, eating from the tree of the knowledge of good and evil.

Reality is formed with his thinking of separateness, replete with the strength of Pharaoh's horses and chariots (the ego's strength and tactics), buried within the waters of consciousness of the human mind—an unstable condition that would follow them into the wilderness.

3:49 More Metaphors ...

"The eye is the lamp of the body"

"Let thine eye be single"

This singular "eye" is the pineal gland.

Five virgins had oil in their lamps; five did not. The five that did not have oil could not borrow from the five that did. This is because the pineal gland, when stimulated/activated, secretes an oily substance. Each person must do their own "work" to activate this "eye" – it cannot be borrowed.

The pineal gland has long been associated with your spiritual rebirth into the intuited worlds.

Spiritual truth cannot be apprehended with the physical eyes of dualism but may be attained through the single eye of union.

No one is exempt. We all must make the journey and we are all capable of doing so. We must "lift our eyes" to see.

3:50 So Many Denominations

There are so many Christian denominations worldwide, each one espousing differing "beliefs" that are supposedly essential to and for salvation. If Christians can't agree on basic doctrine, then what hope does the world have to get it right?

I understand that many fundamentalists are passionate about their beliefs, as I was for most of my life. I sounded just like many fundamentalists in my defense of what I thought was "the" gospel message. I cited the same passages, labeled many "heretics" who did not believe like me, used the scriptures like a whip and beat and thumped many a head with the Bible.

At the end of the day, my religion did not have much confluence with the actual teachings of Jesus, so I decided to go back to the basics.

I recently had a discussion with an old neighborhood friend about reincarnation. We went back and forth with scriptures and it came down to this: John the Baptist denied that he was Elijah, but Jesus said that John was Elijah. I asked my friend which person she believed, John or Jesus? She did not answer.

Too many Christians have formed doctrine unsoundly, basing their foundation upon what has been filtered down through the early Catholic Church, but mainly through modern fundamentalist movements. The crusades said believe like us; convert or die. Fundamentalism says believe, convert, or go to Hell.

Much of fundamentalism is dreadfully stained with dogma and not the sound teaching of Jesus. I encourage fundamentalists to return to the "red letters" and begin there as their foundation. They will see the dramatic departure religion has embarked upon, dragging human consciousness through darkness, hopelessness and despair.

It does not take a lot of effort, just take a look at history to see the influence and domination that the early church enforced and the need for the subsequent reformation movements to adjust the damage done by the heavy hand of control. There are remnants of fear-based theology alive and well within the ranks of Christianity. It is this fear and its systems of belief that are once again being purged from human consciousness as the teaching of the Christ are coming front and center. At the heart of the message of Jesus is LOVE. TOLERANCE. NON-JUDGMENT. KINGDOM. UNION.

Unfortunately, at the heart of mainline fundamentalism is FEAR. INTOLERANCE. JUDGMENT. HELL. SEPARATION. With this view, we might indeed ask ourselves, which system is anti-Christ?

3:51 I Had a Vision of a Huge Bubble

Back in 2003, I had a vision of a huge bubble. I asked what it was, and I was told it was "God." Then I saw many other bubbles within the big bubble, and again I asked what it was …? I was told these bubbles were different belief systems like Scientology, Judaism, Christianity, Islam, Catholicism, Buddhism, Wiccan, Pagan, Pantheism, etc. and that all were "in" God (or Allah, Mithras, Zeus, Jehovah, etc.)

It should be noted that within this huge bubble sphere called the many names of God, there are innumerable spheres (bubbles) of influence. Each sphere has a different vibration, experience, information, timeline and history to it. We can jump from sphere to sphere if we desire, and do this often, as our consciousness unfolds. For example, one may begin life as a Catholic and end up a Wiccan, or vice-versa. There are also systems that do not contain a deity, like Atheism. In the place of a deity is the human ego, or self.

One sphere of influence does not cancel out another, even if the information and experiences within each seem contradictory. For example, one may contain a historical Jesus and in the next, Jesus is understood as a prophet. Another views Jesus as an allegorical "type" and not an historical person at all.

Another may call him an ascended master that has already "graduated" from the Earth school. One may worship him as a savior that saves them from the wrath of God, and another sees him as I AM – their own true identity.

Just the same, some may see Allah as the "God" and Mohammed as the saving prophet. There are many names to this "hero" and many paths that lead to understanding. Most are systemic organizations that pander to the human ego and its need to be right.

None of these "spheres" of belief are wrong, even though there are "bubbles" that cannot see beyond their own sphere of influence and they are convinced that there is nothing more to apprehend. These concepts are in place for our own unfolding conscious development. And again, we remain within the restrictiveness of our self-imposed bubble of belief as long as we desire.

I was encapsulated within the fundamentalist Christian bubble for 43 years. The ruling deity within that sphere is Jehovah or God (not to be confused with the Father that Jesus spoke of).

Now, understanding that this sphere contains all beliefs and experiences, and none are wrong, it is important to note this: there is an environment where this grand sphere exists that is beyond thought; it is beyond any bubble of belief; it is the environment of pure potential.

This environment is the creative potential of the prime source, the progenitor, or "Father," as Jesus called him/it. It is energy. It is love. And there is only one path to this source, and that is outside of the bubble! Outside the bubbles of human egocentric institutions! Outside of intolerance! Outside of judgment! Outside of all belief of separation! This was and is the path that so many messengers modeled for us – it is the way of love.

Thought must be encapsulated into spheres for the purposes of education via creation. By our world's history, we can see what it is that we have created, and by extension, what we are creating via many spheres of thought and belief. Think about that for a moment. What have we created within our own bubbles of belief?

Any religion that teaches separation is within a bubble that someday must *pop* in order for those within to return to the source of all.

3:52 My Husband Left the Church Before I Did

My husband actually left the church system about 6 months before my exit; however, we were not on the same page spiritually. It was a very hard decade, until we came to a place of confluence.

I had to realize that agreement was not necessary for happiness. I think that I was so programmed to proselytize that I thought we all had to believe alike, having found THE truth. Little did I know that "my" truth would continually evolve and is, indeed, still evolving.

We are exposed to concepts and ideas as we can bear them. AND, there is room in "all that is" for every one of them! What a treasure that nugget has been for me, personally! We all have different paths to walk and all with different navigation systems. Success or failure is not an option, because it is truly the journey that counts, not the destination.

Two great quotes from friends recently said, "A person cannot 'un-see' once they have seen," and, "The root has broken the pot." Indeed, Christ the root has broken the way out from restriction and into freedom. We cannot wear our clothing from childhood, as it no longer "fits," but in its time was perfect for our frame.

3:53 There Are Twelve "Disciples" of the Christ

There are twelve "disciples" of the Christ. The Christ walked the Earth to find and regather these disciples; or figuratively, aspects of his multidimensional self.

These "disciples" are aspects of our multidimensional capability – we are capable of inter-dimensional travel, like Melchizedek; we are immortal and have the ability to step in and out of time and mortality. Like the example of the Christ, we may "lay down our (physical) body (vehicle) and pick it up again."

These disciples are "fishers" of men. The fish is the symbol of the Age of Pisces, the era in which the human is pulled up from the seas of dense human consciousness residing in duality. The multidimensional self will aid in this ascension and awakening process.

These disciples are figurative for the twelve strands of our DNA that are being re-bundled, re-established, re-wired, producing a litany of physical manifestations as our spiritual DNA comes on-line. Two-stranded DNA keeps us anchored in duality and mortality. Things are changing, morphing, as this beautiful energy body sputters and coughs into activation – much like a lawnmower in springtime for the first cut after a long winter's rest. It is like riding a bike. It is intuitive. You will remember.

Many are finding commonality in the strange symptoms as this energy body is activated. Like gears in a rusty machine, the kundalini acts like oil to the chakra-gears, these spinning wheels of light ignite and spin out all the old energy from past wounds, trauma and pain. And we feel it. We cry. We ache. The body organs are shocked. All of them.

The redemptive plan for mankind takes place now as the silver coin has been found within the mouth of the fish. Silver represents REDEMPTION. The Age of Pisces surrenders its booty – You.

P.S. This devolution into matter as a two-stranded, limited and mortal being was absolutely necessary for our education as fledgling God-men. Resurrection, ascension, transfiguration is here.

3:54 God and Jesus Established the Modern Church?

Someone recently told me that God/Jesus established the modern-day church and that Jesus taught in synagogues and temples. He asked about being vehemently opposed to attending church.

My reply:

> *Jesus taught in the synagogues until they forced him out and tried to seize him. After these attempts, Jesus taught outside of any building dedicated to religious practices.*

I am not "vehemently" opposed to attending church services; I simply choose not to go. It no longer serves me, and I don't see a pattern for church in the scripture (not that I would need one).

When people (such as yourself) try to make people behave in a manner they deem as correct and cite scripture (errantly) to justify their instruction... this is when I feel I must reply with fact. Jesus NEVER started a church, as defined by the modern assemblies. He, in fact, helped us leave them by demonstration. Jesus rebelled against the status quo religious order and reinforced the nature of a loving, non-judgmental and accepting Father. Those who are unwilling or unable to see this have been indoctrinated by a religious system.

I don't hate the church; I AM the church.

SECTION FOUR

FOUR

4:55 Walk on Water!

There is a lot of teaching out there that states that our entire existence is an illusion and, as such, we should not give credence to it, or that we should practice nonresistance. I get that! And nonresistance is essential in many situations! While I understand the necessity to understand the nature of our temporal existence, it is NOT AN ILLUSION.

In the examples that are recorded about the acts of Jesus, he practiced nonresistance most of the time, but there were a few examples where nonresistance would not have been appropriate.

For example, to the numerous people he healed, he did not say, "Do not resist, what you are experiencing is not real."

To the moneychangers in the temple, he did not say, "It's okay to defile my Father's house because it is all an illusion anyway; carry on."

Present-day circumstances, as when a mother catches her boyfriend molesting her two-year-old child – does she practice nonresistance and say, "It's okay, honey; none of this is real?"

Does a man who accidentally shoots his friend while hunting declare, "Ah, it's a good thing this is all an illusion!"

No; that is madness. While we are immersed (baptized) into human consciousness, there are lessons to learn. This existence is not for naught.

There is thinking out there that I believe severely handicaps our divine ability to manage through our growth by denying the existence of the problem. There is a KEY. And this key is to allow the circumstances of our life without JUDGMENT.

Judgment engages our chakras to "fire up" when our judgment remains in the nether regions (Hell - the lower three chakras). When we are "moved" with fear, survivalism and emotionalism (the lowest three chakras; red, orange and yellow, respectively) we will create more HELL.

Righteous judgment occurs when our emotions move from the heart and upwards. It is said that Jesus had zeal – righteous judgment – and was "moved" with compassion (COME! PASSION!). This is because he lived and moved and had his being in the upper chakras, where decisions are made from compassion and understanding the holistic view of creation.

These upper chakras emit a different frequency – their colors are that of blue and indigo; the colors of water – fluidity. This is why Jesus walked on "water" and calls on Peter, one of the shadow selves of Christ, to come out and to join him in the journey. Walking on water is mastery of the emotions, recognizing that they are powerful and not to be dissolved, but to come into willful submission (SUB-MISSION) to the Christ.

We should not be as a "ship tossed by the wind and waves of the sea," but rather, we need to learn to master the emotions by employing them in our mission as creators in training!

> Acts 5:15 *As a result, people brought the sick into the streets and laid them on beds and mats so that at least Peter's shadow might fall on some of them as he passed by.*

> Matthew 4:16 *The people living in darkness have seen a great light; on those living in the land of the shadow of death a light has dawned.*

4:56 Never Having Been to Any Organized Church

A person never having been to any organized church, born in and belonging to the uncivilized clans of the jungle, can commune with the "higher power" and come to know the I AM within.

Structured religion did not teach me the greatness of the I AM within, it taught me that this higher power was without. It was only when I left the institution that I began to see.

That said, it served me as the womb, the woman of Revelation 12 that gave birth to the Christ and then subsequently retreats to the wilderness where she is fed and nourished by God. Religion is a womb, and at the same time, may serve as a midwife. I was forcefully expelled with violent contractions at the hand of the human ego – within myself and from without.

There is a need for some to experience this restriction of religion. Even Wicca is a religion. It is a structure described by Miriam Webster as "a pursuit or interest to which someone ascribes supreme importance." This object of extreme importance may lead us without or within.

Most of mankind has focused outwardly and will continue to do so until the time of awakening, or "the appointed time." Mankind cannot stop this powerful event that is now upon the Earth, any more than he could stop every plant from growing and producing seed. We are coming to maturity with or without structured religion. Most will shed organized systems like the husk of a seed that is no longer needed and that can no longer contain the burgeoning contents. It is a vibrational occurrence that, once it begins, will rattle our cages of confinement, no matter what they are.

4:57 The Awakening Sleeper

Change is sometimes threatening, for we perceive separation and difference. "That person, over there, thinks differently than I do, so one of us must be wrong." As human beings, we have this endowment of EGO, an aspect of us that must be right in its quest for understanding, for if it is not right, then it sees itself as wrong, and weaker or less than the other. It is the ego's job to discern similarities and differences.

In scripture it is said that, "The kingdom will not come with observation." That small i of self must decrease so that the aspect of us that does not OBSERVE with human eyes will come forward. Observation is for matter-based reality, which invokes judgment. Intuition must begin to supersede observation in our material world.

If we begin to willfully participate in the process of conscious evolution in non-judgment, we will do more to promote movement and/or advancement than to offer words that may be construed as criticism or rebuke (these are triggers for the ego to engage). It will also pave the way for our intuitive mind to speak up while the ego is disengaged from judging.

It is from this observing position in non-judgment that we do not become the snares ourselves; the place from where opposition or resistance fortifies a position of consciousness, so that stagnation does not occur.

Let's not build defenses with words, but carefully consider one another while allowing what is beneficial to remain. That which is growing in us is watered through non-judgment and love. This willful effort will help position the ego in the place of a submissive servant, rather than a domineering taskmaster.

Our judgment will not cause us to awaken. The sleeper (intuitive mind – Christ) awakes with a kiss, not a slap.

4:58 Okay. So, Maybe I Shouldn't Be Watching the News …

This morning I was flipping through channels and came upon FOX News blasting a person for suggesting we help ISIS instead of killing them; that killing was not the answer, but rather that we might consider giving economic support by helping to create jobs in the nations that have a high population of radical insurgents.

The commentators laughed and said something about "killing them with love" and what a joke that was. One special guest held up the cross around her neck and said that she wears it every day in support of those beheaded and martyred for their Christian faith and that she will not forget …

I could not help but think, "What WOULD Jesus do?"

I took a deep breath and thought to myself, "No more news for you."

4:59 I Spoke with a Desperate and Fearful Woman

I spoke with a desperate and fearful woman yesterday, who asked if I still did deliverance ministry (exorcism). I replied, "Not in the traditional sense." I encouraged her to not submit herself to religious systems that are "fear-based" and that promote doctrines of Hell, eternal torture and separation from God.

I went on to say that the Bible states over 600 times, "Fear not" and "be of good courage" and that it was ironic that Christianity is largely based on fear. I asked if she saw the irony in this...?

I told her that Satan and demons had no power over her, and that she was more than a conqueror in Christ. I told her that she has been given all authority over darkness, and that she was a child of THE KING.

She implied that I was "new age" and that she was too afraid to believe that way.

4:60 Anchoring Frequencies

I am convinced that we are "anchoring" higher dimensional frequencies within our bodies. We are walking, living, breathing, human tuning forks that are imbued with something "extradimensional". As human anchors, these frequencies will "sound out", much like a mama whale sounds out to search for her young and to guide them to her.

In this way, those next in line for transition will be affected by the countenance (energy field) of those anchors and will begin to house (anchor) the frequencies, as well.

These frequencies are from beyond our vibrational settings and will affect our physical make-up. Some will experience unusual things, but the more and more of us who anchor these frequencies, the more common it will become, and our bodies will adapt. They always do.

4:61 "Eating" From the Tree

"Eating" from the tree of the knowledge of good and evil, produces a state of consciousness that brings the introduction of time and, subsequently, mortality. Our consciousness is dense and heavy, and this consciousness pulls everything downward through thought.

So, when we eat from the tree, we surely die. Changing the way we think will introduce a buoyancy to our planet, enabling us to shift dimensions.

Gravity introduces time and time introduces mortality.

"Eating" from the tree of life introduces eternity.

Shifting our thought is akin to having our name changed from Jacob to Israel.

4:62 On Manifesting ...

I think we choose events that will ultimately bring us to the point of awakening. Once awakened, we can and do bring things into our experience that we want, rather than by creating through default.

Upon awakening, we begin to manifest much faster than before. It is almost like our safety net of time collapses and we are now responsible for the thoughts we think and the emotions we send out that begin to forge our reality.

4:63 You Are a God-man

Indeed. You are a God-man (Emmanuel) in training. Everything you think about, and apply the appropriate emotional value to, will eventually manifest in your life, somewhere. Be aware that "(God) will not be mocked. You will reap what you sow." Remember that? Different language, but the same truth. Tend to your garden. If you have sown things you do not wish to grow, pluck them out!

4:64 The Issue of Blood

You are the woman with the "issue" of blood. The woman that bled for twelve years (her cycle – your cycle traveling through the twelve ages of the zodiac) is you, oh, human being! – with your mortal life in your blood. When Christ is "touched", we are healed. The mortal becomes immortal once again.

4:65 If I Had a Dollar

If I had a dollar for every fundamentalist who quoted 1 John 4:5, I could pay one healthy tithe to any church.

> 1 John 4:1-5 (King James Version of the Bible)*4 Beloved, believe not every spirit, but try the spirits whether they are of God: because many false prophets are gone out into the world.*
>
> *2 Hereby know ye the Spirit of God: Every spirit that confesses that Jesus Christ is come in the flesh is of God:*
>
> *3 And every spirit that confesses not that Jesus Christ is come in the flesh is not of God: and this is that spirit of antichrist, whereof ye have heard that it should come; and even now already is it in the world.*

Look at that verse again. I have a question: Has Christ come in YOUR flesh? If not, are you of God? Could this verse actually allude to the "Christ in you, the hope of glory" understanding, instead of in one man's manifestation?

I used to believe the scripture was mainly literal and slightly figurative, but then I began to search it out – I mean, really search and compare to other (much) older texts and religions. The Bible and the stories are not unique, nor are they exclusive to Israel. It is the story of all of humanity. And this story (even the end of the story!) is hidden in plain sight through allegory.

So many allude to the sacrifice of Christ and the shedding of blood being necessary and paramount to believe and to remit sin; however, the shedding of blood is (figuratively) your mortal life, as you surrender your ego to death (the ego has caused your spirit body to slow way down so that it actually manifests in matter).

There is no remission of sin (not what you think it is). Sin is this dimensional (and mortal) level where there is continual judgment between good and evil as humanity eats of the tree we are told not to. Sin is not various acts; it is a mode of being. Just as Christ is not a person (but, all people having a trans-figurative experience); it is a mode of being, as well.

4:66 To My Fundamentalist Friends:

Christ is not a last name. If you would like to study the word, it might benefit you to understand where I am coming from. Christ is a verb, not a noun. It is a mode of being. Jesus was a pattern for us, in that he submitted his human will to that of the

Divine will. Once this occurs, the human aspect of us becomes wed, as in marriage to the Divine. The union spoke of in the Bible occurs within us.

You may have a limited view of what Christ is because you have been indoctrinated. I was where you are for over 40 years of my life. I am not there anymore. I am no longer motivated by the fear that the organized fundamentalist church threatened me with. And neither should you be. I read the dogma about Hell being a real place created for the fallen angels, being bought with blood, and how Hell is our destiny and we will be doomed if we do not accept the "gift." Does that really make sense to you? Do you really believe in a God that will torture and torment you if you do not accept a gift?

I used to believe the same way but have gone through almost 20 years of deprogramming to regain my sanity. All it takes is willingness to put fear under your feet. The rest is easy. God is love. Nothing more; nothing less. He is not the tyrant that the fundamentalist church has taught you about. There is a reason that for every person converted to Christianity, four leave the faith. People are not buying it. And you don't have to, either.

4:67 There Are Twelve Cycles That Occur

There are twelve cycles that occur (one ascending and one descending) over twenty-four thousand years. Each time, they last roughly two thousand years each.

Our solar system moves through this cycle (called the Precession of the Equinox), as it makes an ellipsis with another star, our second sun.

This second sun is very far away, but yet still influences our spiritual consciousness, just as our sun influences and tends to our physical being.

As we move away from this dual star/sun, we become less enlightened (the descending twelve thousand years).

As we move toward this dual star/sun we awaken again (ascending twelve thousand years). We are presently on the ascending path.

These twenty-four cycles correspond with the Yugas. The Golden Age is where we are most enlightened; then we descend.

The Silver Age offers enlightenment, but a slow devolution into darkness.

In the Bronze Age, we have a vague memory of the Silver and Golden Ages.

It is during this time, when the sign of Virgo is prominent – the Virgin produces the Christ. The Christ is birthed anew (into baseness/manger) into our consciousness and works to re-store and resurrect the frail human counterpart.

The Iron Age is the place of outer darkness and weeping and gnashing of teeth. Life expectancy is about 23 years.

Then, as we traverse through this futile period, we begin to see hope once again with the Bronze Age (the Industrial Revolution).

This is where we are. We are at the base level era on our way toward enlightenment.

There is something called alchemy, where base metal is turned into gold.

You asked the question – can we skip any ages, or do we have to go through them all?

Alchemy…

The creature was made subject to futility, not willingly, but by the ONE who subjected it in hope. The immersion into this cycle is the symbol of baptism. We, as Divinity, have been made subject to death through this twenty-four-thousand-year cycle. Now it is time to remember and to come up and out of those waters.

4:68 Feelings and Emotions Are a Choice

Feelings and emotions are a choice we make to utilize. I have feelings erupt every day and it is my choice to live either below the heart chakra (red, orange and yellow – Hell) which is the egocentric mode of being, or we can live above the heart (blue, purple and indigo – Heaven) the colors of the waters of transcending consciousness, and thereby we "walk on the water".

When the emotions pull us down into the lower depths (despair, confusion, hopelessness, etc.) we are "in Hell"; hence the red, orange and yellow "flames".

There is a great gulf between the lower, hellish emotions and the higher ones, and it is called the heart. The heart is like the Panama Canal. We allow ships in to be raised to a higher sea level, just like we surrender our emotions to be transmuted. The heart is a sophisticated mechanism that is able to change the energy of the emotion, thereby serving, rather than destroying, our ship, as it is tossed to and fro by the waves of the sea.

4:69 Tame Your Dragon

It's in you. Tame your Dragon – like the Disney film, "How to Train Your Dragon." It is a noteworthy film, and one through which we can learn much about this necessary and vital aspect of ourselves – the EGO.

Many cite this passage and say it is about the Devil (Satan). And it is – but just what is Satan; that great dragon?

> Revelation 12: 3 *And there appeared another wonder in heaven; and behold a great red dragon, having seven heads and ten horns, and seven crowns upon his heads. 4 And his tail drew the third part of the stars of heaven, and did cast them to the earth: and the dragon stood before the woman which was ready to be delivered, for to devour her child as soon as it was born.*

I did an exhaustive study back in 1999. The text says, "the third part of the stars." That is the soul/mind of all of mankind. It fell to the 3rd density which, simply put, is our mortal mode of being. Not one-third – the THIRD part. This means the egocentric aspect of all humankind.

Our "third part" – that which was installed last or third in order – as man became a "living soul." It is this nature that eats from the tree that judges between good and evil and, as such, the soul embodies the framework of the human.

Each of us has this dragon within, the human will/ego that must have its cross experience in order to experience resurrection. This is the symbolism behind the serpent on the pole – it is our own spinal column, and this energy must rise up from the fear, the fight-or-flight nest that "lies" between the lower extremities of the body trunk.

It is allegory. To take the scripture literally brings death. The letter kills.

The Bible is a mystery book. Forsake the history, embrace the mystery!

4:70 Sound Doctrine

> *For a time will come when men will not put up with sound doctrine. Instead, to suit their own desires, they will gather around them a great number of teachers to say what their itching ears want to hear. They will turn their ears away from the truth and turn aside to myths.* 2 Timothy 4:3

Well, this verse was written some 2000 years ago, and it could be logically argued (with great historical support) that the sound doctrines of Jesus Christ were diminished into doctrines of man and demons a long time ago. I am presently watching a DVD about the Christian myth, a diversion from the gnostic and esoteric teachings of the Christ.

The Christian myth, enforced by Rome to ensure order and compliance in an advancing (albeit disorderly) empire, was enacted as a national religion in 313 AD. One could argue that the sound doctrine of Jesus Christ was diminished at the hands of the Roman Emperor Constantine as he sought to contrive and maintain control of his people.

A new Christianity was birthed, including doctrines of the Trinity and Hell, among many others that were clearly a mixture of Paganism and Christianity. This blending of doctrines, ideologies and beliefs is what we now know as modern Christianity.

Now that there is a return to the unblemished teachings of Jesus Christ, the church-at-large cries "foul!" because their fear-based religion with behavioral theology is beginning to crumble and give way to the unconditional love of God.

4:71 When the Bible is Not Taken Literally ...

The teaching within is reflected in many other mystical and or spiritual texts that pre- and postdate the Bible.

It is the story of human consciousness unfolding. Even if you don't believe in a literal Jesus (and that is fine with me!) the words given within the text are transformative – being "born again" is seeing things through a different perspective, just as the word "repent" means "to change the way you think."

There are endless, damaging doctrines that teach that we have to raise our hands and walk an aisle and accept Jesus into our heart to be saved – that is dogma, and produces a limited life. The promise of eternal reward places the responsibility of transformation outside of one's self and is a process that relegates transformation until after death.

The teaching about being born again is simply this: we must experience the shift from egocentric humanity to our divine and eternal nature. This is where our humanity intersects our divinity and the humanity willingly "dies" in order to resurrect. It is the cross experience; not for one, but for all. This is where our ego experiences death, so that it might resurrect a servant to the divine nature. If we remain in our humanity and never experience this inversion process, then we will remain where we are – in death.

You see, all the examples and statements in scripture can and should be interpreted mystically. In that interpretation, there are untold mysteries. If taken literally … well, then you end up with division, war, hatred, violence and injustice.

I understand that there are many who refuse to even look at the Bible because they have been thumped by it. I, myself, could not even pick it up for years, but now can appreciate the rich, poetic and mystical qualities within it. We are the subject of the stories about Jesus. We are the Christ that has been born in baseness, within the swaddling blankets of biology – the stable of humanity. It's all about you.

4:72 Panic and Anxiety Attacks

For those who suffer with panic and anxiety attacks, this may help:

As kundalini rises through the chakra channel, sometimes, as it passes through the 3rd chakra (emotions, kidneys, adrenals), adrenalin is released, and anxiety appears.

These are energy currencies that are seeking release from (current and past) life experiences, and many may feel this process as anxiety, because of the effect that adrenalin has on the nervous system.

Speak to the energy movement. Bless it. Do not offer resistance. Tell it to move. Breathe. Be a screen door and let it pass through. In offering resistance, you become a storm door and the energy remains trapped.

SECTION FIVE

FIVE

5:73 A Friend Who Does Not Like Me to Quote the Bible ...

Words like 'Divine, 'born again,' 'Dies,' 'Christ,' 'Cross' are all-too-obvious Bible references, whether they be mystical or ancient regurgitations. My point is, why bother with the Bible at all, unless you are either still stuck in deity belief or are using it as a manipulative technique to sell something, or it just feels good to hang on to what is familiar?"

My response:

Christ is not a term reserved for Christianity – it was around centuries before, and simply means "anointed." Anointing for all, not just for one. It is a spiritual term, however, that implies a title of sorts for those who seek esoteric understanding. It was not, and never should be, considered a religious term.

The term "cross" far predates Christianity, as well. Easily enough to research, it has application in many cultures and beliefs. But, to me, it simply means the intersection of spirit and man, divinity and ego.

Eternal nature, as well, is not a Christian term.

In my book, I write how the Bible is not a Christian book, but has sort of been "hijacked" by the faith as their own. It is first and foremost a mystery book, not a history book. Jesus (a mythical figure?) was not a Christian; he was not even a good Jew. Within the Bible, he states pre-existence prior to Abraham, who is considered the father of Judaism.

The definition of a myth (mythical person) is this: something that never was, yet always is. The pattern of Jesus Christ is indeed archetypical – it is the story of you.

Finally, the term "born-again" is a Christian term with A LOT of attached dogmatic baggage. The term, correctly translated, is "born from above" and simply means to elevate ones thinking above the norm.

My desire is to help those people who are transitioning out from the manipulation and control found in most religions, to see that they, themselves, are the subject of the myth.

The Bible is filled with mystery, as well as many other texts and books written down through the ages. I choose to glean from them all and choose not to draw a line in concrete as to what I allow myself to read and intuit. When lines are drawn, growth stops, and we become oxbow lakes filled with putrid stagnant waters. It is nice to flow with understanding, allowing everything into view that brings joy and growth.

5:74 Jesus Was Not Political

Jesus was not political at all. He didn't stump for political candidates, favoring one Caesar over another, but rather, stated, "Give to Caesar what is Caesar's." In other words, pay your taxes, although you are "sons of the kingdom" and "not under the law." He stated, "My kingdom is not of this world" – we are told to be "in" the world, but not "of" the world.

As of 1996, after being within fundamentalism for almost 40 years, having attended hundreds and hundreds of church services in many different Christian denominations or sects all over the country, the church had not been political up until then. That was my experience.

In October of 1996, Fox News burst upon the scene with the "religious right" with what it claimed was "fair and balanced news" to counteract the growing popularity of the ever-present CNN with their "far left" opinions.

So, back to my original question... What happened to the church that it became so politically charged to the point that its leaders are being called on the carpet for holding a political opinion in view for their congregations to embrace/follow? Clearly, a violation of the tax-exempt 501C3 public charity guidelines.

It is obvious that, somewhere in the late 1990s, something changed within the fabric of fundamentalism, and I am still pondering what it was.

My conclusion is this: If we focus on the world – the bad shape that it may or may not be in -- we will create more of what we focus on. We are told to "lift our eyes" and to think on things that are "joyful." If we really understood the incredible creative power of our humanity endowed with the creator within, we would stop throwing our valuable emotional currency at the bad circumstances of life.

5:75 When You Focus on Controversy

When one focuses on the controversy condemning homosexual marriage, it is a clear indicator of the age that their consciousness occupies.

> *"In the age to come there is neither Jew nor Greek, male or female; you are neither taken nor given in marriage."*
> Jesus

5:76 On Leaving Christianity – To My Detractors:

I, too, was dogmatic, unmoving, rigid, motivated by fear, brainwashed and conditioned to believe someone else's idea of God. Then something wonderful happened: I let it all go.

I let Jesus go – my idea of him and all of the doctrines I had wrapped myself in – forsaking it all to know the truth. I repented. I changed the way that I think.

I began to search for love, non-judgment, tolerance and acceptance; the very attributes of Christ.

I cannot go back to the idea of a punishing God; one who tells us to love and to forgive our enemies while he tortures his in everlasting torment. No, my religion no longer makes sense. I have found Christ – he is formed within the womb of man, wrapped in the swaddling of our very own flesh and blood.

Yes, I found him; always in my heart; not trying to get in but trying to get out to express through me... him.

5:77 I Let Everything Go

I decided back in 2005 to let everything that I thought I knew about Christianity, God, or Jesus, go. It was a time of personal transition and crisis, and I knew that I was breaking down – spiritually speaking. I looked into the word "repent" and saw that it meant "to turn around and to change the way that you think." And I did.

There is a scripture where Jesus said, "It is better for you if I go away ... I will send the comforter to you." I made the decision to let Jesus, and everything I was taught about him, go. I was so totally confused by what I had been taught about God – this tyrant who loved and hated, was jealous, incited rape and murder, dismemberment and genocide. Really? Nope. I couldn't do it anymore. It just didn't make sense.

This, it seems, is a prerequisite for repentance – "to change the way you think." Everyone will begin to question the tenets of their faith at some time. We cannot help but outgrow our clothing from our childhood.

Then, I began to look at scripture more figuratively, especially the mysterious parables that Jesus taught – were they were all figurative? He encouraged us to "lift our eyes." What did that mean? Were we to look skyward all the time or did it mean to access a different space in our conscious awareness? I asked for help in interpreting the scriptures – not according to any Bible commentary, but what was the Spirit speaking directly to me?

Peace began to wash over me as I sojourned out from fear and into love and acceptance.

The mysteries come from meeting Christ in the "upper room" – that is, in your own higher thinking. This is where the "unveiling" takes place. There is a veil between the two hemispheres of the brain called the corpus collosum. It is referred to in the medical community as the "veil." It acts as a mediator between the left and right hemispheres of the brain, the bride and the groom. Once the veil is "rent" we can have access to both sides of the brain and our intuitive function really kicks in. This is where we meet with "Christ" as Christ is the amalgamation – the byproduct of union.

As far as the absolutes of Christianity …

Jesus was not a Christian, or even a good Jew, for that matter. He said, "Before Abraham was, I AM." Abraham was the founder of Judaism, so Jesus was stating his existence even before the founding of Judaism. He was neither Christian nor Jew.

In my searching, I discovered much of Christianity that was simply not true but had been inherited from Constantine and the Council at Nicaea. I had to learn for myself, like the forming of the butterfly from the liquid carcass; the breakdown of the caterpillar. No one could do this for me, and no one could help me free myself from the cocoon, lest I miss the struggle that forced the life's blood into my metaphorical wings.

The term Christian was around long before Jesus, and simply eludes to an enlightened being. Our enlightenment was nullified when we began to embrace the traditions of men and the doctrines of "men and demons."

5:78 You Are a Beacon

It is very important that we understand things that are happening inside of our bodies.

There are those beings that have incarnated as resonators and beacons to broadcast a vibration or frequency that is higher than typical third-dimensional reality/duality or "eating"/partaking of the knowledge of good and evil.

As we begin to cease judging events of our lives as good or evil, the fabric of the third dimension is compromised because human judgment is what holds reality "in place".

These beings are fully human but are occupied by energy that is somewhat "higher" in the frequency spectrum. These are the "first-fruits" – those who awaken from their position beneath the soil of the Earth (human understanding and consciousness) and sprout what it is that they are; Christ.

Jesus was called the "firstborn of many brethren" and Paul said that he travailed in labor until Christ is formed IN us. This Christ is now beginning to awaken and mature within the womb of our humanity.

This Christ consciousness is not bound for Earth, but rather, is the savior of the Earth.

The ransom has been paid by the shedding of our blood (human DNA), as the son of perdition (self-ego) relinquishes its throne so that the Christ may reign.

This produces the realm or dimension that is called "the kingdom" or the 5th dimensional level. It is the frequency of the heavens between dimensional levels that we are manifesting, becoming a vibrational bridge between the kingdom of Heaven and Earth.

This upgraded frequency places a demand on our physical bodies and, as such, our electromagnetic field is trying to adapt, becoming a bridge in our energy spectrum from one age to the next.

5:79 Stance on Abortion

I remember being asked a while back if I had a stance on abortion. The people I was meeting with were staunch pro-choice. I told them that I was in favor of responsible procreation and non-violent behavior so, therefore, I would focus upon a kind and loving society.

I went on to explain that if I am against abortion and I picket Planned Parenthood, then I am bringing my focus, attention, thought and emotion into a creative process that will actually create the very thing that I have set my focus upon – in this case I would create the need to resist abortion. Do you follow?

If I set my focus, attention, thought and emotion by thinking "I need money," I will create the "need" for more money. If I set my focus on plenty, I will have plenty. If I set my focus, attention, thought and emotion on the need to close Planned Parenthood, I will create more "need" to close Planned Parenthood.

In other words, I will create more of what I do not want – even more Planned Parenthood clinics. Do you follow the process?

Instead, those called to employ their creative abilities must shift their focus on what it is that they DO want. If you don't want to see abortion clinics and films of late term abortions, then think on things that are pure, lovely and just. Resistance is futile. Jesus said, "Resist NOT evil." In our resistance is persistence.

We have to ask ourselves, if we are manufacturers, creators, distributors of emotional currency, and emotional currency is pure creative potential, then what should we set our focus upon???

If you watch the news and see horrific images and you allow your focus and emotion to remain upon the images, replaying them in your mind, you are seeding the universe with a request. If I watch the news, any news offering injustice of any sort, and I give my energy in the form of my focus and emotions to what I view, then I am enlisting the creative potential within me, the microcosm, within the universe, the macrocosm, to accomplish and to create the object of my attention.

Herein lies the mystery of creation. You are the I AM. You are pure creative potential housed within the framework of the human being. The I AM enlists the mechanism that can focus thought and emotion – the human mind!

The I AM is looking for a submissive helpmate – one who will not be distracted by the lower level emotions, but will rather focus on the good things, thereby creating what it focuses upon.

Not all are called at this time, but there are those who are called to transition the ages. This is accomplished by intentional focus. This is the Melchizedek Priest that will help bridge the gap between the ages. We must focus on what it is that WE WANT TO SEE in order to bring it into manifestation.

5:80 Throwing Good Emotional Currency

Your emotions ARE currency. Just imagine that when you get upset you are reaching into your bank account within and scooping up a handful of gold and then throwing it at the given situation, thereby GUARANTEEING that you will SUSTAIN what it is that you are focusing upon.

You may act upon something, but when you enlist your emotions, you are in JUDGMENT. Act without judgment and emotions. Let that valuable currency flow through the heart chakra, and in doing so, you will have changed the frequency of that emotion. It can then be enlisted with compassion and be more able to affect change rapidly – collapsing time itself to serve the I AM that you are.

In so doing, the effector is judging with RIGHTEOUS JUDGMENT and the position of the effector is at the Judgment seat of CHRIST. We must stop throwing good emotional currency at the bad circumstances of life.

5:81 Jonah

Jonah in the belly of the great fish... Metaphorically, Jonah is corporeal humanity in the age of Pisces (in astrological symbolism, Pisces is the fish, so humanity is in the belly, or the middle of, the age of Pisces). We are being called to repentance; to change the way that we think; to be spared from continued and seemingly irrevocable mortality. It is said that in the belly, Jonah passed the gates of Sheol. We are in Hell, folks. The Age of Pisces is where we learn obedience to the voice of I AM within. Pisces has indeed "vomited" us out and now we are faced with the task of obedience. One needs to ask, what is it that we are to be in obedience to?

5:82 Briefly, on Baptism

It is important to see the act of baptism as metaphoric, rather than literal, act.

When baptism is performed, it serves the purpose of awakening the Divinity within humanity of its choice to be willfully immersed into mortality within human consciousness.

This act of willful immersion into humanity comes with a price that must be paid by the Divine. It is necessary to acquire a body. There will not be salvation (resurrecting to immortality) unless there is immersion into the waters of humanity.

It must forget its identity while mortal, until the time of awakening, and not one minute before:

> *I charge you, O ye daughters of Jerusalem, by the roes, and by the hinds*
> *of the field, that ye stir not up, nor awake my love, till he please.*
>   Song of Solomon 2:7

5:83 A Woman Who Wants Me to Follow Jesus

Elizabeth, I devoted 43 years of my life as a follower, teacher, speaker, lay counselor and minister to Christianity. I know the Bible very well, and have been an avid student still, and I am over 60 years young.

I had wonderful experiences within Christianity and am most thankful for them. Now I understand that Jesus was not a Christian, nor was he a good Jew. The I AM that he claimed to be far eclipsed any religion. I no longer follow any religious persuasion, but rather, I choose to love unconditionally and fear nothing.

I no longer subscribe to a God that tells me to love my enemies while he tortures his. I began to challenge the teachings within Christianity that did not reflect the love that Jesus spoke of, and I am FREE.

5:84 Many of You Are Feeling the Shift

Many of you have felt, and are feeling, the most recent shift that is upon us. We have been entering into the most significant time of "ascension" as the restrictions of this passing phase of influence have lifted. Many have felt the manifestation of the "brass ceiling" that has been over our consciousness, unable to lift their heads above this barrier of depression and sorrow. Now it is GONE. This vibrational restriction over the consciousness of the planet is GONE. A natural buoyancy has returned to us as we have plumbed the depths in consciousness and have now been vomited out of the whale of the belly (the great Fish – the Piscean Age). The Age of Pisces has given way to the incoming influence of the Aquarian age. We have spoken of it for decades and written songs to this advent, but now we can FEEL it. It is palpable! How about you?

5:85 A Word for You ...

There is cataclysm within your body. What is happening to you cannot be seen with the physical "I" – it can only be understood by the intuitive mind.

You will feel pain. You will feel unease. You will feel adjustment. And, as these physical adjustments take place, your consciousness will begin to shift en masse. Yes, cataclysm indeed.

You are being recalibrated, reengineered; a new creation fit and compatible to the frequency of the age appearing and upon us.

5:86 The Root Has Broken the Pot

Once you leave systemic fundamentalism, you can't go back. A friend of mine says, "The root has broken the pot."

When the consciousness of Christ begins to grow, like the mustard seed, it begins to take over the garden; what you learn of freedom and love far eclipses the former restriction of fear and judgment.

My God does not encourage me to forgive my enemies while he torments his.

My God did not insist on killing his son, torturing him, so that I may be forgiven.

My God loves me unconditionally, showers me with grace, and lets me see him each and every day, in your beautiful face and in mine.

5:87 High Vibe Tribe!

As consciousness shifts to become more loving and less judgmental, we may notice changes in our physical makeup, as well. As we move from fear to love, the frequency we emit escalates! Practicing non-judgment and love will organically raise your internal vibration!

The most significant shift in our planet's history is occurring. At different points on our historical timeline, we have experienced leaps in our conscious evolution which bring the advent of increasing internal vibration and frequency. When these leaps in consciousness occur, they may bring with them physiological adjustments; notably, a change in skull shape and size, overall stature and cognitive abilities. These changes can be seen in retrospect and occur over long and sweeping periods of time. Our body adjusts to these increases in frequency as time marches on.

However, time seems to be speeding up! Have you noticed this? And with this advent, physiological and cognitive changes seem more pronounced. In particular, intuitive faculties have been activated and, as with any exercise, this ability expands with use.

Test yourself – test your intuitive abilities. Who is calling you on your telephone? Take a guess. Which key will open the lock when you have two keys that are identical? Does your intuition forewarn you of traffic ahead? A response from a friend? A dinner invitation?

How are you responding to the changes in your physiology? Many are reporting unusual body aches, pains, vibrations, auditory tones, headaches, pressure, heartbeat fluctuations and palpitations, various sensations, dizziness etc. From personal experience, it is best to remain joyful as we integrate these incoming and interstellar frequencies.

If you have concerns, see a doctor. If you have no concerns, JUST BREATHE.

And remember, SHIFT HAPPENS.

5:88 You Are a Multidimensional Being

You are a multidimensional being with twelve tones/aspects to your "self". These are disciples (if you will) and are here to serve you and to learn with you. You have agreed to this journey, with all of its twists and turns, highs and lows.

Yours is the story of the birthing, dying and resurrecting God-man. This planet sustains this story, and helps you reap your development and evolution.

Your story is amazing, and I thank you from the bottom of my heart for BEING.

There. How's that?

5:89 Regarding Deprogramming

It is a process to come out from any form of legalism, especially fundamentalism, because of the repetitive nature of the indoctrination process. Fundamentalism employs programming through repetition that helps reinforce dogmatic principles, establishing neural pathways in the brain with threats of separation or damnation. It is insidious. This is why we see "knee-jerk" responses by those fundamentalists who are threatened by anything outside of their established dogmatic order. I can predict with accuracy what a fundamentalist will quote from their dogma or scripture in response to a given challenge. I can do this, because I was one of them. It has taken me since 1999 to deprogram.

Scripture says (isn't it ironic that I quote scripture?) over 600 times to "Fear not; be of good courage", and yet most of the 38,000 to 41,000 differing and disagreeing Christian denominations are based on fear. I think the phrase "spiritually healthy fear" might be a bit of an oxymoron. Fear is the lowest frequency (if you will) in our emotional spectrum. I had to decide long ago that one cannot overcome deception with fear.

I think you are in a very good place. It is a part of most spiritual paths to overcome fear and to learn to listen to your own spiritual guidance (the Holy Spirit). Here is another scripture: "There will come a time when no man will teach you..." I believe this is because we are leaving the age of the institutional church (as was the pattern of the Christ) and what we are learning is not taught because it is no longer an intellectual and ego-centric path (left-brained). We are now learning, sojourning into the intuited worlds of spirit (right-brained). This is the "single eye" that Jesus spoke of.

Trust your inner voice. Follow love, joy, peace, kindness. You will find your way.

5:90 Are You an Energetic Mediator?

Many are experiencing discomfort in their emotions and in their bodies. You are struggling to understand what is happening. There is another "wave" of healers that has been activated in the last couple of months.

As your energy begins to move within your physical and etheric body, you may feel this movement and the accompanying pain. This energy is the "serpent on the pole" (or spinal column) that is recorded in the book of Exodus. This powerful symbol of energy is the movement of the Christ as it brings healing to the Earth's collective energy field.

Many of you felt this combustible energetic movement and suffered from breathlessness, fatigue, volatile emotions, trembling, shaking and physical pain.

What you felt was the collective output of grief, the very human response to trauma. You have helped "mediate" this outflow by transmuting the flow through your body – helping the global reaction and sending it upward. At this time of transition, the Earth can simply not afford to be swamped in grief, and so you ARE. You are here. You have agreed to come and mediate energy from within your framework – and you are quite adept at it, having mediated planetary ascension elsewhere. You are heavenly militia.

It is imperative to recognize your gift. Do not identify with the negative energy but receive it as a gift and raise it upward as an offering to all that is. Remember, there is no human suffering in vain – all has value. When dense emotional energy remains in the body, it cannot become buoyant enough to transcend. This is your task. Hold love, joy, peace, patience, kindness, benevolence, and meekness in your heart as you receive your gift, and it will be transformed, restructured and re-bundled in the swaddle of high energetic currency. This is the stuff of global change. You will succeed in your mission.

The Earth's path is fixed for ascension and there is little to stop it now.

The following is information I have received for a friend who is feeling these changes:

"You have abilities that are latent. It usually takes discomfort to move one into discovery. Once you enter discovery there is no turning back. Your body and your senses become indicators for action. What you sense, is. Information is given for you to act. It is up to you to put thoughtful intention to flight and spiritual movement to action.

"You will learn the language of your body; each part has significance and meaning. You will learn to trust your language and indicators. Your body speaks.

"Creation waits for your conscious participation in the unfolding of times. Each of you plays a part, and each part is precious and reflects the whole, like a hologram.

"Intention is everything. Set your mind to understand and you will.

"There are energy mediators installed for this time. *You are one such mediator."

With love and highest expectation of your accomplishment,
Barbara

SECTION**SIX**

SIX

6:91 The Accident

It is this "gap" between logic and intuition that I am called to bridge. I feel this also means to bring the metaphorical (intuitive understanding) of the mystical script, found within parables and other texts, to light. If we interpret literally, we miss the mystery of the "coming" of Christ. This has been the main impetus in my journey coming out of fundamentalism. *Literalism has left the building.* It has become difficult not to see the symbolism that surrounds us. We must begin the journey out of history and enter into mystery. Throughout this material, I will bring metaphoric interpretation into focus to help bridge the gap between logic and our intuitive mind, using language and imagery.

It is vital to understand that, as participants in this unfolding drama, we have an elevated view to grasp the purpose for experiencing good and evil. Victimhood plants you squarely into duality, whereas being a participant catapults you into understanding the creative processes of the age to come. No matter what has happened in your life, you must remember this: these things do not happen TO you; they happen FOR you. We are transitioning in consciousness, out of this passing age and into the next. Come with me, over the expanse of the gap, and help me build the bridge into the age to come!

Years after his motorcycle accident, my son, Chris, came over rather ecstatic one day, pulled off his shirt and told me to "really look" at his angel tattoo that he had inked BEFORE THE ACCIDENT! I shrugged my shoulders and said, "It looks like your angel tattoo."

He said emphatically, "No, Mom, really LOOK at it; what do you see, or better yet, what do you NOT see?"

I was amazed when he pointed out to me that the angel tattoo was actually missing a hand and a foot, just as he is now. They had never been tattooed in place.

6:92 I Have Read About the "Atlantean Rift"

I have read about the "Atlantean Rift" in Drunvalo Melchizedek's books. It is said that humans of a higher vibration, through their advanced technology, accidentally compromised the fabric between dimensions and the beings that occupied the neighboring vibration seeped through into our dimension, mingling with us and causing humanity to fall prey to a dark agenda. The fall.

Also, we have an account in the *Bible of Nephilim* of "Sons of God" that somehow penetrated dimensional boundaries, as well, and mated with human women, spawning a race of giants that led to mankind being evil continually – prompting the flooding of the planet.

A lot in these writings resonates with me on a very neutral level. I neither embrace nor dismiss. Who may know for sure?

What has been revealed to me is this:

We have been given a dimension to occupy, to learn the value of our emotions and that they do most certainly flow out from us as a type of creative and sustaining currency.

We are beings that, through some penetrative act, have become endowed with higher dimensional energy – God, the Divine, Spirit. We are gods creating and maintaining our own environment (and beyond), up until now, completely unconscious.

We are the mechanism (physical body and mind mingled with God, the Divine, Spirit) that will allow for the creation of material worlds. It is through the physical body, through the human chakras, that material domains exist. We are human generators of frequency that constructs our material worlds.

In order to transition into these roles of creators and sustainers, we must raise our own frequency, become buoyant enough to float to the top of our spectrum and resurrect the body vehicle out from mortality. Presently, we are too low in our vibration and will continue in the time loop continuum until we "raise the body from the dead". This is accomplished with supreme simplicity:

Be happy.
Don't judge.
Choose love.

It is through these edicts that we save the body. The vibrational output that will issue forth from our own generating system will cause this mortal to put on immortality – this corruptible to put on incorruption. And it will happen in the twinkling of an eye or enlightenment.

6:93 New Year's Eve

I had a rather strange thing happen this past New Year's Eve…

Lying in bed at 1:30 in the morning and deeply disturbed about something, I tossed and turned.

Then I heard a text alert on my phone (remember, it is 1:30 a.m.!).

It was from a phone number that I was unfamiliar with, and this is what it said:

> *"As you go into the new year, recognize that there is no objective reality.*
> *Your reality is entirely subjective, meaning that it always manifests as you think –*
>
> *"So, think only positive loving thoughts.*
>
> *"Always keep in mind that you are a beautiful being of light – a loved daughter of heavenly parents.*
>
> *"Also, remember that you are a princess, destined to become a queen just like your mother in* Heaven. *"*

I responded with, *"Who is this?"*

He replied with his full name, and I realized that he is a gentleman that I had spoken with just one time, months ago.

I am beginning the new year with recording the synchronicities that happen on a daily basis and I challenge you all to do the same.

6:94 Meditation?

I am way too squirmy to meditate. I used to try really hard, but my mind races, and then I fall asleep if I am too still. So, I do art. I have found that my mind gets quiet enough, and when my right brain is engaged in creativity, I receive the necessary "downloads". Making jewelry (of late) really helps a lot. I have heard that most people who are awakening deeply appreciate a creative outlet – it engages the right hemisphere and coaxes the left into quietness and "sub-mission".

There are many ways to meditate in this manner – gardening, woodworking, painting, and even the new craze called Zentangle (detailed coloring books for adults). The reason these things are so popular is that it is meditation! So, those who engage in some sort of art form are opening their intuitive portal and are receiving interdimensional information through creativity. It does not necessarily come in the form of words, but it can. Usually interdimensional communication comes through color, vibration, frequency, etc., and is assimilated into language through the left hemisphere – the helpmate. So, we receive these downloads of information unbeknownst to us. We awaken one day with insight, unaware of where it came from.

Also, you probably hear the tones in your head/ears. That is, likewise, communication from outside of our plane.

I have done the "*OM*" thing, as well, but prefer art. My mind jumps around way too much if my hands are not occupied, trying to create something. I have learned to appreciate that about me, rather than to beat myself up over it. Creativity is my meditation. Heck, even organizing the refrigerator is meditation!

6:95 Orgasm – A Mechanism for Creating

I always try to be sensitive, to write about what Spirit is impressing upon me, and this morning is no different.

I don't want to approach this subject clinically or in great detail. I want to be concise and brief and to let your own guidance lead you in this awakening knowledge.

Orgasm brings vital life energy to the body during the physical procreating processes. I want to focus on procreating (although there are obvious other benefits to sex).

In the same way, orgasm brings vital life energy to the creation process metaphysically. Something marvelous and mysterious takes place during these moments of bliss, does it not?

USE these moments to create what it is that you desire to see manifest in your life.

In the moments leading up to and during orgasm, HOLD YOUR THOUGHTS ON WHAT IT IS THAT YOUR HEART DESIRES MOST, and watch it then begin to manifest in your life.

Understanding this process expedites your creative processes.

That's it. Get to work!

6:96 Our Education on Planet Earth

As youngsters, we cannot really appreciate our education within the school systems until long after we have graduated. It is the same here on planet Earth.

The Earth – and the environment of duality – is purposeful and necessary for the Spark of Divinity invested in humanity, as well as for the ego within man.

The Earth school provides the necessary immersion into mortality for the purpose of cultivating the pearl of Christ consciousness within the human. Divinity needs a mechanism – a vehicle that can focus thought and emotion – and that vehicle is the mind of the human with the ego as its steering wheel; the prime navigational device.

All along, this masterful plan has been about cultivating a servant. Divinity as unexpressed consciousness in materiality (sheer energy) needed a vessel through which to occupy space in the material world. Once it found a means to penetrate the material form (the biology of human DNA), it needed to foster necessary relational capacity, courting a spouse – a willing helpmate and a partner – through whom the immaterial could inhabit and find expression in the material world.

This beautiful and perfect helpmate is the human being. It is YOU.

6:97 Trapped Inside a Religious System

I included this excerpt from my book Escaping Christianity ~ Finding Christ because of the relevancy of the times. I hope you enjoy it:

Not long ago, my husband, Lyle, set the trap in our back yard with corn, a meal that hogs love. Unfortunately, deer and other wild animals love cornmeal too. Lyle usually mixes a small amount of diesel fuel in with the corn so that the other animals will not be drawn within the cage and become trapped inside. Feral hogs, it seems, don't mind the sweet smell and taste of diesel, and eat the corn anyway. This time, however, he forgot to include the fuel. We woke up the next morning hearing strange yelps from the pasture and looked out to see a beautiful buck trapped inside the hog pen. Harry, our Great Dane, was beside himself, wanting to go out to investigate the latest game in the pokey. We had to restrain the one-hundred-eighty-five-pound Harry inside the house while we went out to free the buck.

As we approached the cage, the buck was flailing around wildly, trying to escape, and causing a great deal of harm to himself. We stopped moving toward him, hoping he would calm down, but it became evident that we just needed to get the cage opened as quickly as possible and set him free. Lyle had difficulty getting hold of the gate because the buck was ramming his head and snaring his rack in the top of the cage, moving it several inches each time he struck. His rack stood over a foot above his head, and any way he turned he would tangle within the steel grid and hurt himself. The trap is less than four feet high and the buck struggled to stand within it. He charged the cage again, and again, and again.

We opened the door, but the buck was too scared, too hurt, and too wild. Lyle told me to go to the opposite side of the pen, hoping that the buck, being afraid of me, would turn away, see the open gate and leave. However, the most amazing thing happened; as I arrived at the other end of the cage, the buck stopped his violent movements and stood perfectly still, watching me intently. He was bleeding badly from his nose and air was bubbling out through the bloody and torn sinus cartilage just below his left eye. I bent over slowly to look at him. His head and rack lowered to match my gaze. There we were, standing less than 18 inches apart, eye-to-eye; still.

I was overcome with compassion and a lump formed in my throat. This beautiful creature stood before me badly damaged and battered. With our eyes locked I blinked away tears and said softly,

> *"I am so sorry, poor thing...I am so sorry. You are okay; be still. You're okay. You need to put your head down, turn around and leave ... the door is open. Put your head down, turn around and leave; the door is open. You are free, beautiful boy, you are free."*

His eyes did not leave mine, and he watched me ever so carefully. I slowly lowered my eyes to the ground. I swallowed hard seeing his self-inflicted wounds bleeding profusely and making a puddle onto the grass below. In the wee hours of the morning, still and quiet, I could hear the patting of the blood as it hit the ground.

A minute or so had passed, and my back ached from bending over. I moved ever so slightly to straighten and suddenly the buck put his head down and with a swooping motion he turned around and exited the cage running swiftly toward the open pasture, his beautiful white tail disappearing in the brush.

Lyle and I walked inside, utterly amazed at what had just happened. We sat at the kitchen table sipping our coffee, when suddenly I realized that this battered and wild animal was a reflection of me. Looking into the eyes of the deer and telling him to be still and that he was okay, felt now like I had been speaking to myself. After numerous painful experiences within the church system, where I had the emotional stuffing knocked out of me, I saw me – beaten and battered by my own doing – fighting and resisting the system, instead of leaving it completely behind. *"Put your head down, turn around and walk out of the door."* Those were words for me, and for anyone who has tried to pull circumstances past their season of relevance. Finally, after years of battling the dogmatic fundamentalist systems and the subsequent relationships formed within them, I have put my head down, turned around and walked out the open door.

Everything changed when I left fundamentalism; my world view, what I saw as truth, and my understanding of who we are and why we are here. I was filled with wonder at the increasing and holistic view I was beginning to see. It was like I had climbed this big hill overlooking a beautiful view and I was peering out through the parting trees at something magnificent. Our story is broad and vast, and the implications of such truth will severely threaten the prevailing religious systems. For those spiritual seekers outside of these religious structures, inversion is necessary. We must begin to see our cultural mythologies not as external and historical events, but rather, as glimpses into our internal spiritual construct and its principles, aiding us in our awakening; our evolutionary processes and ultimate reconciliation of our purpose here on planet Earth. You have planned and charted your course to be here at this moment in time – and you are right on time.

6:98 Decades Spent Within Christian Fundamentalism

I have learned so much in my life, in the decades spent within Christianity. But somewhere along my journey, the flow of love was diverted into the love of dogma. I floated along the tributaries named "judgment" and "intolerance". I deemed others as less knowledgeable than myself. And I stood in the place of judging them as saved and unsaved.

Yes, somewhere in this vast river of Christian consciousness I began to *believe* what was spoken and repeated that was not in keeping with the love of Christ, rather than to test the "spirit" behind the dogma.

> *"I am the way, the truth and the life and no one comes to the Father but by me."*

This became the mantra of Christianity to hang their hat on, deeming Christ to be elitist, separatist, judgmental and intolerant; just like us.

We failed to recognize that this "way" was love and non-judgment – just like the teachings of Jesus. Instead, we adopted dogma:

1. Raise your hand at the altar call
2. Walk the aisle for all to see (If you confess me before others, I will confess you before my Father)
3. Say the sinner's prayer (Where did that one come from?)
4. Get baptized (sprinkled or dunked)
5. Speak in tongues (Interpreted erroneously as being "filled with the spirit" or being "spirit-filled")

(These things may vary from denomination to denomination, but loosely are practiced.)

If these things are done, you are saved. You will go to Heaven and escape Hell.

The "way" of Christ is Love. Love the Creator. Love one another as yourself. Other than this, there is NO OTHER REQUIREMENT.

The Father is within and is the primordial force of creation. You may not get to this force, this power, this kingdom unless you surrender to LOVE.

That's it.

Christianity is not in keeping with the teaching of its namesake. We have veered off of the path. We have lost touch with our first LOVE. We have become separatist, divisive, intolerant and judgmental. Yes, Jesus came to bring a "sword and division". This edict to love will clearly separate those led by the law and those led by the heart.

Wake up, Christianity!

6:99 Jesus Did Not Start Christianity

Jesus did not start, or even create, Christianity. Man did that. Jesus was not a Christian.

I have come to understand the extreme control of the early Roman Catholic Church, along with Constantine, that formed doctrines that are not in keeping with the teachings of Jesus Christ. The Church is in need of an extreme makeover. We have been embracing incredible falsehood.

I decided to study for myself and not to embrace someone else's idea of God. I let the Holy Spirit teach me. The church down through history had to undergo reformation; it had to go through RE-FORM.

The church must come away from the teachings and doctrines that are not in keeping with the original texts and teaching of Jesus.

After a while, truth becomes mired with dogma, and that perpetual flow of spirit is relegated to an "oxbow lake". An oxbow lake is when waters turn putrid, having been separated from the perpetual flow of spirit, giving heed to doctrines of man and demons – additions from the egocentric mind of man.

6:100 Those Within Dogmatic Beliefs

Those within the dogmatic beliefs of fundamentalism pick and choose what they believe in, and usually at the behest of their fundamentalist leaders. It doesn't take one much to see the truth in my statement. Fundamentalist Christian dogma has instituted rituals and doctrines that have nothing; nothing to do with the words and teachings of Christ. Jesus sat with the sinners. Paul taught separation from them (until, that is, he awakened and counted all that he taught and learned "dung"). So, the question begs to be asked, *"Who do you follow, Paul or Jesus?"*

Furthermore, the advent of the life and teachings of Jesus were like a bomb dropped in the Bible. So diametrically opposed are most of his teachings to the rest of the Bible, that we fail to bridge the gap in understanding that fact.

Jesus came to rescue those held hostage within the grasp of religion by introducing love, non-judgment and tolerance. He fulfilled all of the requirements of the law when he expressed unconditional love.

This is to be our journey in consciousness, as well. We are to "follow" Christ.

Jesus actually manifested the next age outside of time itself. He spoke often of the age to come, because he embodied it. He plopped down, smack dab into a religious society that was holding the hearts and minds of men captive through ritualized religion and fear.

He came to set men free from such tyranny. The bomb dropped was consciousness clearly evolved past the environment it found itself within; it was, in fact, from another time, another age, even another dimension.

And He called that dimension, "The Kingdom."

6:101 The Bible Produces Vivid Imagery

This imagery is supposed to help the mind that dwells within the material world understand the principles within the IMMATERIAL realms or consciousness, if you will.

For example: SATAN.

Those within fundamentalism view Satan as a BEING that is at war with God. THE ADVERSARY. It is a BEING, but it DOES NOT EXIST OUTSIDE of YOU.

There is a war with the SPIRITUAL MAN as it is opposed by the MATERIAL MIND within man. That adversary is none other than the intellect that uses the knowledge of good and evil to inhabit, understand and to manipulate the world of matter. Because we "eat" from this tree (consciousness) our lifespan is limited. We are MORTAL and limited to approximately 120 years of age (Genesis 6).

Divinity or Spirit continually offers to the human being signs, symbols and allegory (figurative offerings) to AWAKEN that latent part of us (Spirit) that does not dwell within the intellect.

Intellect (what the mind thinks it knows) discerns through the knowledge of good and evil; our serpent nature. This is our primary operating system.

However, we are being "courted" by the part of us that is Divine and Spirit, gently awakening within us the spark that we have been impregnated, through the virgin soil of humanity and biology, where the babe is cradled.

In order to awaken, we must begin to interpret the signs! Lift your eyes! How many times have we been told to do this??!

Sarah and Abram pregnant! Sarah/CERE. Abram/BRUM. CEREBRUM! This babe is born within the constructs of the human mind.

ASK SEEK KNOCK to have the eyes and ears of SPIRIT opened. It's that simple. But the religious mind will resist, hanging onto its need to be right rather than righteous, grasping world of form, a FORM of godliness, yet denying its power. Denying the Christ within becoming the ANTI-CHRIST.

The ANTI-CHRIST is within us all until we cease to deny that Christ has come in the flesh – OURS.

6:102 A Letter from William:

"You are fabricating a different reality for yourself. When your son almost died, and you had that weird experience... you should have turned to God for guidance. Instead you followed some weird "spirit" which has led you away from a reliance and need to see Jesus as your Savior. I feel sorry for you. If only you had the freedom God had provided freely in Christ...the knowledge and trust in Christ as Savior from sin. We are all dying, some faster than others, some suddenly, but must be prepared with faith...which is like a beggar clinging to a gift of priceless worth...after all...that is heaven...but for those who reject such a Savior...they get what they asked for...an eternity away from love. You don't want to go where love can't follow. So where can I mail a Bible commentary that can start you on the path to heaven?"

Here is my reply to him, a man named William:

I challenge you. I challenge your comfortable places. I make you uncomfortable, because you need consensus to feel safe in your dogma.

So, I hear threats of Hell, death and separation and that if I don't turn away from my sin (which is what, by the way?) that I will get what I deserve...

King David said, "If I make my bed in Sheol thou art with me." You see, William, there is not a place where love can't find me, comfort me, cradle me.

Jesus said the "Kingdom is within you." So how can I miss it? There is nothing that can separate me from the love of God. Not you. Not your dogma.

I am in my sixties. I have studied the Bible *and read about every commentary out there for the last 50+ years. But there comes a time when "No man will teach you, save the Holy Spirit". I made the decision long ago to study for myself and not to rely on someone else's understanding. I had to rely on the Christ within me, the comforter – the same comforter that held me in the throes of trauma during my son's accident. You may call that Spirit "weird", but I call it love.*

"A person with an argument is no match for one with an experience." That's how I feel with this exchange between you and me. You are no match for me. I know what I have. I know what true freedom feels like, and I am sure that if you continue to seek, that you will, likewise, one day, find.

6:103 A Little Humor

Recently, a woman that I do not know stated this one-word response to me:

> *"Heresy"*

My response:

> *"Pharisee"*

Ya gotta keep your sense of humor here folks...

6:104 To All of You Forerunners!

To all of you forerunners out there who have had to shrink back because of the religious bullies out there; TODAY is your day of liberation!

I received this prophetic word back in June of 1994, and today it is FOR EVERY FORERUNNER out there. I can't tell you what I am feeling right now! So much LOVE! POWER! and AUTHORITY! Read this! It's for you too! Here is an excerpt:

> *"For the Lord says I am going to give you now a new anointing of keeping the pace, pace-making, trendsetting, in ways that you have a new anointed initiative to set the RIGHT THINGS IN ORDER. WALK IN IT FIRST, knowing that you are forerunners. There will be abuse that comes to forerunners; but the Lord says YOU WILL STAND IN THEIR FACE AND NOT BE ABUSED! With Joshua and Caleb, the whole congregation rose up to stone them when they gave a report of the promised land; the Lord says you are the good report! The good reporters that I will anoint and bless, and you will say, 'THEY WILL BE BREAD FOR US.'*
>
> *So, understand this: I am enlarging your borders. I am broadening your feet beneath you. A NEW WAY has been opened. A door has been opened that no one can close. I am giving you the KEY OF DAVID. What he opens no one can shut. He shuts what no man can open."*

Be encouraged! Claim your spiritual heritage as a forerunner who sees around the corner! This is YOUR GIFT TO THE WORLD! Even if they don't listen at first, SPEAK ANYWAY! Your truth is going forth as seed that will NOT RETURN VOID.

6:105 Get Bold!

Get bold, get free from toxic relationships ... I consider this paramount in freeing yourself from religious and other abuse.

Hotchkiss' Seven Deadly Sins of Narcissism – In her 2003 book, *Why is it Always About You?* clinical social worker and psychotherapist Sandy Hotchkiss identified what she called the seven deadly sins of narcissism:

Shamelessness: Shame is the feeling that lurks beneath all unhealthy narcissism, and the inability to process shame in healthy ways.

Magical thinking: Narcissists see themselves as perfect, using distortion and illusion known as magical thinking. They also use projection to dump shame onto others.

Arrogance: A narcissist who is feeling deflated may re-inflate by diminishing, debasing, or degrading somebody else.

Envy: A narcissist may secure a sense of superiority in the face of another person's ability by using contempt to minimize the other person.

Entitlement: Narcissists hold unreasonable expectations of particularly favorable treatment and automatic compliance because they consider themselves special. Failure to comply is considered an attack on their superiority, and the perpetrator is considered an "awkward" or "difficult" person. Defiance of their will is a narcissistic injury that can trigger narcissistic rage.

Exploitation: Can take many forms, but always involves the exploitation of others without regard for their feelings or interests. Often the other person is in a subservient position where resistance would be difficult, or even impossible. Sometimes the subservience is not so much real as assumed.

Bad boundaries: Narcissists do not recognize that they have boundaries and that others are separate and are not extensions of themselves. Others either exist to meet their needs or may as well not exist at all. Those who provide narcissistic supply to the narcissist are treated as if they are part of the narcissist and are expected to live up to those expectations. In the mind of a narcissist, there is no boundary between self and other.

6:106 We Will Always Judge, to Some Extent

We will always judge, and we judge every day on a multitude of issues. I think the key is that we stop engaging our lower three chakras (the 1st, 2nd and 3rd – fear, survivalism and emotionalism, respectively). These three emotional centers are what create and sustain our present reality and are the mechanisms that are triggered into action when we "eat from the tree" of the knowledge of good and evil.

Therefore, for the awakening soul, we recognize that whatever we judge, IS. If we deem something evil and we release the emotional currency from our chakras, we set in motion and create more potential of the very thing that we have just deemed evil.

With all of that said, it is normal for the human being (the ego) to discern between good and evil. This is the primary operating system of being human IN THIS AGE. But the awakening human is called to transition the age and recognizes that he, while he judges between good and evil, is not only creating this present age, but sustaining it. It is through non-judgment that we begin to forge the path and pattern in thinking of the age to come.

There are those who are called to maintain this age and there are those who are called to transcend it – building a bridge in consciousness for humanity to shift and to evolve in consciousness. Each must discern his call.

It takes a while for it to soak in, because we are focusing mechanisms. The ego was created for just such a thing. But the ego, while on its own mission, will continually create what it focuses on. Therefore, the mission of the Christ (within) will cause the human to come to the place of surrender and submission to the Christ mind. This is the union spoken of in scripture: "Nevertheless, not my will, but thy will be done." It is our cross experience.

The human is now recognizing that the Christ savior is not "out there" somewhere but lies cocooned within humanity – growing into the full measure and stature of the Christ. This mustard seed is growing within. We are the saviors the world is waiting for. It is time to awaken.

Emmanuel = God with man.

6:107 Now Ledge

I remember when we were in the ER waiting room during my son's accident, and I felt as though I was stepping up to a precipice (a very high ledge) and was being given the opportunity to leap off of it.

I did.

And, I flew.

Knowledge = NOW, LEDGE.

Each of us is being given the opportunity to think differently – to surrender into the now moment of knowing. This is a game changer. Things look differently when you see with your single eye. It requires a leap; a leap of faith.

When we begin to open up to the spirit, the environment we find ourselves within will require a different measure of discernment than what we have operated in before. Love begins to speak from all around us – flowers, birds, trees and even bugs begin to vibrate toward us, speaking mysteries to us. Love opens things. It is a key. Appreciation apprehends us and tears of gladness flow. We are Divinity living amongst humanity, and creation is both speaking and emanating from us.

And nothing is the same.

6:108 The Shadow of God That Has Been Cast by Men

I read stories and testimonies of drug addicts, prostitutes and gang members finding God and redeeming their lives. Once mired in darkness, they now serve the Lord.

I personally know of several people whose lives are forever changed because they have committed their lives to serving the God of Christianity. Having been convinced of their sin and sinful ways, they hear of the mercy of a loving God to forgive, heal and restore them. Having been convinced of eternal separation and torture, they submit to the system that opens their arms wide to them. And they are loved.

And the system works.

The prostitute has exchanged one pimp for another.

Think about it. While prostituting, a woman has to work, and must give a share of her earnings to her pimp under the threat of beatings and, ultimately, death. Within fear-based Christianity, one must "tithe" to the system to remain in right standing with the church. If you do not tithe, you may receive a letter asking why you do not give, and even why your children do not give in children's church. Sound familiar? Some systems stop at this, but others take it even further. Many will hear messages from the pulpit that are coercive to gain more funds from followers.

This form of manipulation keeps people under the threat of separation – separation from God, separation from Heaven, family members and friends. I was there. The system worked for me; until it didn't. The following events were all my fault. I fully recognize that I brought the "shit-storm" down on my own head. I had pimped myself out. Being very immature, I was drunk with the authority that I had been offered and had agreed to cast my council votes the way I was told to.

Being in church leadership, I eventually challenged the authority in my church and found myself being emotionally battered. In an odd twist, I was called into a private meeting where I was told to sit and take the verbal tongue-lashing and, if I did not, that I would be treated like I was divorced from authority and told that I would not be looked at or talked to. I was devastated. I have not spoken of this event to anyone outside of family and close friends, until today.

Meetings were held behind my back. Whispers that cast doubt on my reputation – the system defaulted into damage control.

We ultimately left the church, and I was invited to a meeting outside of church where they said they wanted to "love on me and give me encouragement." The meeting turned out to be a time of belittling and accusation, with a trusted board member resigning from my ministry and heavy persuasion and direction telling me to get back into church and to submit to the pastor. But I could not go back.

It is so wonderful to know God outside of Christianity. I am thankful to recognize the measure of control that Christianity had over me, and to realize that Jesus was not a Christian and did not come to start what we now know as the modern-day church. Yes, the system works; until it doesn't. For whatever reason, I was allowed to see the insidious side of "church." Not all are like this, but these events were enough for me to never want to go back.

Unfortunately, most people judge God by those who claim to follow him. So, when one does feel the need to move away from the system, he flushes himself from the very thought of God because of the people and systems that claim to represent him.

Most people in our world know only the shadow of God that has been cast by men.

Get able. Get free. Get authentic relationships. Find God within the temple made without hands. In you.

And ... FORGIVE. Even though I write passionately about these things, I have forgiven. These examples were my absolute best teachers, and I would not be where I am today without them.

Moving on.

SECTION SEVEN

SEVEN

7:109 When You Judge the Path of Another...

Be mindful of your judgments. When you look at someone and mentally disapprove of their actions and pronounce a judgment, you are selecting the threads, colors and texture to be added to your own life's tapestry.

As humanity endowed with divinity, your judgment is highly creative. Your judgment of a certain situation is vibrational, and you are sending instruction to the master weaver, giving orders for future experiences that you have requested through this vibration. The universal force within you and around you is vibrational in nature and responds to the frequency coming out from your body. If you are expressing hatred and disapproval, you are sending a vibrational request and, as Divinity, surely the universe will respond to you and you will receive what you request.

If you are viewing a given situation with appreciation, allowing and acceptance, you will receive the same.

We are largely unconscious of this process. We think that judgment is just an opinion, but it is so much more than that.

This is a great mystery – it is how this dimension is maintained – created daily by our continual judgments, and is why Jesus said, "DO NOT JUDGE. The judgment with which you judge another will fall upon your own head." Jesus was giving us keen instruction on how to transition into the kingdom, leaving the world of duality – judging between good and evil – behind. So profound is this!

7:110 It is a New Day

It is a new day. New days bring advancing light, illuminating your path, directing your course and preparing you for transfiguration.

You have chosen to be here at this time and have charted your course perfectly. You are the ones who will bridge the gap, carrying the frequencies of both dimensions within your mental, emotional, spiritual and physical bodies. You are, indeed, an anomaly.

Do you understand why it has been so difficult?

But, take heart dear ones; you have done this before, and because of this experience in your repertoire, you have elected to return to help this next graduating class.

You are helping to anchor this incoming light, which enters your sphere with great impact, pulsating with the heartbeat of the universe.

Just as in cellular mitosis, the emerging cell takes DNA from both spheres and becomes an amalgamation of both influences. You will carry the frequencies of the old and new and, as such, become the vibrational link between dimensions. This is what it means to "Bridge the Gap."

Much of what you hear will not have been "heard" in this present timeline. It will be a first for consciousness in your octave. The information will percolate just below your conscious awareness and will seep into your vocabulary and mind. You will sometimes wonder at the words you think and speak; but rest assured, it is YOU who is speaking to YOU from an elevated position, where scope is expanded and understanding prevails. So, trust in the guidance that is offered to you at this time, for there is no better source than YOU.

You have walked this way before you were you, so the journey will become increasingly familiar. It may be the first time for your present incarnation, but not for your multidimensional self. The Christ will call his disciples, and they will gather in the upper room, and they will unite as one.

The New Jerusalem emerges.

7:111 A Man Who Says Christ is Not Within Us ...

John, it is this very mindset that disqualifies one of eternal life (not going to Heaven when you die, but rather, immortality NOW). Hear me out.

You must believe in Christ. Christ is a VERB and is the title bestowed upon one whose mind has been illumined. It means "anointing by pressing in." It is the occurrence when the Spirit apprehends the flesh and the mortal awakens to the indwelling Spirit of God. This anointing is a CHRISTENING and happens only when one BELIEVES.

"I am the WAY, the TRUTH and the LIFE, and no one comes to the father (not Heaven, but the father, the source principle of all eternal creation), but by me"– this is NOT IN A SET OF DOCTRINES FORMED BY A FEAR-BASED RELIGION! It is the belief that Christ is actively being formed in you – CHRIST being a conscious awareness of your true identity. It is like a king being groomed and crowned. A title of an enlightened being will not be granted to someone who refuses to believe in the indwelling presence of GOD.

5 Let this mind be in you, which was also in Christ Jesus:

6 Who, being in the form of God, thought it not robbery to be equal with God:

7 But made himself of no reputation, and took upon him the form of a servant, and was made in the likeness of men:

8 And being found in fashion as a man, he humbled himself, and became obedient unto death, even the death of the cross.

9 Wherefore God also hath highly exalted him, and given him a name which is above every name:

10 That at the name of Jesus every knee should bow, of things in Heaven, and things in earth, and things under the earth.

Philippians 2:5-10

(The "knee" is our surrender of the ego to the Christ within).

We all must come to the cross, where we crucify the old man of flesh and yield to the Divine presence that dwells within us.

It is only then that resurrection will occur. Until then, doubt and unbelief will reign, and men will be deceived by doctrines of man and demons surrendering the faith to what will tickle their ears, thereby embracing another gospel.

7:112 The Oxbow Lake

I love the picture that an oxbow lake provides. An oxbow lake forms when a river overflows its banks. When the river recedes, the oxbow lake remains in a typical u-shaped pattern but is cut off from the continual flow of the source and, as such, its waters turn putrid.

As such, a lot of religions are metaphorical oxbow lakes. The lake is akin to the limited intellectual mind and its attempt to know, via their ego, that which is unknowable to it.

Only when the ego makes the conscious decision to yield to the mind's ability to intuit truth, can it know the Divine and, more importantly, the Divine within. This is reconnecting with the source of all.

7:113 It is The Story of the Ages

The story is offered to you in many forms, cultures and myths and throughout many lifetimes. You made a plan, and you are working the plan.

You see, you are God. The Divine. You are "All that is."

You (Divinity) devised a rather brilliant strategy on how to put yourself inside of biology. Yes, you, Son of Man (your physical self), have been inoculated with something ... holy. This is the part in the story where Mary (humanity) is "overshadowed" by a Divine and eternal principle; God.

And at some level of consciousness, you, Mary, are an accomplice because, as you said, "Let it be unto me as you have spoken."

And Divinity penetrated your DNA.

Man went from Neanderthal to Homo Erectus. Man is now endowed with inspiration and imagination; the very attributes of God.

And so, it is. The Son of Man now has the potential to become the Son of God.

The Son of Man is humanity expressed through slumbering Divinity ~ The Son of God is Divinity expressed through awakened humanity.

And the Son of Man grows in understanding.

And the Son of Man learns through the things that it experiences, and mostly through the things that it suffers.

The Son of Man awakens to the reality that it has a very legitimate part in the created things. It learns that whatever it focuses on and reacts to emotionally, it creates. The mechanism, mankind, is learning to create and is understanding that the very reality that surrounds it has been, likewise, created. It is an environment from which to learn how to exercise its Godhood.

The Son of Man realizes it has "skin" in the game. It awakens to the knowledge that it is not a victim; but rather, a participant, in this Divine drama.

It then begins to experiment with thought and focused emotion. It creates more and more environments to experience. It has learned well through the atmosphere called duality, whereby it knows between good and evil, and discerning between the two has cast the currency of judgment toward the creative process.

It awakens to the knowledge that it must overcome the egocentric need to judge between what it discerns to be positive and negative, thereby surrendering the human operating system; and in surrender, begins to compromise the very fabric of human life. It willingly surrenders the life it has known to crucifixion. It dies the death. It is entombed within the matrix of the Earth and soon emerges a new being.

It is born again.

From above.

It has become Christed within the CHRYSALIS, the crucible of the womb of its mother. It has broken down its own DNA to resurrect the human that has died within the husk of the frame to become the Son of God.

As we view the caterpillar – grasp its journey to the cocoon – we see our own death and resurrection.

Everything within the butterfly was innate within the caterpillar. Vibration began the process of metamorphosis.

Vibration will begin your journey, as well.

Vibration elevates when we choose love, non-judgment and appreciation. When a human surrenders its hate and intolerance, it is only natural that its vibrational make-up escalates.

This is the resurrection process.

It is innate within you.

There is no fooling this intelligence within you. The resurrection process may only be "triggered" when your vibration reaches the tipping point.

The Divine within you activates. It is through non-judgment and love that it will activate the causeway to the impending dimension called "The Kingdom."

BRIDGE THE GAP between the dimensional boundaries.

Do it with love.

Love never fails.

Your Divine self has been percolating beneath your conscious awareness and is emergent.

It is time.

7:114 Christ is Come, in the Flesh – Yours

The ONE story of all mankind: I use scripture to help bridge the gap for the folks (millions) who are leaving evangelistic and fundamentalist Christianity. I find this helps them understand that The Bible is a mystery book, not a history book.

The Bible plays nicely into many (if not all) mythos. There is only ONE story, and the Bible helps those with a scriptural background see and understand this story. It also helps those whose heads have been thumped by it, who may never have been indoctrinated into the historical application.

The ONE story is this: *God is misunderstood.* We have anthropomorphized this current of energy; this highly charged "love" frequency; this dark matter; and called it "God". This energy, being NO-THING but a frequency, sound waves … desired expression in SOME-THING.

And so, the material universe and material worlds were born. God is the matrix. The matrix is a womb of energy where things are born into being. This energy is in ALL THINGS. It has created and chosen the human being as a means of expression, no-thing into some-thing, and through the human being, IT is.

The Earth is a beautiful incubator of energy and creation. The highly charged "love" frequency penetrated this virgin field of potential and has merged with biology. It is the force that animates the body, giving charge to the brain, nervous system and heart. When a human being recognizes that the force that animates the body is this love energy, and submits/succumbs to it, this being is then called "Christ."

The human ego relinquishes its role as master of the body and becomes the willing servant of all (symbolized by the donkey bearing Jesus to death and Jesus symbolizing us – the potential habitation for this energy). It is the ego that focuses thought and emotion; the two essential components required to create realities; and it surrenders to death (to its SELF/limitation) so that it might experience resurrection.

Christ is a verb, a mode of being, a title; not a last name for one man, or a title reserved for one man, but for all. This mode of being is able to collapse the birth/death loop of time and enter into immortality. This energy has then ransomed for itself a helpmate, a being from which it may discover, explore and inhabit the material universes.

This is our story repeated in all cultures, in all languages and highly distorted by religion, relegating this process to only a few, fighting an external devil which, indeed, is just the human ego.

7:115 Who is the Beast in the Book of Revelation?

The beast is man, indeed, when "under" the leadership of its base, instinctual and egocentric mind. The anti-Christ is in all; especially those (and we have all been here) who refuse to acknowledge that "Christ is come in the flesh." This is because we are beaten down; told we are no-good sinners. We fail to see the GOOD NEWS that Christ is all, and IN ALL.

> *1Beloved, believe not every spirit, but try the spirits whether they are of God: because many false prophets are gone out into the world. 2Hereby know ye the Spirit of God: Every spirit that confesses that Jesus Christ is come in the flesh is of God: 3And every spirit that confesses not that Jesus Christ is come in the flesh is not of God: and this is that spirit of antichrist, whereof ye have heard that it should come; and even now already is it in the world. 4Ye are of God, little children, and have overcome them: because greater is he that is in you, than he that is in the world. 5They are of the world: therefore, speak they of the world, and the world heareth them. 6We are of God: he that knows God heareth us; he that is not of God heareth not us. Hereby know we the spirit of truth, and the spirit of error.*
>
> 1 John 4:1-6

7:116 There is Great Benefit in Raising Your Frequency

There is great benefit in raising your frequency and, as a byproduct of raising your frequency, you will be the recipient of information that has been coded into your DNA – this frequency is what accompanies love, non-judgment and appreciation. This is a "key" to the "kingdom" of possibilities that are dormant within you.

Our DNA is waiting for our conscious participation in its evolutionary process. This adaptation is waiting for our command to morph into our next state of being. WE MUST WILL IT TO BEGIN.

Just as a ship does not move out from the harbor into the sea without the command from the captain, you must signal the activation of your DNA. Your DNA will percolate with vibration while releasing mysteries into the well of your consciousness. We alone carry the information for our journey. This map is indelibly written into our intuitive consciousness. It is here that we begin the journey.

7:117 I Was Unable to Pick up a Bible, for Years

I was unable (or at least unwilling) to pick up a Bible, for years. I associated it with Christianity and all the abuses misapplications/translations found within fundamentalism (generally speaking). Then I began to appreciate the mystical side of it, understanding that it is not a Christian book (although it has been sort of hijacked by Christianity), and interpreted literally, which has wrought a whole lot of problems – including what the general population believe and perceive about it.

So, while I don't require consensus, I do feel it is important to be a voice that offers something different than what many believe about the Bible. I may use the stories and quote from it, but it is usually those who have bad experiences within Christianity that have trouble with reading and receiving from its content. It is so much more than what we think, and it is a book that has, in part, borrowed from Egyptian culture; and Egypt, in turn, has probably borrowed from Sumer, etc. What we have are mysterious texts that run parallel to one another because they are all telling the same story. It is a book about you. Inside and out.

7:118 The Christ Rode a Donkey to the Crucifixion

The Christ rode a donkey to the crucifixion. The donkey is the ego willingly going to the cross (where our humanity intersects our divinity).

The Christ returns on a white stallion. The white stallion is the redeemed ego, the willing helpmate that has risen from the dead in a new form. The robe, "dipped in blood," that the Christ wears is your skin filled with capillaries, veins and arteries

I.love.metaphor

7:119 God is Not Who/What We Think It Is

God is not who/what we think it is. God is a word that comes from the German word for "good." The term that describes the actual name of the creator is ineffable because it encompasses far too much for the limited human mind to comprehend.

There are excellent books titled, *The Ancient Secret of the Flower of Life*, Vol. 1&2, by Drunvalo Melchizedek. In them, he describes the journey of its prime creator and its journey into the material world. Also, another exceptional book is *The Third Millennium,* by Ken Carey (my favorite!). This beautiful journey of the creative principle (God, Source, Divinity, etc.) is a purposeful one as it searches for its lover; its helpmate; the human soul; that occupies flesh and blood. Without exception, this is the love story, albeit told in different culturalisms that are within all of the world's myths and recorded in the Bible and other extra-biblical accounts.

These stories are told down through the ages to remind humanity that we are, collectively, the subjects of the myths. We are the Son that was given, we are the Christ. With an inverted lens, the stories have not occurred outside of us but rather they reveal our internal, spiritual and Divine development. Christ in you, the hope of glory.

This story, this grand play, is not illusion; to call it such is to fear the reality behind the props. There is purpose in all things created, all feelings felt, all things good and evil. None of it – not one iota of our existence – is without purpose. In fact, to not see the purpose is, in itself, vanity; and creation is considered illusory.

We, the God-men, have been given the garden to tend when the primal cause stepped away from the "vineyard. " Prime source gave us, humanity, the keys to the kingdom, and we have been the driving force ever since. This, however, does not mean that we were not present when Divinity hung the stars, constructed the universe, our galaxy, our solar system – for we were hidden in potential.

Now we are Divinity expressed in matter – in the material realm – getting ready to shed the containment of the egocentric nature, as it willingly relinquishes its role as master of the human and partners, instead, with divinity … producing a couple; a bride and groom. This is why Jesus called himself the "bridegroom" – because union had already occurred within him – he, returning to set the pattern in place for a consciousness that had long since forgotten its source, its call and purpose to fill the universe with glory.

7:120 Desire is Far Different than Belief

Desire is far different than belief.

Desire creates more desire toward your object of desire.

Belief creates what you believe in.

John 16:23-24:

Modern translation:

"Whatsoever you ask the Father in my name, he will give it to you.
Hitherto have ye asked nothing in my name:
ask and ye shall receive, that your joy may be full."

Aramaic retranslation:

"All things that you ask straightly, directly, from inside my name, you will be given.
So far you have not done this. Ask without hidden motive and BE SURROUNDED BY YOUR ANSWER. BE ENVELOPED BY WHAT YOU DESIRE, that your gladness be full."

How are we surrounded by our answer?

How are we enveloped by what we desire?

We must, from our very being, VIBRATE the fulfilled request, believing that we are already in possession of the object of our desire.

Desire alone is not enough. Desire begets desire.

When we see ourselves as the Christ (or inside the nature of Christ), we create what we see.

The nature of Christ reveals UNION – when the masculine (the seed, the idea, the inspiration) is planted within the feminine womb (the matrix of possibility!). This is the NAME and, more accurately, the NATURE of CHRIST.

When we see ourselves as separate and petitioning, begging, asking something outside of us, we fail.

Simplistically, as in the example of the spotted and striped goats in Genesis 30, Laban wanted more goats that were streaked and speckled, so he lay branches in their drinking water so that when they drank and MATED (masculine and feminine) they saw their reflections. They believed themselves to have streaks and speckles, and that is the very thing they PRODUCED.

This is PROFOUND.

> *Genesis 30:37 Jacob, however, took fresh-cut branches from poplar, almond and plane trees and made white stripes on them by peeling the bark and exposing the white inner wood of the branches. 38Then he placed the peeled branches in all the watering troughs, so that they would be directly in front of the flocks when they came to drink. When the flocks were in heat and came to drink, 39they mated in front of the branches. And they bore young that were streaked or speckled or spotted.*

When we create by joining masculine and feminine energies within (the seed and the womb of creation), we create what we believe.

When practicing the art of creating, believing trumps desire every time.

7:121 Taught Through Repetition

I was willingly brainwashed by Christianity.

I was taught, through repetition, that I was separate from God; a sinner; going to Hell – no matter what the fruit of my life showed. I could be the most benevolent, kind and loving person on the planet, but if I did not have a personal relationship with Jesus and accept him into my heart, I was doomed.

I was shown, through example, that I needed to raise my hand and walk an aisle during an altar call, say the sinner's prayer and accept Jesus into my heart, and that if I did not, I would be denying Jesus and, therefore, Jesus would deny me before the Father.

I was taught that Hell was eternal torture in fire.

Then I woke up.

7:122 Losing Christian Friends

Losing friends due to evolving spiritual beliefs is an organic manifestation of growth. It does not make them wrong and you right; it just means that there is a vibrational incompatibility.

During a rather intense time of transitioning friendships, I was told, through my guides, that I was a dissonant sound to them. To them, my evolving views were like fingernails on a chalkboard. As we leave behind fear, judgment and intolerance, forsaking all for LOVE, something miraculous begins to happen within us. We begin to fall out of resonance with this passing age and begin to enter the age to come, or the Kingdom age, if you will.

It's a good thing; and your "friends" will eventually experience the same, as they make their own transition. We cannot help but become who we are; that is, Christ in you, the hope of glory. Each man in his order. Be encouraged!

7:123 We Are Emergent

In response to a friend experiencing unusual physical symptoms:

Termed "ascension symptoms", what you are experiencing is pretty common and unsettling. However, for me and many, there is a "knowing" during these episodes that comes from a higher place in consciousness, that all is well.

I personally think that as we choose love and leave behind judgment, our personal vibration escalates, and our nervous system sometimes bears the brunt of the change.

You are right; there is a lot of information out there on these strange physical manifestations. It brings peace knowing that we are not alone, and that the body is in the midst of activating a different bioelectric signature. The new creation is emergent.

7:124 New Shoes

The soul that you are wants to hang onto those comfy shoes, even though they no longer support you.

The love that you are shows you how wonderful the new pair can be and gives you the courage to step out of the old and into the new.

7:125 As for the Enemies of the United States:

There is no us and them – only the one. It is in perceiving separation and individuality that the ego flourishes, deeming this one or that one greater or less than.

If we continue to see an enemy, we fail to see ourselves as we truly are.

Down through the ages, mankind has identified adversaries and fought for what they felt threatened them.

Mankind needed an adversary.

Governments need adversaries.

Governments incite fear and trepidation, rather than the message of Jesus Christ and other most notable dignitaries of spirituality. In fear, strategies are formed to gain more wealth; more land.

These dignitaries give insight into the kingdom age; the next age if you will – the age where there is no separation between man and man, God and man.

If we continue to resist what we perceive as evil, when will that wheel stop?

It doesn't.

The ego will always need a foe.

This is why Jesus stated, "Do not resist evil", because in our resistance, what we perceive as evil flourishes.

Trust me; our perceived adversaries view us the same way. We are the evil ones. And who or what is to say that we are not?

SELAH

"There is no path to peace. Peace is the way."

7:126 Letter to a Friend, Regarding Government

"You are correct – a government cannot act as an awakened individual, because that is not its role. We are under tutelage and overseers until maturity, as the scripture states. Until then, we are treated as children who are 'no better than slaves' as scripture states, as well. And as slaves, we must bow to the dictates of our master.

Jesus came to awaken us and to give us keys to the next age in consciousness. We cannot migrate into the new without releasing the old. This is the mystery of the new wine skin. There is a place for government while we need oversight, but Jesus modeled a way for us out of such systems, as we become of age. Until the time appointed, we are to render to Caesar what is his, but the sons of the kingdom owe nothing. We are strangers and foreigners in this world. We are told to be in the world, but not of the world.

Now, on to your comment and, as you know, or may remember; this question comes up often when I travel and speak, because it is hard for the mind to perceive of what they deem as inaction:

> *'Barbara, if an illegal alien murdered your precious loved one, you would not expect the government to forgive them!'*

My reply is this:

> *If you are called to judge, then judge well.*

If you are called to transition the age, then stop judging.

In judgment, there is creativity – whatever the human focuses upon and applies the appropriate emotional value to for that judgment, it creates more of what it focuses upon. So, to your comment; if I judge with anger, hatred, revenge and the like, then I will create more experiences and circumstances of what I am feeling.

I, alone, am responsible for disbursement of my energetic currency. I cannot tell a government how or why to judge, if it chooses to do so. I must walk in forgiveness, so that I am careful not to create more of what has hurt me and others. The government will act upon the laws that have been put in place by the people who support it. So, little by little, things will change, and have been changing.

If I, as an awakened human being, move in forgiveness, then surely this movement will gain momentum, as love trumps all else. Eventually, our government must reflect the will of the people or it will find itself out of a job.

It is our responsibility to move, as Christ did, in the Earth and eventually, by acting peaceably and with love, the scales will tip, and a new age will be established. Until then, if we continue with an eye for an eye, we will find ourselves under the law of an immature consciousness, the very law that Jesus came to set us free from. The Old Testament is a great metaphor for those under the rule of an egocentric system, and that system has no choice but to bring DEATH.

Our present government system manipulates through the media with fear and drama. If we focus on that, then that is what will be created. It's that simple. As God-men, we must awaken to this reality. The "powers that be" control the masses and get exactly what they plan for. In this way, power structures are established, and the game RISK continues."

SECTION EIGHT

EIGHT

8:127 The Pattern Has Been Set

When the egocentric life of self surrenders to the cross (that is where our humanity intersects our Divinity – where the horizontal life of mortality surrenders to the vertical life of Divinity), the work is finished.

The caterpillar emerges from its state of death – its earthbound existence – and begins to break free from the encumbrance of the tomb – its self-imposed restriction (the cocoon – your flesh and blood body).

Interesting to note that the cocoon is spun silk, 3000 feet of unbroken thread from the caterpillar – the attire fit for a queen, according to the Bible.

It is finished. It is what we came here to accomplish. To shed the earthly clothing of mortality, to embrace the garment of light, and to walk as immortals is our "work".

The cross did not happen to one man BUT IS THE PATTERN FOR ALL MEN; the last Adam, (an eternal) life-giving Spirit.

8:128 Appreciating Nature More?

Are you paying closer attention to the miracles of life that happen all around you?

One day, I saw a glimmer of reflected light on the deck outside; I found myself on my hands and knees looking at a wounded dragonfly, as it struggled on the ground. A deep stirring of gratitude came up from somewhere inside me for this wounded and dying thing. Its wings were iridescent and beautiful, like little rainbows.

Last week, a big dog lumbered into our yard, walking strenuously. I thought it belonged to our new neighbor; he said they might come to visit our Great Dane, Harry. Finding myself too busy to go outside in the heat, I watched her badly swollen frame struggle toward home. The next morning, Lyle and I found her face down in the pond. She had come here to die. A tag identifies her and her owner. She is named "Ruby."

Lyle makes arrangements with the owner to bury her out by the side and back of the yard, where the wolves from the previous property owner lie. Gravestones from the 1990s mark their rest: Boo, Pippy, Luna and Woof. Three other markers are in disrepair; they are cracked and crumbled to where I can barely read their names anymore.

I find it interesting that Ruby came here, to us. Lyle takes the time on his tractor to dig deep. He marks her place with two big rocks. The owner comes, at the end of the day, to say, "Thank you," and wants to see where she is. The sun is setting over the pond, as we ride in the ATV to the hill near the back pasture. We sit in silence, and he says a quiet, "Goodbye, Ruby."

The owner takes a call from his son, away at college, and tells him of the news; I can only guess his silence means he is a thoughtful listener. It was his son's dog for 11 years.

Days later, a barn owl swoops in front of our 4-wheel-drive vehicle, clutching a limp rat in his talons. Lyle, our three grandsons, and I watch in silent awe as he flies higher and higher with his booty. I am growing more and more aware of the cycle of life and death on this land, and a deep appreciation fills me.

Months ago, a hawk flies overhead and drops a snake; it lands on the fence line and swings back and forth as we ride by. The bird settles to a nearby branch, perches, and watches us. The snake is lifeless.

I listened to Abraham (channeled through Esther Hicks) talk of animals and the life/death cycle. Abraham said, "I assure you, not one of these animals comes here that have not agreed to die and be food for another animal or human. It is part of their experience."

Again, appreciation swells.

8:129 Embrace Your Lessons

You are a 12-dimensional being having a 3rd + 4th dimensional experience. You are presently transitioning into the 5th dimension. A shift is in process. As you let go of fear – all fear – you will move buoyantly toward the consciousness that makes up the 5th dimension. As you consider the 12 disciples that surround the Christ in the upper room, you will understand your future, for the disciples are disciplines that you are learning while here. The mastering of these disciplines is necessary for your growth and transition.

Embrace your lessons.

You are Peter (the one that hears the voice of the father); you are Thomas (the one that doubts); you are Luke (the physician within); you are Judas (the one that delivers you up to death, time and time again)… You are the I AM that existed before Abraham was (before all religions). You are a sophisticated biology that houses Divinity within. You are both Jacob and the angel he struggled with. You are.

8:130 The Tithe (10%)

I write of a people group that I call the "tithe". It is roughly 10% of the population that will not be a part of religious structures built on the framework of fear and separation.

There are roughly "89%" of people that practice "cognitive dissonance" and are stuck in systems of ego and fear. They will not change their views and beliefs, even when presented with incontrovertible proof that what they believe in is false. If the "89%" number is accurate (speaking of those who are stuck in systems of ego and fear), then this "tithe" that is 10% of humanity may be accurate!

This "tithe" will depart from religious structures or will have never joined them.

This tithe will pave the way in consciousness out from fear and into the next age of non-judgment, allowing and acceptance.

Their personal vibrations, linked with many others, will create an unstoppable cadence that will pierce the dimensional boundaries, allowing mass consciousness to seep out, much like when a dam is compromised.

This 10% is the priesthood that will be the conscious "link" between this present age and next.

In the Old Testament pattern, we see the priest as the "go-between", and this is what this "tithe" will manifest:

> This people group will not be made subject to fear.

> This people group will surrender all egocentricity to love.

> This people group will not continue to create the fabric of this present age of darkness and duality through their human judgment of any given circumstances.

> This tithe will bridge the gap between heaven (the 5th dimensional level) and humankind.

This tithe is not "better" or "worse" than anyone else; they are just first to "crossover" the metaphorical Jordan River, from death to life. Remember, in the story, the Priests, carrying the presence of Divinity, cross over FIRST, causing the waters (symbolically water is human consciousness) to divide in order for them to step in and to create a safe passageway for others to follow.

That is why you FEEL DIFFERENT. You are DIFFERENT.

8:131 Memory Loss? Fuzzy Thinking? Forgetfulness?

You may be operating out of your intuitive mind.

If you are operating out of your intuitive mind, it may not be accessing the mind that holds memory.

There needs to be a bridge established between the intuitive mind and the mind of YOU, the personality.

Right now, we are becoming more and more aware of both minds within as we float between the two.

The intuitive mind is quickly formed information that you "feel".

The personality mind has to think, and process information gleaned through past experience. It is slower to percolate to the surface of your awareness than intuition.

For now, we are learning to navigate into, though, and out of the intuitive mind.

The next step is to establish the link that allows both minds to work in tandem.

The unified mind has both components working through synergy. It is called the "Christ."

The process is called UNION; and the two shall become one. Two are walking, one is taken (in marriage), and ONE is left.

This is the marriage spoken of in scripture.

You mind is the helpmate of the Divine Nature.

8:132 We All Have Our Demons to Shed

> *"If I by the finger of God, cast out demons, then surely the Kingdom of God is at hand."*
>
> Luke 11:20

These "demons" are negative ballast that keeps us afloat; buoyant, yet strategically submerged into the waters of duality – knowing good from evil. It is time to release the old fears that have kept us anchored in the garden, "eating from the tree of the knowledge of good and evil."

It is time to step boldly into this new area of consciousness that allows us, with divine guidance, to overcome the many enemies of our flesh. We have so many "ites" that lie in the heart of our promised land that must be conquered. These enemies keep us in restriction until we recognize that they are all WITHIN.

We must become inner landscape strategists, listening to the voice of our own intuition, honing that skill until we hear the command to clear the land of formerly held beliefs and strongholds.

These strongholds are imbedded in our consciousness and are linked to our physical bodies. As we clear, we must OCCUPY that "land," *"lest the beasts of the field multiply against us."*
(Exodus 3:29). As you change your thinking, your whole being – body, soul and spirit – will change, as a result.

Let's do this!

8:133 Have You Stolen the Life of Another

Have you exerted yourself strongly enough to cause another person (against their will) to bend or change, marring the fabric of their nature, to suit your will? Do you see how this is treacherous, stealing the life of another human being simply because you had to have your way or because you thought your way was best? An employee? A friend, or perhaps someone you love?

Those who practice deep control and manipulation usually cannot see their efforts. They grasp control of the painter's hand and brush, and the self-portrait becomes marred and skewed according to the vision of the dominator; the image ultimately becoming the creation of another ego. This is a life taken by dominance and is no less insidious than a life taken by other means.

Recognize dominance in you or over you and free yourself.

8:134 What is SIN?

This is a mystery; to participate in judgment is what sustains the world, as we know it. Jesus was trying to reveal a secret; that judgment, in accordance with the law, is actually what drives and sustains sin.

But let's not stop there. We need to take a deeper look to see what sin actually is. Most think that sin is any number of acts, but it is so much more than that. Actions are only symptoms of an underlying condition. Duality is SIN.

Sin is living according to mortal and limited standards dictated by the ego within man that discerns culturally between right and wrong. WE ALL LIVE IN SIN.

Sin is the environment that is created when we are under the control and dominion of our ego.

It is said "there is no remission [of sin] without the shedding of blood" (Matthew 26:28). Metaphorically, the shedding of blood is death to the life of self (ego), so that we might be raised to a new life free from the environment of sin.

Here is a mystery – The Apostle Paul writes this:

> *The sting of death is sin; and the strength of sin is the law.*
> 1 Corinthians 15:56

Paul states that SIN GETS ITS STRENGTH FROM THE LAW.

Paul, the overseer of the fledgling seed of Divinity within the human, was given the task to bridge the gap between the ages as the human migrated out from the law and into grace. The fundamentalist does not perceive that it is he who wanders in the wilderness of human and egocentric judgment and is sentenced to death (mortality).

We die in the wilderness, just like the pattern set in the Old Testament story, because of our unbelief in this very principle. Those not so entrenched in religion step out from judgment easily, while the fundamentalists find it difficult to let go of their need to be "right."

8:135 Walking on Water

When we allow our emotions to be pulled to and fro, we truly are puppets in the hands of those who seek to control us. We must shift our focus to the things not seen with physical eyes; to a standard far above the mundane politicos of our day and recognize that we are citizens of another dimension.

Water represents status quo consciousness of the day. We are beckoned to walk above the water and not to be consumed by it. This is the path of the Christ.

This is a mystery and is the meaning behind being "in the world, but not of the world."

8:136 I Surrender to the Simple Things

I surrender to the simple things.

Today I needed to see love in action.

I chastised my granddaughter for not listening to me. When I came to her, releasing her from her debt to the corner, she had tears in her eyes.

I picked her up and held her on my lap, and we rocked in the chair, silently.

We read a book, had a tea party, she examined me with her doctor's kit and applied stickers to my nose. She covered me with a blanket and sang me to sleep ... or so she thought.

My eyes were closed, and I was thankful for the simple things; for seeing her love for me in action.

In our country today, it is so easy to be pulled apart, rather than to be pulled together.

Pull together. Take the time to listen, even though you feel you are not being listened to.

You may just end up listening to a most beautiful song ... with stickers on your nose.

8:137 When We Say We Know it all

If you are in the midst of transition, you are in a good place. Shifting and transitioning is the hallmark of spiritual unfolding. There must be a continual migration from belief to belief, and then from knowledge to knowing.

Most of our mindsets are in need of adjustment, and for those whose hearts and minds are open, adjustment will occur.

A willing and open heart is what invokes guidance toward us. When we say we know all... such things stifle and muzzle the voice of truth.

8:138 I Am the Way

"I am the way, the truth and the light and no one comes to the Father but by me."

John 14:6

Fundamentalist Christianity asserts that one must get "saved" and submit to the church's idea of salvation. We need to understand what Jesus meant when he said, "... no one comes to the Father but by me."

The "by me" is what needs clarification, because there is great latitude taken by most Christian fundamentalists as to what this exactly means.

Does it mean that you must raise a hand, walk an aisle and accept Jesus into your heart?

If yes, then why did Jesus never give instructions to do that?

Each person needs to discern for him or herself what this "way" means and not let a religion that has its basis in fear interpret for them.

Could this "way" mean the "way" Jesus lived his life? If this is true, then we must examine what it is like to willingly die to self, to be non-judgmental, inclusionary and fearless.

8:139 Christians: The World is Watching You

Over the millennia, your various Christian religious sects HAVE changed and MORPHED into what they are today. All things change, even the God that you and that the Bible says "Changeth not" (Just look at the difference between Jehovah and Elohims– they are not one and the same).

Jesus sought to introduce us to his Father and to display the traits of unconditional love and non-judgment, which are NOT the traits displayed in the Old Testament. Modern Christianity is confused; blending the traditions of old with the new. We must see beyond the historical accounts to discover their covert and hidden meanings, if we are to progress spiritually.

Christianity has been and is based in the "F" word – FEAR.

The Bible, itself, commands us to "Fear not" and to "Be of good courage" over 600 times, and yet Christianity, as a faith, is so terribly fearful.

We fear being taken over by refugees, or Muslims; that our weapons will be taken; that our borders will weaken; that our food source will become scarce; that there will be no water. Did Jesus not say, "Take no thought of what you should eat..."; that the "...hairs on our heads are numbered? ..."; and "He cares for the sparrow and clothes the fields with Lilies...”? And yet, most of the world's wars are led by the religious and based on the fear of lack.

Yes, Christians, the world's eyes are upon you. You might want to re-read the red letters of the New Testament to rediscover the message of Jesus. His words are not unlike what many of the world's spiritual (not religious) leaders are saying. The words will change the world, but only when human will embraces love and inclusion. We are all ONE.

8:140 When You Really Understand

When you really understand that your thoughts and emotions create the world around you, you will stop allowing manipulation by friends, family, enemies and the mass media (including false news).

Until then, you will continue to reap and to experience what you have sewn into the energetic atmosphere.

Chaotic thoughts? Chaotic life.

Angry thoughts? Angry life.

Victim thoughts? Victim in life.

Unhealthy thought life? Unhealthy physical life.

Peaceful thoughts? Peaceful life.

Your choice.

8:141 You Create What You Focus On

What you give your attention to providing emotional currency with your thought, you create.

If you are upset about the candidates in our election, and you give your emotions to either side, you create more of what you are emoting.

If you are upset with a person for anything like _____ (pick something!), your thought and emotion, percolating in your awareness, is sending a vibrational request from the universe and it, being under orders to fulfill your vibrational demand, sounds back to you the very frequency of your request, and it will rapidly create what you have emoted.

You must, now more than ever, learn to keep captive negative and unwanted scenarios (thoughts) at the non-creative level. This level is a thought that does not anger you, but rather, is held in a "neutral position"– much like pressing the pedal of the clutch – thereby disengaging the gear that drives this present world of conflict.

The conflict you see around you, the darkness, the depravity etc. – welcome to the world of unbridled thought mingled with emotion. YOURS.

Be not deceived; God is not mocked: (This is the creative component that is activated within YOU when you emote!!!) *"… for whatsoever a man soweth, that shall he also reap."*
(Galatians 6:7)

God is dwelling in you, as you. Whatever command you give through emotion and thought, YOU WILL RECEIVE because you are ONE with GOD.

8:142 Woundedness

There are so many wounded souls out there and most of the people I deal with have been hurt in some way by the system of Christianity. I was one of them.

When I say "system", I am referring to people, mainly, who believe in a systematic approach to knowing, loving and being saved by their idea of God. For the most part, their system does not allow for them to embrace those with differing beliefs, as this is a threat to Christianity and, by extension, a threat to them. Intolerance becomes the order of the day, and this lack of tolerance extends to friendships that had their genesis within the church structure.

When my beliefs began to evolve, I found myself falling horribly short of expectations, and the more I talked about my transitional process and revelations, the more people separated from me.

I talked this over with my husband on several occasions and asked him, "Where did their love for me go? Was their love real? Is this kind of love modeled from the God they serve? What would Jesus do?"

I simply could not believe that all of the love, sweat and tears, invested in them and their children through the years and decades, could be erased because I now saw God differently than they did.

I am sure my story is not unlike many of your stories. I hurt for years, it seems, and suffered from disillusionment. Situation after situation arose for more hurt and pain.

Confusion set in and I began to question the idea of love, mutual respect, and even friendship itself.

Now healing, I have come to this conclusion:

> *It is best to be yourself and those that celebrate and appreciate your truth will be attracted to you.*

That's it. That is my wisdom today.

Recently, a person who has left Christianity became angry with me because I still use the Bible, and specifically, metaphorical understanding of scripture. They are in pain, having suffered abuse within fundamentalism, and from this basis they are unable to see that they are dispensing the same intolerance that was shown to them. Pain becomes circular. Hurt people hurt people.

We need to heal.

Acceptance of the way things are and trusting that this is a process that forms character within us, is half the battle.

If you know someone who has been abused by fundamentalism, listen to them and offer them your unique balm of tolerance and acceptance, wherever they are. It will go a long way toward healing the millions of people that are shedding the bounds of religion and finding the freedom they deserve.

8:143 Judgment

It is time we realize that there is a difference between judgment and righteous judgement. Judgement issues from below the heart at the place of self-servitude. Righteous judgement issues from the heart in the place of selflessness. Loving people removes us from below and places us above. Below is hell and hell begets hell. Above is heaven and heaven begets heaven.

8:144 Melchizedek Priests Offer Their Emotions

Melchizedek priests offer their emotions – their "right" to be offended, hurt, angry, vengeful, hateful, etc., on the altar that is within them. This altar is located at the heart center, and the fires below the altar are the first three energy centers – the flames – the red, orange and yellow chakras. These centers allow us to feel, to emote, and ultimately to create this DIMENSION.

Emotions are the building blocks necessary to procure matter. We create every time we emote.

The Melchizedek priest knows this and slays the fatted calf on the altar of sacrifice.

Once the emotion is slain, the energy is transmuted through the heart chakra and ascends as a pleasing fragrance to the heavens within man.

During this process, the heart chakra, consuming the sacrifice of emotional currency, will sometimes cause the physical heart to sputter. Have you ever heard a fire crackle and see it pop?

So many with heart palpitations, racing heart, arrhythmias. You are a priest forever; offering sacrifices; yours, and for others.

Energy never goes away. It only changes form. It is changing form through the multidimensional configuration of your body. As you surrender your pain, as you choose love over judgment, you are drafted into the priesthood, for you are bridging the gap between the heavens and the Earth. The altar of sacrifice is in your body.

You are a priest forever, after the order of Melchizedek.

As you surrender your right to be human and enter the priesthood, it is because you have been "Chosen from among men that are familiar with suffering."

> *Hebrews 5:1Every high priest is selected from among the people and is appointed to represent the people in matters related to God, to offer gifts and sacrifices for sins.2He is able to deal gently with those who are ignorant and are going astray, since he himself is subject to weakness. 3This is why he has to offer sacrifices for his own sins, as well as for the sins of the people.*

By disengaging your own emotional release, this dimension weakens, and you begin to create the bridge to the next. You have been given by Abram to Melchizedek through the tithe. (Genesis 14).

Roughly 10% of the population of the Earth will disengage and transmute energy through their bodies. They are the mechanism that pulls Heaven to Earth, God to man. This process is all internal. Let it be.

P.S. The next dimension is immortality. This is what it means to be saved.

SECTION NINE

NINE

9:145 Drop the Stone

What would Jesus do? He would say, "Drop the stone." And maybe he would quote Mahatma Gandhi and say, "There is no path to peace; peace is the way."

There are no [easy] answers. But when Jesus told them, "Let he who is without sin cast the first stone," he was speaking of a mystery – a specific consciousness that he embodied – of the coming age; an age he said was "at hand," or within our reach.

NOT TO JUDGE these horrendous situations that have been, and are, occurring at the hands of religious extremists is NOT HUMAN.

We are called to a higher order, a higher consciousness. There must be a people group that will break the way into this consciousness as peace makers.

Retaliation and war are symptomatic of lower consciousness. It is a place that we all must pass through on our way to enlightenment. There is a time for war in the history of our world. And there is a time for PEACE.

By Jesus stating, "Do not judge LEST YOU BE JUDGED IN THE SAME WAY" he is speaking the most profound mystery. Whatever we judge and resist will return to us, and the reason is that [judgment] offers a specific frequency that will request to the universe THE SAME IN RETURN.

The universe recognizes a vibration, whether it be peace, love or joy, or hate, vengeance or fear. It does not recognize our flawed human logic as the Old Testament edict of "an eye for an eye."

Rather, we must "Come up here" and see what this admonition from Jesus meant when he said, "Be in the world but not OF the world."

If you are called to wage war, then wage it well. If you are called as a peacemaker that heralds the age to come, then let your trumpet sound!

9:146 Who is Christ, and Where is the Upper Room?

Who are the 12 that he gathered and that he met with in the upper room?

We are being built into a multidimensional habitation.

The 12 are joining the Christ in the upper room.

12 brothers. 12 tribes. 12 stones on the priest's ephod. 12 disciples.

12 levels to the New Jerusalem.

Do you think this is a building; a construct that exists outside of you?

You are the Christ. You are the 12.

The disciples of the Christ are now being gathered about you. Can you feel their presence? There is a multidimensional merge happening within you.

You are in the process of becoming complete. A being that can house the fullness Divinity.

The new Heaven and the new Earth are a new consciousness and an eternal, immortal body.

> *Revelation 21:1Then I saw "a new heaven and a new earth, for the first heaven and the first earth had passed away, and there was no longer any sea. 2I saw the Holy City, the new Jerusalem, coming down out of heaven from God, prepared as a bride beautifully dressed for her husband. 3And I heard a loud voice from the throne saying, "Look! God's dwelling place is now among the people, and he will dwell with them. They will be his people, and God himself will be with them and be their God. 4He will wipe every tear from their eyes. There will be no more death or mourning or crying or pain, for the old order of things has passed away."*

9:147 There is an Electromagnetic Grid that Covers the Earth

This grid holds Earth memory in place. It is the same formulation of energy that holds the memory of each human being. You can easily see global memory divided into nations and regions. For example, the Jewish people hold the memory of the Holocaust and behave in a manner befitting the wound. It is the same for the wound from the Crusades and the slavery of the African nation within America. There is no need to look very far in our global history, for our planet is scarred with injustice.

Wounds occur every day over people, regions and nations. In December 2016 there was a wound over Fayette, Missouri where a young man took his life because of the extreme bullying that took place at school and work. His boss at the Dairy Queen was charged with Second Degree Involuntary Manslaughter.

The memories of painful events mar the planetary grid and hold fear, hatred, pain, etc., in place. This is why forgiveness is vital to our planetary evolution.

From time to time, this grid is interrupted, and a portal opens in the place where the circuits no longer connect. We find ourselves suddenly free from self-condemnation and the condemnation of others.

A vortical movement from the temporary collapse of the grid ensues and creates a vacuum; like a wormhole that pulls an extra-dimensional envelope through to our dimension. The envelope opens to reveal to us the physics inherent of higher-dimensional space and consciousness.

In this incursion, our bodies are subjected to a current unlike our typical time-space. The Shaker and Quaker religious movements were named due to the unusual movements the body makes under the influence of higher dimensional energy.

There are numerous examples of this happing in our history. Cain Ridge Revival, 1801, in Kentucky, is one such event; and more recently, an event called "The Toronto Blessing" in the 1990s. Other events include: Lakeland Revival, Brownsville Revival, Welsh Revival, Azuza Street Revival, and the Second Great Awakening.

What causes the interruption of the geo-magnetic grid? I am guessing that when unity, non-judgment and unconditional love are focused, those who hold the intention for healing magically and temporarily absorb the grid into their bodies. The sophisticated neural network of the energy healer then reconfigures the energy. This focused intention creates a vibrational elixir that is applied, like a poultice, to the wound.

How is the grid interrupted? The grid is dissolved by beings that, by INTENT, focusing unconditional love and non-judgment, have the ability to place their consciousness into the grid system, temporarily disconnecting the current. This is similar to waving a hand in front of a laser eye. The frequencies of love and non-judgment override all other energies.

It is the electromagnetic quality of consciousness projected that overrides the grid that holds our space-time continuum in place. There are beings that are doing this work secretly, and even unbeknownst to them. As they meditate and hold peaceful loving intention, their current rises to the top of the grid like cream.

This interruption and dissolution of the grid will enable human consciousness to escape the prison of this dimension, to glimpse beyond the veil, into the eternal. It is a necessary interlude that will spur on our conscious evolution.

Events like this have happened over the centuries, and even millennia, and are the catalyst for eventful and lasting change. The envelope stays open temporarily; otherwise the incursion of higher-dimensional space and its frequency would blow our circuits. But, over time, the more and more people who are able to "hold" the frequency of unconditional love and non-judgment will dissolve the old grid.

Upgrades are made slowly, and with the intent to preserve the body vehicle.

9:148 Interview by *Recovering All* (an online magazine)

Barbara has a unique gift of blending scripture with metaphysical concepts. Her journey gives her a variety of insights, drawing from her life experiences and many other resources. Even though her understanding comes from many different avenues, she remains open to learning from others and discussing their journeys and experiences, as well. As we were talking to Barbara, we decided to ask her a few questions; this is her response.

1. Your Background

I grew up in Milwaukee, Wisconsin and its surrounding suburbs. For as long as I can remember, I had this insatiable thirst for God and spirituality in general. I grew up listening to Harry Greenwood, Andrew Culverwell and Terry Barge; charismatic evangelists from England, Nicky Cruz and David Wilkerson; Oral Roberts and Pat Boone, to name some.

When I was very young (six years old), I had an encounter with a white light, where this blindingly beautiful light appeared to me, and (it seemed) came into the side of my right temple. Sounds strange, I know, but it is a child's memory described as best as I can remember. I felt inexplicable excitement and curiosity. When the experience was over, I went running into my parents' bedroom speaking in a different language. I was told it was "speaking in tongues."

At that time, my parents had best friends who had a child born with cancer who was miraculously healed and was written up in the medical journals. She was a true miracle, and this intrigued me and whetted my thirst for the supernatural acts of God.

As a child, our family attended many diverse fellowships including our Lutheran church to Jesus People meetings, Full Gospel Businessman's meetings, home churches, etc. As a little kid, adolescent, teen and young adult, I thought about God all the time, and the presence I would feel was palpable. It was joy. It was hunger.

2. Your Passion - What motivates and drives you?

Discovery. There is nothing in the world like revelation, knowledge and understanding that the creator, who dwells within, reveals truth, as our consciousness can bear it. The Christ that has been given us as a seed deposit will grow and will become the fully matured Christ, the Emmanuel. We can't help becoming what we are. Those who hunger and thirst after truth motivate me to continue to seek and unfold spiritually. I understand that I can make more of an impact if I will participate in the processes that allows me to unfold, much like a flower blooming, rather than to try to convince someone intellectually, with words. We are not navigating into intellectual unfolding, but rather spiritual, intuitive unfolding. In essence, our spiritual being is not enhanced with wise or persuasive words.

> *1 Corinthians 2:4 "And my speech and my preaching were not with persuasive words of human wisdom, but in demonstration of the Spirit and of power, 5 that your faith should not be in the wisdom of men but in the power of God."*

You simply can't force a rose to bloom. You can't preach someone into maturity. You can't behold the total beauty of a rose while it is yet a bud, but you can place it in conditions that are optimal for its unfurling. It is in the rose's nature to bloom. Did you know that the chirping of birds causes flowers to open and blossom? They recognize a distinct sound or vibration in the quality of the birds' song. That is a cool pattern in nature.

And that is my present passion. I read from a wide variety of authors and subjects; I listen to their bird song – basically anyone that I find attractive in a spiritual sense – and I try not to draw boundaries through fear of the unknown. And I am learning to trust my intuitive senses – the spirit of truth – to lead and guide me into all truth. I am forsaking the history for the mystery, and by that, I mean I had to let Jesus "go away" (with fear and trembling) and trust that He would send to me the comforter to lead and guide me into truth outside of the evangelical, charismatic environment I was raised in.

> *John 16:7 "Nevertheless I tell you the truth. It is to your advantage that I go away; for if I do not go away, the Helper will not come to you; but if I depart, I will send Him to you."*

Many people would point to the scripture above as a precursor to the crucifixion, but in addition to literal interpretation, I think it is most expedient and beneficial to see Jesus' words in a mystical sense. After all, Judaism is an Eastern, mystery religion. Here in the western world, we choose to forget that.

> *2 Corinthians 5:16 16 "Wherefore we henceforth know no man after the flesh: even though we have known Christ after the flesh, yet now we know [him so] no more."*

We would be so far ahead of the game, so to speak, if we truly "lifted our eyes" to see and interpret the scriptures with eyes and ears of spirit, rather than our limited intellectual understanding. Jesus often rebuked the Sadducees and the Pharisees for their intellectual base of understanding and perception of spiritual truth. When they were called a "brood of vipers," we can see that He was addressing the egoic serpent nature within all men.

The serpent on the pole is an excellent example to view metaphorically, rather than literally – The people wandering in the wilderness (mortal, egoic life) were being "bit" by serpents (symbolic of the ego, or carnal self-nature) and the cure was to fashion a brazen serpent and fasten it to a pole and raise it up, and every time they were "bit" they were to "look" at the pole for their healing (this was symbolic of the crucified ego, or carnal self-nature). After a while, they began to worship the pole, rather than to look to it, and God ordered them to "utterly" destroy it. What are we to glean from this pattern?

Instead of understanding the work of Jesus the Christ (if you will, bringing the carnal self or ego as master of the body, into death, and resurrecting then as a servant or, better yet, a helpmate, as in Eve, to Spirit) they began to worship the serpent on the pole. Does this sound familiar? We worship the man Jesus, rather than to see what it was that He patterned for us – a way to the Father by bringing our carnal nature into death, promoting the resurrection of the body as a servant to Spirit.

This is the path or way to the Father – the Father is within His Temple; the framework of the human; the Temple made without hands. A submitted ego causes the path to the Father, the creative energy within man, the pearl of great price, the treasure within earthen vessels, the treasure hidden in the field, to open freely to us. This path leads us to the next dimensional level in our conscious evolution. It is the Kingdom. An egoist nature (flesh and blood) will not enter the Kingdom and reap the rich benefits and heritage of a living God. This developing consciousness needs to exit Egypt and the taskmaster Pharaoh, or EGO.

Christ – the amalgamation or wedding of human and the Divine, soul and Spirit, Bride and Groom, masculine and feminine – results in a being called Emmanuel, or "God with man." Jesus patterned this union by bringing his "soul" into death in the Garden of Gethsemane when He said, "Nevertheless, not my will but thy will be done..." and we pray the Lord's Prayer, "... Thy Kingdom come, Thy will be done..."

3. What is your vision?

Well, I guess my vision is to see and to help people understand the mystical patterns in scripture so that we, as humans, ultimately experience the death, resurrection and ascension of that nature that was patterned for those of us presently wandering in the wilderness.

4. Your view of God's Presence and Your view of the Origin of evil.

God's presence is patterned in scripture; first as internal, walking "with" man in the garden; and subsequent to the eating of the Tree of the Knowledge of Good and Evil, we then saw Him (God) as separate and external (the burning bush, the Ark of the Covenant, etc.). Our serpent nature tends to do that. However, I believe this was a necessary descent into base knowledge and the overall message and task of Jesus was to free the captive stuck in the knowledge of good and evil; to pattern Emmanuel; God with man; the treasure in earthen vessels; the pearl of great price.

AND the scripture says that man would become fully exercised in the knowledge of good and evil

> *Hebrews 5:7 "Who in the days of his flesh, having offered up prayers and supplications with strong crying and tears unto him that was able to save him from death, and having been heard for his godly fear, 8 though he was a Son, yet learned obedience by the things which he suffered; 9 and having been made perfect, he became unto all them that obey him the author of eternal salvation; 10 named of God a high priest after the order of Melchizedek. 11 Of whom we have many things to say, and hard of interpretation, seeing ye are become dull of hearing. 12 For when by reason of the time ye ought to be teachers, ye have need again that someone teach you the rudiments of the first principles of the oracles of God; and are become such as have need of milk, and not of solid food. 13 For every one that partakes of milk is without experience of the word of righteousness; for he is a babe.*
>
> *14 But solid food is for full grown men, [even] those who by reason of use have their senses exercised to discern good and evil."*

In order to enter into maturity (solid food for full grown men) there must first be a rite of passage in the realm that discerns good from evil and, therefore, the divergence into mortality and the LAW was a necessary one. The Christ (speaking corporately now) descended into mortality from a higher position, to have this corporate man's mortal senses fully exercised in the knowledge of good and evil, so that they might discern the same. This is a necessary education for the developing Emmanuel, or God-man if you will, because of where we are headed after this harvest. (Selah!) The consciousness of "all that is" inserted himself into human flesh and blood for the purposes of becoming fully human and so that the body of flesh and blood might "be saved" for the next adventure coming down the pike (another big SELAH). In order to remember our origin, Jesus fixed the pattern in the Lord's Supper.

He "broke bread" = signifying the sacrifice of the immortal state; the broken immortal becoming fully human.

We place the broken bread in our mouths and swallow it = signifying the journey of Spirit into flesh, the throat signifies "the grave" and the belly signifies the realm of Hell and death or Sheol (mortality).

He drank the cup = signifying the acceptance of the task, the slowing down of the body of light into the slower vibration of blood.

And finally said, "Do this in remembrance of me" (The Christ) and Christ in you, the hope of Glory. This practiced ritual will lead the intentionally slumbering Spirit within man to awaken and to remember the purpose for the divergence into mortality.

The ritual and pattern of His (our) baptism is the same:

The descent of one nature into water (water represents dense human consciousness) and resurrection out of that consciousness and reconnected with your highest self (Christ - the Holy Spirit descending like a dove).

Getting back to the origin of evil, my thoughts are that if God wanted this creature to understand the nature of duality, good and evil, then it (the realm of good and evil) must be created and the creature then must be subjected to it. Carl Sagan said, "If you want to make an apple pie from scratch, you must first create the universe."

> *Romans 8:17 "...and if children, then heirs – heirs of God and joint heirs with Christ, if indeed we suffer with Him, that we may also be glorified together. 18 For I consider that the sufferings of this present time are not worthy to be compared with the glory which shall be revealed in us. 19 For the earnest expectation of the creation eagerly waits for the revealing of the sons of God. 20 For the creation was subjected to futility, not willingly, but because of Him who subjected it in hope; 21 because the creation itself also will be delivered from the bondage of corruption into the glorious liberty of the children of God. 22 For we know that the whole creation groans and labors with birth pangs together until now. 23 Not only that, but we also who have the first fruits of the Spirit, even we ourselves groan within ourselves, eagerly waiting for the adoption, the redemption of our body."*

Simply put, Evil is because man says it is so. When we focus on something and deem or judge it to be evil, then it is. To understand this, we must grasp that, as human beings endowed with light, God, Christ, the treasure, the pearl, etc., we are created just like the creator, and we indeed create. And we create (albeit currently by default) by focused thought, the corresponding emotional value and JUDGMENT. We must understand that while the ego within man is on the throne (the Son of perdition), in our judgments we create the realm of duality, the knowledge of good and evil. In order to transcend this realm or this present age, we MUST CEASE TO JUDGE. In our judgment is resistance and in resistance there is focused thought and emotion which thereby causes whatever we focus on, to flourish. This is why we are exhorted to "think on things that are pure, lovely and of a good report" and "set your mind on things above" and "take every thought captive unto the obedience of Christ." Jesus said, "...resist not evil."

> *Matthew 5:39 "But I say unto you, that ye resist not evil: but whosoever shall smite thee on thy right cheek, turn to him the other also."*

So as for the origin of evil one might say, "I have met the Devil and he is me."

As we shift our focus in this manner, we are in keeping with the teaching thrust of Jesus to see things not as external realities, but rather, internal spiritual principles. This is the way of escaping the egoic, carnal centered realm. Jesus said, *"I have lost none except the Son of Perdition (John 17:12)."* Our egoic existence is that Son.

5. What is the New Paradigm of Deliverance? (mental health)

The scripture above, regarding futility, dovetails into your next question. If we understand the purposeful devolution into futility, we can then begin to understand that there is divine purpose in suffering. All human suffering comes with great purpose. I can't stress that enough. If we can see through this lens of divine purpose, then it helps move us from being a victim of circumstances to participant in this divine drama we call life. That is liberating.

There is a lack of suffering that needs to be filled up...

> *Colossians 1:24 "Now I rejoice in my sufferings for your sake and fill up on my part that which is lacking of the afflictions of Christ in my flesh for his body's sake, which is the church."*

Suffering produces something of such great value that from our present circumstances we cannot yet see...

If you are asking my views on "deliverance" per se, this is my thought – Jesus said in *Luke 11:20, "But if I cast out demons with the finger of God, surely the kingdom of God has come upon you."*

This tells me that demons have no place in the Kingdom. They are cast out as the Kingdom comes upon us. The Kingdom dimension carries a higher vibration and the lower vibrations cannot be thrust through - but are either cast out or transmuted to a higher vibrational level. Energy does not disappear - it changes form. That's a whole other conversation, but suffice it to say that if we are transitioning into the Kingdom dimension; if we are focused on things that are pure, lovely and of a good report; if we are focused on things above; then demons and demonology have no place in our consciousness. Demons become a non-issue, having been dealt with prior to our emerging into the Kingdom dimension. This is a process.

6. Where is God leading you?

Every day is a new experience. Every day I experience an expansion, or at least a shift in my understanding of spiritual principles. My path seems to be to put one foot in front of the other and just keep walking through doors that open. That is an exciting place to be.

7. Where do you see the future Church headed?

I think there is a sector of the modern church beginning to understand the principles of Spirit based on two commandments: Love God and Love one another as yourself. They are walking free from the Law. This sector is advancing, while the traditional structures assumed to be "the Church" are deteriorating. This "woman" is getting ready to expel the child from her belly. She is purposeful and necessary.

The structures based on fear will not advance into the age to come, where the requirement is courage and love. Any movement based on fear, especially the fear of eternal judgment, is under the jurisdiction of an old wineskin. Fear-based consciousness restricts. The root (Christ) is breaking the pot. The old restrictive environment found in the traditional Church structures cannot contain the maturing Christ. I see the division Jesus spoke of in *Luke 12:51 "Suppose ye that I am come to give peace on earth? I tell you, Nay; but rather division."* Ultimately, this is a very good thing.

This maturing Christ is the firstborn of many brethren - Christ is the head of the body - your body. This newborn babe called Christ will lead "them" and "them" is the human under the steady influence of your higher self. The "head" of the body is your Christ nature, and this Christ that is the head of the body is not an external being separate from yourself - Christ is internal. That is why scripture warns of those who say to look here or there for the Christ. We have to stop waiting and looking for an external source to save us. We are the saviors the world is waiting for. Christ is in us – the hope of glory. This is a beautiful world, and it is only getting better as we begin the ascension processes.

I was riding on the back of a Harley Davidson in Oahu, Hawaii back in 2009 when I pondered *Hebrews 6:1* where we are admonished to leave the discussion of the elementary principles of Christ, and one of those things to leave was to leave "FAITH TOWARD GOD."

I was puzzled by this and inquired as we rode through the beautiful rain forest of Oahu. I felt God speak to me clearly once again and say, "The key to understanding this admonishment is in the word 'TOWARD,' as it implies direction outward." This initial understanding of an external God was a necessary one, but now we are to know that God is in us, as us. the Bible, as we know it, maps this journey in consciousness. We depart from the task master of our flesh (ego/Pharaoh), wander in the wilderness a while, until the old generation that doubted our true inheritance has died, and then we boldly cross over Jordan to enter into promise (immortality). Initially our consciousness was only able to bear the presence of the Most High on our shoulders, and we wandered from camp to camp, dwelling in temporary tabernacles (our mortality), but now is the time to cross over! The creator has invested much into our biological, intellectual and emotional evolution. It is now our unfolding reality to recognize that we are the dwelling place of the Most High God.

This merging of the consciousness of God and Man is what produces the Christ, as patterned by Jesus. To this we can shout, "Joy to the World! The Lord is come! Let Earth receive her King! Let every Heart, prepare Him room! Let the veil be rent in every mind as the marriage of God and man (Emmanuel) begins!"

9:149 The Last Supper ... Metaphorically Speaking

In the Last Supper, Jesus referred to the bread that he was holding as his "body" and then he "broke" it. Metaphorically, Jesus was telling us that his immortal status was surrendered, or broken, when he descended dimensional levels, and wrapped his Divine self in this body of death or mortality.

His immortal body was "broken" for us. Viewing this as a template, we see that it was our immortal or celestial body that was, likewise, broken – or at least surrendered – while Divinity within us sojourns into humanity. We must re-member.

As a human race endowed with Divinity we must, for a time, forget who we are in order to be fully invested into creature-hood. Our human senses get us drunk and our egocentric self becomes addicted and lost in sensory overload in a world fueled by good and evil – or duality.

Like a seed in the ground that never germinates, we need activation to sprout. We need a "savior" to come remind us of who and what we are, and to set a pattern or "way" for our own awakening and ascension. These "saviors" have appeared in many cultures and religions down through the ages.

In the story of Jesus, we may see this historically; which is not wrong, but Jesus modeled something within ourselves that we cannot see. The Christ's appearance is within our upper room, descending down from Heaven; a body of immortality broken, but eventually redeemed, as this egoist life of self ultimately surrenders.

9:150 Even Outside of the Church System …

Even outside of the church system, I felt a measure of control in my personal life. It seemed that fundamentalism reaches deeply into the fabric of the lives of those within it. As I began to overcome some of the fear in my personal and professional life, I no longer felt the need to submit to the authority of the church. I learned about Divinity outside of the church system. I was like a bloodhound – locked onto a scent – and I was relentless and fearless as I progressed, like a person blind from birth; I could suddenly see. My dogmatic dominoes began to fall with each one gathering inertia, tipping over the next, and the next.

9:151 Never Underestimate

I was in a restaurant in Round Rock, Texas, with a couple of wonderful friends. After we ate, I glanced over at a man with a few books at his table, including a laptop and a NIV Bible. He sat alone, and I asked if he was a pastor or speaker, to which he replied, "No."

During our conversation, we discovered that he was estranged from his son, and we gathered that their separation had to do with a clash in beliefs. After some discussion, my friend asked him, "If your son did not believe as you do, would you sentence him to an eternity of torture and separation from you?"

He did not reply with an answer.

I asked, "Do you judge your son?" This was an attempt to gauge his knowledge of the teaching of Jesus, where he admonishes us not to judge another.

He replied, "He judges me."

He chided me for not taking in the whole word of God and said that I cannot "cherry pick" it and take only what I wanted from it. I replied, "Do you follow the God that said to rape women, kill children and dismember men?"

He did not answer that, either.

After a lengthy exchange of concepts, his within fundamentalism (mainly about Hell, judgment and obedience) and ours way outside of it (love, non-judgment and tolerance), he wrapped up our conversation with this:

> "Hey look, we are approaching the end times and they are even now upon us, and you could walk out of here and get hit by a truck and die. Where are you going to spend eternity?"

I said, "Isn't it interesting that your Bible states more than 600 times to 'Fear not' and 'be of good courage,' and yet Christianity has its basis in fear?"

He said, "Christianity is not based on fear."

I replied, "You just threatened me with eternal separation and torture in Hell."

He then said that we should go back home and read the Bible a little more, and that whether or not we were aware of it, seeds had been planted in us.

I replied, "And in you as well."

You cannot force someone to comprehend a message that they are not yet ready to receive.

Still, you must never underestimate the power of planting a seed.

9:152 You Are Not Victims

Wake up.

You have every component necessary to change the way that you think. It is a matter of will.

The way you think has everything to do with where you find yourself.

Redirect your thought.

Redirect what you focus on.

Disconnect from all of the DRAMA.

You are gods.

What you focus on, YOU CREATE.

You send out frequency from your body, and the universe is configured to answer your request with like frequency.

If you focus on hurt and pain guess what you will receive???

Lift your eyes.

Do not focus on what you have. Focus on what you want, by imagining you have it.

This is a recalibration of your consciousness.

Ask what you will and surround yourself with the frequency of already having it.

It cannot fail.

This is craftsmanship, and you are a master at it.

Love yourself enough to disconnect from the drama. By focusing on what is wrong, painful, hurtful etc., IT IS controlling your life, your destiny and what manifests around you.

The UNIVERSE is only obeying your every command. These commands are not issued from language. IT IS THE VIBRATION THAT IS EMITTED FROM YOUR BODY WHEN YOU HAVE EMOTION AND REACT TO THE BAD CIRCUMSTANCES OF LIFE.

The universe recognizes the signature of emotion and RESPONDS with the exact same frequency. IT SOUNDS BACK TO YOU WITH THE SAME FREQUENCY THAT YOU SENT FROM YOUR BODY, THROUGH EMOTION.

We are focusing mechanisms, so when something bad happens, we focus on it and create more of it.

Once we awaken to this truth, we can and will change our world, because what happens internally in our thought systems directly impacts what we see outside of ourselves. Our thought is the operating system of our reality!

As a man thinketh, so IS HE.

9:153 This Is Us

I was watching the television series called "*This is Us.*" In the last episode I saw, the two main characters (husband and wife) are arguing simultaneously. In the argument, each told their version of the story while yelling at the other. As I was processing the information from within the argument, I was taking sides ... for each of them. They each, from their own perspective, were absolutely right.

This is how it is for most (if not all) conflict. To be truly empathic, we must be able to put ourselves in another's shoes and walk in them, to understand their perspective.

And not all perspectives are rational, but they are VALID.

The following is a synopsis about perspective.

Self to self:

> During conflict, this person's thoughts are centered on how things affect themselves only. This person often feels a victim to the actions of others.

Self to others:

> During conflict, this person is beginning to understand how others may perceive things, and to understand another person's point of view, while surrendering their own (for the sake of being empathetic). They try to "put the shoe on the other foot."

Others to others:

> The person operating in "others to others" mode has the ability to see and forecast the ramifications of interpersonal action and reaction [of other people] in their relationships with another. They understand the emotions cultivated from both sides of the interaction. When another person hurts them, their first course of action is to understand why that person behaved the way they did.

Where do you fit in the three of these areas, when conflict arises?

Remember, the ego is powerful and will, at all cost, self-protect. This is why we must yield the mind and all its constructs to LOVE.

9:154 Angry Lately?

I have received a couple of messages about anger and the inability to function through its waves.

I think we are beginning to transmute a lot of planetary energy. This happens ONLY through the human chakra system. We are the PRIESTS that are able to offer the beast (human emotions that are dense and negative) on the altar.

This altar is within the human physiological endocrine system that correlates with the chakra system. As anger manifests, and as we slay that beast, it is then offered as a sacrifice – the flames are the red (base chakra), the orange (second chakra) and the yellow (the third chakra).

These lower three are responsible for fear, fight, flight, survivalism and emotionalism. Emotions are what are responsible for the creation and distribution of energy that moves quantum bits of matter, that subsequently creates the world we live in.

The priest knows this and begins to disconnect from emotion; offering it as a sacrifice. Often, the priest will attract, hold and move this dense energy from other people, places and things.

In neutral, the energy moves up the chakra column and is transmuted in the heart and high heart, literally changing formulation, going through transfiguration and ultimately resurrection, as it approaches the heavens within man.

9:155 Christianity is the Only Religion That Threatens

Christianity is the only religion I know of that threatens one with eternal torture if you do not believe in it. Not Jesus ... "it." Because of this, Christianity will someday need a "come to Jesus" meeting. We must begin to understand that the knowing (not belief) must be in "the Son"; that is, the human being, as it becomes aware of the creator inhabiting the temple made without hands, the human body. You must know that Christ is in you. Christ is the immortal aspect of creation that inhabits YOU.

All of the doctrines and dogmas found within Christianity have their basis in truth, albeit seen through a glass, darkly. The stories found within scripture have an element of truth, if you want to see them literally (reinforcing mortality). Scripture, when viewed figuratively (as we must do in interpreting the parables), is packed with TRUTH and the message that we all seek after-life eternal.

This is my role: to bridge the gap between literalism (fundamentalism) and mysticism. We all must have an awakening, and because of the atmospheric change that happens when we do, we normally adopt the system that we find ourselves within. Fear, mingled with truth, will produce an egocentric system (mortality); however, love is still found within and is faithful to the seeker as he migrates through the halls of human egocentric consciousness.

It should be the goal of every person to seek righteousness, and righteousness (love) is found everywhere. We do not have to be threatened with Hell to apprehend spiritual truths. Love birthed within us is enough.

9:156 A Crop is Seeded

Our planet's foundation is like a farmer's field; a crop is seeded, germinates, grows, and is ultimately harvested.

This happens over, and over, and over, and over …

The seed that is the divine drops from the ethers and plummets to the Earth where it dies, is buried and breaks.

Something of a miracle pushes outward from within the husk of death, and it goes down. Down.

Roots begin to reach for the life that darkness provides. It is now anchored to time and mortality.

The structure is steady now, and the germ turns upward to search for the life above the soil.

For the sun.

And the wind.

And the rain.

All necessary to build strength and stamina; growing all the while.

"Here we grow again," the seed says.

We are a living allegory.

9:157 In Regard to Evolving Spiritual Concepts

In regard to evolving spiritual concepts, I was asked if I travel and teach. I replied that things are different from this perspective, because the knowledge cannot be taught – it is KNOWN – and is inside of everyone and accessible for those who make a way for the revelation to flow.

This way is made by the metaphorical John the Baptist – that Spirit of Elijah within you that drives you, that makes a way through the swamps of human intellect with the "voice" that cries out from the wilderness – all of our pet doctrines and understandings must give way so that the babe of Christ may be birthed and ultimately rest within the intuitive mind within human consciousness. This Christ is the amalgamation that has brought together the celestial with the terrestrial. Divinity within biology.

These are exciting times as we embrace the Christ that is nesting, growing and wrapped in the swaddle of our very own flesh and blood. All of our triumphs and tragedies have been forming something precious within us. This new creation is Christ, both God and man, that the Universe has been expecting from Earth.

We are the womb.

9:158 Is the Love of God Unconditional, Or Not?

Is the love of God unconditional, or not?

Christianity says it is, but with one condition ...

The love of God was so great, that he came to Earth in the form of a man,

and the one condition is this:

We must believe that

the anger of God with man and sin was so great

that this man (God) tortured himself by being beaten, whipped, stabbed and nailed to a cross,

dying there and going to another torture chamber (created by God) that is Hell,

and then springing back to life once he destroyed the Devil (that he also created),

and if we don't believe this story,

then the great love of this Father will send you to be tortured for all eternity in fire.

And as Christians, we wonder why rational, logical people think we are nuts ...

9:159 The Fishbowl

Those who take the Bible literally, refusing to see beyond the historical account, aren't able to see the treasures that these figurative writings hold. They fear the mystical content of scripture, calling it occult, and live within the fishbowl of literalism.

The scripture itself alludes to allegory at least five times. (Ezekiel 17:2, Galatians 4:24, Proverbs 1:6, John 10:6 and John 16:29). So, we must view some (if not most) of scripture as having metaphorical or allegorical value. The principal style of the teachings of Jesus is allegory or parable, and Jesus even warns that you must have "ears to hear and eyes to see" and that you must "lift your eyes."

The Bible is filled with mystery, but many other cultures and myths – some written before the Bible – actually speak of the SAME THINGS. There is a central Christ figure in them, referred to by Joseph Campbell as the "Hero of a Thousand Faces," appearing in all of our world's religions, pointing to the SAME TRUTH. Viewed metaphorically, we find Divinity's love story with mankind secretly (occultly) planted within all of our world's religions, waiting to be uncovered (CULT-ivated), like the pearl within the oyster.

The problem with us Christians is that we feel like our Jesus is the only path to this secret knowledge, whereas the awakened individual who sees this mystery understands the depth and breadth of the love story to encompass ALL into Christ. This individual jumps the rim of the fishbowl and sees CHRIST as all in all, the progenitor; not of Hebrew origin, but one who holds the UNIVERSE and beyond in its grasp.

The awakened understand that it is not ritual, not raising a hand and accepting Jesus into your heart or adopting a set of doctrinal standards imposed by any number of Christian denominations (an estimated 38,000 to 41,000 of them), but it is understanding the pattern set in his life, and that pattern or "WAY" is the unconditional love he expressed and his unequivocal teaching of non-judgment. Jesus did not call us to enter the fishbowl, but rather, calls us to leap outside of it, offering love, tolerance and non-judgment to all. This is not the way of our world. This is the way of the kingdom.

This way is not Hebrew, or any other worldly nationality, because the lineage of Christ is not hemmed in by any cultural or historical setting. To do such is to be the source of all wars and strife. Christ is the state of consciousness that recognizes the interconnectivity of all men, and that mankind is indeed imbued with the Divine. This understanding is not global, but rather universal. We must lift our eyes beyond the fishbowl and see that the whole Earth is yielding a crop whose origin is that of the stars and beyond.

This origin is encoded into all myths; myths that will guide us into our heritage as Christ in the Earth. Just as seed is planted in the garden, we cannot help but become who and what we are. Separation, judgment, elitism and intolerance are not the fruit that comes from Christ, but rather the ego, the serpent found within all of our gardens that lures us into thinking apart from our Divine nature.

You may recall the event where Jesus overturned the money-changers' tables within the temple. This figuratively represents the egocentric structures within all of mankind that seek gain beyond the simple truth that he offered. It is an indictment against egocentric behavior within all of mankind.

Adhering to an historical, rather than mystical, view will keep mankind forever waiting for the return of Christ outside of himself, a place where Jesus told us NOT TO LOOK.

You are the Son that has been sent to save the world. You are a unique amalgamation of the Divine and man. You must believe that you are so much more than a human – you are the manifestation of Christ in the Earth – and through your belief, the world will be saved. Being "saved" is not about escaping the wrath of Hell by raising your hand, walking an aisle and accepting Jesus into your heart. It is believing that the Divine is already within.

You are here to offer "SALVATION" to the Earth. This is not to go to Heaven after you die. The awakened individual must set his mind on things above to discover the meaning of this salvation.

Awake, oh sleeper!

9:160 For Those Suffering the Loss of a Loved One:

I don't know of one person who hasn't lost someone they loved – a parent, grandparent, friend, brother, sister or child. Death is hard, but it is a part of life. You are experiencing something called GRIEF. It takes many forms, in as many people who suffer from it.

No one can tell you how long it lasts; it is different for each of us.

Remember the feel of it. Remember how it gripped your thoughts, your mind, your emotions.

Remember how it tore your heart out time and time again.

There now.

Go help someone else who is suffering from it.

Because you know how they feel.

Hug them.

Tell them you understand.

Tell them you are sorry.

Life can be hard.

Pull yourself up and do it all over again.

Greet the day and receive the valuable lessons and memories that only it can bring.

Breathe.

Live as your loved one would have wanted you to.

Then grief finds its way down from your list of priorities.

And you smile again.

9:161 For Those Who Have Been Betrayed:

Your mind cannot stay in pain and betrayal. That is a death sentence that your body will eventually acquiesce.

You must rise up and out of victimhood and recognize that things are as they should be, and that your life experiences are leading you out of humanhood and into godhood.

9:162 On Allowing ...

I love the word "allowing."

It neither judges something as good or evil, right or wrong but "allows" the circumstance to be viewed/perceived in neutrality.

This neutral position does not fuel the creative fires of conflict by our emotional output, but rather holds it in a space of non-creation.

In this place of non-creation, the ego observes the conflict, rather than reacting to it.

SECTION TEN

TEN

10:163 The Two Ages

There are presently two ages that exist within the consciousness of mankind – three, if you count the overlapping place between the two spheres (or ages).

The sphere on the left represents this present age, and the one on the right is the age to come – 5th Dimension, Age of Aquarius or Kingdom, if you will.

The overlapping place is where both ages are experienced. This is where we are.

On the left, we have consciousness that eats from the tree of the knowledge of good and evil and is largely fear-based and egocentric, as humankind continually focuses upon duality.

It is an egocentric consciousness that is likened to living under the "law" of the Old Testament, reward and punishment, etc.

We are beginning to transition out from the age that requires judgment between good and evil to maintain and sustain our present reality or age. This is why there are so many heralding the call to non-judgment and unconditional love. These two things are principal drivers of the age to come and will create, maintain and sustain this new age.

The overlapping place is the place of birth for a new consciousness. This new creation is birthed through humanity, and it will grow until one day it overtakes the way we think, much like the parable of the mustard seed planted in the garden.

This present system of knowing and judging between good and evil will resist this new age, as all old systems tend to resist the new. They will think on a national basis, be fear-based and have the mindset of protectionism. However, it is time to think globally. For those who already think globally, it is best not to shame or demean those who are not where you are. That is egocentric divisiveness.

You must ask yourself, are you working with what is breaking down (this passing age) or with what is breaking through (the age to come)?

It is at this juncture where we are given the opportunity to come into union with the Divine spark, the deposit of God within us. It is the marriage between the human and the Divine. This union will birth a new order of beings called Christ or Emmanuel; that is, God within man.

10:164 One Day

One day, Christian fundamentalism and its doctrines no longer made sense to me, and I couldn't see the love of Christ through much of the dogma that I embraced as fact. That doesn't mean it is wrong, but it was growing uncomfortable for me, much like when my little shoes no longer fit my growing feet.

I had prayed for wisdom for a whole decade – whenever anyone asked how they could pray for me, I asked them to pray for wisdom. I received several confirming prophecies from various prophets (some rather well-known) that I would go through a tremendous shift, where I could no longer see things as I once saw them. They spoke of severe rejection from the status quo church structure (even said it would be like a "bone-crushing" experience, which it was); that I would have to keep going and forgive them for mischaracterization and slander against me and my ministry, and that they simply could not see... yet.

When the root breaks the pot, you cannot return to the old structure.

Fear no longer has a hold of me through dogmatic beliefs, and I see the teachings specifically saying not to look "outside" for the Christ. This is all an internal process to have the nature of Christ grow up within us. We cannot continue to cry out for a "king" when we have all we need inside.

Love is inclusive. Love is giving. Love is non-judgmental. Love is not territorial. Love does not insist on its own way. Love is the opposite of fear. There is only one requirement, and that is to become what you behold. We must be born from above (the accurate interpretation – not "born again"), out from fear and limitation and into love itself. This means we surrender the old wineskin (eating from the tree of judging between good and evil) for the new and embrace love without borders. This means we see the mystery beyond the history. This means we understand the meaning of John 17. WE ARE ONE.

10:165 She Did Not Buy into New Age Beliefs ...

She wrote that she did not buy into new age beliefs:

No one is asking you to buy anything. That's the beauty of love – it places no demands, no threats of Hell, nor eternal separation. These are manufactured doctrines of the early church that sought a means to control the masses. Fear is a great motivator, and threats of Hell still work today; however, the Christian church is in decline, as former adherents are choosing love, rather than law.

But if the love you speak of brings unity, then why do Christians remain so divided? Not only from themselves (38,000-plus different and disagreeing Christian denominations) but from others, threatening and warning of deception and Hell (torture) if you don't believe the same as they?

Jesus did not start the Christian religion and was not, himself, a Christian. His message was to bring freedom from any and all religious law, was it not?

And as far as Hell ... I began to question why God would command us to love and to forgive our enemies, while he tortures his for eternity?

You and I are not so different. You have a seeker's heart and mind. Do not fear, as the Bible encourages us over 600 times to do and move boldly into the truth that is written upon your heart. It is there to apprehend, however veiled through tradition and dogmatic belief structures.

Remember the great reformation was brought about with great price by those who saw beyond the grip of fear implemented by the early church. There comes a time for adjustment when consciousness can no longer fit within the confines of illogical doctrines.

This is the mystery of the new wineskin. Those remaining with the old structure cannot grow and expand with the volatile movement of revelation. The old wineskin simply cannot expand, and thus the need to surrender it.

And the beauty of this movement can only be stopped by fear – the same fear that kept the sojourners in the wilderness from apprehending the land of promise.

Be fearless and follow the voice of the one that cried out in the wilderness to make straight the "way" of the Lord.

This way? Non-judgment. Tolerance. Unconditional love. Fearlessness.

10:166 Precession of the Equinox

Let's mention precession of the equinox – the backward movement of the zodiac band that appears to encircle the Earth, where a different constellation appears in our eastern sky roughly every 2,000 years.

Why is this important? The stars affect us! We are presently observing the constellation of Aquarius coming into view and Pisces fading. Until now, science has based this apparent backward movement of the constellations on the wobble of the Earth, but recently another theory has emerged that is 41 times more accurate than previously held models and ideas.

This theory involves a binary partner to our sun. People love relationships and so do stars! Our star just may have a mate that is a partner in a gravitational relationship!

As we move into a long period of enlightenment, we are remembering that our whole solar system moves in a giant ellipse; our sun moving closer to and then away from its lover in a spectacular dance. This dance moves our consciousness through a great clock, experiencing 12,000 years of enlightenment and 12,000 years of darkness – just like our 24-hour day cycle.

10:167 Letter to The Editor

I attended the graduation for College Station High School recently, at Reed Arena. Coach gave an uplifting and very positive opening speech for the Class of 2017. I couldn't help but be thankful for the quality men and women placed in leadership positions guiding our young people.

Then, near the end of his speech, he made the following statement: "... and Jesus Christ saved my soul."

This saddened me; please allow me to explain why:

Our governmental structure is one of the most sophisticated in the world, forged by men of extreme integrity. My family believes in fighting for those standards, including the Separation of Church and State.

I question the motive of any persons circumventing this standard to promote ideology within a government institution, especially when it influences our nation's young people. Furthermore, weighty consideration must be given when the ideology is promoted by an authority figure.

The question begs to be asked: if another person or group attempted to promote ideals in our public schools that contradict Christianity, how would Christians feel? I know how I felt. I am a recovering Christian fundamentalist who spent forty-three years of my life submerged within that culture. I have worked diligently for eighteen years to regain critical thinking while undoing programming, dogma and rhetoric that had been forced upon my adolescent and adult mind. This programming included damnation, separation from family and friends and threats of torture in Hell for noncompliance.

I have recently come to terms with the phrase "saved" and the rigid doctrine of salvation, when I asked myself why God would command us to forgive and to love our enemies while he tortures his in eternal fire? The answer is this:

"Nothing can separate us from the love of God." Nothing. Romans 8:38

10:168 "In Seeing, They Do Not See"

"In seeing, they do not see." This was said of the Pharisees, and yet, even the Pharisee is not external from us. We only feel it is separate, like the finger is pointing at someone separate from ourselves. That is what the word Pharisee means: Separated ones

We are all Pharisees when we are asleep and living literally.

Ah, the journey of the ego.

10:169 Chasing Demons

A few months after my son, Chris, was in an accident, where he lost his left arm and leg, he was told that because he was not in a church, the enemy caused his accident.

How can I serve a God that would allow this because my child did not go to a church?

How can my God be made so little that the Devil could inflict such harm? Is God sovereign or not?

What about the people who do go to church that are hurt and killed? Are they subject to the wiles of the Devil, as well?

Please do not cite where we need to pray for our nation to appease the wrath of God, because I am not under the law, but under grace. And praying in the spirit without ceasing looks nothing like we think it does. Most of us pray in the flesh and move in the flesh. Furthermore, praying in the spirit is not speaking in tongues. Spirit CANNOT BE UTTERED by human vocal cords.

This flesh is what needs intercession. Our critical circumstances are a reflection of our internal landscape. But even this suggests cause and effect, a byproduct of the law.

When Jesus said,

> *"But if I drive out demons by the finger of God, then the kingdom of God is at hand."* Luke 11:20

This tells me, as we get ready to transition into the kingdom, that the ballast of evil will be released from creation with ease. Furthermore, it tells me that there is NO

PLACE for demons in the kingdom age. So, if you are chasing demons, what age are you in? You are not subject to evil. You are children of the kingdom and of light!

10:170 Who is the Best President of the United States?

I loved keynote speaker Robert Gates' reply when questioned at my husband's Texas A&M University MBA graduating class of 2006. As you may know, Mr. Gates was President Gates at Texas A&M University just before resigning to become the Secretary of Defense, from 2006-2011. Prior to his tenure at Texas A&M, he had worked for six other sitting United States presidents from both sides of the aisle.

Mr. Gates was asked, "Who was the best president that you have served?"

His reply, as best as I can remember, went like this: "Each president that I served under had the strengths and gifts needed at that particular time in our nation's history – something that can only be ascertained in retrospect."

Wow!

While I cannot say for sure what, if anything, is needed from President Trump, it may be beneficial for us (if for nothing else than our personal health) to focus our valuable energy and emotions in a manner other than what has been the rancor of past decades. This rancor has caused a severely deep rift in the fabric of our political system and, indeed, in American consciousness. What we resist, persists. If you desire change, you must be the change you desire to see.

10:171 I Think We Come Here to Learn ...

I think we come to learn how to manufacture and distribute emotional currency.

We get to experience all the variations of emotion through our experiences and discover how to emote to create what we want. (When we are unaware that our emotions create, we sometimes create what we don't want.)

When the component of judgment (between good and evil) is dismissed, we are left with currency without a lien; that is, the ability to create circumstances that are not tied to mortality.

10:172 We All Have Bad Thoughts ...

We all have bad or negative thoughts.

It is part of being human.

To the extent that you listen and entertain bad thoughts will determine your state of mind.

Happiness, peace and contentment may vanish in the face of negativity.

Allowing bad thoughts to marinate will infiltrate your thinking, much like a good steak receives the marinade. It permeates the tissue of the meat and changes it forever.

You must slough off the thoughts that seek to stain your wellbeing. If bad thoughts are allowed to remain within your consciousness, repeating them over and over, you cannot help but manifest them. Like coffee in a percolator, it will percolate over the coffee grounds and produce a product.

Bad thoughts cannot help but manifest when our consciousness incubates and percolates over negativity. You will end up with a coffee cup full of self-hatred, malaise, low self-esteem, sickness and dis-ease.

Practice healthy self-care. Right now, select twenty things that are positive about yourself, for example:

I am a good person
I am a good friend
I nurture those around me
I am an advocate to those in need
I am kind
I am strong
I have a good sense of humor
I am organized
I am fun to be around
I am compassionate
I am forgiving
I can admit when I am wrong
I am easy to love
I am a peacemaker
I make friends easily
I am a great listener
I put the needs of others first
I am talented
I have great energy
I can laugh at myself

Now, say these things to yourself and let those good and positive things MARINATE!

It is not up to someone else to say these things to you. It will mean A LOT more if YOU say these things to YOU.

Practice this type of self-care and see the difference it will make in your mental, physical and spiritual state.

You are worthy to hear these words.

10:173 More on the Precession of the Equinox

The Precession of the Equinox is a term that denotes something remarkable in the sky! The twelve constellations in our Zodiac are moving from right to left, with a different constellation prominent in the sky behind the sun approximately every 2,000 years, as evidenced at the vernal equinox. So, there is a grand cycle that influences the rise and fall of many Earth civilizations over a 24,000-year period – each constellation appears in prominence for roughly 2.000 years, then passes to the next.

The mounting evidence reveals that this great cycle of time is propelled by our sun's gravitational relationship with another star. This viewpoint is that our sun is in a binary relationship with another star that is very far (relatively speaking) from us and is outside of our solar system. The elliptical movement of our sun in its dance with this other star pulls us through the twelve constellations (at roughly 2,000 years for each constellation) which, in turn, give us an education in both light and dark ages, depending on the energetic influence of the constellation.

For example: 6,000 years ago, we know that the prominent constellation at the vernal equinox was Taurus, and consciousness had the general characteristics of the "bull."

Then, 4,000 years ago, the prominent constellation was Aries, and consciousness expressed like characteristics of the ram.

Then again, 2,000 years later, Pisces was prominent, and we experienced many Christed figures arriving on the scene through the great portal of the Vesica Pisces that would prepare us for a plunge into the dark waters of consciousness, as we experienced the dark ages.

Now, another 2,000 years later, we are transitioning into the Age of Aquarius (the constellation where we see a man pouring water out of a pitcher), where out of mankind will pour our old, darkened consciousness, and we ready ourselves for a new way of being. Love over law. Just like in birth, when the water breaks and the babe is forced to breathe anew, so will we. We are entering into a most exciting time!

10:174 A Fundamentalist Calling Me New Age and Gnostic

We all have a resident Divine power – that is the purpose for a Spirit driven life. This is the meaning behind, "Christ in you" and Paul "laboring and in travail until Christ is formed in you."

Yes, we all have this seed-like deposit that we may nurture, like the mustard seed within the garden, or it may be eaten by birds or choked with weeds. Each one must determine what those metaphors mean. For me, religious piety and submission to world systems that control the masses through fear were the weeds and the birds; these things seek to enslave the mind through threats of separation and torment unless consensus is achieved. These are the hallmark traits of fundamentalism. God forbid we should think for ourselves! This is a reference to the intuitive gift that Einstein so aptly wrote of.

This passing age has produced world religions that have brainwashed and enslaved the masses. Thankfully, this age is passing, and a new age has begun. This is the age that Jesus not only told us to look for, but encouraged us to occupy, utilizing the new wineskin and abandoning the old. It is the age that he himself lived in and manifested.

This new wineskin is flexible and able to expand with the volatility that comes with revelation. New wine combusts and will burst the old skin, as we were warned it would. Jesus was our pattern; a model of what would happen as the old is challenged. Cries of heresy! Blasphemy! Evil! This man claims to be God!

But it was said of him:

> *5 Let this mind be in you, which was also in Christ Jesus:*
> *6 Who, being in the form of God, thought it not robbery to be equal with God:*
> *7 But made himself of no reputation, and took upon him the form of a servant, and was made in the likeness of men:*
> *8 And being found in fashion as a man, he humbled himself, and became obedient unto death, even the death of the cross.*
> Philippians 2:5-8

It was also said of him that he was the pattern son. The things that happened to Christ will happen to those who believe. They do not happen to one man, but to all who seek to crucify the old nature, and with it, the old wineskin.

You see, you have forgotten your own journey as the lamb slain before the world's foundation was set. You, as the Divine spark, agreed to appear as Divinity couched in humanhood in the environment of mortality. You surrendered your immortal life by breaking the very structure of your eternal nature so that you might penetrate the virgin soil of biology as a seed and grow up within the creature called man. Therefore, we are told to take the bread and break it, swallowing the brokenness and descending into the belly of darkened humanity, waiting for this divine nature, albeit broken, to grow within the framework of the human being. "Do this in remembrance of me" the Christ in you; the hope of glory.

Remember.

The same pattern may be realized within the ritual of baptism. It is not about getting wet. It is about the journey of the Christ being immersed under the waters of darkened consciousness, holding its Divine breath until the time of awakening and resurrection.

Likewise, we are told to join him, the Christ, as he walked above the waters symbolizing lower human consciousness.

These are mysteries apprehended by those that seek.

Call me what you may, as they did the same to Christ. The old order will always be threatened by, and seek to disqualify, the new. It is the path and pattern we have been shown.

Jesus had to leave behind organized and systematic religion and those beginning to awaken will do the same. These forerunners will set the tone and tempo, building the bridge for the masses to follow during the great falling away. The son of perdition (the human ego and all its world structures) will surrender the throne when confronted with the burgeoning consciousness of Christ in you, the hope of Glory.

10:175 Symbolically, Rather Than Literally

More and more people are beginning to look at the Bible as a book that should be interpreted symbolically, rather than historically or literally. Of course, there are those within fundamentalism who will embrace talking snakes and donkeys and remain in limited understanding. Rather, if we are flexible, we are able to see these invaluable truths that span the ages that have been recorded for us and our evolving consciousness, through allegory. Interestingly, these truths speak to all, no matter the cultural conditioning or religious affiliation. Truth does not discriminate.

The scripture compares itself to "allegory" at least five times. (Ezekiel 17:2, Galatians 4:24, Proverbs 1:6, John 10:6 and John 16:29).

I decided, back in 2005, to let everything that I thought I knew about Christianity/God/Jesus go. It was a time of personal transition and crisis and I knew that I was breaking down – spiritually speaking. I looked into the word "repent" and saw that it meant "to turn around and to change the way that you think." And I did. Unfolding consciousness will not be satisfied without asking, seeking and knocking on the doors of truth. I knew that I was about to leap from my lily pad of fundamentalism and into the pond.

There is a scripture where Jesus said, "It is better for you if I go away… I will send the comforter to you." I made the decision to let him, Jesus and everything I was taught about him, go. I was so totally confused by what I had been taught about God – this tyrant that loved and hated, was jealous, incited rape and murder, dismemberment and genocide. Really? Nope. I couldn't do it anymore. It just didn't make sense. This, it seems is a prerequisite for repentance – "to change the way you think." As consciousness expands, most will begin to question what they believe, as we cannot help but outgrow the clothing from childhood.

Then I began to look at scripture more figuratively, especially the mysterious parables that Jesus taught. He encouraged us to "lift our eyes." What did that mean? Are we to look skyward all the time, or did it mean to access a different space in our conscious awareness, to tap into another area of the brain? I asked for help in interpreting the scriptures – not according to any Bible commentary, but what was the Spirit speaking directly to me?

Peace began to wash over me as I moved out from fear-based religious doctrines and into love and acceptance.

The mysteries come from meeting Christ in the "upper room" – that is, in your own higher thinking. This is where the "unveiling" takes place. There is a veil between the two hemispheres of the brain called the corpus collosum. It is referred to in the medical community as the "veil." It acts as a mediator between the left and right hemispheres of the brain – the bride and the groom. Once the veil is "rent" we can have access to both sides of the brain and our intuitive function really kicks in. This is where we meet with "Christ," as Christ is the amalgamation – the byproduct of union.

In my searching, I discovered much of Christianity that was simply not true but had been inherited from those like Constantine and the Council at Nicaea. I had to learn for myself, like the forming of the butterfly from the liquid carcass of the trans-morphic caterpillar. No one could do this for me, and no one could help me free myself from the cocoon, lest I miss the struggle that forced the life's blood into my metaphorical wings.

Look.

See.

Your tent pegs have been broadened. Stretch, reach and soar.

Fly, you God-men.

Fly.

10:176 Reply to a Christian ...

First, I hope that you can appreciate the sincerity in my reply here to you. Maybe we all need to experience being within and without religious systems to have a well-rounded education. I spent 43 years inside the system and studied scripture for most of that time, although it was not necessarily independent study. By that, I mean that as I read and went to various Sunday schools, home churches and adult study groups, I learned what other people – other teachers – thought of a given scripture, and I mostly adopted their interpretation. It was only in the late 1990s when I began to do independent study and, like you, asked for the Holy Spirit to teach me and to guide me into truth.

I began to see more than what I had been taught by other people. I saw that, although it may have happened literally, if I didn't see beyond the history into the mystery, I was missing something profound and hidden, like a pearl within the oyster.

I don't mean this to sound demeaning, but Joseph, I used to sound like you. I had almost the very same rhetoric; and I say rhetoric, because it is canned. We repeat what we have heard. Your responses are from the system and learned through repetition, just like I had over many decades. It is a primary means of control that works like this:

> Talk of separation, and sometimes the system resorts to teaching of torture in Hell as a consequence for non-compliance

> Talk of being "left behind"

> Talk of being backslidden or deceived if one questions mainline doctrine and strays outside of the accepted dogma. This mainline doctrine has evolved over the centuries with many pockets of Christianity fragmenting into between 38,000 and 41,000 different and/or disagreeing sects.

The metaphorical interpretation of scripture beyond literalism bears many mysteries to those willing to "lift their eyes."

Over the years (almost two decades now) when those involved within fundamentalism wish to communicate, as you have done here (mainly through citing scripture), one of the most interesting things is this:

> *I am being confronted with a literal interpretation of scripture by those wishing to make their point, while I no longer see scripture literally. So, it presents a conundrum, almost like we are speaking two different languages.*

I have a wealth of scriptural knowledge and a track record of vigorous study and teaching within fundamentalism (43 years), so I totally understand your view, having believed the same things and even citing the same scriptures as you have here when I sought to sway another who strayed outside the acceptable "box".

I don't think there is anything wrong with where you are and what you believe. It is just not right for me. You have heard the proverbial story of the blindfolded people all touching and describing a different part of an elephant. The one describing the tusk is not wrong, as opposed to the one grasping the ear. They have two different viewpoints from which to describe what they are feeling and touching. I am moving as you are, to touch and feel different aspects of the message of the ages, some of which is contained in a book, but most of which is found within, where it has been recorded on the heart.

So, let's just say I am not touching the same elephant part as you, and it's okay.

The second point that I want to make is that during my tenure within fundamentalism my decisions, my life, was based in fear: fear of missing out, fear of being left behind, fear of separation and punishment. Now I know that nothing can separate me from the love of God and that the letter (literalism) kills. If I put myself under one item of the law, then I am responsible for keeping all of it. Hence, the need for Christ. In you. The hope of Glory. With this mind in me, I am free.

10:177 A Christian Questioning Hell, the Seals and Scrolls ...

Anytime eternal punishment is mentioned, we must try to view things holistically; or easier said, we must try to view the whole drama that we are playing out.

First up, you said the following:

> *"It seems you guys want to pick and choose what Scriptures you think apply to your way of thinking. But we have to take the Word of God as a whole. Every word of it is relevant today as it applies to the plan of redemption AND the judgment on Evil and Sin."*

I agree! We must take it wholly; but if we take it literally, then we have a God that incites rape of women, murder of children, arranged marriages (i.e., if a man rapes a woman then she is his), dismemberment, plundering, genocide, etc. Would you agree that this God, if scripture is taken literally, is quite a tyrant? I think any rationally minded Christian would agree that the scriptural references to the above are quite a contrast from the Father that Jesus spoke and taught us about. If God "changeth not," then we have quite a conundrum on our hands.

The answers are not cut and dried. There are many opinions of why our Old Testament records the above. Among those opinions is mine which is simply that it is mostly allegorical, as Galatians 4:21-26 states:

> *21Tell me, you who want to be under the law, are you not aware of what the law says? 22For it is written that Abraham had two sons, one by the slave woman and the other by the free woman. 23His son by the slave woman was born according to the flesh, but his son by the free woman was born as the result of a divine promise.*
>
> *24These things are being taken figuratively: The women represent two covenants. One covenant is from Mount Sinai and bears children who are to be slaves: This is Hagar. 25Now Hagar stands for Mount Sinai in Arabia and corresponds to the present city of Jerusalem, because she is in slavery with her children. 26But the Jerusalem that is above is free, and she is our mother.*

and 1 Corinthians 10:9-12

> *9We should not test Christ, as some of them did – and were killed by snakes. 10And do not grumble, as some of them did – and were killed by the destroying angel.*
>
> *11These things happened to them as examples (metaphor, allegory) and were written down as warnings for us, on whom the culmination of the ages has come. 12So, if you think you are standing firm, be careful that you don't fall!*

Joseph, the whole of scripture will open up to us once we begin to view these stories as allegory or, at the very least, mystery. Some of it may be historic or literal, but the majority is to be taken mystically. Many of the foundational stories (Adam and Eve, the Garden of Eden, the fall, the flood, the wilderness etc.,) were borrowed from much earlier Egyptian and Sumerian texts. They are not original or unique to the Bible.

Now, concerning the scripture you questioned, I can only give you my opinion:

41 "Then he will say to those on his left, 'Depart from me, you who are cursed, into the eternal fire prepared for the devil and his angels. 42 For I was hungry and you gave me nothing to eat, I was thirsty and you gave me nothing to drink, 43 I was a stranger and you did not invite me in, I needed clothes and you did not clothe me, I was sick and in prison and you did not look after me.'

When we see "left", as opposed to "right", the Bible (and many other ancient texts) are referring to the ego within man. The rebuke is to the man or woman who does not tend or nurture the spirit within. Ego loves the law, literalism, the letter, the intellect. Spirit loves the rich intuited fields, that which cannot be seen or discerned with the five physical senses; hence the directive to "lift our eyes." The seed that is Christ is sown into each man and the choice is made to nurture that aspect of who we are.

If one does not nurture and care for the spirit, then they must return to the mortal worlds of flesh and blood until they do. The Devil and his angels are nothing more than the egocentric dalliance of man within the worlds of matter. They will return to the futile fields of carnality until they mature. The Devil is a metaphor for YOU (me) as long as you (we) remain in egocentricity.

We can see these entities as external, and they will be. They will appear externally as long as we need them to. But in reality, the whole of scripture is what lies within the consciousness of the human being. All of it. The Christ is birthed within you, within humanity, through the virgin form of human consciousness; Virgin because never before had the Divine penetrated the DNA of humanity to find within the worlds of matter a helpmate; the human form from which to experience and navigate the material worlds.

And your second verse, from Revelation 5:

2And I saw a mighty angel proclaiming in a loud voice, "Who is worthy to break the seals and open the scroll?" 3But no one in heaven or on earth or under the earth could open the scroll or even look inside it. 4I wept and wept because no one was found who was worthy to open the scroll or look inside. 5Then one of the elders said to me, "Do not weep! See, the Lion of the tribe of Judah, the Root of David, has triumphed. He is able to open the scroll and its seven seals."

6Then I saw a Lamb, looking as if it had been slain, standing at the center of the throne, encircled by the four living creatures and the elders. The Lamb had seven horns and seven eyes, which are the seven spirits of God sent out into all the earth. 7He went and took the scroll from the right hand of him who sat on the throne. 8And when

> *he had taken it, the four living creatures and the twenty-four elders fell down before the Lamb. Each one had a harp and they were holding golden bowls full of incense, which are the prayers of God's people.*
>
> *9And they sang a new song, saying: "You are worthy to take the scroll and to open its seals, because you were slain, and with your blood you purchased for God-persons from every tribe and language and people and nation.*
>
> *10You have made them to be a kingdom and priests to serve our God, and they will reign on the earth."*

I did an extensive study on this passage, and to go into detail would be time prohibitive. I will gladly send you my book that will go into much more detail, but I will give you an abbreviated version here:

No egocentric man is able to open the scrolls – the scrolls are internal within the consciousness of mankind and record the mysteries of the ages. The worthy one is the Christ in you – the hope of glory, that must experience death to self and be resurrected to new life; that is, where fear does not rule, and the intuited mind is wide open. The Lion of the tribe of Judah is an astronomical reference to the Age of Leo as it pertains to the Kingship of the human being.

The seven seals are over the seven scrolls that is the human chakra system which aligns with the endocrine system and that are positioned along the spine. When the chakras are activated it brings healing to the body, much like the serpent on the pole brought healing to those wandering in the wilderness when it was "raised up." The pole is a metaphor for our spinal column, where the endocrine glands are positioned. This activation will produce the Merkabah (Merkavah, if compared to the chariot that Ezekiel was carried away in). Jesus and other masters had a fully functioning light body (Merkabah) which enabled them to move from place to place, inter-dimensionally. This is why Phillip was able to disappear and reappear miles away in the same moment.

Remember, "The things you see me do you will do and greater…" Jesus said that. And it will be; but not if we remain in fear and under an egocentric idea of God.

The twenty-four elders are the twelve paired cranial nerves within the skull. The book of Revelation is a medical mystery book.

10:178 Another Letter to a Fundamentalist

You repeat a lot of the same things that I used to when I was involved in fundamentalism. It is part of your journey, all of our journey, as we are awakening from the deep sleep of fear-based thinking and programming. I no longer see God as you do, and for some reason that threatens you because you need me and others like me to agree with you in order for you to feel safe in your beliefs. Otherwise, why would you be moved to reply?

Christianity, by and large, needs consensus to feel safe because, deep down inside of it, there is conflict and contradiction. However, your responses are typical, and even normal, as I have heard from many like you; like I was, over the years of having my Facebook page. To even begin to think that you might have embraced error is very hard for you to swallow. Neural pathways have been created in your thinking that will not allow unconditional love to infiltrate easily. You have been controlled, manipulated and dominated by fear. Behind every teaching of separation or damnation is FEAR.

This conflict is because of what you have embraced; doctrines and dogma that do not resonate with I AM, but rather, are based in fear – the opposite of love. In your heart, you know that I AM would never torture human beings in a literal fire, but what are you to believe when you have been taught these things by people you love, respect and trust?

Christian fundamentalism teaches separation, damnation and torture. To teach such things is emotional abuse, especially when taught to children, as it was to me. It is a mixture of truth and error; error that comes from interpreting things literally, that were never meant to be taken that way.

This is why Christianity is failing, along with other fundamentalist religions. People are waking up to the controlling mechanism of dogma that can no longer rule over human consciousness. Love is triumphant over fear.

You sound very angry, and maybe that anger comes from submitting yourself to someone else's idea of God. Maybe you are tired of towing the heaviness of the law around like a weight strapped around your ankle. All I know is that I don't see or sense the love of your God in your words, so why should I listen to you?

You have the truth within you, and if you take the time, you will hear it as it percolates up and through the dogma you have tried to wrap it in. Love never fails, and it won't fail you.

10:179 Fragile Aspects

It is important to allow the fragile aspects of ourselves to have a voice. Betrayal. These wounds don't heal with time. They fester. Opening the musty box of unresolved pain allows for freshness to apprehend the wounds that have been wrapped in the grave clothes of retrospect.

Betrayal is the most difficult of wounds to heal, because we can never find validation from those who did the betraying. They have buried their guilt so far below denial and self-justification that they cannot see – will not see – their part in your pain. The ego will simply not allow it. We ALL immerse our guilt under the putrid waters of self-justification.

In the departure years we wander in the wilderness stepping on the fiery serpents of egocentric life. Battered, bitten and dying, we turn to the image of the ascended serpent on the pole, and awaken to the knowledge that the musty box must open, and its contents must spill out. In the open air these memories become faint, just as the smell of death fades meekly over time.

No one is coming for you. No one will defend you. We die alone. No one will appear to bind up your wounds like the Good Samaritan, for the Good Samaritan is within you, awaiting your surrender on the highway of injustice. From your brokenness the germ will appear, and plant itself in the manure of this passing phase.

And it will thrive.

And it will call itself "Christ."

And it will ascend.

10:180 Self-Care

A friend recently asked, "What is the most important practice in the art of self-care?"

I replied: "Letting go of expectations."

SECTION ELEVEN

ELEVEN

11:181 A Paradox

What a paradox! I have never been one to draw boundaries, and subsequently, I think I suffered because of it. When I was younger, I always placed the value on someone else: How would they feel toward me if I put my foot down in one area or another? Would they reject me? Don't get me wrong; I had some boundaries where the line was not crossed, regardless of what another person thought. But regarding everyday encounters, it seemed I had let fear, rather than healthy boundaries, rule over me.

That is low self-esteem. Very low.

I felt I could work around whatever brought discomfort to me.

As I grew older, I thought that I was savvy, having learned how to be political rather than learning how to set boundaries. Who needed boundaries, right?

Now, I have finally come to the point of wanting to set some boundaries while understanding that every boundary comes with a price. Giving a lot of consideration to the issue, I finally decided to set a boundary with a good friend of mine. I had made a substantial intellectual and emotional investment thinking about it for months and needed to make a move to resolve it. It was time!

Then, while watching TV last night, I heard this quote:

> *"Boundaries don't keep people out,*
> *they fence you in.*
> *Life is messy;*
> *It is how we are made.*
> *You can waste your life drawing lines,*
> *or you can live your life crossing them.*
> *If you are willing to take the chance,*
> *the view from the other side is spectacular."*
>   A quote from the television show *Grey's Anatomy*)

So now what do I do? This quote hit me like a love arrow in my heart. I have worked so hard to love and to love unconditionally, so how in the world could I even think about drawing boundaries?

I feel as though I am coming full circle. Before, I didn't draw healthy boundaries out of fear. Now, I choose not to draw boundaries out of love and ultimate forgiveness. I am learning from every experience and being given the opportunity to embrace pain and to make it bless me.

11:182 The Jesus I Know

The Jesus Christ I know does not require me to attend a church or to pay admission fees.

The Jesus Christ I know does not tell me to separate myself from those who don't "believe" like me, but rather, encourages me to be a light to the world.

The Jesus Christ I know does not care for dogma.

The Jesus Christ I know does not threaten me with Hell.

The Jesus Christ I know does not threaten me with separation.

The Jesus Christ I know does not threaten me with condemnation, nor does he condemn me.

The Jesus I know does not wait to accept me only if I accept him.

The Jesus I know is already within my heart, my soul and body as Christ; this Christ only asks that I believe that I am the dwelling place of I AM.

The Christ I know wants me to understand the allegory of the virgin birth and that it is I, Mary (humanity), that has been impregnated with something Holy and Divine.

The Christ within allows me to see that God has been wrapped within my flesh and blood and that I AM.

The Christ within allows me to see that the Bible is my story. The Old Testament is my old story, while I perceived God as tyrannical and something to be feared.

The Christ within allows me to see that the New Testament is my new story, as I begin to embrace the Father that Loves me. rather than seeks to punish me by burning me alive…forever.

The Christ within allows me to see that the story of Jesus is my story.

The Christ within allows me to see the content in all of the scriptures as a metaphoric and chronographic depiction of the human journey, growth and education in this world.

The Christ within allows me to see that the cross is my event horizon. It is the place where I must choose to die to my human identity so that Christ may live.

The Christ in me allows me to understand that the very human aspect of who I AM does not remain in this "grave" but is resurrected to new life as a servant AND equal partner of my divine nature.

The Christ in me allows me to see the events described in Matthew 24 and in the book of Revelation as a personal tribulation, as the old me breaks down like a caterpillar, like the worm of the Earth, but only to be created again in the cocoon of Heaven, birthed anew in my identity of the risen Christ.

I AM.

11:183 Empaths! Healers! Shamans!

YOU ARE A MAGNET!!!

Is your judgment making you sick??? YOUR DISCOMFORT IS AN INDICATOR!

Even the slightest judgment (something that allows your emotions to move in a negative way) may be attracting that same energy (from another person, place or thing) into your body. You have the innate ability to remove it organically, but if you offer the same frequency of fear, anger, sorrow, despair, etc., then it has found a home and will remain within you.

THIS IS BECAUSE YOU ARE A HEALER!!!

You have the ability to transmute and to move negative energy off of people, places and things, and if you provide a negative vibration through judgement that is compatible with the energy of who and what you are healing, IT WILL STAY WITHIN YOUR BODY. Again, YOU ARE A MAGNET!

An energy body that has been activated is like a fan that pulls in air from the backside and expels it out the frontside. However, if the environment is a "closed system", then the air will just circulate over and over within. This is akin to a toilet that is full of crap but never flushes! It just swirls around and around, and you experience the same old S%#T. You need to open the exhaust portal, get the Roto-Rooter out and allow all of the negative energy to be released from your energy sphere.

Opening the exhaust portal is accomplished with, love, joy, peace, patience, kindness hope, grace, forgiveness, meekness – UNCONDITIONAL LOVE AND

NON-JUDGMENT, etc.! The empath must rise above the fray and actualize CHRIST!

Judgment locks the portal closed and clogs the toilet! You can tell immediately if you are in judgment because you will feel NEGATIVE EMOTION! This has happened to me over the last decade when I have felt pity or sorrow for a given circumstance and I feel a "pulling down" and get depressed and full of despair. My own energy must be transmuted through non-judgment of a given situation so that I may continue to heal people, places and things. You must become adept at recognizing that what you are feeling in the way of your emotions just may be someone else's negative ballast that needs to be transmuted. As a healer, you can do this, but not if you continue to judge what you feel and to ascribe it to your own life circumstances! That clogs the toilet!

Emotions are indicators and provide the opportunity to disengage the pain body from the puppet strings of judgment! Negativity affects the physical body and is the source of all dis-ease.

ASK, "Is my judgment making me sick???"

When we stay in forgiveness, love, tolerance, etc., it is like the floodgates are opened and negative energy will sail through your energy sphere without obstruction! You will not be affected by it. HOWEVER, if you provide a compatible negative frequency of your own, then the negative energy that would normally sail through your sphere of influence will get bogged down rather than experience the transmutation that the healer is capable of.

If you are a healer, empath, shaman – whatever you want to be called – then you have the ability to heal this dimension of its negative ballast.

If you get into judgment, then your emotions from your lower three chakras are active rather than passive, and they will attract and RETAIN negative energy within you. And the clogged toilet bowl effect kicks in!

Choose love! Choose happiness! Choose forgiveness! Choose joy! Choose hope!

When you find yourself bogged down with negative energy, look up! Laugh! Find joy! DO NOT JUDGE. LOVE UNCONDITIONALLY! You will find what you attract!

11:184 Jacob Wrestling and IS RA EL

For those familiar with the Old Testament story of Jacob's wrestling with the angel (messenger), bringing about the change in his name from Jacob to Israel: Some thoughts and questions for you this morning…

If Jacob (which means *supplanter*; one who seizes the place of another metaphorically. Jacob is our own ego that has seized the throne of I AM temporarily) wrestles with the Divine messenger and Jacob's name is changed to Israel – what does that mean?

> IS RA EL
> Is (Isis, Isus, Jesus) – Means "came from the creation of the universe"
> Ra – The sun god, "The one who was there at the beginning"
> El – The Divine, God

So, Jacob being representative of all egocentric mankind (ego-driven life) has his name/nature changed through the struggle with the messenger to IS RA EL. (It should be noted that this struggle is INTERNAL).

We are created egocentric beings that, through struggle, awaken to our true identity.

At the creation of the material Universe – we were there at the beginning. We are God, expressed in physical form.

> Is = Feminine
> Ra = Masculine
> El = the birth of the Divine through the union of Is and Ra

Come up and out of the waters, ye Godmen! Your baptism into humanity is finished. Your labor is over. You are the womb-man that births the Christ.

11:185 Love Never Fails

We may be pro-war, until one of our children enlists. We may be anti-gay, until one of our children declares their homosexuality. We may be for the death penalty, until one of our children is sentenced to death. We may be pro-abortion, until a long-awaited grandchild is on the way. We may be against euthanasia, until we see our beloved suffer endlessly. When it gets personal, hearts bloom. Let's not wait to evolve. Choose to love today. No more boundaries. If we must draw boundaries, let us draw them in sand, not concrete. Love. Never. Fails.

11:186 What Sense Does it Make?

Listen up!

What sense does it make to be commanded by God to forgive and to love our enemies while he tortures his for eternity?

That is not God. That is religion. It is what separates and divides relatives, friends, families, neighbors, churches, countries and our WORLD, and is the source of all wars, conflict and strife.

When political parties are mingled with religious affiliations, we will fall, without fail.

Our country was not founded on Christianity; it was founded on freedom from religious oppression.

Jesus was hardest on the religious.
Religion will not serve us.
Religion will divide us.
Religion will conquer us.
Only love will serve us.
Only love will unite us.
Only love will not fail us.
Open your eyes.

And by the way, your non-religion and persecution of Christians will not serve us either. It is the SAME as religious oppression. Intolerance is a stain upon our consciousness.
Stop the madness. Your country and the world NEEDS you.

Wake up America.

11:187 Controlling Doctrines

Down through the ages, fundamentalists have created many controlling doctrines to support their system of religion, building upon limited revelation and acquiring consciousness constructed with fear. Being saved has nothing to do with raising a hand, reciting a prayer, or behaving according to some cultural and moral code of ethics employed by over 38,000 disagreeing Christian denominations. Heck, if Christians can't agree on dogma, what chance do they have of getting it right?

The saving of the body has everything to do with the purpose for our journey in consciousness as Divinity, couched within the human being, leaving behind and evolving out of egocentric fear-based and survivalist mentalities and learning to love one another. Being saved is not what we think it is.

Jesus modeled a path out of fundamentalist religion by breaking the rules and by being hardest on the religious people, especially leaders. Jesus and John the Baptist called the religious folk "a brood of vipers" – terminology that is a metaphor for egocentricity or fear-based consciousness, referring to the "serpent." The first appearance of this viper is, of course, in The Garden of Eden, when the serpent spoke to Eve. Metaphorically, this is not some external enemy named Satan or Lucifer; this is our own egocentric nature speaking from within, luring us to eat the fruit of selfishness and establishing us into duality, or knowing good from evil. Eating this "fruit" would begin our journey out of immortality and into time, mortality and ultimately, death.

11:188 Come Sit with Me

I heard a true story this past week that I wanted to share with you. My friend told me of a circumstance in which she found herself. I have changed the names of the people in the story.

There was a group of eight women that belonged to a specialized social group. This group of women got together before their scheduled monthly meeting for a dinner out. When Angela arrived at the restaurant, there were only five of the group members sitting at the table. She joined them and asked where the founder of the group was. They replied that they had purposely excluded the founder, and their reason was judgmental. Angela asked where the other non-present member was and got a vague answer that she knew was not true. They had excluded two people from their little group.

Angela stood up and abruptly stated this:

"I did not participate with this shit in high school and I won't do it now!"

As I listened to this story, I felt the whole gambit of emotions. I thought things like, "Way to go, Angela!" And, "YES! She told those mean girls off!" and "I hate cliques and they deserved to have someone tell them off!"

I have been on the receiving end of "mean girl" behavior. They deserved a taste of their own medicine, I thought. A while back I watched the movie *Mean Girls,* starring Lindsay Lohan, in which a very insecure girl garners enough hutzpah to retaliate against a group of mean girls. The movie shows how young we are when we begin the process of "social sorting."

Sadly, I identified with the story Angela told because I had been every person in the drama. I have been accepted and rejected. It's too painful to label myself a "mean girl," but when I found myself on the inside of a group I did not stand up for "the rejected." I guess that makes me a "mean girl."

I long to be like Angela, though, standing up to those women. She was right; behavior like that is reminiscent of high school cliques. That is how it starts. We learn to sort, reject and accept, reward and punish according to local and national societal norms and pressures. And we hurt people.

The moral of this story? We all need to find the "mean girl" within that we keep alive with our tasty morsels of insecurity and self-justification. We need a "come to Jesus" meeting and to learn, truly learn, how to love people beyond our politics, beyond our religion and social affiliations. May we all set aside our weapons that have been forged in the fires of rejection and see one another as we are – souls that need to be loved, accepted and appreciated.

Come sit with me by the light of the fire. Love me there where the light is dim.

11:189 Sometimes I Get a Little Irritated

Sometimes I wonder, what is wrong with me? Why do I get a little irritated when I see someone pray in public? Plead the blood over someone? Even raise their hands in worship and adoration? I know that they danced in the Old Testament... Wasn't Jesus adverse to someone, anyone, worshipping him? So why do I feel a twinge when I see these things?

I did ALL THESE THINGS. I understand why I did them and maybe that is why it bothers me a little.

Are these and other practices even in the Bible, or have they become part of Christian fundamentalism through conditioning, modeling and peer pressure? Is it cultural? And if it is, why?

I remember when someone raised their hands for the first time in worship, rather than standing stoically; we considered it a "win". They were finally one of "us".

I have just named three practices that are not instructed or scripturally sound. I am comparing the practice to scriptural soundness because most of fundamentalism uses scripture to validate their practices. Can you name more practices that have been created by modern fundamentalism?

Curious.

11:190 The Princess and the Pea

I keep two personal filing cabinets in my home. One is in my desk and readily accessible and contains active files. The other is about 10 feet from my desk and contains inactive, or rarely accessed, files.

I have been thinking a lot about emotional pain and how memories resurface that invoke an emotional response. I was telling my husband this morning that some of the pain that resurfaces does not seem rational or, at the very least, are memories that I thought have already been healed. Not so. These are memories that should be kept in the "inactive file".

Healing comes in layers, and at the deepest layer, we can see that painful memories shape our present reality. Sort of like the *Princess and the Pea* story – she felt the pain of a small pea so far beneath the layers of her mattresses that it affected her rest. We are the same. We keep things so far buried beneath the layers of our consciousness that sometimes it takes the removal of all of the coverings to discover the pea.

In the fairy tale, the prince is searching for his beloved, and only a true princess is able to feel the pain beneath the mattresses she lay upon. The prince rejoices when he finds a princess who can feel the buried pain, and so they are married.

What does this say about the masculine and feminine within us all? The feminine is required to "feel the pain."

What does this speak to you?

I am learning that pain is there for a reason, and that in order to navigate through life and relationships, we must not add another layer of mattress to our bed, but rather, our pain is a qualification for AWAKENING AND MARRIAGE. Somehow, the masculine needs the sensitivity of the feminine, but all too often women are dismissed as "too emotional" or for having a "memory like an elephant." But in reality, he needs her. Masculine needs feminine to be complete. The creation and movement of emotional current serves as the currency of creating reality. It is through the creation and distribution of emotion that reality is created. Our emotional current is currency that we "pay" in order that reality manifests.

Now for the good stuff:

We learn through the things that we suffer. Emotional pain serves as an alarm clock to awaken us to the reality that what we focus upon, we create. The gap of time that exists between our thoughtful focus and its ultimate manifestation is diminishing.

We now know that what we thoughtfully focus on, providing the emotional current through memory, we create.

So now the task of the feminine energy is to focus upon union between the masculine and feminine so that conscious creation manifests. We now know that we must not cover over or even do away with emotional pain, but it must find its place in our "inactive files" so that we do not continue to focus on what it is THAT WE DO NOT WANT; the things which brought about so much pain to begin with. Let us put pain in the inactive file and recognize that it has served to awaken this restless princess to union.

11:191 Feeling Someone Else's Pain?

How can you tell if you are feeling someone else's pain?

An empath is defined as this: a person with the paranormal ability to apprehend the mental or emotional state of another individual.

Being an empath can be tricky, because the empathic person walks through life feeling emotional overload that most often is not derived from their personal experience. They are feeling the pain (or energy) of another person. The empath may feel energy from places or things, as well, that hold the energy in specific configurations unique to the environment. We know, through research, that even plants contain memory, and we are told in the Bible that the ground "cries out" when or where innocent blood has been shed.

So, who are these people that can absorb the negative emotional ballast from other people, places and things? Why are they here? Where did they come from? What do they do with the energy they absorb?

Just as a paper towel absorbs the mess of a spilled drink, the empath absorbs the emotional spillage of wounded people, places and things, thereby reducing the trauma and promoting healing.

An empath discovering their unique gift may silently think, "Why am I feeling this way?" We have a sorrowful feeling and we may link the emotion to the latest hurt or drama that has occurred within our own life. When we do this, we miss the opportunity to understand that our empathic energy body has just received the emotional "dirty laundry" from someone else and this dirty laundry looks just like OUR LAUNDRY! This is why it is so important NOT to identify with the emotion by falling into agreement with it while we recall the stories of our own personal wounding.

A normal person will think about a hurtful event and it will conjure up painful emotions, whereas an empath WILL FEEL THE EMOTION BEFORE THINKING OF A HURTFUL EVENT.

This is a key indicator that we have received someone else's "dirty laundry" to process – when we feel the emotion before thinking about the painful event. All of a sudden, the emotional payload is just there.

For some, emotional "dirty laundry" is not felt in the emotions, but rather, they have a physical reaction such as nausea, dizziness and various pain when and where they have absorbed emotional spillage.

The task of the empath is always the same – they have received the dirty laundry to CLEAN it. Somehow, there is a vibrational capacity within the empath to change the current of the energy that is released into the atmosphere through the expulsion of emotion. Emotion is a powerful creative force, and if the spillage is left unattended, it will create circumstances after its kind. For example, if someone has suffered the trauma of rape and remains unhealed, the emotional configuration/vibration that comes out from their body sends a request to the universe to create using the same configuration. So, the emotion that is released is one of trauma, violence and victimhood. The universe does not discriminate but gives to us circumstances that will eventually manifest the same energetic configuration. All energy has a unique signature and the universe, through the Law of Attraction, hastens to give to us (us being the generator of the vibration) what we "request". Our requests are not with words, but with vibration. We create what we emit through our emotions.

The empath, in essence, must hold the vibration in a neutral space, not judging what they feel, being careful to raise the frequency upward; like it has captured the vibration and put it in an internal elevator. In this way, the energy is not free to create after its kind, but rather, goes through a trans-MUTING process where the frequency of fear, anger, jealousy, violence, prejudice, etc. is trans-MUTED. The energy "held" in non-judgment, while the empath offers unconditional love, peace, joy, patience, etc., cleans the vibrational signature, allowing it to ascend. The excess energy then is free to roam, usually into higher dimensional planes. It has served its purpose and is now enabling a buoyancy to return to the Earth, permitting it to ascend.

This is the rich symbolism behind the serpent on the pole in the book of Numbers, Chapter 21. The energy (serpent) that killed those wandering in the wilderness was transmuted when they affixed an image onto a pole and lifted it UP. When they looked to the image of the serpent (emotions) rising on a pole, they were healed.

11:192 Like the Caterpillar

Like the caterpillar as it morphs to a butterfly, we are consuming the internal parts and are reforming/resurrecting the body vehicle from the inside out … This is an excellent quote from my friend Joseph Danna about the internal changes occurring now within your body!!!

Read on!

> *"… and we too will metamorphose. Oneness, being all-pervasive of course, also means the mind/body is a unit…and as the mind changes so does the body. I have heard hormones referred to as "God's chemicals." At a certain point in the caterpillar's life, a hormone is released to bring on the metamorphosis. It seems feasible that at a point in our evolution, a drawing in of higher frequency thought energy may be the required fertilization for God's chemicals to be released in us. Maybe there's more to transformation than we know…"*

Oh! I so agree with Joe on this viewpoint! I have struggled to understand these hormonal changes and my source has intimated that there are many changes afoot in the manufacture and distribution of our hormonal output. These changes occur organically as our frequency/vibration elevates from fear to love unconditional.

As in Matthew 24. we read of catastrophic changes occurring as the end of the age draws near. We misinterpret these catastrophes as happening externally, when in reality, they occur within the body vehicle.

I have heard from so many who are having difficulty with the physical changes occurring within the body's electrical system which, as you know, has a lot to do with our hormone production.

So, know this: as it pertains to the resurrection of the body vehicle, we are to be encouraged as it says in 1 Thessalonians 4:

> *"For the Lord himself shall descend from heaven with a shout (Christ in you will descend from higher dimensions with a frequency alteration), with the voice of the archangel (a higher dimensional tone!), and with the trump of God (the chakra wheel of light from the next higher plane): and the dead in Christ shall rise first: Then we which are alive and remain shall be caught up together with them in the clouds, to meet the Lord in the air (Christ in the heavens – a higher immortal state!): and so shall we ever be with the Lord. Wherefore comfort one another with these words."*

We must comfort one another in the days ahead because the caterpillar is cocooning, and its interior is breaking down. We are consuming the internal parts and are reforming/resurrecting the body vehicle from the inside out. THIS MAY BRING A LEVEL OF PHYSICAL DISCOMFORT, as all of our body's electrical systems will recalibrate!!! All of them! We will see, and are seeing, massive variances in heart rates, hormone production and distribution, and even muscular-skeletal reformation, including a lot of dizziness that comes from a recalibration and or movement of the Otoconia crystalline structures within the inner ear. They are moving like an antenna shifts to pick up signals from a different source. A floating feeling will ensue when this happens.

Please, I encourage you to read Matthew 24 with metaphysical eyes. This chapter is all about the destruction of the temple in the last days and the temple IS YOU. We are reforming, cocooning, recalibrating, and being rewired. New neural pathways are opening because you have chosen LOVE over FEAR. As consciousness within the brain shifts, it cannot help but produce changes within the body. We are in the beginning stages of resurrection. This is your purpose. You are winding down the mystery of the ages as the dying and resurrecting God-man. This did not happen to one man but is occurring in ALL MEN.

11:193 A Detailed Map

> *"The worlds people, through religions and mythologies, provide to the human a detailed map of their own unfolding consciousness. If we could just step outside of them [religions and mythologies] we could see the patterns they represent and awaken to the process of our conscious evolution."*
>
> Barbara Symons

11:194 A Level of Discomfort

When you feel a level of discomfort in lieu of revelation knowledge being dispensed, it is almost certain that the finger of God has been placed on the pulse of a doctrine within your consciousness not suitable for the age to come.

> *But if I with the finger of God cast out devils, no doubt the kingdom of God is come upon you.*
>
> Luke 11:20

11:195 Halloween

I was a typical kid and adult who celebrated Halloween every year with candy and Trick-or-Treating. It was never a big deal, just a time of fun and innocence. Then came my indoctrination into fundamentalism …

After to moving into our new home in College Station, Texas, I called a locksmith to change the locks. I had a couple of very large hefty garbage sacks (full of leaves) that were orange and looked like jack-o-lanterns placed in the front yard of our house. After changing the locks, he inquired if I was a Christian/believer and was saved. I said, "Yes." He then gave me a rather stern rebuke and told me to get rid of the jack-o-lantern trash bags out front because they would draw demons to my home. He told me stories of darkness and how I needed to protect my children and invited me to his church for the "fall festival" rather than to let them go trick-or-treating. Young and impressionable, down the rabbit hole I went.

For almost a decade I lived, moved and had my being in FEAR. I became a deliverance minister (exorcist) within that church and saw many, many examples of possession that reinforced my belief and focus in darkness.

I could go on for pages, but the following is succinct. Jesus spoke this:

> *"If I by the finger of God cast out demons then surely the kingdom is at hand."*   Luke 11:20

This tells me one very important thing: There is NO PLACE FOR DEMONS IN THE KINGDOM AGE!

So, my focus has dramatically changed. Jim Swilley says this:

> *"Now I've come full circle...I'm happy to just call it Halloween and enjoy it for what it is...the devil is a non-issue in my life, and I think that a major part of embracing the light is accepting the darkness for what it is...I view everything through the paradigm of the Tree of Life, as opposed to seeing everything through the paradigm of the Tree of the Knowledge of Good and Evil, so I live in a non-judgmental mindset..."*

Bam! Jim nailed it.

Now I understand that what I focus upon, I will have. If I focus upon darkness, then that is what I will see. If I focus upon the light, then that is what I will have. It's that simple.

I was in a Cracker Barrel restaurant with my 5-year-old granddaughter a few years back. She saw a beautiful "princess dress" that she had to have. I purchased it for her. Years ago, and fears ago, I would have never bought it. Now, I celebrate her innocence, focusing on the light of Christ within this loving little soul.

11:196 The Appearance of Christ Brings Division

The appearance of Christ brings division.

There is no way around it because the "Christ" is not compatible with mainstream humanity.

In the New Testament pattern, the appearance of Christ divided the religious from the righteous, did it not?

This is exactly what we have today. Look at our national stage; how polarized we have become!

I see it happening, even within my family, as politics slithers into our relationships and a sword is drawn between those we love.

You speak peace between Democrats and Republicans, and what happens? Swords are drawn.

You speak unity between fundamentalist "Christians" and Muslims, and what happens? Swords are drawn.

You drop a love bomb in the middle of warmongers, and what happens? Swords are drawn.

You bring up politics at the dinner table, and what happens? Swords are drawn.

> *Do you think I came to bring peace on earth? No, I tell you, but division. From now on there will be five in one family divided against each other, three against two and two against three. They will be divided, father against son and son against father, mother against daughter and daughter against mother, mother-in-law against daughter-in-law and daughter-in-law against mother-in-law."*
> Luke 12:51-53

The rule of law in our world is determined by what is discerned as good or evil.

Christ's message is to say don't judge between good and evil, for it is in this judgment that your world exists. Judging between good and evil is what keeps conflict on our world stage.

The message of Christ brought cataclysm to the ruling religious order, for this message compromised their platform, their authority, their powerful rule. And Christ was killed for it. But in the killing of Christ came a powerful demonstration.

You cannot defeat love. This message lives. It does not happen to one man, but to all of humanity.

> *"If the same spirit (love) that raised Christ from the dead dwells in you, it will quicken your mortal body."* from Romans 8:11

And so, it is.

11:197 People Say Odd Things in the Midst of Trauma

People say all sorts of odd things in the midst of trauma, most of it is an attempt to understand what cannot be. You may know my story: when my son Chris lost his two limbs in a motorcycle accident, he was told that if he had been going to church, God would have protected him. Chris handled that situation with grace and love – a better demonstration of the love of Christ I have not yet seen.

I remember when a voice spoke to me out to the mist of internal hysteria while Chris was in the operating room. It said, "There is no human suffering in vain. All suffering has value."

And this I believe. If we are to manifest Christ within, as Paul stated, then we must understand that suffering is a prerequisite for our learning. "He, (the Christ) learned obedience through the things that he suffered." My prayer is that we begin to see the bigger picture and to understand that we are not victims here, but participants, actively ushering in the kingdom age as we shelter the babe of Christ within humanity.

11:198 A Recovering Charismatic Christian Fundamentalist

I spent the first 43 years of my life heavily involved within Christian fundamentalism. At my last church I was on the Board of Elders and in charge of Deliverance Ministries (exorcism). Then, one day I began to question the Christian concept of Hell, eternal punishment and separation. I thought, why would God encourage us to love, forgive and to pray for our enemies while he sends his to eternal torment in fire?

My Christian idea of God was unstable, and I found Christian doctrines to be erroneous. Like tipping dominoes, my dogmatic beliefs were tumbling, each one providing inertia for the next. My questions raised eyebrows and challenged the basis for Christian dogma. Now, outside of organized religion, I can clearly see the manipulation and programming that Christianity (and other religions) instills.

Recently, I was asked how Christians and former Christians might find "Christ" once outside of the church system. This question requires that I define what Christ is. and by defining it, one sees what it is not. It should be noted that my basis for understanding scripture is mystical, rather than historical. Therefore, I had to let the historical Jesus "go" so that I might see the mystery beyond the history.

Once letting go of the historical Jesus, it was paramount for me to understand the word "Christ." It is automatic to think that when one says "Christ" that they are referring to Jesus. Some actually think "Christ" is a surname, of sorts. However, I have read that the word "Christ" was around centuries before the advent of Jesus and was used to describe a person who was an initiate into mysticism and anointed with special understanding.

The word "Christ" actually means to anoint, to rub or to press into. and is not exclusive to Jesus. The word "Christ" might be considered a verb, because it expresses a mode of being. This very visual concept of "rubbing or pressing into" shows us the act bringing two things together. In metaphorical understanding, "Christ" expresses union between God and man and Jesus is a pattern for this union.

The "Christ" or "Christed one" is a human being that recognizes its oneness with God. As such, the egocentric mind yields to the nature or mind of "Christ" as it willingly surrenders its role as master of the body to become the servant of the Divine. This is the cross experience, where horizontal humanity surrenders to vertical Divinity. It is death to the ego.
The egocentric mind seeks to experience eternity and immortality provided by "Christ." It understands the necessity to yield to its eternal counterpart that can ultimately lead it to expansiveness beyond the physical domains. This is resurrection of the ego.

God has penetrated and inoculated the corporeal Mary with Divinity; that is, the human race; and is resting within humanity, within the swaddle of our beautiful biology. We are beginning to awaken to this and other mysteries that have been metaphorically hidden in plain sight. God, in its infinite creative potential, found a way to join us, to fold up the wisdom of the multiverse and hide inside this biological Eden. Divinity has been incubating, growing inside of the body vehicle, so that it can experience the material domains with us and through us, and acquire for itself a helpmate – a physical body from which to navigate the material domains.

Divinity, this so called "father" better termed as "progenitor," is waiting for our conscious participation in union. No one person may access this potent creative force that lies within without the cross experience. It is aware of the indwelling of the creative force of the multiverse, the immortal counterpart of humanity. It is the human ego in submission to the Creator of all things. It is Emmanuel – God with man.

> *I am the way, the truth and the light and no one comes to the Father but by me.*   John 14:6

Fundamentalist Christianity asserts that one must get "saved" and submit to the church's idea of salvation. We need to understand what Jesus meant when he said, "no one comes to the Father but by me." The "by me" is what needs clarification, because there is great latitude taken by fundamentalism. Does it mean that you must raise a hand, walk an aisle and accept Jesus into your heart? If yes, then why did Jesus never give instructions to do that?

I believe the life of Jesus modeled a path of transcendence through and out of egocentric humanity and into our core identity, Divinity. This is the "way" that he walked. Jesus spoke of love unconditional and non-judgment, and this path leads straight to the powerful creative force within called "father." This path leads to freedom from fear-based religions where the followers ignorantly adhere to literalism, rather than the symbolism behind it. This "way" is offered to all and is patterned and found in a multitude of religions and cultures. Christianity does not have the market cornered on Heaven.

Albert Einstein said, "The intuitive mind is a sacred gift and the rational mind is a faithful servant. We have created a society that honors the servant and has forgotten the gift." This intuitive mind is the pearl of great price; it is God found within the husk of the human shell.

The pattern of Jesus serves to remind us, to show us the way back to the sacred gift. The servant is our egocentric intellect and its mode of operation is fear, while it flourishes in fear-based systems. The gift is the intuitive mind, and it is fearless. This is where Divinity flourishes. It is Christ.

The mystery of the ages is the dying and resurrecting God-man. This story is found in all of the world's major religions. Do you see it?

SECTION TWELVE

TWELVE

12:199 Is It Live, Or Is It Memorex?

Is it live or is it Memorex?

For those of you old enough to remember, cassette – and even reel-to-reel – tape recording devices were commonplace from the 1950s to the 1980s. Tape was magnetized with sound and recorded anything you wanted to hear. With the flip of a switch you could erase whatever had been recorded, and you could re-record on the tape.

We descended into this world with our memories recorded in our consciousness; but as we moved closer and closer to this dimension, our memories were erased, and we forgot who and what we are.

Joseph Campbell was the foremost author on the subject of myths in the mid-20th century, and he tells us that when we see water in myths it is representative of consciousness. Consciousness is simply this; it is what we are aware of. That says a lot, and consciousness is jam-packed full of what we, as human beings, are aware of. From the insignificant to the significant, the knowledge is recorded in our present memory base.

We have had our previous memory base erased as we were lowered into the physical world. What we had previously known was erased as we entered into the severely dense electromagnetic field of physical life. Like the tape in a recorder, the recording on the Memorex brand tape was erased, and purposely so. In order to have a fully human experience, we had to forget our origin.

But we have something of a memory… a ritual was instituted to remind us that we have been lowered into the dense and watery consciousness of being human.

Baptism. It's not what you think it is.

We are immersed under the waters of being human, holding our divine breath while submerged in the drama of physical and mortal life, only to someday come up and out of those waters and to REMEMBER …

The same goes for communion. The bread (from Heaven – another dimension) is broken and is swallowed into the belly (descending into death, becoming mortal). We are told to "Do this in remembrance of me…"

In remembrance of you.

The Christ.

Having been given as the only begotten.

To save the world.

Having become one of them.

Becoming all things to all men.

> *"Let this mind be in you, which was also in Christ Jesus:*
> *Who, being in the form of God, thought it not robbery to be equal*
> *with God:*
> *But made himself of no reputation, and took upon him the form of a*
> *servant, and was made in the likeness of men."*
> Philippians 2: 5-7

12:200 Therefore, Remember

There are those who have come here, to our planet, to help people overcome the negative energy that is so prevalent here.

Negativity is everywhere. Wherever you focus your energy; taking a knee during the anthem, the political divide, the wars, the drugs, the various abuses… folks, when you focus your energy here, that is what you will create more of. It is that simple.

So, there are those "eaters" of negative energy who are here, helping the planet by the millions. You know innately if you are one of them. They are the highly sensitive people out there, the empaths. You can feel the sorrow and pain of others, even in places and things. You are on a mission.

In order for you to continually transmute and change the formation of negativity, you must remember who and what you are, and do not fall into the pit of negativity by identifying with it. If you keep yourself buoyant, you will transmute negativity with ease.

Therefore, remember.

Remember that you have a unique bioelectric configuration within your body and sphere of influence.

Thank you for your service.

12:201 Blood on the Doorposts

Blood on the doorposts to be spared from death of the firstborn is a metaphor for the physical act of union – penetrating the birth portal of the virgin. The barrier of the broken hymen coats the "doorposts" with blood. This powerful symbol is why a virginal female will shed blood during her first sexual penetration.

A very quick glimpse into the symbolism of the Passover.

Union between the divine and the virgin soil of humanity is required to enter into immortality where the firstborn (the physical us) does not have to die.

12:202 A Little Buddha Statue

A little Buddha statue brought an end to a 25-year-long friendship.

We remodeled our bathroom in 2016 and I found a lovely little statue at the furniture store. I did not know at the time what it meant, but I liked it even more when I found that it is depicting the Buddhist Mudra for peace.

Peace.

My fundamentalist Christian friend of 25 years came to see the remodel, and shortly thereafter told me that she could no longer be my friend because I had a Buddha in my bathroom. True story.

Within Christianity there is so much misunderstanding regarding the Buddhist message. From the teachings of Jesus, one could easily make the connection that he may have been a practicing Buddhist. Buddhism is a peace-loving way of life. I hesitate to call it a religion, although many do. It is more a lifestyle that you may practice along with whatever religion you claim to be your own.

My understanding of Buddhism is this:

> We suffer because we want things.
> We want things because we see lack.
> We focus on what we lack and thereby create more lack by this focus.
> Therefore, the end of desire brings about the end of suffering.

This is why many third world nations are found to be among the happiest nations on Earth. They simply are not distracted by need and desire.

How can a Christian see the Buddhist way of life as evil? I have made many new friends from outside of the Christian community in our city, and I will tell you that they are some of the purest-hearted souls out there. I am thankful for what I have.

12:203 Severe Mercy

It has never been about sex. The Bible speaks of stories that divulge the mysteries of the universe that, when taken literally, result in death – always death. But if viewed in terms of energy (masculine and feminine not male and female), it reveals the dance of creation.

Taken literally, when a male and female copulate it produces physical life within the womb. When taken mystically, the masculine penetrating feminine energy produces eternal life within the womb-man, not male or female, but both so unified that they are a genderless form. An eternal form. One that is self-replicating, if you will.

This is where we are headed.

It was an act of severe mercy in Genesis 2 to separate us into male and female where we can view this mystery as it plays out in physicality. The egocentric nature within form may now "see" by a pattern that has been displayed for it through male and female.

We perceive with our five senses externally that which is internal and hidden. Our internal workings are displayed through patterns in the natural.

12:204 A Letter to Barbara

> *"The misguided souls just keep coming at you from all sides, and yet you stand. I shared your book the other day and it's the first time I have found the courage of my own to openly admit that I have escaped Christianity. My friends have kept quiet. My children have, also. Many of them are still believing all they have been taught. Thank you. I'm enjoying your book. Everything you write resonates with me and rings true. There are some things I am still pondering, but I have no doubt you have an enlightened consciousness."*

My response:

> *It can be brutal, but I was told to "bridge the gap," and so I stand. I understand that the "gap" is a boundary in consciousness that is difficult for the mind to penetrate. And so, I sow seeds and know that*

"all that is" is faithful to bring the increase. Thanks for your kind message.

In addition, I have pages of transcribed "prophesies" where I was told that I would be a source of controversy, that I would be rejected, that I would see things differently, and that mysteries that had been long hidden would be revealed through me. I was told that rejection would come from unlikely sources (some from my best friends) and that these experiences would be "bone-crushing."

Well, they have been. But I stand firm in my resolve to deliver the message. The hearer is responsible after that.

To those who are "receivers" of mysteries and "resonators" of the same, I salute you.

Carry on.

12:205 Every Ego's Struggle for Relevance

The key to becoming its most relevant state is to become irrelevant.

It is in irrelevance that the ego assumes its greatest role; It finally awakens to the mystery of the dog chasing its tail.

It has been busy creating the world of duality; simply, its focus on that which captivates for self-promotion.

It has its intersection – the world cross – where the horizontal surrenders to the vertical.

It dies as the master of the human self – the terrestrial shell.
It resurrects a servant – an equal partner with the celestial body.

Union. A divine incursion. A penetration. An incubation.

A new creation that is both terrestrial and celestial is birthing.

You are being readied for inter-dimensional habitation.

Your DNA is morphing;

Adapting.

12:206 Twelve Densities

I recently read an e-mail from a friend who feels his spiritual journey coming to an end and it struck a chord in me about something I began to see a few years back, while reading *The Nature of Personal Reality* by Seth (through Jane Roberts), chapter four, about multiple densities occupying the same body – taking turns "coming up" to have and to fulfill various experiences while human.

My thoughts are: There are twelve densities/aspects of our consciousness, just like there are twelve zodiac signs around our solar system/sun, twelve levels to the New Jerusalem, twelve tribes, twelve brothers, twelve stones on the ephod, twelve disciples of the Christ. The disciples that surround the Christ (the great cloud of witnesses) all served different purposes; for example, Judas betrays the Christ and delivers him up to death. How many times have we delivered ourselves up to death ... ?

In *The Parable of the Mustard Seed*, it is said that the mustard seed begins small and grows so large that the "birds" of heaven come to nest in its branches – the consciousness of the Christ matures through testing, trial and suffering, and then another "aspect" or energy comes in to nest/add to the vibrational makeup of the developing God-man. This is the change we see in people when we say, "He is a totally different person than he used to be." It is because one aspect fulfills its purpose, steps down, and then another steps up to the plate – still you, but with a new set of experiences to fulfill.

All of these aspects are here with us 100% of the time, but maybe not so prominent – like the priest consulting the ephod for wisdom; he wore the ephod on his chest and would enquire and the stones would light up, depending upon the question and answer asked and answered. Each with a different impetus for life and living.

I think that sometimes in the cycles of "reincarnation" this truth of multiple aspects occupying the same essence can play out multiple time in one physical lifetime. In the traditional understanding of reincarnation, our multiple lives play out in different bodies, different times. But sometimes, I believe that one aspect can surrender its stand, and another take the helm. Spiritual rebirth – born again.

Just a few thoughts on this.

12:207 Conscious Evolution

What a catch phrase! This is most unusual terminology for Christians, and it is vital that we understand what this means.

Too often Christians get so hung up in their own language or "Christianese" that they become out of touch with the general population.

What is consciousness? How does it apply to Christianity? How is it evolving? Simply put, consciousness means a human being becoming aware. It is the act of unfolding intuitively and intellectually, en masse.

Throughout the ages, human consciousness has experienced steady, constant stages of becoming aware. Lately, consciousness has been experiencing quantum leaps in awareness in many areas. For example, in the last 100 years women now have voting rights, the concept of this not always being the case is ridiculously foreign for today's young people. We have also seen democracy spread, civil rights flourish, men on the moon and phenomenal advances in understanding, not only our galaxy, but our universe, as well.

Likewise, spiritual advances are occurring rapidly for those who are willing to step outside of their dogma. Jesus warned that we would require a new wineskin to contain the new wine. Our old ways of receiving and digesting revelation need serious updating, lest we miss the Messiah in our midst. Simple adherence to dogma will jeopardize present knowledge being revealed to those who have these "ears to hear." Dogma is the practice of unquestioned beliefs.

In 1999, I began to question the word "saved." Today it means something completely different to me than it did over a decade ago, simply because I put the term and the concept on the chopping block. How could the process of something so marvelous as the body material becoming the body immortal be relegated to something so trite as an accepted invitation to an altar call? How can our glorious inheritance of eternity be reduced to its embrace only after death? How can we continue to externalize our concept of the kingdom when Jesus said it was *inside* of us? We have missed so many clues to these mysteries because we are afraid to let our old comfort systems of belief die; and die, they must, if we are to experience conscious resurrection.

What are these dogmatic links in your chain that keep you pinned to the stake, going around in circles? What are your unquestioned beliefs that deep inside you know just don't make sense? What are you so afraid of that you maintain a spirituality based on fear? Fear of not getting it right, fear of not being good enough or fear of rejection will keep you linked to the stake, hindering your progression in spiritual understanding. Dogmas will suffocate you and reduce you to robotic adherence to someone else's idea of God. Would you free yourself today and ask the Holy Spirit within you what specific doctrines need to be placed on the chopping block? Remember, even the God-ordained serpent on the pole was smashed to pieces by divine edict because its worship was dragged past its season of relevance.

12:208 The Catapult of PAIN

I find that painful and mortal woundings catapult me into places beyond where I have been. We can allow them to move us or we can choose to remain in our salty wash of tears.

So often, I find I must will myself to accept and understand that they are necessary for my journey. Once I do, I can feel momentum building, my awareness increasing, and then I find myself moving once again onto the next set of circumstances that, in turn, add to the richness of the tapestry I am creating.

In my book I write of the "oxbow lake" that is the bow-shaped pool formed when a river overflows its bank in times of flooding. When the river recedes, the lake remains. However, it is cut-off from the perpetual flow of life. The waters turn putrid.

Yes, we must continue to move, to pioneer and to return to the rapids of our unfolding consciousness.

All of our lives' experiences serve us well.

12:209 Through Tears

Are you a female that has struggled for relevance? Have you been taken advantage of, taken for granted, abused physically, emotionally, mentally or physically? Have you been crying a lot? Feeling oppressed?

These and other related issues are surfacing within the feminine consciousness. In women who have been victimized, pain is rising and infiltrating mass consciousness. If you are empathic, you will feel the collective pain of misogyny.

Collective pain is being released through tears. Let them flow.

In the midst of this correction, a tempered heart is your mainframe. Women will lead the way in a world where many people groups have been oppressed.

It is time that we arise with healing. Consciousness is undergoing a major correction, and it is up to us to handle this correction with grace, strength and integrity.

Rise up. This is your time.

12:210 Metaphor is a Thief ...

The word "seed" carries with it remarkable symbolism. Jesus used the word "seed" many times as he sought to relay a powerful image and to reveal the process of Divinity's investment into humanity, into the garden of man's consciousness.

This germination and growth process has spanned millennia, and is now reaching its "coming of age." This Divine consciousness that has been embedded into the human being uses intuition to aid in its interpretation of reality; it utilizes symbolism and metaphor, bypassing limited human reasoning and employing it as a servant, only when necessary. A servant, because it yields its limited understanding to the divine portion of consciousness that sees way beyond the trappings of the mind.

The intuitive mind is activated and comes as a "thief in the night" to apprehend spiritual truths in unfolding human consciousness by doing away with literalism. "Night" represents our darkened consciousness.

This "Christ" consciousness appears suddenly and becomes the premiere operating system within our human consciousness. Once activated, Christ consciousness becomes the mode of being. It is impossible to turn back to the old operating system once it has "crashed."

To help awaken fear-bound consciousness, Jesus came to them, to stimulate their intuitive faculties by using rich, symbolic language that must bypass the intellectual ego, like a "thief in the night" to reveal latent Divinity, the pearl of great price, hidden within man. It is said, "Behold I come as a thief" (Revelation 16:15)

Metaphor is a thief that gently robs us of our literalism while we transition into the intuited worlds that wait anxiously for our conscious habitation.

12:211 More on Christmas

By now, most informed people know that the story of Jesus born of a virgin in a manger did not happen on December 24th- 25th.

We know that this is a story of time immemorial of the dying and resurrecting God-man that eclipses Christianity; in fact, predates it in many myths and cultures.

The Sun moves southward from its highest position at the Summer Solstice (June 21st) in our constellating sky in its trek toward the Winter Solstice where, on December 21st, it comes to rest in the constellation called the Southern Crux or "Cross."

For approximately three days it rests there, unmoving.

Then, on December 24th- 25th, the Sun begins to move northward, reversing its position. It "resurrects," per se, and begins its northward trek toward the Summer Solstice. As such, it is said that the sun (son) dies on the cross, is buried, and in three days rises from the dead.

This is an astrological event that represents something far more encompassing than what Christians believe.

This is our story.

God (the Divine Principle, Source) found a way to fold itself, penetrate and occupy the virgin soil of our biology – the swaddling of flesh and blood.

Impeccable Spirit, eternal and all-encompassing, is born into lowly physical form to occupy, inhabit and explore. God finds for itself a helpmate, one that can interpret the sensory world of matter through its five senses – YOU.

A helpmate that does not condemn, but rather, with awakening, will bring the offer of eternal life to our limited and mortal frame.

You are the Virgin. You are the Manger. And you are the Christ that has come to save the world.

You only need believe. And when belief comes to an end, you KNOW.

Not in a prayer of accepting Jesus into your heart and escaping Hell as the result.

You must believe/know the creator rests, abides and lives in you and through you.

While we sleep, dreaming our dreams of separation and good and evil, we sleep in drama. When we awake, we resurrect the mortal flesh, redeeming our Spirit body with the capacity to understand our physical existence.

We have lived the drama.

We have occupied Hell. (There is a Hell, and this is it!)

We have on our Curriculum Vitae lifetimes of experience on planet Earth. And now we have VISION.

Our gift to the universe and to God lies in our ability to FEEL and to EMOTE. Through our vast experiences submersed under the waters of human baptism, we have learned, and we have learned well. We awaken with an arsenal – weaponry fit for the creating and sustaining of material worlds.

The GOD-MAN AWAKENS. That is the true Christmas Story.

12:212 Forgiveness

Forgiveness ... Forgiveness has great value, eternal value, sometimes beyond human comprehension. The benefits of forgiveness affect the physical, emotional and mental bodies and, not least of all, it benefits your spiritual body.

So why do we hang onto injustices as if they are a lifeline, when they are more like an anchor strapped to our ankle? Ah ... the ego. The sense of self we derive when we continually see ourselves as separate from one another provides an opportune canvas for us to paint our backdrop of pain.

Oh, and what a memory for recall the ego has – photographic, in fact – albeit tainted with self-perception. Each stroke of the brush with recall adds to the canvas until the beauty of the portrait is marred. The brush becomes a blade, disfiguring the life, as the painter becomes the painted, splashed with the blackness of betrayal, abuse and rejection.

The original sketching with weakness of voice speaks through the bloody mire, "You are not a victim, you are a participant. There is no human suffering in vain. All suffering produces something of great value in the Earth."

And the gift from suffering is released when the desire for justification is silenced.

12:213 The Flood

The flood was a reset of human DNA and energy body. Before the flood, we had been interfered with by para-dimensional beings, according to Genesis Chapter 6: the Nephilim. Gods. Human beings were continually evil, and so a divine reset was in order.

I am not sure about a literal flood, but I know that water represents a specific consciousness that saturated and penetrated the planet.

In place of our former energy body, we were given the chakra system – the rainbow.

The story of the flood says that God gave the rainbow as a sign and said never again would he obliterate the planet with water.

Human consciousness would no longer be controlled by this former influence but would now have the ability to move freely up and out of "hell" (the flame-colored, lower three chakras: red, orange and yellow), which symbolizes the human subject to instinctual fear and unchecked emotions.

Moving out of "hell" and into the heart (green) is where energy is transmuted. Then, onto blue, which symbolizes "walking on the water"– a higher state of being.

This is the ascension process. This is resurrection. This is the rapture.

12:214 The Birth of Christ Did Not Happen to One Man

We have yet to fully grasp that this birth of Christ did not happen to just one man, but to all of humankind. The Earth has been incubating the God-man as Mary (you) has committed to birth the Christ. This commitment did not happen 2,000 years ago; it happens NOW.

One of the name meanings for Mary is "wished for child". Isn't that interesting that Mary not only wishes for the child but agrees to be "overshadowed" by something mysterious and Divine.

"Let it be unto me as you have spoken."

We hold this agreement and foreknowledge as we are overshadowed by the Divine. We have come into union and are gestating the Christ within.

Joy to the world; the LORD has come
Let Earth receive her KING

Emmanuel means "God with man" or God-man. This is the purpose for planet Earth, to impregnate biology, to gestate and to birth the being that is both God and man.

This is your destiny.

Jacob saw this when he rested his head on a rock (symbolizes intuited revelatory information) and saw God standing "above" the spiral staircase (DNA molecule) and also saw angels ascending and descending upon that staircase. Jacob saw the human DNA molecule where Divinity not only is but moves within.

Jacob declares, "Surely, God is in this place and I did not know it; therefore, I shall name this place Bethel" (Beth El, or house of God). God (Divinity) dwells in you, within your DNA.

You are Mary. You are the manger. Your biology is the swaddling clothing of the Christ.

12:215 There Are Two Types of Bodies

There are two types of bodies – terrestrial (congealed light or biology) and celestial (energy and light).

Humans are terrestrial.

Para or multidimensional beings are celestial.

Divinity is pure LOVE energy and light that seeks manifestation in material, biological worlds, and, as such, needs a helper to do this.

Divinity creates a plan, the material universe, and an environment (Earth) and material body (you), shielded by vibration, to execute the plan.

The body must have a mind/soul to survive as a human body, and so individual aspects of Divinity, fractals of the ONE, took up residence within the body vehicle.

It thinks, judges and creates according to the intelligence invested into it, given to it as a gift.

The symbolism of the gifts given to the Christ child (you); Frankincense, Myrrh and Gold:

> **Frankincense** is a symbol of holiness and righteousness. The gift of frankincense to the Christ child was symbolic of His willingness to become a sacrifice, wholly giving Himself up, analogous to a burnt offering.

> **Myrrh** is a symbol of suffering, for the tree must first be bruised, Myrrh weeps from the bruise, the sap scraped from the bruise. It must harden, and then be crushed, to release the aroma.

> **Gold** is, technically (and alchemically) speaking, a soft, shiny, yellow, heavy, malleable, ductile metal. It is also a trivalent and a univalent, which means it is a transitional metal. As a transitional metal, gold is symbolic of flexibility on our spiritual path. One of the more valued elements, gold represents perfection in all matter, on any level. It also symbolizes humankind's quest to perfect, illuminate and refine his/herself. Because of its resistance to heat and acid, gold is a symbol of immutability, eternity and perfection.

The human, fully equipped with its gifts, sets out on its quest, as the Divine within sojourns right along with it.

The human is subjected to all things and learns and perceives, judges, emotes and creates.

This is the necessary devolution into matter and education of both the human and the Divine.

Now it is time to awaken.

The human realizes that the personality is just an aspect of the Divine within.

It intuitively knows that to stop the world from spinning, the hamster wheel from turning, it must surrender its very human traits of judging, emoting from the judgment and ultimately creating the environment of the classroom called Earth.

Now it is equipped with knowledge.

Now it is equipped with experience.

Now it is equipped with the good stuff necessary to create,

and it can tap into this treasure within its earthen vessel (the progenitor, creator, father) when it follows the path and pattern of the Christ.

It is seen as death. Selflessness.

It is only by following this pattern of death that it may experience resurrection.

Resurrection will bring about the new creation that is now fully conscious, that it is both God and man.

Emmanuel.

"I am the way, the truth and the life and no one comes to the father (the untethered ability to create ANYTHING if focused upon) but through me" (Christ – the suffering servant that willingly dies to being human, is selfless, is compassionate, chooses LOVE and does not judge or condemn).

12:216 You Are a Multidimensional Being, Part 2

You are a multidimensional being.

There is more to you than you.

As Christ matured (30 years of age means dedication to a task or calling) he set out to gather his twelve disciples (or, viewed metaphorically, he gathered fractals of himself) and taught them figurative and allegorical mysteries: He taught them how to perceive reality with the intuitive and intellectual mind. He taught them how to be physical and material yet maintain their etheric divinity. He displayed for us Emmanuel; God and man in one body.

You are doing the same.

There are aspects of yourself that were scattered at birth. You are reclaiming your birthright now by gathering these "lost" aspects of yourself that are surprisingly near.

These fractals are now ready to join you, as you have been made a "fisher of men."

What do the disciples represent? Simon/Peter could hear the voice of the Father in Heaven (within). This is the aspect within you that is quite capable of listening to the voice that does not use words. It is your intuitive knowing.

Christ said to Simon, "Who do you say that I AM?" Simon answers, "You are the Christ." Christ says, "Flesh and blood did not reveal this to you but my Father in heaven."

This disciple must be found within us in order for us to hear the Father's voice.

Next, we have Luke, the physician. Luke is able to heal the body.

Matthew is good with numbers, and makes sure that while in the body, you tend to earthly affairs.

John is the aspect of you that is loyal beyond ego.

Judas will deliver you up to death, time and time again, as many times as it takes for you to lose your life so that you may find your life.

Timothy is weakness in your flesh. Weakness is allowed for a time, so that your spirit may soar.

I have recently been made aware of an aspect of myself that has been called to me, the Christ. This aspect is "herald." Not a name, but a function. It is a forerunning aspect that must break the way into new (old) information and revelation. It is the aspect of me that can never be late and that is never satisfied for long with what I learn. I must keep moving, pace-making, trendsetting. It has been with me always.

What are your aspects? Are you finding yourself?

You are being built into a multidimensional habitation. The book of revelation says that this habitation is twelve levels.

The priests in the Old Testament wore a vest-type covering called an ephod that had twelve stones. The priest would inquire of the vest and the stones would answer by lighting up. These stones are fractals of you.

These twelve surround the Christ in the "upper room;" that is, your higher consciousness.

As we depart from fear and from judgment and leave behind the former things forsaking them for unconditional love, our vibration escalates. This frequency attracts those aspects of ourselves that are ready to join us and cause us to ascend. Do you feel it?

SECTION THIRTEEN

THIRTEEN

13:217 To My Lovely Friends …

To those who are chasing mysteries like crumbs on a trail

those who are changing, morphing travail

To those who have experienced spiritual shaming

offering forgiveness rather than blaming

Here's to you, the brave ones keep going

Turning faith, not into belief, but rather, to knowing

Yours is a forerunning path, for sure

You blaze the trail with hearts that are pure

Thanks for the hours, the days and years

That you have spent bathed in tears

Your work will reveal the magnificent pearl

Buried in all, as hearts unfurl

Though your work, 'til now, is silent and stealth

an abundance you will reap, beyond any wealth

Keep going, keep going

The seeds you are sowing

Will grow to the skies

and nourish the wise

A blessing you are!

Whether near or far

An angel cloaked, in the swaddling of flesh

Soaring on solar winds that are fresh

You are Joseph, you are Mary, you are Christ, you are me

Once the bondsman, once the slave; but now, you are free.

13:218 Channeling YOU

On the subject of channeling through writing, I would like to offer my view. There are many different voices out there, some claiming to speak for entities beyond our present comprehension. I have benefitted from many of these brave souls. However, this is not the type of channeling I want to address here. I want to write about learning to hear your own voice, a part of you that exists in a higher vibrational plane that has the benefit of seeing from a more holistic and encompassing view.

This voice is always there but may require cultivation to hear. It is the still small voice spoken of in ancient texts. If you are not unlike me, most often this voice is stifled by the louder, more "out-front and center" voice of the ego.

This is why books like *The Power of Now: A Guide to Spiritual Enlightenment (Eckhart Tolle),* and many others about learning to meditate and still the mind, are so important. This stilling of the egocentric and always "on" mind will enable you to hear the proverbial "voice in the wilderness." This voice percolates up through the willfully stilled waters of human consciousness and speaks mysteries to us, things that cannot be discerned by or through our logic-based mind. This voice is intelligent beyond our dimension and can see around the corners of time.

Allow me to walk you through how this type of channeling comes through for me.

Oftentimes, upon awakening, I will hear a phrase or a group of words that will repeat over and over in my mind. If I ignore this gentle prompt, sometimes my index finger will tap on something (anywhere it may rest) involuntarily. This is a signal for me – sort of like when your computer or phone will chime when you've received mail. I get up and go to the computer and write the phrase or group of words and, voila! The message begins to come through. I enter some sort of stream – like jumping into a rushing river, rather than standing on the riverbank – and I type until I am through. The result is a message from an escalated view of things past, present or future.

For example, as a recovering fundamentalist Christian, I went through a season of losing some very dear friends. I was pretty devastated by the losses and was wallowing in self-pity and sorrow. I kept on hearing the phrase "concentric circles." Below is a portion of what I heard:

"It is time you begin to understand your sphere of influence. As you transition through the concentric circles of consciousness, each sphere contains a level of vibration or resonance that you operate within. As you transition into broader spheres of influence, the vibratory resonance changes. These vibratory resonances are comprised largely from people and their relationships with you. As shift occurs, you will see new relationships form and old relationships cease.

You have been particularly resistant and or reticent to free yourself from relationships from this passing phase or "sphere" of influence. Because of this resistance and lack of vision and understanding, steps have been taken to ensure the separation in relationships, much like a scissor will cut a pattern out of cloth. You have been set aside for a particular function in this age and this function will not come to completion with the frequencies of interference from traditional religion, control, fear, doubt, pity and unbelief.

We understand love at its highest form and know that you will, in time, come to know this form. Highest love is void of the fear of loss, including the loss of relationships. It is imperative that you let go and move forward into the next level of resonance."
End of transmission

Notice that in reference to the source, the text uses the pronoun "we." I believe this refers to the multiplicity of source. It is ONE but it is also ALL.

As I typed this message, I cried. The words were touching the deepest parts of my soul, my emotions, my brokenness. They also set the stage for many more people that separated from me because of my evolving spiritual views. I was able to understand the purpose, and in understanding it, I saw MY PURPOSE.

We all are given the task of overcoming obstacles that would impede our spiritual growth. Each person needs to ascertain their weaknesses and fears and to plow through them with courage. If we would just take the time to center ourselves in silence, even if only for a few minutes, we will begin to hear strategies for success. That voice is always there; ready, willing and able to respond to our desires. That voice is heavily invested in you, for it IS YOU, providing guidance like a lighthouse in a fog-veiled bay. We must take chances and risks. Ships are meant to be sailed and not to remain tethered in the bay. Louisa May Alcott said this:

"I am not afraid of storms for I am learning to sail my ship."

And so, it is.

13:219 Sensitives, Empaths, Healers, Lightworkers and Servers

There is a lot of information out there on Sensitives/Empaths/Healers/Lightworkers/Servers, etc. I think it is an emerging field of study, with little research actually done, because of the intermingled and very wide range of physical, emotional and spiritual components present in those people that seem to soak up energy from other people, places, and even things.

There simply are no guidelines for these unwitting souls, and it seems to me that each person must "run the gauntlet" individually.

This is what I know about people who have this "gift" (and *it is* a gift):

- It cannot be controlled

- A healthy and organic diet helps

- Medication, when appropriate

- A strong connection with individual spiritual guides

- A strong connection with other Sensitives that are neutral (neutral, meaning not judgmental or resistant to their gift)

- Grounding (or "Earthing," a book by Ober, Sinatra and Zucker) helps; that is, being in nature, barefoot whenever possible and allowing the resonance and energy of the Earth to absorb excess energy

- An understanding that what they innately possess is a gift to the world that helps alleviate suffering

- Symptoms seem to exacerbate around the full moon.

- A will to understand the gift and to tap into the memory of what to do when one soaks up negative energy (we all know what to do but have not necessarily accessed the celestial ability that has been hard-wired into our physiology to complete the task).

- Remembering will come when urgency and need arise, if we stay focused on the task and remember this innate ability.

- We must never identify with the negative energy that we soak up (in other words, think it is our own energy manifesting through any set of personal circumstances).

- Neutrality and joy will help move negative energy through and up the chakra channel, changing the configuration of negative energy to positive.

- Remembering that the gift given is to displace negative energy. The negative energy sometimes bounds toward the Sensitive, recognizing that the Sensitive is a portal (a safe house of sorts) to reconfigure itself and to ultimately be released into other dimensions through the multidimensional make-up of the Sensitive. They act as "elevators", receiving negative energy through lower chakras (depending on the frequency), traveling up through the heart chakra, where it undergoes reconfiguration via love, and experiences release in the upper channels.

One may look at the lock and dam aspect of the Panama Canal, where the ship enters the lock and is elevated with the release of water into the lock, and then released into a higher body of water. Such is the nature of transmutation of energy within the body of the gifted Sensitive.

I hope this helps.

13:220 The Word of God ...

What is the "Word of God?" I can remember pastors and preachers over the decades holding up the Bible and giving it this title by saying, "The Word of God says..." When did this title come about? Is it something we have acquiesced into our knowledge base or does it have foundation somewhere in the Bible itself? It's funny, because I still catch myself saying things like, "Well, the Word says…" and I don't even believe that way anymore! Talk about programming!

We simply cannot use it as a moral compass standard, lest we condone slavery, rape, inequality in the sexes, murder, pillaging ...

So how can we embrace some of it as the "Word of God," but not all? Where do we draw the line? Somehow, by giving the Bible the title of "The Word of God," we embrace and propagate cultural initiatives. For example, there are some sects where women cannot cut their hair or wear makeup because of references about Jezebel painting her eyes, and hair as a "woman's glory." Some sects do not permit women to teach, and others insist on guidelines for food consumption, dress and social behaviors.

We regulate being a "Christian" as someone who has accepted Jesus into their heart as their personal Lord and Savior, a practice that insures a heavenly reward. But there is no scripture that requires this modern evangelic practice...

We must believe ... We must be baptized ... Jesus is the way...

Yes, Jesus said, "I am the way, the truth and the life, and no one comes to the Father but by me..." What is this way and where is the Father? Jesus said the Father is within, and that HE does not dwell in buildings made with hands...

Within us.

What is this "WAY?"

Should we look more to the example and pattern that Jesus set, and follow IT, rather than to practice a non-biblical reciting of the sinner's prayer?

Come! Let us reason together ...

This "Way" is what got Jesus in so much trouble with the ruling religious order of the day, because this pattern threatened its existence. Much like today, when traditional Christian fundamentalism is challenged, cries of HERESY! FALSE PROPHET! ANTI-CHRIST! DECEIVER! are heard ... Isn't it ironic that Jesus never warned of such things? Go search for yourself.

What is this "WAY" that Jesus identified as THE way to the Father???

Jesus broke the hierarchical rules. He said we did not have to follow the "LAW." He ate and socialized with those from outside the societal norms. He said, "DO NOT JUDGE." He taught us to break from tradition. He taught us that the Kingdom was WITHIN. He said if they say that the Christ is in the field and to come greet him, DO NOT BELIEVE THEM! Certainly, this applies to any perceived "second coming!" This is because the appearing of Christ is within YOU.

It is not external. The Christ is being formed within you.

So, do you know of someone breaking tradition among you? Do you know of someone having mercy on the woman caught in adultery? (Incidentally, this woman is an archetype of all religious systems that require you to join them – it is that which we metaphorically "fornicate" when we join ourselves to other "lovers"). It can be when we join ourselves to any system that requires fear of something ... anything!

Jesus spoke mysteries and called them such. For us to take even this example literally, we miss the point of his message.

Be fearless. Look at these mysterious messages with fresh eyes not weakened from lenses that interpret for you. Meet him there, in the "upper room."

13:221 Just Stop

There is something happening to the consciousness of America.

Allow me to define consciousness: The state of being awake and aware of one's surroundings; the awareness or perception of something by a person.

We are living in one of the most polarized nations on the globe. We are some of the most divided and fractioned societies on Earth and there are two institutions that harbor MOST of the blame for this schism:

FOX News and CNN.

These two are NOT NEWS ORGANIZATIONS. They are political brainwashing machines designed to incite schism. That's right, designed. They are "news commentary" rather than news reporting.

I have traveled many different continents and watched the news all over the world, and there is nothing like CNN and Fox News anywhere else. America is being fed biased information from VERY OPINIONATED and agenda-filled sources.

I know of a woman (she used to be one of my best friends) who in 2015 announced that her and her husband were seriously thinking of moving to Mexico because of what was happening in America. Their logic was directly from sound bites attributed to Fox News.

Turn off your TVs. I purposely watched NO NEWS for almost a decade. From 2008 until 2017, I watched little to no news. Now I read a little BBC on my phone, but I refuse to watch these two brainwashing channels. You cannot help but be affected, if these two channels are your steady diet.

Wake up, America!

13:222 Shakespeare Nugget

> *"For there is nothing either good or bad but thinking makes it so."*
> Shakespeare.

Our thinking, judging and projecting is what creates the world we live in. Therefore, let us think positively, judge righteously and project beautifully.

13:223 The Water Bearer

Jesus said we are to follow the water bearer to celebrate the Passover (Passover means the first born does not have to die because the blood was painted on the portal, the symbol for unity; that is, the broken hymen coating the vaginal portal after virginal sex).

The water bearer is the Age of Aquarius. So, Christ was pointing to an astrological event that would signal the coming transition into the age of immortality.

Unity will result in that the firstborn (the man born of water or natural birth) no longer being mortal or having to die.

The water bearer shows the water being poured out of the vessel. To me this "water" symbolizes very human-filled consciousness – the type of duality consciousness that has flourished, creating and sustaining this present age of good and evil. In order for us to enter into unity, out from duality, judgment between good and evil must be poured out, no longer within us. We are to "follow" Aquarius and everything that it represents in order to "celebrate" Passover.

Lastly, each constellation is like a giant syllabus that will herald what we will learn in each age.

When asked where to celebrate the Passover, Jesus said to look for, and to follow, the water bearer that would lead them to the place to celebrate – the upper room – higher consciousness.

The water bearer is a point in linear time when the constellation Aquarius (the water bearer) is prominent in the eastern sky.

This constellation shows a human "pouring out" the water from the vessel. Metaphorically, the vessel is us, and the water being poured out is very human, ego-driven consciousness. We are being poured out of the consciousness that has driven the previous ages – egocentricity – the judgment between good and evil that has propelled the growth and unfolding of consciousness up to this point.

Let us remember, our education in the knowledge and judgment between good and evil is NECESSARY if we are to go on to perfection.

> *Hebrews 5:11 We have much to say about this, but it is hard to make*
> *it clear to you because you no longer try to understand. 12 In fact,*

though by this time you ought to be teachers, you need someone to teach you the elementary truths of God's word all over again. You need milk, not solid food! 13 Anyone who lives on milk, being still an infant, is not acquainted with the teaching about righteousness. 14 But solid food is for the mature, who by constant use have trained themselves to distinguish good from evil.

We see that we need to be trained in good and evil! It is necessary if we are to go "on" to perfection!

Hebrews 6 Therefore, leaving the discussion of the elementary principles of Christ, let us go on to perfection, not laying again the foundation of repentance from dead works and of faith toward God, 2 of the doctrine of baptisms, of laying on of hands, of resurrection of the dead, and of eternal judgment. 3 And this we will[a] do if God permits.

4 For it is impossible for those who were once enlightened, and have tasted the heavenly gift, and have become partakers of the Holy Spirit, 5 and have tasted the good word of God and the powers of the age to come, 6 if they fall away,[b] to renew them again to repentance, since they crucify again for themselves the Son of God, and put Him to an open shame.

13:224 A Substantial Shift

There is a substantial shift taking place within us, within our thinking. There have been toxic people that have been a part of our learning syllabus. You know them. Nothing good (except education!!!) can come from your affiliation with someone who is narcissistic, self-promoting, controlling and abusive. We all have someone like that in our repertoire for higher learning. To depart from such relationships may require extreme mental maneuvers, but it is TIME!

Part of our journey is to learn to step around these briar bushes, rather than to be ensnared by them. We may only learn of their damaging effects if we "touch" them.

Cut your losses and put them behind you. They have been worthy teachers, but they are no longer worthy "of" you.

13:225 Backing Up

A line is drawn, there is sand before you. You are shown the line and told to jump as far as you can without crossing the line before you begin your jump.

Intuitively, the jumper studies the line and backs up as far as possible, to get a good running start, to ensure that they achieve the greatest distance with their leap.

Is backing up wrong?

We are poised for the greatest leap in consciousness that our world has ever seen.

Discern the times.

Do not resist "backing up". You are not losing ground.

Gain understanding that backing up will ensure the greatest trajectory of the leap.

13:226 Addicted to Fear?

Are you addicted to fear?

Negative news is damaging to your soul.

The brain is a focusing mechanism, which is why we rubber-neck as we pass by an accident. We simply must observe trauma if it is unfolding before us.

News organizations know this, much in the same way that the fundamentalist church knows this. If we are kept with the threat of annihilation hanging over our heads, then we will return to the source of the threat. IT IS HOW THE HUMAN BRAIN WORKS.

Fear restricts and confines. Love allows for freedom and expansion.

Be wise about what you give your attention to.

The powers that be also know that you are a creator, and that whatever you focus upon, providing the appropriate emotional quotient, YOU WILL CREATE.

Your energy output from your body is the fabric of this world. Your judgment directs the output and applies the energetic current to any given set of circumstances.

This energetic output is akin to the energetic current that is within your electrical outlets. Whatever you desire to "power on" is done through this circuitry, when you insert a plug into the outlet.

IN THE SAME WAY, those powers that feed off of your energetic signature will plug into YOU and DRAIN YOUR ENERGETIC RESOURCES.

It is how they survive and is why they must keep the world's tree of "good and evil" alive and well.

In order to transcend the age, you must unplug from the source that drives this age.

And that source is judging between good and evil.

Jesus said this, "The Judgment with which you judge another will fall on your own head."

And, so it is.

13:227 Did You Know ...

If you are unawake, still slumbering, fully human, non-transcendent, still learning, still fighting and still seeing a God as outside of yourself, still fearful – there is a book that describes right where you are:

The Old Testament – the old you

Did you know that, if you are starting to stir from your sleep, meeting the Christ in the upper room (your mind), learning that you are actually Mother Mary, who has been penetrated by something mysterious and Divine, and that you will birth the Christ, die the death (to ego/self), and resurrect the new creation that is both Divine and Man – there is a book that describes right where you are?

The New Testament – the new you

Did you know that, once you awaken, you are awake, not dreaming, fully God and fully man, transcending, non-resistant and unmoved, scrolls opened (chakras activated), mysteries revealed, the Christ triumphant – there is a book that describes right where you are??

Revelation – the completed you

The Earth school is a platform where you learn to interface with the material worlds and experience emotions (energy in motion) by creating situations where you will manufacture and distribute emotional currency – the stuff of the "Gods"– and thus, create material worlds.

You need a full palette of color; light and dark, and everything in between.

This education plays out in time.
You are in the perfect environment.

You put yourself here.

You signed up for this.

You have chosen your syllabus.

Learn well, Gods. Learn well.

When you are through, you will cry out and the "Lord" will release you from the belly of the whale, the Age of Pisces, The Matrix, the Womb.

13:228 They Told Me That My Son Chose to Lose His Limbs

When they told me that my son chose to lose his limbs, I did not believe it.

However, they continued and said that when we made these choices, we were pre-incarnate.

In other words, the intelligence that was my son, and a forerunner to his physical incarnation, made those choices. I had made the choice, as well.

We were not yet human and did not make choices like a human does.

From that unbiased and un-indoctrinated consciousness in good and evil, we made decisions based in purpose, not pain.

"There is no suffering in vain. All suffering has value ... you must remember ..."

13:229 Our DNA

Our DNA was tampered with. The schematic for Divinity inhabiting its helpmate was overlaid as we, as Mary, were overshadowed.

We know that Christ indwells us – and that when we are in submission to that greater and eternal part of us, we become "wed", and our identity is Christ.

Human + God = CHRIST

Christ means "anoint" and "to rub or press in."

This is the process when the human biological part of us is infused with Divinity. We become inseparable.

This is Mary, having been overshadowed by a Divine messenger and became impregnated with a holy thing. We are Mary.

Our DNA was tampered with. The schematic for Divinity inhabiting its helpmate was overlaid as we were overshadowed.

This Holy thing has been growing within the human framework and its essence is overtaking this garden.

It is the mustard seed, the pearl of great price, the leaven within the yeast.

This understanding is you, as the slumbering Jacob with his head resting on the "rock" of revealed knowledge. As Jacob slept, he saw the spiral staircase of our DNA molecule and observed the God of all that is standing above it and messenger angels ascending and descending upon it. He proclaimed, "Surely God is in this place (our DNA) and I did not know it. Therefore, this place shall be called BETH-EL (house of God)." Genesis 28:16

We are the dwelling place of Divinity.

13:230 The Seed

As we transition through various levels of understanding and relationship with "All that is" (God is a German word for "good". and even scripture says that this creator is unnamable! But I still call him God when trying to relate to others), I have found that it is important that I not see someone as right or wrong in their beliefs, because I think that we are all wonderfully accepted and seeing accurately, depending on our individual perspective and vantage point.

That was a hard lesson for me to learn, as passionate and zealous as I was, and am! If someone is a seed, and Jesus compared us to this analogy, then their outward perspective is one of dormancy, and even death, until they are planted – then it is darkness. Suddenly, they descend deeper into that darkness and reap the treasures that are found there – the minerals and moisture from the soil or our earthly carnal experiences. A strong root system is built, and again, a shift occurs, and their direction is turned upward, where this sapling breaks the plane of the earth. A neighboring mighty oak cannot pull the sapling upward for it would mean its destruction. The sapling – through time, water and weathering – will grow to be what is encoded in its DNA.

It is important to remember the origin of the seed, as well, for it fell from the mature, mighty oak ...

We cannot help but become who and what we are. We grow and unfold, and no one knows how.

As for those believing that Jesus never existed, it matters not to me. I experienced a great shift when this voice came to me and said, "Let me go."

> *John 16:7 Nevertheless I tell you the truth. It is to your advantage that I go away; for if I do not go away, the Helper will not come to you; but if I depart, I will send Him to you. 8 And when He has come, He will convict the world of sin, and of righteousness, and of judgment: 9 of sin, because they do not believe in Me; 10 of righteousness, because I go to My Father and you see Me no more; 11 of judgment, because the ruler of this world is judged. 12 I still have many things to say to you, but you cannot bear them now. 13 However, when He, the Spirit of truth, has come, He will guide you into all truth; for He will not speak on His own authority, but whatever He hears He will speak; and He will tell you things to come. 14 He will glorify Me, for He will take of what is Mine and declare it to you.*

We can interpret this in many ways. For me, the key to understanding the perspective of those not believing in the historical Jesus is that they have experienced repentance (which means to turn around and change the way that you think). It is a divine inversion when we realize that everything in scripture is actually inside of you – the ego needs to see things as external in order to grasp the mysteries of scripture. Then, one day, in the twinkling of an eye (enlightenment), the shift occurs, and we realize that the history is actually a mystery and that this Christ is you.

Paul labored intensely with this little seed (human consciousness), as he was in travail for us, even now, to see that Christ be formed in us.

There is a book by Deepak Chopra called *The Third Jesus,* where he classifies three beings called Jesus. If you have not read it, it is a worthwhile read. He speaks of the historical Jesus, the Jesus of Christianity and the cosmic Christ.

It is necessary for the fledgling seed of man's consciousness to see a pattern, and so the pattern is here with us in book form (The Bible), so that the intellect can read and decipher what it chooses to believe, historical or mystical. If I believe in Jesus as a human, it is of no consequence, as long as I understand that Christ is come in the flesh (yours and mine). It is of no consequence if I believe he did not come in historical form, as long as I believe he has come in the flesh (yours and mine). It is of no consequence if I see a cosmic Christ (Christ all in all) as long as I believe he is appearing in you and me.

Belief is all that is required – not in a man, per se, but what is in you; what your true identity is as spirit that is having quite a human experience. This is the Christ, the Emmanuel (God with man). Presently, this Christ is slumbering in the manger of humanity wrapped in the swaddling of our beautiful biology. He, this Christ, is growing within and at some point, we must put away those necessary things/beliefs from our youth so that the Christ might appear in us.

This is why Jesus warned us not to believe it when someone says, "Look, there is the Christ!" Because this appearing will not be external from us, but rather, will be within the framework of man.

13:231 The Limited Mind/Ego

The mind/ego is limited to discernment through the five senses and the physical world. It (the mind/ego) is feminine; it is the womb-man.

Its function is to provide the framework to incubate the two components (egg and sperm or human and Divinity).

It is the material helpmate of the Divine. The feminine/ego/mind aspect must open and yield willingly to receive the seed so that it may grow within the framework of the human.

The ego/mind recognizes the need to submit (wives submit to your husbands) in order to birth the new creation that is luminous. It births the synergy of the God-man, Emmanuel.

Once penetrated, the womb-man incubates the creature that is both human and Divine. It gives of itself, and the Divine gives of itself to create the new ONE.

It births the creature that is both God and man.

The mind is the servant within the earthly material plane and, as such, is limited. The mind/ego has been master of the body, but it is now time to yield to death at the cross, the intersection of the mortal life and the immortal life, surrendering its rights to the body.

Once the ego surrenders to death, it is then raised triumphantly and is in partnership to the Divine as it navigates through the material plane with its helpmate – the human/God-man.

13:232 Under the Spell

When the consciousness of the human is under the spell of materializing influences (that is the dynamic principles that hold energy bound in matter), your thinking is likewise bound/restricted to fear. Fear contracts.

Thinking was never intended to be sub "merged" with fear. We were to USE fear as a servant to help us create the material worlds because, while creating, lower frequency holds/binds energy in matter, matter within energy. But when our consciousness sank and thinking sub "merged", it became trapped under the dome of a fear-based reality (show). So, fear, in turn, becomes the basis of our creations, and as such, is limited to 120 years. Fear-based creating will only last so long. THIS IS BY MERCIFUL DESIGN.

Many think that we just need to get rid of the EGO, but this is NOT SO.

Your ego is beautiful and beautifully evolved but trapped under the "dome". The "dome" represents mortal and limited creation under the governance of TIME.

The ego is the mechanism that can FOCUS THOUGHT and EMOTION. The human creates whatever it focuses upon.

IT IS THE MECHANISM.

It will create and create CONTINUALLY wherever it is. Therefore, if it is trapped under the dome of fear, it will create a fear-based reality.

Awakening will liberate the EGO. The human then becomes conscious that whatever it focuses upon it will create and then willfully chooses to focus on "things ABOVE".

For those so inclined, this "merge" with fear is relayed in the story of Gomer as she was "merged" with other lovers. The commandment to Hosea was to marry her anyway. Gomer was sensuous and given over to pleasure, as are we as we are captivated and merged with the material world.

13:233 The Word "False"

I want to look at the word "false" as it is being used a lot to describe the ego as the "false self." This is not an accurate way to describe this most precious aspect of the Divine.

False means this: not according to truth or fact; incorrect; deliberately made or meant to deceive

Let me attempt to define the ego in as few words as possible: The ego is what enables us to focus thought and emotion as it determines what is good or bad. From this culturally discerned perspective comes all conflict. This friction that comes from the creation of conflict is a necessary part of our education in duality.

We are awakening to the understanding that we are far more than our ego; the way we think should not be relegated only to our earthbound five senses. Now we are becoming aware of our "higher self" that is beyond the material world and that is connected to all in a collective consciousness that transcends the physical dimension.

Here comes the rub. Being aware of this greater self does not negate or cancel out the part of us that remains focused in the material world. Many are labeling this self the "false self," and it is simply not so.

The ego which focuses thought and emotion is the HELPMATE for the greater self that wishes a tangible environment from which to experience matter.

We are to work in tandem. Heretofore, the ego has thought itself alone and disconnected from "God" or Divinity, when in reality it is the essence of God, albeit individualized and "separated" in the limited mind.

This separation is useful until our education is complete. Sort of like a Spanish immersion course where the English-speaking student is dropped off in Mexico with a family that will only speak Spanish, the student must quickly learn how to speak the language. This is Divinity as it is immersed (baptized) into the material domains. It is learning in us, as individualized cells of the greater body.

Once these two minds wed (the material mind and the immaterial mind, or the mortal and immortal, or the terrestrial and celestial) we will have a new creature – the God-man, the Emmanuel – which simply means "God with man."

Union is a beautiful pattern. Who gets married and then nullifies their wife? We see that pattern in some human marriages hundreds of years ago (in primitive human history), but as we have evolved, the feminine has a vital role as an equal partner.

13:234 Path to Enlightenment

Be human and egocentric

Be free from the ego (leave lower education modules)

Be nothing (this is akin to being a teenager lying on a couch – don't stay on the couch)

Get bored being nothing

Find creativity (your source)

Create (copulate/interact with source)

Be something (Birth Christ)

Walk as an enlightened being creating and filling the dimensions of matter

SECTION FOURTEEN

FOURTEEN

14:235 Women, Be Silent

"Women, be silent in church" and "I do not suffer a woman to teach." SYMBOLS! Paul said these are mysteries – Not directives to women and men, but mysteries! The ego (the womb-man) must learn its "place", not to be done away with, as some suggest, but to yield to the Divine mind so that it may become the helpmate, a co-partner with Divinity to form and fill the material worlds. This is to reach stillness through many forms of meditation, including art!

14:236 As We Progress

As we progress, we will begin to see that the whole of our physical existence mirrors that of the etheric or celestial venues.

Therefore, it is vital that we interpret our physical dimension as it mirrors the principles of the nonphysical dimension.

It is by the physical that we "see" the nonphysical.

All of physical nature is a pattern or template of the nonphysical.

Creation through nature demonstrates principles that are unseen by the human.

It is through physical patterns that we begin to see the nonphysical and unseen by our five physical senses.

These physical patterns will help bring the physical, mental and biologic being to a place of understanding what is unseen by physical eyes.

It is through this understanding that our intuitive "eye" will open. A bridge will appear between dimensions, between the physical and nonphysical.

We are called to "bridge the gap" between dimensions.

14:237 Transmutation:

- The action of changing or the state of being changed into another form
- The conversion or transformation of one species into another
The Transmutation of Error:

- Changing the state of an error

The error occurred that during our willful descent, our memory was compromised and our innate power to work in tandem with the forces of materialization were surrendered to a victimhood mentality.

The error occurred when we became incompatible with the vibration that held our eternal memory and we forgot who and what we are as creators of the material domains. Subsequently, we cannot access our eternal memory as our present fear-based vibration does not "match" the frequency of eternity.

In this forgetting, we saw ourselves as victims of the "gods" and, as such, were paralyzed by their whims – and so became victims, rather than participants.

As egocentricity and fear became the operating system of the day, we surrendered our power to the forces that we came to regulate. These elemental forces became gods to fulfill our conspiracies.

They, nevertheless, are subject to us and await our conscious habitation. And the tipping point adds weight to its inertia as each person awakens to the knowledge that the human being is THE RULING POWER of the material worlds.

As we step away from human judgment, our vibration escalates and the propensity to match the frequency of eternity appears, as well as the new creation species – the human that is also Divine.

14:238 Curriculum Vitae

When we think of "The Fall" it is good to remember that this "fall" was recorded in historical/spiritual texts:

> *Romans 8:20 For the creation was subjected to futility, not by its own choice, but by the will of the one who subjected it, in hope.*

Within Mithraism, Cautes and Cautopates were symbols carved in statues (torch up/torch down) denoting times of enlightenment and, conversely, darkness. They can be symbols of high culture and low culture as in the "fall."

What is important to remember is that this baptism into dense human consciousness was by design, as part of our curriculum vitae on planet Earth.

14:239 My Life's Purpose

The purpose for my life is to break open systems that keep the mind in restriction. If that messes with your religion, well then, good – I've done my job.

We are trapped within illusion, within religious dogma, concepts and ideas that are limited to the five senses and that are someone else's idea of things.

May our single eye open.

14:240 You Define You

"You tend to see yourself as others treat you."

Don't do that.

Don't let another's treatment of you take on life in and through you. Their treatment of you does not define you.

You define you.

14:241 An Accelerated Pace

I am breathing deeply these days.

I feel like I am learning at an accelerated pace all the things that I have asked, that I have wondered about from what I knew of "God."

My experience of God has been very wide and varied, as I was in the Christian system for 43 years of my life. So, I don't share or even think flippantly on this subject. My view is what most would call well-rounded, if not complete.

Lutheran, Full Gospel, Jesus People, Assembly of God, Catholic, Methodist, Presbyterian, Bible Church and a host of Non-Denominational churches, Christian fundamentalism – I have attended and been a member of many as a "born again" believer. I have experienced or been a part of many more Christian systems, as well, but these aforementioned are the main ones.

Something happened to me in the late 1990s that is best described as disillusionment. My view of God was restricted into the box of systematic Christianity and I was challenging those boundaries. Specifically, my experiences were ever-growing beyond what was accepted and those who recognized it sought to restrain my learning, and even to pull me back inside the box.

And I was struggling to be the entity, the new creation, that God intended. That I intended. My mind was, it seemed, no longer in restriction. There are many that have had the same experience as me. Likewise, they are beginning to spread their butterfly wings, lest they die in the struggle to overcome their cocoon of "beliefs".

I had broken free of beliefs and I have been gently transitioning into KNOWING. My consciousness had shifted out from fear and fear-based beliefs into a broader, wider and more complete understanding of this magnificent universe.

I had been growing beyond the boundaries of my Christian skin, perceiving the love of the creator outside of and beyond my imposed set of beliefs.

Now I see those who are just beginning their journey into systematic religion, like me, must endure their time in the crucible. It is the pattern of Christ. We see, through the Bible, that Jesus set the pattern as he broke the bond of religious encumbrance and tells us to follow him. Yes, that is what the pattern displays.

Jesus did not desire to create, establish or institute a religion; he broke free of it. In many ways, the religious systems recognize that there has been the "seed" of divinity invested into each one of us that, in order to maintain control, seeks to control that growth of "Christ in you." This is the insidious side of the system of Christianity that bears little design of Jesus within its DNA. It will keep you ever looking externally for your savior, when all the while, it is within.

Matthew 24:

> *23Then if any man shall say unto you, Lo, here is Christ, or there; believe it not. 24For there shall arise false Christs, and false prophets, and shall shew great signs and wonders; insomuch that, if it were possible, they shall deceive the very elect.*
>
> *25Behold, I have told you before.*
>
> *26Wherefore if they shall say unto you, Behold, he is in the desert; go not forth: behold, he is in the secret chambers; believe it not. 27For as the lightning cometh out of the east, and shineth even unto the west; so shall also the coming of the Son of man be.*

The "east" is your intuitive mind, the mind that is not based in time and in the material worlds. This is where you will meet the Christ. The intuitive mind must develop its place in the universe before it seeks to crossover to the "west" or the limited, logic-based consciousness of mankind.

The coming of Christ is not outside of you. It is within your consciousness. It is a journey we all must take to see the nature of divinity formed within the carcass of our humanity.

> *28For wheresoever the carcass is, there will the eagles be gathered together.*

When the time comes to break free of your cocoon, do it. Don't let them break your wings. Remember, the religious system crucified Christ. That is the pattern.

If you refuse their restriction, they will abandon you and leave you to "die" alone. But, little do they know, that it is by design that you struggle, and your struggle will force the life's blood to the tips of your wings, and you will fly.

This is the death on the cross where your terrestrial life, as you know it, comes to an end so that you may be born again, from above, unrestricted, resurrected.

14:242 Myths – The Original Story of Us

It is interesting to view these things, these myths, whether human or not, as the story of us.

The love of the creator (who is initially immaterial), joins us in the fields of matter (our beautiful domain), and tells us of its descent into our mortal world through these myths:

> In Asia Attis was born of the Virgin Cybele.

> In Syria, Adonis was born of the Virgin called Myrrh.

> In Alexandria, Aion is born of the virgin Kore.

> In Greece, Dionysus is born of the virgin Semele.

All of the aforementioned predate Jesus.

The love of Divinity has even ventured to hang the stars in beautiful constellations to tell OUR story. And what a story it is!

The Divine who slumbers within is awakening to this reality. That it, the immaterial spirit, planned a willful descent into biology, creating for itself a cross.

> *"The cross was a sacred symbol to the ancients. Its four arms represented the four elements of the physical world: earth, water, air and fire.*
>
> *The fifth element, spirit, was bound to materiality by these four elements.*
>
> *The figure of a man nailed to a four-armed cross would, therefore, have signified the predicament of the initiate (those awakening to the understanding of the symbols, myth and allegory) as a soul bound to a physical body.*
>
> *The four nails used to crucify a man through the hands and feet would have been symbolic of our sensual desires, which attach the soul to the world of the four elements."*
>
> From the book titled, *The Jesus Mysteries,*
> by Timothy Freke and Peter Gandy.

We are awakening to all of these cultural stories and myths – that they are actually telling us of our journey.

We, as Spirit, descended into the mortal and vibrationally dense world of matter.

Unless we drink the cup and eat the bread (to become fully mortal attached to and through a physical body), we will not obtain for ourselves a helpmate, a form that could be raised incorruptible, a mortal destined for immortality. This mortal will have been fully knowledgeable in duality – a necessary prerequisite for godhood.

14:243 Seismic Shift

A while back, on the evening news, Scott Pelley reported that Christianity in America is experiencing a seismic shift and that for everyone convert to Christianity, four leave the religion. The scripture below states that this (the great falling away) will happen before the coming of Christ:

> *2 Thessalonians 2:3 "Let no man deceive you by any means; for that day shall not come except there come a falling away first, and that man of sin be revealed, the son of perdition."*

Is it just possible that this "son of perdition" (the egocentric and fear-based nature of all mankind) is revealed as we recognize these corrupt and errant fear-based systems that we participate within? That all that is within the mind of mankind that seeks to manipulate and control with fear will be exposed as the real "ANTI-CHRIST?? "

Anti-Christ is just that. Those who are anti-Christ – anti-love, anti-peace. This is not external! All of us bear the mark of the beast, the 666 – 6 molecules of carbon, 6 molecules of oxygen, 6 molecules of hydrogen. These are the building blocks of all "flesh", and where there is flesh, there is FEAR.

Wake up! Your transfiguration awaits!

Perfect love casts out all fear.

14:244 Socrates

"The secret to change is to focus all of your energy, not on fighting the old, but on building the new."
Socrates

I woke up this morning thinking about my former belief system and the absurdity of some of the "doctrines" found within Christianity. As the day progressed, I read the above quote. I loved it and realized I have a lot of mental real estate dedicated to fighting the old system. Therefore, I decided to give voice to my present-day knowledge (not belief!):

I know that I am loved and accepted, no matter how many Christians say that I am unworthy.

I know that Christianity and the teachings of Jesus are not the same. As a matter of fact, they are diametrically opposed on many issues.

I know that I will never burn and be tortured forever in Hell.

I know that the universe conspires to bless me, and that if I focus on good things, that good things will come to me.

I know that there is evil in the world, and that evil will torture the minds and hearts of those who give it latitude.

Jesus said, "If I, by the finger of God, cast out demons, then surely the Kingdom is at hand." Therefore, I know that in the Kingdom, there is no evil.

I know that the "Kingdom" is a higher state of mind.

I know that the Creator is intrinsic within me, and that we cannot be separated, no matter how many times I am told I am a sinner that needs saving. Therefore, I know that raising a hand and accepting Jesus into my heart is dogma.

I know that the one standing at the door, knocking to come in, is ME. This me is the identity of Divinity that I must accept. Knowing that I am much more than a biological human being, I am God that has invested itself into flesh and blood.

I know I am Mary (meaning "wished for child"), having been penetrated by celestial DNA.

I know I am giving birth to myself.

I know I AM.

14:245 The Bridge Appears

I love mornings.

This morning as I sit sipping my coffee (decaf, of course), I am listening to the sound of the bullfrog that has graced our pond of late, sounding his instrument – a low-burrowing and steady intermittent hum. I have read that when you hear the sound of a frog that it is "… the start of a steady transformational process, a movement from an old life to a new." I have not seen him but am told he is epically proportioned; the largest that my husband has ever seen. I try to pay close attention to nature, as it is transformative, and brings to us information and vibration necessary for our own metamorphosis.

And so, I am impressed to write these things down for you.

Moving from old to new, this passing age into the age to come, there will be changes – and at times, very sudden changes – as we leave behind our former understanding. Acquiring the new set of lenses and donning them affords us clarity of our own disposition; who are we and why are we here?

This message is not for everyone… yet. It is for those who have begun the exodus out from the former glory, pioneering the way into greater bliss. This message is simple for you. You must save your body. The way to save the body is through the reNEWing of your mind. It is from the mind that ALL creation takes place, so your mind must be reprogrammed; that is, to save a helpmate for the Divine.

Heretofore, we have believed that we must die. Not so. Even though we are told that we are eternal beings, yet we see the vehicle we inhabit return to decay time and time again… but what of this new era where moth and rust does not destroy? There is another dwelling, another dimension that we must migrate into. However, there is a purposeful buffer zone between dimensions.

Your task is to bridge the gap between dimensions. The Earth school and the dimension it inhabits is MORTAL and limited; assigned an expiration date on purpose. Here on Earth, we are learning to exercise our godhood, our inherent abilities as beings endowed with the powers of the age to come. We are becoming more and more aware of this innate ability to create and recognize that the shackles of time limitation and expiration dates are reserved only for those un-awakened souls that have yet to reach the morning stretch.

Upon awakening, the shackles of time and mortality are thrown off like an unbridled stallion bounding its way toward liberation. "This mortal must put on immortality and the corruptible must put on incorruption." MUST.

The driver of this age is knowing good from evil. Knowing CONTRAST. This knowing is NECESSARY as we begin to understand the mechanics of creation, the movement of quantum matter by the focus of our thought and emotion. HOWEVER!!! To transition the age, we must let go of the reigns! We must stop eating from the "tree" that knows good from evil and enter into the all-important era of non-judgment. This is the message of the Christ and is what it will take to DISENGAGE THE EGO from this dimension. We must change gears, and this new gear will propel us into the next dimensional level!

Disengagement will bring persecution from the prevailing mass consciousness, but you must not be distracted from your task. As you surrender judgment, your personal vibration will begin to ascend within your body and begin to create your light body, your MERKABAH, just like the chariot of Elijah.

And the bridge appears.

14:246 The Jesus People

I remember, back in the 1960s, a group called the Jesus People; a peaceful, but radical, current of young folks declaring Jesus is Lord and that there is only "one way" to get to Heaven and it was through him.

I bought it. I was a part of them; religiously attending youth groups, and as one who distributed their newspaper, called *"Street Level."*

Christianity teaches that you must accept Jesus into your heart to be saved. This is their hallmark concept; that, after hearing a plea to get a pass into Heaven and to escape Hell, you raise your hand and recite the sinner's prayer, repent from your sins and accept Jesus into your heart. There. That's it. You are safe.

"I am the way, the truth and the life and no one comes to the father but by me..."
Yes, Jesus said that. But what did he mean?

Could it be that he, as the "pattern son" did just that? Set a pattern, I mean. What was
this pattern?

> Acceptance
> Tolerance
> Love
> Non-Judgment
> Mercy
> Kindness
> Benevolence

Christianity would rather you raise your hand and, of course, behave to their
particular brand of Christianity. Whether or not to cut your hair, own guns, vote
Republican, wear makeup, pay your tithe, abstain from alcohol and R-rated movies
… oh, and the list can go on, ad infinitum.

No, people. Come on now.

The way to the father, the source of all things good (which, by the way, is inside of
you) is accessible 24/7 through LOVE, not raising a hand, walking an aisle and
reciting a prayer.

All may access this powerful creative source, no matter what your religion,
persuasion or affiliation.

Time to awaken.

14:247 Go and Multiply

It is not about sex.

"Go and multiply and fill the earth ..."

Male and female are symbols for spirit and ego, and these two energies are within
every single human being.

The Bible is a book of mysteries and is not about history.

"Go multiply and fill the earth..." viewed mystically, has to do with you as an
individual – we are to populate the Earth with Christ as the masculine and feminine
energies within each one of us comes into union, or rather, "agreement".

This is an internal mystery.

The masculine and feminine energies are found within every single human being, just as it is within our creator, for it is in that image we are created.

> *"My little children, of whom I travail in birth again until Christ be formed in you ..."* Galatians 4:19

This is the second birth, or the "born again" experience, as it is often called.

It has nothing to do with human sex, other than it serves as a pattern for us to observe externally, THAT WHICH TAKES PLACE INTERNALLY.

We must lift our eyes to discern the seeable patterns found all around us, to understand that which takes place internally.

This is how we glimpse into the domains of spirit; by observing what is seen and overlaying it, like a template, into the unseen.

The masculine (spirit) must wed the feminine (ego) in order that Christ is conceived in the midst of humanity; that is, within you.

It is not about raising a hand and walking an aisle or living according to some doctrinal ideas formed by any number of denominations and religions.

It is simply this:

> Death to the egocentric self (i.e., selfishness, meanness, revenge, anger, pride of self, etc., etc., etc.)

This is how "Christ" is formed in you: The ego is feminine in nature because it is the "womb" of creation. Everything that is created here on Earth is created through the womb of consciousness within the human being.

The ego yields to Divinity and incubates its seed of love, non-judgment and tolerance. This combination of the human and the Divine produces the God-man, Emmanuel (God within man) or Christ.

This process is the ego, as it willingly yields to the Spirit; and Christ is subsequently birthed from that union.

Once Christ is birthed, the world – as we know it – ends, and a new world begins.

14:248 Escalating Frequency

It is very important that we understand things that are happening inside of our bodies.

There are those beings that have incarnated as resonators and beacons to broadcast a vibration or frequency that is higher than typical third dimensional reality/duality or "eating" – partaking of the knowledge of good and evil.

As we begin to cease judging events of our lives as good or evil, the fabric of the third dimension is compromised because human judgment is what holds reality "in place."

These beings are fully human, but are occupied by energy that is somewhat "higher" in the frequency spectrum – these are the "first-fruits"; those who awaken from their position beneath the soil of the earth (human understanding and consciousness) and sprout what it is that they are – Christ.

Jesus was called the "firstborn of many brethren" and Paul said that he travailed in labor until Christ is formed IN us. This Christ is now beginning to awaken and mature within the womb of our humanity.

This Christ consciousness is not bound for earth, but rather is the savior of the earth.

The ransom has been paid by the shedding of our blood (human DNA), as the son of perdition (self-ego) relinquishes its throne so that the Christ may reign.

This produces the realm or dimension that is called "the kingdom" or the 5th dimensional level. It is the frequency of the heavens between dimensional levels that we are manifesting, becoming a vibrational bridge between the kingdom of Heaven and earth.

This upgraded frequency places a demand on our physical bodies, and as such, our electromagnetic field is trying to adapt, becoming a bridge in our energy spectrum from one age to the next.

I hope this helps.

14:249 $54-Million Jets

I remember the news report on how Jesse Duplantis is asking his "flock" for a $54-million jet so that he could travel the world for Jesus.

Why I think fundamentalist Christianity is the way it is: Fishbowl mentality, relationships and social culture. You are singular minded with typical Christian fundie "think" because you segregate yourselves from everyone else.

Be in the world, people. It doesn't mean you have to be "of"' it. This means, you don't have to participate in the dregs of societal community.

Be in the world, and radiate love – the kind of love that will change the world. But when you segregate yourselves, you become myopic and victim to scams like having to buy your pastor a 54-million-dollar jet to fly around the world for Jesus and think that it is normal.

54 million dollars can buy a lot of grain.

Wake up, people!

14:250 Do People Tend to Behave Like Their Parents?

Would you rather be the child of a father who would torture you for eternity if you disobeyed him, or the child of a father who forgives you?

People tend to behave like their parents ...

No wonder we have so much division, separation and intolerance in our world. Wake up, Christianity. YOUR father is unforgiving – THE ANTITHESIS OF HIMSELF when he, through Christ said, "Forgive."

The progenitor, the source of all, loves me, and there is nothing that can separate me from that love, for I AM LOVE.

Christianity teaches a God that is irreconcilable with himself.

14:251 Genius

It is expanding to accept differing concepts and ideas continually. It is restrictive to think that one has it all "right".

There will never be an end to experience. Jesus spoke of the necessity of the new wineskin. The old has stretched as far as it can and cannot contain the volatile expansion that comes with revelation.

The ONE has its place in our evolution but is not the goal. How can it be? We are forever individuated, having been replicated and primed for expansion.

But, recognizing that we share in union; that is, making the TWO ONE is the purpose for the symbolism of the babe born in the stable – you – where God has joined us, and we have yielded in union. We are this metaphorical manger.

Now, we conceive, again and again bringing forth from our own universal womb what is inherently both God and man. Christ. This is the stuff of Genius.

That love found a way to explore and inhabit the material planes in and through a helpmate – the human being.

That said, there are those whose ultimate purpose is not to be Emmanuel, and those will return to blend with the ONE. It is our choice.

> Some purchase land.
> Some remove the rocks.
> Some till the soil.
> Some plant the seed.
> Some are the bounty.
> Some reap the harvest.

It is not so important for the reaper to convince the tiller to be a reaper.

We must appreciate all and recognize we are all, in all fulfilling the purpose for which genius is.

14:252 Why I Am Impressed by the Holistic Community …

To me, holistic defined means, "A regard for the whole person; body, mind and spirit."

I spent many years within Christian fundamentalism, where genuine and sincere effort was made for unity, and to some degree it was achieved; but only within the ranks of the Christian religion with this caveat: Generally, Christians only socialized with other Christians with whom they shared enough commonality of beliefs for consensus.

Recently, at the holistic fair in our community, I got to observe many people from all walks of life express their desire of health for the whole person – not just physical, but mental and spiritual health, as well. No one there was trying to proselytize another person. Rather, there seemed to be a sincere effort to extend themselves; to truly understand other beliefs and practices outside of their own.

Our community is very conservative (and fearful!), with practices like yoga, acupuncture, meditation, intuitive readings, etc., not so common. Two of the best quotes I have heard are these:

> *"In an age where information is so readily available, to remain ignorant is a choice,"*

and

> *"Contempt, prior to investigation, is the height of ignorance."*

I was one who condemned holistic practices because I was ignorant. I "ignored" them, because I thought they were evil. And yet, some of the intuitive arts were practiced within Christianity, but labeled differently – like "prophesy" instead of channeling and "a word of knowledge" instead of psychic abilities, or the "laying on of hands" instead of Reiki.

Recently, I had a 22-year very strong friendship come to an end (via text, no less). The final straw was when she saw a Buddha statue (making the hand gesture that means "Peace") in my newly remodeled bathroom. To me, this lacks the character, love and tolerance of Christ and is not emulating the Jesus I would follow. With little exception, there is more Christ-like behavior within the holistic "come-unity" than what I had experienced within my 43-year-long tenure within fundamentalism. It should also be noted that Jesus was intolerant towards one people group. Do you remember which one? That's right – the religious folk.

In general, Christian fundamentalism practices "sectual pollination" where they only associate with those of their own ilk and, as such, suffer from a myopic view of community, humanity and the world.

I am proud to be a part of the holistic COME-UNITY in our city and impressed by the very Christ-like practice of non-judgment, tolerance, acceptance and love found within so many.

Good on ya!

SECTION FIFTEEN

FIFTEEN

15:253 Desire Precedes Leaving Organized Religion

There must be a desire, a hunger and a willingness to learn – qualities that come from humility and brokenness. Many have fallen upon the rock that is Christ and have been broken – many, many people. There are many now within religion who are making the decision to exodus, to keep moving, just as we have.

Ours is a perspective that may be considered "new age," and indeed, it is. Jesus did not caution us about new age, he told us to LOOK for it. This is a NEW age and we are apprehending all that has been intended for our growth and for our conscious evolution. Many, many souls are navigating the spiritual path outside of systemic religion.

Many within systemic religion were initially drawn within the organized structure because, at one time, the church had the freshest revelation, having experienced the overflow in abundance from Spirit. But now, as the river recedes, the waters collected into separate pools, where they seem to be cut off from the perpetual flow that comes from the richness of intuited streams. Now, what remains are Oxbow Lakes, without the fresh water supply necessary to keep them from becoming putrid, unmoving and stale. And the system does not want to let go of its parishioners, so those leaving are scrutinized and labeled, as I have been. Deceived. Witch. New Age. Satanist.

The reformation deluge movements are necessary to propel the population, to shake them; but if we stay within the remaining Oxbow Lake structures, history shows that religion becomes controlling, abusive and restrictive, but mostly instills fear while rigidly adhering to a translation of the letter that kills.

It should also be said that each individual must discern his or her place in this unfolding drama. We are headed into the tribulation period (and many have been there for a while), some looking externally for these signs to manifest and others embracing the internal process, as their body undergoes transfiguration and sheds the containment of the past that is comprised of the frequency of limitation and fear. Tribulation, indeed!

There are two very broad places for consciousness to occupy. They are:

1. That which is breaking down (this world and its systems) and each person knows intrinsically where his or her place is at this juncture of time. That does not mean that those working with this passing age cannot transition into that which is breaking through, it just means that they know in this moment the space that their

consciousness occupies. These will fight to maintain their equilibrium in this disintegrating age, continually eating from the tree that discerns between good and evil.

2. That which is breaking through (the new [kingdom] age that Jesus spoke of).

These recognize that neither position in consciousness is wrong, as they no longer "eat" from the tree that produces the knowledge of good and evil. Therefore, all is good, useful and expedient to bring about the transition into the next age. They disengage from judging, thereby raising their personal frequency that will eventually rise to compatibility with the age to come.

They understand that there must be the restrictive womb (systemic religion) that brings the babe to bear, so they appreciate the system that birthed them, and in so doing, do not judge those maternal systems. They are not exempt from entering into the age to come, but rather, honored to be a part of the structure that both incubated and birthed the Christ. We read in Revelation 12 that this woman that births the Christ is well cared for, albeit she will remain in the wilderness for a time…

The "woman" is the structure (womb) that allowed us to grow until the environment became too restrictive – consciousness then passes through the narrow way and is birthed out from this structure.

For many, it is the church; for others, it may be an abusive relationship or a job that, out of fear of lack, they remain there. Symbolically, the "woman" is all structures of fear that keep us in restriction, for one reason or another.

Once the woman (this incubating structure) gives birth, it itself retreats into the "wilderness" (another term for egocentricity that has not yielded to the other voice/mind of Christ – the one John cried out for to prepare its coming).

This is a divine place that the structure (fear-based mentalities) retreat into, but just for a "time, time, and half a time." (Daniel and Revelation)

The fundamentalist church that induces fear of missing Heaven and going to Hell, is one such structure. It is a consciousness that can no longer control or restrict the burgeoning consciousness of the Christ.

15:254 Christianity is in Crisis

Christianity is in crisis. As we grow in stature and knowledge of this all-encompassing love of God, we are beginning to shed the falseness that religion has applied. Over the centuries, we have been coated with thick, dark paint as our understanding of spiritual principles has been covered. Each passing century has afforded us another layer of paint, applied by charismatic leaders expressing their opinions. These same tattoo on our psyche with threats of Hell and damnation.

We are like a fresco in need of rejuvenation. We are in need of a good scraping so that the original beauty might be brought to the forefront again. After all, what sense does it make for an all-loving Deity that tells us to love our enemies all the while he burns his to a crisp??? What has happened to us? Who or what has bewitched us from following the pure word of truth?

Where is this "turning the other cheek" that Jesus spoke of, and where does "Nothing can separate us from the love of God" come into play? Does his love hurt, like an abusive lover that after a good beating says, "You made me do it!"?

Surely, we have misinterpreted scripture and have failed to see types and shadows within this figurative prose. Surely, our English translation does not do justice to the rich Aramaic language Jesus used.

Ah, but to digress from these popular translations, one is accused and defiled while we hurl accusations of "Heresy!" Are we not JUST LIKE THE PHARISEES that Jesus called a "brood of vipers" … coiling to strike with venomous teeth...?

Yes, our egocentric nature; the serpent, the one who must defend the "I" of self, the one that must be right, the one who cannot bend like a healthy tree in a storm. This "I" of self breaks, instead, because it has become rigid and unmoving, not watered by the latter rains of change.

Let us see clearly the patterns in scripture and recognize that the story of the Pharisaical resistance is not constrained within far-off history. This pattern plays itself out repeatedly as the winds of change blow upon the embers sparked by lightning as the heavens touch the Earth.

Blow upon me winds of change and burn up the dross of my egocentric life. Help me to see and to embrace the changes upon us as the bones of the Christ grow with the pains of the passing age…

I yield myself to death again, as I see the futility that surrounds. Resurrect this life again; I plead that I may see you plainly in me!

15:255 Your World is Attractive

Your world is attractive at its CORE.

Beings that are not physical SEEK to experience your attractive world because it is at the center of creation. You are at the center of all creation.

Your thoughts are electric in NATURE.

But thoughts without their helpmate (the MAGNETIC NATURE of EMOTION) will not create at all.

You may not be aware of this, but when you have a thought it is always accompanied by an emotional value. This emotional value comingles with the thought, much like the act of sex.

Think in terms of masculine and feminine, rather than male and female.

Thought is masculine and emotion is feminine.

Together they copulate to form the object of their attention.

You see this played out at a physical level, as this is how another human being is created. It is a pattern given to you so that you may clearly see that which remains invisible to you.

What you think on, coupled with the appropriate emotional value, you will create.

This is how the world keeps on spinning, recreating itself every second, because there are 7.5 billion creators thinking and emoting, thinking and emoting.

Why is there war, hatred, killing, vengeance, retribution, anger and malice, etc.?

Why do you THINK there are these things?

These things ARE because a portion of 7.5 billion creators are thinking of them and emoting as they think. Some feel victimized at the hands of an angry mob. But you are all cells of the same organism acting, thinking and emoting – all the TIME.

TIME serves you in this manner, as you are learning to create. You are also victimized by your creation – a very effective means to learn PAIN.

Oh, if you could see the attractiveness of pain. It is your greatest teacher. If you could USE it, rather than be victimized by it, your world would be on the fastest track to enlightenment.

Time serves as a gestational tool so that you may see and GROW within it. Just as it takes nine months of gestation to form a child, your creative endeavors also take TIME to manifest.

A side note:

This information is drawn much like a cold beer on tap.

You may draw upon extra-dimensional information anytime you wish. It is akin to reaching up to a shelf that requires you to stand on your tippy toes to reach the object of your desire. In the same way, anyone of you may "channel" or "prophesize", for the information is intrinsic IN YOU.

We prefer the cold beer on tap analogy, but some of you think that you must obtain a "higher" position in consciousness. In some ways this is true, but not necessarily higher. You must reach for the information, but we prefer that you reach THROUGH and within, rather than "up."

Those famous prophets of old and the channelers of today are no different than you. Kryon and Abraham are aspects of the collective that give voice through individuals. It matters not HOW the information reaches you, but it is preferred that you each pour your own drink!

15:256 God is Not a Republican

God is not a Republican. God is not a Democrat. Jesus couldn't have cared less who was in political power when he walked the earth. While he honored the likes of Caesar, Pilate and Herod, he did not embrace their systems. He did not embrace Judaism or Christianity, either. He continually broke the time-honored Jewish traditions. And, how could he embrace Christianity? It was not an official religion until 313 AD.

Jesus said, "Before Abraham was, I AM." Abraham was considered the Father of Judaism and Jesus was stating his pre-eminence before this ancient religion was birthed.

We are so silly to think that our fate rests in the hands of mere men.

For those who cite the Old Testament and a God that hears if we fast and pray hard enough ... to those I say, "Understand the nature of Jehovah!" This was a ruling deity of the day for man to identify with. In eating from the Tree of the Knowledge of Good and Evil (duality), mankind needed a God that was dual; that would reward and punish, love and hate, give life and take life. This was our fledgling egoist nature, and this is why Jehovah was introduced in Genesis, Chapter Two, after the "fall." This was not the Father of Jesus. Elohim(s) is the Father of Jesus. Jesus came to release human consciousness from the old order of things found within the Old Testament patterns.

As Christians, we continually blend the old with the new to form our spiritual governance. We need to recognize the implications of the law and move fully into grace. The New Testament offers the way of escape from the law, and yet we are still bound and governed by the fear of Jehovic patterns.

The law served us well, and we bear the imprints of it in our collective consciousness, but it is time to move and embrace the "age to come," as Jesus put it. Things will not look the same. Let's migrate out of the wilderness, recognizing that even it has served us, and move firmly into promise. Ego's in check? Let's cross over!

15:257 Stop Resisting Evil ....

"As a man thinketh in his heart so is he ..." Proverbs 23:7 Whatever a man thinks, he creates.

Whatever a person focuses on; that, he shall have.

This is such a simple concept, and yet we have not grasped it. Jesus said, "Resist NOT evil." WHY did he say that? And why do we continue to resist it?

Jesus knew that in our resistance and focus, we will create more of what we are actually NOT wanting. THINK ABOUT THAT.

Let me explain further: The human being is endowed with this "pearl" of great price, something that has been forming within the human race for eons. This "treasure", hidden within the human field, is the ability to create! Whatever the human focuses his/her thoughts and emotions upon, he/she creates MORE of what he/she thinks about.

Let's say a woman experiences betrayal and thinks about the circumstances of the betrayal, time and time again, and feels the pain, and sheds the tears because of the pain she re-lives. There is a deep cry coming from within her being that is actually requesting; ASKING to be betrayed! The universe does not discriminate! It hears the vibrational request because a human being is focusing thought and emotional currency into being betrayed!!! And the answer is, "YES!!!"

I have recently removed several postings on my timeline about supporting a movement to stop human trafficking, gun control etc. The unfortunate thing is that if people focus on human trafficking and view provocative pictures and stories that move them to frustration, anxiety, fear, hopelessness, anger, etc., then THAT IS WHAT THEY ARE CREATING!!!

Scripture says to take every thought captive and to think on things that are pure, lovely and of a good report.

This woman that is focusing on the betrayal and the sorrow she feels, is actually sending a detailed plea for more! She must cease focusing on betrayal and begin focusing on loyalty and integrity in order to receive it!

If we truly grasp the mechanics of creation, then we will maintain our focus on GOOD things. Focusing on things we deem as evil will attract it to us and we will ultimately receive whatever it is that we "ask" for.

The reason we focus on the negative things is because we have an ego that recognizes right and wrong, good and evil. We must remove this "Son of Perdition" from the throne of our humanity, to become a servant to us, rather than a master of us.

15:258 About Diet ...

I think as our consciousness evolves, we find ourselves leaning more and more toward plant-based diets and away from red and other meats.

Consciousness is becoming kinder and gentler in many ways. As we are less warlike and vengeful, the less we need the characteristics of the "beasts" we consume. Our diets evolve organically as we change the way we think and ACT.

> Jesus said, *"Blessed is the lion which becomes man when consumed by man ..."*
>
> (7) Gospel of Thomas

I think this is a mystery that reveals that the consciousness of the beast that is consumed, manifests in the eater.

You may look at what the animal represents and understand that those same characteristics will manifest through you. Consider the bull. Then consider the salmon.

That is an eye-opener.

For many who are struggling to incorporate a more plant-based diet into their lives, I think it is wise to let your body lead you, and not to become legalistic about it. I still eat red meat on occasion but prefer lighter foods.

15:259 Trump

Every time you are negative toward another human being, it literally reflects BACK ONTO YOU.

Energy will seek its source to return to. Our words create, and do not return to the creator void, without fulfilling their intent.

What then, are you speaking over yourself?

I was recently at a gathering of 1,600 enlightened people at a science and spirituality conference in Canada. Of course, there were jokes about our President, and I found my energy cascading with every slam.

(It should be said that I did not vote for any candidate.)

After five days of various negative comments, I raised my hand during the question and answer panel and asked this of the all-star panel:

> *"Over the last week we are learning how powerful we are and that we create our reality. With this in mind, what is our responsibility toward President Trump?"*

15:260 When Have You Chosen to Awaken?

I have an inner drive that I can only now see is a "calling". This inner drive is to speak and write about the abuses found within fundamentalism, religious and other.

Fundamentalism robs us of our intuition and our ability to discern for ourselves. Fundamentalism, through fear of rejection, demands that we submit and conform to a particular order of beliefs. These beliefs are cultivated by individuals who feel strongly about a given set of criteria and who have the desire to create a following.

Fundamentalism is polarizing, and it is what I am called to liquidate by identifying its characteristics in our thinking and in our various belief systems.

I was born for this, and I awakened, through pain, within Christian fundamentalism in 1999.

15:261 Don't Stay Bitter

In the outstanding book titled, *The Book of Awakening,* Mark Nepo writes of a man who grew up under apartheid. He was taught by his ancestors "not to stay bitter or vengeful, for hate eats up the heart, and with a damaged heart, life is not possible."

We are each confronted with the same dilemma: "How to feel the pain of living without denying it, and without letting that pain define us. Ultimately, no matter the burden we are given, once whittled to the bone, we are faced with a never-ending choice: to become the wound or to heal."

Back in the late 1990s we slept on an under-filled waterbed, and sometime during the night my hip came to rest on the heating mechanism under the waterbed mattress. I awakened suddenly, with excruciating pain, having just been burned deeply from an electrical short in the heating element.

Weeks went by and the burn would not heal. I had a deep open sore about the size of a 50-cent piece that oozed and wept. The wound had consumed my time, with cleaning it and trying to find appropriate clothing that did not irritate it. I finally went to the doctor, who recommended that the burned tissue be excised. He said that without surgery, the wound would have little chance to heal.

It was an outpatient procedure, with several shots of Novocain injections. They surgically removed the damaged tissue, deep into the subcutaneous layer of skin, and sewed the wound closed. And I healed.

Much in the same way, many of us lament over emotional wounds that will not heal. We meditate. We forgive. We go to counseling and sometimes the best efforts do not bring about healing. The damage is just too deep, and we begin to embody the wound. It defines us.

What merciful thing may you do for yourself to excise your wound? What must be cut away so that healing begins?

15:262 External vs Internal

There is an external path and an internal path. We perceive externally until the ego has learned through the things it experiences. The following describes the internal path:

> *Therefore leaving the principles of the doctrine of Christ, let us go on unto perfection; not laying again the foundation of repentance from dead works, and of faith toward God, Of the doctrine of baptisms,*

*and of laying on of hands, and of resurrection of the dead, and of
eternal judgment. And this will we do, if God permit.* Hebrews 6:1- 3

Let's look at the admonition in this scripture to leave "the principle of faith toward
God."

While on vacation in Hawaii, we had rented a Harley Davidson motorcycle and rode
all over the Island of Oahu. I love riding on the back of a motorcycle. My mind goes
blank, as there is nothing for me to do other than to take in the beauty around me –
it's like a form of meditation. As we rode through the rainforest, I was thinking about
this scripture in Hebrews, as I had been stumped by it for weeks.

Why, I asked, would we be told to leave behind faith toward God? The wind had a
gentle mist about it, tingling my skin as we rode, and I heard that voice within say
this:

> *"The key to understanding the message behind this scripture lies in
> the word 'toward' for it implies directionality outward from you. You
> are misapplying your faith to an external position."*

I came to understand this voice as the "I AM" within – hearing I am within you, as
you.

Again, our externalization of God was necessary until the Divine penetrated the
framework of man. Now, our worship should be an act of becoming: Becoming
fearless; Becoming non-judgmental; Becoming love; Embodying forgiveness;
Loving the Divine. This is the cosmic Christ! It is the unique amalgamation of God
and man that is uniquely Christ.

Are we God? No. We are not the totality of God. I heard it said that if God were the
ocean, we are a glass dipped in the ocean. Is the ocean within the glass? Yes. Are we
the totality of the ocean? No. We are over 7 billion individual expressions of the
Divine, yet we are all ONE.

The human frame has given animation to the Divine in the material world. We are
the helpmate. We are Eve.

15:263 More on the Ritual of Baptism

Baptism is a SYMBOL.

It is a ritual that, when performed, will demonstrate a foundational spiritual
principle.

It looks like a person submersed under the water for a second or two and then coming up drenched. Whether in a baptismal font, pool or natural body of water like a lake, river or ocean, submerging a person underwater is supposed to symbolize something of great importance.

I think it is a mystery.

We are supposed to "see" something more than a ritual. We are supposed to see that we, as Divine beings, have taken the journey into biological form and have been sub-merged into humanhood.

Sub: under
Merge: absorption by a corporation of one or more others; also, any of various methods of combining two or more organizations (such as business concerns); to dip

The two organizations that have merged are that of Divinity and the human under the "waters" (consciousness) of being a physical, mortal being.

So, we see that the act of baptism is for us to remember that we, as Divinity, have taken the "plunge" into being human – a position in consciousness where we are holding our DIVINE breath until the time of resurrection, coming up and out of the waters of being mortally human.

It is to remind us while we are submerged under the sea of forgetfulness, where our Divine inventory and memory is suspended due to the incompatibility our divine memory and our earthbound frequency. We only remember what we have learned while being human.

This ritual is to remind you of your decision to willingly forget your Divinity and to become identified in death; that is, to be a human.

15:264 The Profound Symbolism of Communion

Are you a DIVINE BEING?

Have you surrendered your DIVINE FORM for that of a human being?

Did you step out of immortality into biological form?

Are you the BABE born in the MANGER of humanity?

This is the SYMBOLISM of COME-union

Christ (not Jesus, although he is also Christ) is the amalgamation of the DIVINE and MAN.

Christ defined is a DIVINE BEING that has taken up residence and ultimately has accrued a partnership with a human being.

The CHRIST (you) said, "I AM the BREAD that CAME DOWN from HEAVEN."

A DIVINE BEING descended down from Heaven and entered biology. Christ "humbled himself, taking the FORM of a SERVANT."

This is the SYMBOLISM OF come-union.

The bread (your immortal form and nature) was BROKEN and SWALLOWED.

The throat is called the "GRAVE."

The grave is being MORTAL.

The bread enters the belly or SHEOL. This is also the symbolism of JONAH being swallowed up of the great FISH (the Age of Pisces) while he learns obedience to the Divine voice within.

DO THIS in remembrance of me (you – the Christ).

Break the bread – the symbolism of your broken divinity.

Swallow the broken bread chased by the symbol of blood – the wine; your MORTALITY.

And remember your journey into the material worlds.

You are here to find a helpmate to navigate the worlds of form.

RE MEMBER.

IT IS ALL SYMBOLISM.

15:265 Parting the Red Sea

I love the metaphorical aspect of the parting of the Red Sea. The two halves of the brain separated, divided, just like the Red Sea. The coming together of these two halves is the union that is spoken of.

It takes both halves becoming "one" to produce the Christ. A divine synergy is created through union, where the sum of the two is worth more than the individual halves.

The parting of the Red Sea signified the beginning of wandering in duality and egocentricity. Then, once finished in the wilderness, we cross again back over the parted waters of the Jordan, the boundary of death into life.

This is such a fascinating concept/symbol. The Bible is not a Christian book, it is a mystery book that outlines, through story and allegory, the journey that the divine takes couched within humanhood.

Take, for example, this article about the parting of the Red Sea – it reveals that our brain developed a thick band of neural networking fibers to help us utilize logic (left) and intuition (right) while we journeyed into, were baptized into separation/wilderness.

This happened while our solar system departed the close proximity to our dual sun, Sirius, the star that stimulates our intuitive mind in its 24,000-year ellipse.

This is when we experience the baptism into futility, when the mind cannot perceive of anything it cannot experience with the five senses. This neural networking veil helps the human navigate dense human consciousness as we travel through the dark ages.

15:266 Letter to a Fundamentalist

This will sound harsh and it is not meant to – I say this with love, respect and appreciation of where you are. You are as I was for 43 years – asleep. It is a necessary slumber, just as Jesus slept in the boat and as did the beloved in the Song of Solomon.

It is an imposed and purposeful slumber that will allow you the opportunity to grow. I know when my grandkids are in a growth spurt, because they eat and sleep a lot!

You have cited many, many scriptural verses, most of which you are largely unaware of their meaning. They are seen "in part". You have read them or have been taught them by well-meaning teachers or preachers. However, the "kingdom" (which is a higher level of awakened consciousness) does not come to you by "observation"; that is, it cannot be discerned by the five senses and cannot be learned via logic or through the intellectual mind. Another mind must grow within you, and that is the mind of Christ – not Jesus, but Christ, which is an amalgamation of the Divine (what you may call God) and man. This is the time "when no man shall teach you."

I was like you, as well, reciting scripture, thinking I was defending the faith, sometimes criticizing those who held a different viewpoint than me. I came to understand that there are between 38,000 and 41,000 different (and sometimes vehemently disagreeing) sects within Christianity. I had to humbly submit to the fact that I may not have it all right. As I began to yield to that concept and humble myself, it was only then that I began to awaken. I did not awaken by listening to someone like me.

There has never been one person asleep in religion, in all my years of speaking and teaching, who has ever said, "I might be wrong." It is simply not permissible by the ego to give up ground to anyone, especially when you think your eternal salvation is at stake. This is because there is no third party in awakening – it is between you and God. It is an internal and intuitive process.

This process begins when the ego yields to a broader perspective than what it has accrued through head knowledge. This is the symbolism of the donkey (ego) that bears Jesus to death on the cross, where your egocentric thinking (the horizontal beam of the cross) yields to that of your divine self (the vertical beam of the cross.)

Everyone must come to the cross, and until you do, resurrection will not occur. Each in his own order. It is ALL GOOD.

15:267 Like Fingernails on a Chalkboard...

Like fingernails on a chalkboard...

That is what hearing anything about God and Jesus felt like in the years after I left the church system. What in the world was happening to me?

I felt so ruffled inside if I saw a televangelist asking for money or heard someone quote Bible verses ... even to see someone pray over their food in a restaurant. Fingernails dragging across a blackboard. I would cringe.

Early on, I described this process like losing a program like "Word" or "PowerPoint" on my computer. I simply could not access the program and I was irritated when someone else did. Little did I know then, that is exactly what happened to me. I was deprogrammed in the blink of an eye.

I recall someone asking me about a mutual acquaintance – was she saved or not? I thought I was having some sort of neurological event, because I honestly did not know what the word "saved" meant. As I stood there searching for understanding, my friend asked, "What is wrong with you?" My face flushed as I panicked, searching for words. My eyes scanned the room and I thought, "okay, there is a table and a chair, a rug and my coffee cup." I didn't lose other words… what happened to "saved?"

In a very short frame of time, I lost my own "salvation" as all of those self-imposed religious concepts simply left me. I no longer knew about Hell, Heaven, the rapture, baptism, Satan, demons, etc. They were … gone. Something was happening to me, and it began with a wrecking ball named Ian Chellan, an Apostle from the World Breakthrough Network, who blew through town challenging traditional dogma.

One day, just before he spoke to a group of about 35 people in my home, he said this:

> *"For those of you that think Satan and Lucifer are one and the same, I am here to tell you that they are not. But don't believe me, search and study for yourself."*

I did, and the rest is history. As I searched, I saw that TREMENDOUS latitude and mistranslation had been applied in the various scriptures to create and promote this diabolical doctrine. I thought, Lord, if I had this wrong, then what else is wrong?

Suddenly, autopilot took over, because my searching and questioning were genuine. My doctrines of man and demons began to tumble like dominoes.

15:268 Miracles

Miracles tend to validate whatever system of belief you find yourself within.

If something miraculous occurs, the God of your particular religious institution did it; so, if the miraculous happens within paganism, the Divine entity of that culture gets credit. If a miracle happens within Christian fundamentalism, then that God gets credit.

These miraculous acts validate our chosen standard of belief.

And witnessing the miraculous begins the process of indoctrination, brainwashing and mind programming.

Within any given belief or practice, peer pressure undergirds the indoctrination processes. This is because religion requires consensus to dull the effect of cognitive dissonance.

Cognitive dissonance is what one feels when they are told something, but they KNOW BETTER.

For example, we know that a loving God will not torture and burn someone forever and ever, yet people believe these doctrines because they are supported by passionate believers who have been told these things by people who they love and trust.

Stop the madness.

15:269 Remember Your Task

You fluctuate between this age and the age to come, between head knowledge and heart knowing, between ego and spirit, between humanity and divinity.

You straddle the worlds.

Remember your come-union with humanity.

Remember your baptism into the Earth.

You are an Earth-walker.

Remember your task!

15:270 Beauty for Ashes

> *"Every now and then, I experience waves of sadness over the loss of relationships from my Christian past. There are those who have cut me off like a diseased part of a tree, and I have no choice but to surrender to the burn pile.*
>
> *When these waves come, I realize that it is me, calling up from the ashes and surrendering little bits and pieces of my heart, tearful goodbyes to the shared memories, to the love. I have asked myself a hundred times, "where did their love for me go?" – my tender heart bruised from their inability to love me like Jesus does.*

As I move farther away leaving, those belief structures behind, the view of this passing age grows ever dim. With time, I am content to keep moving forward, knowing that all of our wounds serve us. I know that in this sort of surrender, beauty may be seen in the ashes."

The above communication was written in 2014. I am amazed at the healing power of time. Leaving Christianity and the subsequent disenfranchisement was difficult, but the wounds have finally healed, and the pain of lost love has grown dull.

I do see purpose in all of this and know that, through suffering, I am an initiate as I walk the path of Christ. This was a hard thing for me to learn, but I did learn, and I now value this precious pearl enough to surrender all else to find it.

"Remember the word I spoke to you: 'A servant is not greater than his master.' If they (the religious) persecuted me, they will also persecute you." John 15:20

SECTION SIXTEEN

SIXTEEN

16:271 A Message for Empaths

A message received after numerous questions about empathic abilities and the feeling of transmuting energy, personally and with others:

This is unprecedented. Stop looking outward for answers, as this is a new way. You are way makers and trendsetters. A new way has been opened to you, a methodology to help "drain the swamp," so to speak; to help the Earth's atmosphere clean itself from dark or dense energy. This dark energy forms itself into structures that inhibit thought and keep the human mind encapsulated; fear, anxiety, panic, hatred, unforgiveness, rage, addiction, etc., are examples. Have you ever witnessed someone unable to move out from a system of bad thinking???

The synergy that works within you is unprecedented. Your energy swirls like a gathering storm and acts as a propellant to draw new energy in and to force old energy out. The energy configuration is like the working of a set of lungs. It is a divine exchange. Your energy configuration "breathes".

Out with the old, and in with the new. A new alchemic structure is replacing the old as this divine exchange takes place. It is an upgrade from your old structures that were based in mortality. Little by little, this new vortex will install itself, multiplying and advancing along with the advent of your upgraded energy. You would do well to focus more intention here. It is called "alchemic" because it has the ability to signal the change in atomic structures morphing their configuration from this age (dimension) to the next.

This alchemic structure is within and without you. The circumference of the structure eclipses the border of your bodies. There is an energetic signature that is created by you. You each have a specific key or frequency that produces a harmony, a vibrational signature. Your key activates the vortex. You planned this well. And the vortex is large and, much like an etheric tornado, will sweep "things" into its, wake pulling it upward violently and reconfiguring its structure in the process. Energy naturally reconfigures with vortical movement. If you could see what we see, the unseen workings of your energy body, you would stand amazed as we do. You are quite spectacular. It is like a super-cell tornado, and huge swaths of land are impacted, and structures demolished. You reap structural energetic destruction and displacement. And it is good.

Heretofore, this appears happenstance, but we are here to tell you that it cannot help but happen when your key activates the vortex. Each of you continuously receives and continuously transmutes. At times the "package" may require some heavy lifting. UPS even designates parcels as "heavy" so that the delivery men may get help when necessary.

At times, energy that is ready for release looks for this energetic signature and struggles through the opening of the portal, and sometimes it is much like someone squeezing through the closing of elevator doors. It cannot help but upset your energetic apple cart, as there is a great vibrational differential between their signature and yours. It is a lot to transmute but, because your outlying intelligence resides out of time itself, you will "feel" the unction long before your "hopper" is full. It is predictive and can see around corners. Hence, you will feel energetic shifting. The movement of this energetic shifting brings discomfort to your body vehicle. Just as the barometric pressure drops before a storm, it is an uncomfortable indicator that something is brewing in the atmosphere. Look to discomfort. It is your indicator. You set the program up this way and it has proven to be an efficient means of notification. It is a physical "email" that has arrived in your body's inbox. You must become adept at reading the signs through the inbox of your body AND THROUGH YOUR EMOTIONS. You've got mail!

As you continue your journey in consciousness, you traverse familiar pitfalls and straddle them with ease. This makes the process of "breathing" so much easier. Like a runner who has fine-tuned their body, so must you condition your energetic lungs. As you are conditioned, the process will get easier. We promise.

And we also encourage you to get creative. You may see that this energy is malleable to your will and must obey your thoughtful intention.

As your planet increases in frequency, it acts as a vortical vice, literally squeezing out lower frequency. In your science classes, you learned about the power of centrifugal force. The denser particles always get pulled to the outer circumference. From that position, they have been separated from the finer energetic molecules and are "spun out" of the mixture configuration that comprises Earth's electromagnetic atmosphere.

As an empath, this vortical and energetic movement penetrates your body mass and the surrounding sphere of influence that is around you. So, it is not that energy "chooses" to be released from the energetic atmosphere as much as it is an act of physics following the laws of gravity that govern your planet. In this way, it "looks" or is, rather, drawn in by the laws of gravity.

There is a crypt of sorts, a chamber likened to a Faraday cage, where the energy, once captured, will not retreat. This cage works on the principles of love being the greatest force available to you, and as you know, love conquers fear. As you love, you reconfigure the energy of fear. It does the dance of twirling within your vortex and is loved to "death." It experiences a dis-configuring, is pulled apart like salvaged auto parts in a junkyard. These energy parts are useful in other planes and will be gathered to be configured according to divine plan.

Obviously, love is not unique, and all of those on your planet will activate their individual centrifuge as love conquers fear. You are in the order of firsts – a forerunner – and, in that way, pitfalls must be mastered, hills climbed, valleys crossed, paths cleared. You are not special, necessarily; you are servants from the Melchizedek order. You came into this incarnation fully loaded. The technology of your self-activating centrifuge was just waiting to start, once the internal structures that govern and nurtured your fear were compromised. Once fear is put down, the frequency of love activates the movement of the dance. Others that are not of this order will be led to do the same and led by your example. Their path of learning is not a function of intellect; rather, their higher selves will activate as they observe and see the dance. You were born with the dance within you; they will "see" the dance and do. Twirl your partner round and round! We say this tongue in cheek, but fear has partnered with you in this journey and has been the most necessary component in the art of emoting and creating.

The why of it is this: As your planet increases in the frequency of love, it readies itself for intercourse with the Divine. This union will produce the incubation of the Christ in you.
As you have noticed, the each of you has a function in this equation.

As energy dances, it collects and separates into individual parlors. You call them "organs." The organ works in conjunction with its universal counterpart – sort of like a master computer. You are the micro of the macro and, as above, so below. These holding "cells" called organs breakdown the chemistry of the molecules for dissemination through the central tube. This is why you feel discomfort in certain areas of your body. Send love to them. They are doing a most beautiful work on behalf of the material universe. As it happens within you, it happens in the cosmos. You are helping to construct the dwelling place of I AM within the universal order of things.

16:272 Empaths and Coincidences

I know I am a type of empath. As a former deliverance minister, I know that just about every person, place and even thing can have negative energy either around it or in it. I also know that the frequency of "love" can displace negative energy.

I mentioned to my husband, Lyle, the intense gurgling sound that was coming from both of our innards for over a day while in Santa Fe may not be last night's supper, but that we may be actively transmuting energy. I am very familiar that our body is a microcosm of the macrocosm, and that our organs are reflective of something on a much larger scale; just as we digest physical food, we also may have the empathic ability to digest, and to change the form of negative ballast, thereby relieving the person, place or thing of its negative affect.

Walking around the Indian Market in Santa Fe, we came upon the St. Francis of Assisi Basilica and I snapped a photo of the skies over the top of the church. We went inside the Basilica to take a rest from walking and to enjoy the painted interior, and I looked at the photo I had just taken. To my amazement, I saw what looked like a person blowing something into a hand in the skies over the structure.

This photo was just so fascinating to me. As we returned to our walk around the Indian Market in the Plaza in Santa Fe, I thought I saw James Cromwell; he is the actor that played Warden Hal Moores in the movie "*The Green Mile.*" We both thought he looked just like James Cromwell, and continued our walk.

If you haven't seen it, WATCH IT. The Green Mile is about a wrongly accused death row inmate who has the miraculous empathic ability to remove sickness/negative energy from people, places and things by bringing it into his body and transmuting it. After he takes it in, he blows the negative and transmuted energy out, and it looks like a bunch of flies (a symbol for Beelzebub) come streaming out of his mouth.

Here is the weird part: We returned to our room and laughed at the amount of movement that was occurring in both of our bodies. Not to give too much information here, but we had to open the patio windows in our room for some fresh air. (Yes, this is what transmuting energy looks like in the natural and in the supernatural!)

We plopped down on the bed and Lyle began surfing the TV when we came upon the movie "*The Green Mile.*"

I looked at him and said, "Coincidence????"

16:273 Are You Awake?

You are not a Republican.

You are not a Democrat.

You are asleep.

There is a massive effort to pull your energy into schism. Schism is the creative dynamic of this age. The more you split, the more you divide, separate and create more schism. Sort of like nuclear fusion.

Unite. Love. Create peace. Multiply this, instead.

If you are schismatic, you are part of the problem, not the solution.
16:274 A Powerful Intention!!! Read On!!!

Intention:

> I intend to be whole physically, mentally, spiritually and emotionally, and I ask for every benevolent energetic force to aid me in this process, to expedite my wholeness.
>
> I intend to be free of every influence and or attachment that impedes my sovereignty.
>
> I intend to heal all wounds and access points with the understanding that the release of emotional currency through them only fills the banks of those that seek to keep me in a cycle of breakdown, rather than breakthrough.
>
> I intend for the cessation of every genetic and non-genetic influence that has, with my conscious and unconscious participation, kept my wounds from healing.
>
> I intend that every cycle within my network of neural pathways that has kept me in an unhealthy state be broken, and that the time for manipulating my emotions come to an END.

So be it!

16:275 Are You Predictive?

Are you predictive?

Do you have a predictive mentality?

Do you make decisions based on pain from the past that set a quantum pattern and mandate for your future?

You are more powerful than you think.

We are taught to calculate, to weigh and to measure. We are predictive in nature, and this nature will govern our lives, if left unchecked. Then we end up a product of our own fears and unforgiveness.

Live now.

Presently.

Like you have never been hurt.

16:276 Non-physical Voices

A message to a friend this morning about non-physical voices out there ...

There are a whole lot of voices out there that want a chance to speak, and to be heard, that are not presently physical. I believe there are both light and dark energies that are helping to create and maintain this present age where the knowledge of good and evil flourishes.

I am sure there is a wide variety of celestial beings beyond our world that communicate, as well. In Christianity, I was taught that we (according to OT passages) are not to seek them out through the use of mediums; but what about directly? I believe that consciousness at that point in time was immature – fledgling, if you will – and not ready for such information. Now, it seems I am much more allowing and discerning and able to hear for myself. I ask and intend that only those voices that have my highest and best purpose in mind may speak – in dreams, visions, visitations, etc. I set my intention for benevolent voices; ones that will bring me what I need on this step on my evolutionary ladder in consciousness. Messengers are all around us, and more importantly, within us.

Jacob, with his head on the rock (revealed knowledge), saw angels ascending and descending upon the ladder (translations suggest a spiral ladder) that I believe to be our DNA molecule. Jacob said, "Surely God is HERE, and I did not KNOW it."

Jacob means "supplanter" - one who wrongfully or illegally seizes and holds the place of another. Usurper. Offender (THE EGO!) The EGO does not KNOW that Divinity is within the biology!

Jacob, as he wrestles with the messenger (angel), has his hip joint touched, walks away with a limp, and has his name changed to Israel. That is us in our processes, coming to the end of self-life (ego) and transitioning into our godhood.

16:277 Swallowing the Hook

Yes, the journey out from fundamentalism allows us to tap into the information that we know, somehow, has always been there. It takes a lot of fear to compound a false doctrine into our consciousness and over the truth.

It is not easy to learn false doctrine, so it must be reinforced with lots of fear ... like a gap that forms in the fabric of our consciousness ... and the threads of falsehood are woven into us.

Some of the concepts that we have been taught have some truth within them, so it becomes more palatable to swallow the hook; like the concept of being saved ...

We must save the body, but it is not about going to Heaven when we die – it is about recognizing that we exist in hell, now, in this dimension of decay, where the human condition suffers daily from a perception that we are separate from the Divine. And because reality is formed from our perception, we live as mortal beings in a prison built by our own doing.

> *John 1:1 In the beginning was the Word, and the Word was with God, and the Word was God. 2The same was in the beginning with God. 3All things were made by him; and without him was not anything made that was made. 4In him was life; and the life was the light of men. 5And the light shineth in darkness; and the darkness comprehended it not.*

We see Christ as an external savior; whereas, in fact, we have Christ within, and we were with God in the beginning. This is the knowledge of union that Jesus spoke of and prayed that we would see our "oneness." The darkness is the ego that did not comprehend the light that shines within us.

"All things were made by him ..." We create our own reality and live within the walls of our prison, seeing ourselves as victims rather than participants.

It is time for the understanding of our oneness with the Divine. It is time to see that we are co-creators of our lives. It is time to understand that we have preordained our awakening through difficulty – that we awaken and learn obedience through the things we suffer.

> *Hebrews 5:8 7During the days of Jesus' life on earth, he offered up prayers and petitions with loud cries and tears to the one who could save him from death, and he was heard because of his reverent submission. 8Although he was a son, he learned obedience from what he suffered 9and, once made perfect, he became the source of eternal salvation for all who obey him 10and was designated by God to be high priest in the order of Melchizedek.*

Jesus is the pattern of divinity couched in humanhood; us. Therefore, we must see his life as a pattern, a Melchizedek Priest who came to show us the way to the Father; that creative force that lies within all men. As he is Melchizedek, an immortal being, so are we ...

16:278 Gotta Love

A popular country song has the lyrics, "Gotta love like there is no such thing as a broken heart." I heard this song, and specifically these lyrics, play over and over as I was waking up and simultaneously remembering my bad dream.

There is a position of the heart where it is allowed to love untethered.

It is free from expectation.

It is free from standards.

It is free from ideals.

It is free from hurt.

It just gets to love without the condition that love gets returned to it.

This is a place of freedom.

This love beats with pure positive energy, free from the limiting straps of the ego, the voice that says, "I will love you, but you must first do this for me – you must tend to me first."

There is a place of abandon. To love without condition.

It is unconditional love.

It gets to romp and to play in the fields that this beautiful world creates and allows.

Untethered. Unstuck in the ego's plots and schemes, this love finds a way around obstruction and returns to the free flow of untarnished energy.

Who can you display this kind of love to today?

Is there someone who is undeserving, according to your ego? Let's dismiss the ego from its role as protector of the heart and run with the throttle to the floor. Let's let it do what it was created to do without the governance of self-protection and like there is no such thing as a broken heart.

It is a fearless heart.

Be fearless with your love.

16:279 God is Not an American

Our consciousness is always on the move.

Consider, for a moment: 200,000 years ago, we became conscious of our "familial unit".

Then we became conscious of our "tribe".

Then, region.

Then regional boundaries.

Then, around 3115 BC, we became aware of "nations".

We have been in a national cycle ever since. And we have had WAR over our national boundaries, physical and cultural.

The next logical conscious awareness is "global."

We will recognize that we are ONE PEOPLE.

With this in mind, and with the knowledge that the old always resists the new, how do you think transitioning into global consciousness will occur?

What do you think those with a nationalist mindset will do when their "borders" are threatened?

This is not something new. It is as old as time itself.

Each new crop of humans will go through this evolutionary process in consciousness.

Hence my statement, "God is not an American."

16:280 A Beautiful Quote by Ken Carey

> *"You must leap naked into eternity's promise, stripped of the assurances of time, certain only that the vast benevolence that has given birth to the universe is more worthy of trust than the belief-system deities of the historical order."*

This quote from Chapter 10 page 89 pierced my heart, my soul, my spirit.

Get the book. *The Third Millennium* by Ken Carey

16:281 Imagine

From John Lennon's *Imagine*:

> *Imagine there's no Heaven*
> *It's easy if you try*
> *No Hell below us*
> *Above us only sky*
> *Imagine all the people living for today*
>
> *Imagine there's no countries*
> *It isn't hard to do*
> *Nothing to kill or die for*
> *And no religion too*
> *Imagine all the people living life in peace*
>
> *You, you may say I'm a dreamer,*
> *but I'm not the only one*
> *I hope someday you'll join us*
> *And the world will be as one*
>
> *Imagine no possessions*
> *I wonder if you can*
> *No need for greed or hunger*
> *A brotherhood of man*
> *Imagine all the people sharing all the world*
>
> *You, you may say I'm a dreamer,*
> *but I'm not the only one*
> *I hope someday you'll join us*
> *And the world will live as one*

Truly a man before his time. The consciousness of the world was not ready for such a one. Are you ready now?

There is no Heaven *"out there" somewhere.* Jesus said, "The kingdom of Heaven is within you." If this is true, then there is nothing to be right about, no expansive place where only those who believe like you will be.

There are many mansions in the Father's house. Where is the Father's house? Where does the Father dwell? In you, beloved, and in you are many dimensions – mansions. Heavens.

There is no physical Hell below us. It is a state of consciousness, of depravity. It is where we dwell when we fail to see who and what we are and that is ONE WITH THE FATHER! The Father is the source of all, the PROGENITOR. It is a principle of creation that is WITHIN YOU.

Imagine living for today – no fear of tomorrow. Jesus said, "Be anxious for nothing."

Imagine there are no countries. There will come an appointed time when nationalism will cease, and we will recognize our oneness. Consciousness will expand into globalism and beyond.

Nothing to kill or die for. Jesus said, "Let he who is without sin cast the first stone"

No religion. No structures built and sustained by the ego within man to know and to apprehend that which is unknowable to the mind. Jesus said, "The God who made the world and everything in it is the Lord of Heaven and Earth and does not live in temples built by human hands."

Imagine no possessions, no hunger. Jesus said, "And they had all things in common."

Imagine a brotherhood of man. Jesus said, "I in them and you in me – so that they may be brought to complete unity."

John Lennon was truly a man before his time.

And he was assassinated, as well.

Consciousness crucifies what it does not understand.

It kills what it is threatened by.

The ego does not recognize that it is ONE with GOD.

Until it does, it will be threatened by anything that does not support its view of things.

And there will be war.

Until.

16:282 A Letter to Christianity

Remember Jesus rebuking the Pharisees for their inability to see their own hypocrisy? They enforced the law of their religion past its season of relevance, while Jesus introduced them to grace. He told the people that if they saw him, they have seen the Father, and he prayed that they, too, would one day see their equality with the Father.

The religious sought ways to trap him, rather than to listen to him.

They could not see their equality with God because they saw this Father as "GOD," the tyrant from the Old Testament. They failed to see that Jesus was introducing all of humanity to a radical shift in thinking and perceiving the creator.

What Christianity fails to see is that this was a pattern that Jesus was setting as the "pattern son". This is exactly what is happening as certain individuals are speaking and teaching of "oneness."

You have worked diligently to "earn" your place in Heaven by believing and doing all the right things, as they are defined by your individual religion or religious sect. You are threatened because … you might just be wrong.

At midnight, you might be caught saying, "But Father, I have worked since sunrise and these have only worked since 11:00 PM and you are paying them the same??? That is not fair!!!"

As you are threatened, you call those who speak the SAME MESSAGE AS JESUS "deceived, antichrist, and of Satan." Ugh. In general, Jesus was called the same.

Jesus said, "*I am the way, the truth and the life and no one comes to the Father but by me.*"

You may have interpreted "the way" as raising your hand at an altar call, reciting the sinner's prayer and walking an aisle and accepting Jesus onto your heart (all not scriptural, by the way), rather than letting your need to be right GO and surrendering to love and non-judgment, as was the "WAY" of Jesus!

Miracles abound, inside and outside of Christianity, because the benevolent being of the universe; this "Father," does not choose sides and does not withhold. It is a powerful creative force WITHIN YOU (the "father" means "progenitor," which is at the source of ALL created things) that does not keep score, and certainly will not torture anyone for non-compliance, especially with a religion that does not emulate the teachings of Christ to begin with.

And of Hell? There is a Hell, and this is it.

Oh! The absurdity of it all.

For the love of Christ, wake up, Christianity!

16:283 What is Figurative in The Bible and What is Not?

Roughly six thousand years ago, when the golden calf was destroyed, was it a sign in the heavens for the passing of the Age of Taurus (Taurus is the bull)? This was where and when Taurus was prominent, yet passing in the eastern sky, at the precession of the equinox.

Roughly four thousand years ago, when the ram was caught in the thicket, was it a symbol of the Age of Aries (The Ram)? This was where and when Aries was prominent, yet passing in the eastern sky, at the precession of the equinox.

Did Jonah really get swallowed by a great fish, or is that figurative language that points to the human learning obedience to the voice of "God" during the coming Age of Pisces (Pisces meaning "fish")?

Then, two thousand years later, there was so much symbolism during the advent of Christ with fish, including becoming fishers of men, the Ichthus (symbol of the fish), feeding the thousands with two fish and five loaves, finding silver (the symbol of redemption) inside the fish's mouth. This is where and when Pisces was prominent in the eastern sky, at the precession of the equinox.

Two thousand years ago, when Jesus asked the disciples to follow the man bearing the pitcher of water, was he referring to the coming Age of Aquarius (Aquarius is the celestial sign for the "Water bearer," a person holding and pouring out water from a pitcher)? They were asking Jesus where to celebrate the Passover which, as you know, is where the firstborn does not have to die (this alludes to immortality). What is this firstborn? Is it, metaphorically, our flesh? Was Jesus giving us a hint of what was to come during the now present Age of Aquarius, two thousand years later?

The Bible is FILLED with metaphor, and if we take it literally, we miss the mystery. Contained within the mystery is the resurrection from the dead that is humanity no longer subject to death. Jesus told us to "lift our eyes, for the fields are ripe with harvest" (harvest means completed work). These mysteries are available to us NOW, but only if we LIFT our eyes and see the mysteries hidden in plain sight.

We determine these mysteries through the intuitive mind, the Mind of Christ. "Let this mind be in you ..."

16:284 I Struggle ...

I struggle to understand the emotions that come when I see people practicing fundamentalism from my past church life. Part of me is so thankful to be out of the system that includes mind and thought control, and when I see others in the system, I see myself as I once was.

I feel for Barbara, as she acquiesced to a systematic and religious approach to knowing and longing to fit in. I feel for the many times that, as truth rose up within her to say, "This isn't the path," she swallowed hard to silence the voice, choosing instead to follow blindly.

I feel a loss for the years and decades spent serving a system, belonging, climbing.

I feel remorse.

I feel hurt and anger for those who reject me still; those who said they loved me but, in reality, only loved me if I agreed with them, believed like them. With very few exceptions, they have not modeled to me the one they hold in high esteem.

No, I am not over this, but I am getting better, feeling better and more resolute as I experience true love void of religious insistence.

I think this is all part of the process of dying to the former things so that we may one day completely shed the old. My hope is to do so gracefully.

After all, when you really think about it, isn't this what Jesus did? He broke free from the established religious order. We are to do the same and greater!

16:285 Noah's Ark

Noah means: "rest" or "repose"
Ark means: "beginning; origin; Christ; curves; bows"

Not thinking it to be a literal story, I wondered what is/was Noah's Ark?

I asked this question years ago, in a meditative state of sorts, and I heard that Noah's Ark is a metaphor for the DNA molecule that holds all of creation within it, masculine and feminine species alike.

As the biblical story goes, the Earth was filled with evil inhabitants, so God told Noah to build an ark and to put a male and female of every species within it.

There was a time of "rest" when the Earth was cleansed of impurity by deluge (water represents consciousness), and so we see that the Earth was "flooded". That elevated the "ark" above the waters, or consciousness, if you will. Remember, Jesus walked upon the water, which symbolized a higher state of consciousness, and bid us to do the same.

The Earth's nonhuman inhabitants were spared this type of ethnic cleansing, as the structural DNA was preserved in a state of "rest" or "repose."

Eight was the number of humans supposedly aboard the ark in this story, and eight is the number of new beginnings.

Animals represent emotions and manifest in biological form to reflect to us our nature.

This probably spurs more questions than answers, but for what it's worth, it will make you think.

16:286 Metamorphosis

I watched a short video on the metamorphosis of a caterpillar to a butterfly. When the caterpillar is in its cocooned state, the inside turns into a rich nutrient soup and it actually digests itself.

Isn't that interesting, as we draw a parallel to our own journey to awakening? I am sure I have digested my issues time and time again, consuming, swallowing my own pain, trauma and all the emotions that accompany it. And it seems, at times, that the damn process never ends. These emotions need to be consumed; our pain body devoured until there is nothing left of it, of suffering.

The odd thing is, that as long as we entertain desire, we will have pain and we will suffer. Like the image of the ouroboros.

> *The ouroboros is an ancient symbol depicting a serpent or dragon eating its own tail. Originating in Ancient Egyptian iconography, the ouroboros entered western tradition via Greek magical tradition and was adopted as a symbol in Gnosticism and Hermeticism, and most notably in alchemy. Via medieval alchemical tradition, often taken to symbolize introspection, the eternal return or cyclicality, especially in the sense of something constantly recreating itself. It also represents*

> *the infinite cycle of nature's endless creation and destruction, life and death.*
>
> Taken from *Wikipedia*

So, it is with us; as we journey within, we become the image of the ouroboros, consuming, digesting and recreating ourselves.

16:287 There Are Two of Me

There are two of me.

There are two of you.

There is a struggle between these two as a shift in power is imminent.

My nature is being changed as I see my humanity begin to yield to my Divinity.

One moment I struggle in human affairs in an attempt to hold my place in the way things ought to be.

I try to set boundaries for self-preservation.

The next moment I see things from above, from a view beyond the ego's perch.

And I see all attempts at self-preservation as vain, and choose, instead, to forgive and to love, regardless of my right to self-justify.

And I have peace.

And the clock ticks by an hour or so, and there I am, again, perched as the governor of my soul.

Observing injustices and being offended and hurt.

What is going on?

Jacob is struggling with the Divine messenger, and in the struggle is being defined; Jacob's name will change from "supplanter" (one that seizes the place of another – our ego as it has assumed the role as master of the human, the snake in the garden) to Israel (IS-RA-EL) or "May God prevail; He struggles with God; God perseveres; contends."

I keep on seeing the scales of balance in my mind's eye, and I am recognizing that we are in the midst of the battle for our eternal lives, as the old man (our ego-centric mind) seeks to maintain its place yet must ultimately yield to its counterweight, as more and more clout is added to tip the scales in favor of the Divine mind.

Jacob, as his name is changed to Israel, comes away from the struggle with an impediment – a wounded hip where the messenger touches him in the midst of the wrestle. Could the hips be representative of the scales of balance? And in the struggle, the scales are tipped in favor of the Divine identity?

The struggle is real.

16:288 Breathing Deeply

Today is a day for breathing deeply. There is a lot of negativity in the energetic fields that will lead us to an epic paradox in the collective consciousness. We will come face to face with the adversary, that great Satan that resides within.

Be a screen door, not a storm door. Jesus said, "Resist not evil," for in our resistance comes a strengthening to all we oppose.

In your allowing is buoyancy.

In your resisting, there is sinking.

Rise above the mundane and see, maybe for the first time, your supreme role in the play.

You choose to continue in your role

Or to withdraw from the fray.

Like the Samaritan that lies battered and bloody on the roadside, the Christ within will emerge in your surrender.

SECTION SEVENTEEN

SEVENTEEN

17:289 Time an Illusion?

No illusion here. A learning environment? Yes.

The mind is powerful and sustains and creates reality as we know it. We have exercised a willful dalliance into "time" produced by celestial movement. The celestial movement by design ... ours ... that produces days, weeks, months and years.

Not only do we find ourselves within the terrarium of planetary existence, but we created the solar system and beyond, from which to learn the mechanics associated with TIME.

We simply cannot deny time's existence while we live within it. Our purpose is to finish the syllabus that time employs without denying its purpose. Rather, we should understand the will behind the exercise.

I often describe our dalliance within the framework of time like an English-speaking person dropped off in Mexico for a Spanish immersion course.

As you may know, the student is left with a Spanish-speaking family that will only speak Spanish to the student. It is sink or swim – the student must learn how to live and communicate in an environment that is foreign to them.

And, so it is with us, the new creation that is both celestial and terrestrial, willfully immersed into the doctrine of humanhood. The celestial is vibrationally lulled to sleep and is baptized, or immersed, into flesh and blood, and left there to grow within its framework. The biology is, likewise, inoculated with celestial DNA.

As this "mustard seed" of celestial DNA grows, the mind of man decreases, and the mind of the universe takes over this bio-celestial garden. And we awaken.

17:290 Leap!

There is no limit to the love of our creator, and this love DOES NOT COME WITH CONDITIONS.

There is no prayer that needs to be recited, nor is there a church that needs to be attended. There is no tithe to be paid. If you want to give, give to the local homeless shelter or any of the other dozens of opportunities out there. Don't give to a church that pays a pastor, a mortgage, rent or utilities. If you need a Biblical example, doing such is not scriptural, no matter how you interpret it. If you desire fellowship, look for people that meet in the rent-free locations, like outdoors in nature, on the mountainsides, or in homes. That is the pattern.

There is no Hell to be threatened with by this creator – absolutely not. The doctrines that most evangelical Christians believe is simply not true. Take the time to investigate for yourself. Please.

Do not attempt to convert another person with your belief system; just love people. It is not required that someone believe like you. No, it is not. They must believe in themselves. Yes, in themselves. Christ is growing inside of humanity and it is this mystery that must be understood. Paul said it like this:

> Galatians 4:19 *"My dear children, for whom I am again in the pains of childbirth until Christ is formed in you ..."*

To try to convert someone to your particular brand of Christianity is no better than those described here:

> Matthew 23:15 *"What sorrow awaits you teachers of religious law and you Pharisees. Hypocrites! For you cross land and sea to make one convert, and then you turn that person into twice the child of Hell you yourselves are!"*

Somewhere along the line, Christianity hijacked this concept and distorted it by threatening people with eternal torture in fire or Hell, damnation and separation. But in reality, there is NO THING that can separate you from the love of the Creator. The only thing that can separate you is your thinking that you are separate. (Romans 8:38-39) Not even your concepts of eternal punishment are accurate which by the way isn't eternal at all if it is cast into the lake of fire… (Revelation 20:14)

Hell is simply this: The belief in the knowledge of good and evil, the "tree" we are told not to eat from. It is from the belief in evil that we have it, for what we focus upon, we create! We are told to think on things that are pure and lovely and to take every thought captive. As fundamentalist Christians, you may very well be creating the hellish world that plagues us.

Wake up, Christianity. Your slumber is over!

It is time to LEAP!

17:291 Regarding Programming

It is a process to come out from any form of legalism, especially fundamentalism, because of the repetitive nature of the indoctrination process. Fundamentalism employs programming through repetition that helps reinforce dogmatic principles, establishing neural pathways in the brain with threats of separation or damnation.

A couple of examples are:

Calling the Bible "The word of God"

Stating that belief in Jesus is the only way to gain entrance to Heaven (this means raising your hand and accepting Jesus into your heart as your personal Lord and Savior and being baptized).

ANY study on the scripture alone will reveal the above two items as erroneous, but because they are repeated with enthusiasm and consensus, they are adopted into their library as "truth."

It is insidious. This is why we see "knee-jerk" responses by those fundamentalists who are threatened by anything outside of their established dogmatic order. I can predict, with accuracy, what a fundamentalist will quote from their dogma or scripture in response to a given challenge. I can do this because I was one of them. It has taken me since 1999 to deprogram.

Scripture says (isn't it ironic that I quote scripture?) over 600 times to "Fear not; be of good courage," and yet most of the 38,000 to 41,000 differing and disagreeing Christian denominations are based on fear. I think the phrase "spiritually healthy fear" might be a bit of an oxymoron. Fear is the lowest frequency (if you will) in our emotional spectrum. I had to decide long ago that one cannot overcome deception with fear.

If you are challenging your doctrinally enforced beliefs, I think you are in a very good place. It is a part of most spiritual paths to overcome fear and to learn to listen to your own spiritual guidance (the Holy Spirit).

Here is another scripture: "There will come a time when no man will teach you ..." I believe this is because we are leaving the age of the institutional church (as was the pattern of the Christ) and what we are learning is not taught, because it is no longer an intellectual and egocentric path (left-brained).

We are now learning, sojourning into the intuited worlds of spirit (right-brained). This is the "single eye" that Jesus spoke of.

Trust your inner voice. Follow love, joy, peace, kindness. You will find your way.

17:292 Having Dominion Over the Earth

Having dominion over the "Earth" has been a necessary baptism into the dynamics of creating the material world.

We create by judging and discerning between light and dark/good and evil.

Judgment is the driving factor.

It is the substance that holds this dimension together because it is a decree that comes from the Divine and, what the Divine decrees, IS.

Judgment tethers us to the world where there is a time limit on our creating – including ourselves; and so, we have death, disease, rust, rot, mold and mildew.

There comes a time, however, where judgment must rest, so that the creation may become buoyant and transition out from this school and is thrust between dimensions.

A new place of abiding is created by the focus of emotional currency that has accrued in our dalliance on Earth.

This currency is potent vibrational substance that we may access with memory of our painful or joyful experiences.

Without judgment, that is, with forgiveness, we access the currency without lien, without being tethered to time and mortality.

It is our Earthly escrow account that is made up of the treasures of darkness – our experiences as mortal beings.

It is said, then, that He (the Christ) learned "obedience" (the dynamics that govern the propelling of emotional currency) by the things that HE suffered.

All serves. Pain is the shortest path to learning. To be mortal and to have the GIFT of pain is to have one of the greatest treasures in the Universe.

17:293 The 12 are Gathered

There is a gathering of the twelve disciples and the Christ in the upper room.

The upper room is your heightened state of consciousness.

The twelve are aspects of your multidimensional self that exist in the energetic atmosphere around you. They each serve you in different ways.
From time to time they are gathered.

They are ministered to.

Their feet are washed (symbolizing the removal of evidence of our earthly incarnation).

When they gather, you may feel an energetic upheaval in your body, for this upper room is within you.

You must begin to see that the scriptures are mystical occurrences of divine providence taking place within you NOW, not historical circumstances that occurred in times past.

Ask. Seek. Knock. You have all the answers that you need.

17:294 I'm So in Love!

I'M SO IN LOVE with this BRAVE HUMAN. I've betrayed you. I've not loved you as I should have. I've fed you lies and told you that you weren't good enough.

I've allowed you to be broken. I've watched you run through brick walls and battle for others who, when the time came, would not stand up for you. I couldn't stop individuals that believed the lies from abandoning you, yet I've seen you stand to be a light to the world and to love others, despite it all.

I have watched you issue apologies and forgiveness to those undeserving.

I've stood paralyzed by fear as you faced the loss of reputation alone – I watched you fight for the truth to win out, and I watched you fight for your life when it didn't.

Forgive me for not going to war for you, like you do for others. You are a warrior. A WARRIOR. You are WORTHY, indeed.

You inspire me to transform, as you have. Believe in me, I beg you, even when I have not believed in you!

You are UNSTOPPABLE, yet gracefully broken and standing... still. You are love. You are life. You demonstrate transformation, as I have watched you rise from the ashes again and yet again. I am now a believer, as I have seen resurrection with my own eyes.

With deepest admiration,
You.

17:295 About Men and Women

It has never been about men and women.

It is about masculine and feminine energy.

You have to separate your judgments from the truth of what men and women represent.

You cannot be sensitive, claiming misogyny or misandry.

It is not about your form or your genitals.

We appear as male and female to demonstrate physically, with physical characteristics and functions, MYSTERIES that CANNOT be seen with physical eyes. Men and women represent something mystical, hidden and unseen.

Masculine energy is the seed-giver, the source of all living and human creation, but cannot be successful in its creating without a FORM to pour into. In our physical description, this form is called the WOMB-man or woman.

IT IS NOT ABOUT MEN AND WOMEN, for masculine and feminine energies are innate within all humans!!!!

It is about your ability to RECEIVE from the MASCULINE and to INCUBATE what you RECEIVE within the FEMININE.

OUR PHYSICAL EXAMPLES ARE THERE FOR US TO LEARN THE MYSTERIES OF CREATING.

And learn, we will!

The mysteries are hidden in plain sight, in all of creation.

We are living metaphors.

17:296 Approaching the Holidays

Dear Christian,

Jesus was not born on December 25th.

The world celebrates his coming in December, because it is an astrological sign in the heavens that has been happening for millions, if not billions, of years.

Because of this, many other "saviors" have been said to have been born December 25th.

There is a celestial event that is seen in the northern hemisphere of our planet. June 21st, the summer solstice, is the longest day of the year. Our Sun is at its zenith (so to speak), as this is the longest day of the year.

As the days, weeks, months and seasons progress, the Sun's southward movement in the sky shortens the daylight until, on December 21st, it stops its southward trek. This is the shortest and darkest day of the year. It remains unmoving to the physical eye for approximately three days.

While in this motionless state, it rests with the constellation named "The Southern Cross" as its backdrop.

Then, after three days, it begins its northward trek again, until it reaches its zenith, once again, on June 21st.

This is why it is said that the Sun (son) "died on the cross and, after three days, rose again."

In reality, this isn't the story of many different saviors throughout our planet's history. It is your story.

You are the celestial and shining being, the Son, that reaches your zenith on the Earth. You shine brightly with your sense of self, only to realize that you must decrease so that the divine spark that animates your being may increase.

This is death to self; not physical, but rather, a figurative death to self, selfishness, self-ambition and self-serving. This part of your egocentric nature must yield to the part of you that is selfless.

In so doing, YOU RISE, like a phoenix from the ashes, and you fulfill your destiny as the coming Messiah – the one that can save.

This is your immortally joined self with God. It is the coming of the babe that is birthed in the stable of your very own flesh and blood. Mary – not a singular woman, but all of mankind; her name meaning "wished for child."

And isn't that what we wish for? Ultimate union with God? This is the union that produces the Christ within! Isn't this what the teaching of so many illustrate to us as the Bride yields to the Groom? Who is this babe but the rule of the kingdom within? The soul that has died the death, and has experienced the resurrection, has come.

Joy to the world, the Lord is come! Let Earth receive her King.

17:297 Judgment is Circular

At the end of the day I am convinced of three things:

1. Judgment is circular. In the words of Jesus, "Judge not, lest the judgment with which you judge another fall on your own head."

   This tells me that if I judge another, I may be found guilty (of generally the same thing) at some point in my life (whether I committed the act or not).

   I have experienced enough of this to know this as true. "What you sow, so also shall you reap. God is not mocked." This tells me that I sow (the universal and creative power within me) continually into the receptive universal field of probability every day. I must be a vigilant gatekeeper of my thoughts and actions. "Take every thought captive."

2. We are the God that is not mocked. This creative potential within answers the vibrational codes that we transmit every day. It is law. We create what we focus upon and provide the emotional currency to back the request.

3. If the above two are true, then I must, as an awakening being, choose love and non-judgment, as these two are "keys" (vibrational codes) that will create more of the same. If I really want to dethrone the powers of darkness, then I must BE LIGHT.

17:298 The Most Profound Truth

Christians have the most profound truth.

They have Adam and Eve.
They have the Garden of Eden.
They have the ark that helped them escape the great flood.

They have Moses and the Red Sea crossing.
They have all the great kings in scripture.
They have the Holy of Holies and the Ark of the Covenant.
They have Melchizedek (the immortal priest).
They have the Promised Land.
They have a Savior that resurrected from the dead.
They have the keys to Hell and Death.
They have the seven scrolls in Revelation.
They have Heaven.

What they don't have, is an understanding that all of these things are within them.

17:299 An Ultra-Dimensional Being

Do you believe in a story of a babe born in a manger, or have you apprehended a knowing that you are this babe?

You are an ultra-dimensional being, having been born into a body, into the manger of humanity.

You are wrapped, like a gift, in the swaddling clothing of flesh and blood. And oh, what a gift it is!

You will incarnate for thousands of years, returning again and again, remaining in this realm of death and decay, until the time of resurrection. It is said, the Son died on the cross and descended (the intersection of mortality and immortality), and on the third day rose again… and again, and again.

This immortal being, making himself subject to death and picking up the cross, dies daily.

It is time to awaken, oh sleeper! Remember who you are! You have no bounds, and the grave clothes of mortality cannot keep you in restriction. Wake up and set them aside.

17:300 Religion Says, "Go to Church."

Religion says, "Go to church"
Spirituality says, "You are the church."

Religion says, "You are a sinner."
Spirituality says, "You are perfect and complete."

Religion says, "You must accept Jesus as your personal Lord and Savior."
Spirituality says, "You are the Christ."

Religion says, "You must be baptized in order to be saved."
Spirituality says, "You must remember your journey into human consciousness, and now it is time to come up and out of those waters."

Religion says, "You must eat the body of Jesus and drink his blood."
Spirituality says, "You partake in the nature of Christ every day that you are human yet practice unconditional love and non-judgment."

If you choose to take the literal bread and wine, you do this to remember the journey from immortality into mortality, being swallowed up of death. Into this limited mortal realm, you travel, as the broken bread slides down your throat (the grave) into the belly.

You are Jonah swallowed up of the great fish during this last and passing age of Pisces (the FISH). This is where you have learned obedience to the voice of Divinity, the voice that is awakening, the voice that you are.

Oh! Ye God-men! Awaken!

All of the Bible is symbolic, but most take it literally. There are mysteries hidden in plain sight within the scriptures.

We are told that in order to be "saved" we must be baptized – so Christians practice the ritual of baptism, rather than seeking to understand what baptism MAY REPRESENT figuratively.

So, we have to look at the ritual, but also at what it means to be "saved".

Being saved cannot mean that we go to Heaven when we die, because we are told, "the kingdom of Heaven is within you."

Being saved has everything to do with our mortal state that has been in place since we partook in eating of the tree of the knowledge of good and evil. So now, we must understand what eating the fruit from that tree means. I believe it is simply this: we live by the subtle voice of the serpent; that is, the EGO – the voice within that, if followed, makes us self-serving, selfish and, according to Genesis 6, causes us to "fall" down from Eden (immortality) into mortality, as it says that, "Man is now mortal and his years will now be limited to 120."

Being saved means to commute the death sentence of our lifespans being limited to 120.

Vibrationally speaking, we ascend up from death to life.

Baptism – human consciousness, where we are ego-driven and self-centered – is symbolized by the waters. Whenever we see water in scriptural and other ancient texts, it is representative of how humans think, believe and are aware of.

So, in the ritual of baptism, we see a divine essence lowering itself, and immersed in the waters of being mortal and HUMAN, holding its divine breath until the time of awakening and coming up and out of the waters of dense and limited human consciousness (selfishness). This ritual serves to remind us of this human (and divine) journey.

Along the way, Divinity that dwells within all of us is having a quite human experience within the framework of us, and at the end of the journey, will accrue for itself a helpmate in the form of a physical body from which it may continue to experience the material worlds.

This amalgamation of God and man is called EMMANUEL (God with man).

17:301 The Ego

The ego is the mechanism through which we discern, and ultimately experience, reality.

In terms of conflict I read this quote by Justin Cohen:

> *"The course of conflict is not determined by who initiates it, but by who responds to it."*

The ego interprets the offending criteria and responds to it, thereby inflaming or neutralizing the offense.

Therefore, the ego is creative and creates reality.

The EGO is in charge of ALL emotions. It will distribute the energy from them at will. Therefore, the WILL is what needs adjustment.

I guess the ego has been given a bad rap; not necessarily by the scriptures, but by semi-modern psychologists who ascribe attributes to it.

Human beings can be selfish, arrogant, and self-serving. These are character traits. So are love, patience, benevolence and kindness. The ego has been given the task to oversee all things human.

Think of it this way: a plantation owner buys slaves and mistreats them. His task is to bring the harvest in. He needs slaves to accomplish this great feat. He feeds them, houses them, tends to their basic needs, and sometimes violently beats them. A horrible, deplorable role to play. Now, it is inhuman to own slaves – even ridiculous. We, as Americans, look down on nations that still employ slaves (some slaves are indentured, just because they are women).

The role of those that were tasked to bring in the harvest has changed. And, so has the thrust of that aspect of us that oversees. That is metaphorically what the ego does. It oversees.

In this story, as time moved on, the ego yielded to the change in our national consciousness. Soon it became illegal to own slaves. It may be said that this "master" was ruthless, violent, unrelenting and self-serving, but it may also be noted that he may have been seen as a great plantation owner who was a shrewd businessman, a faithful husband, and a loving father to his children. Such is the task of the ego.

Many things change over the years, and their meaning lost in modern interpretations. For example, steeples are now identifiable with the Christian church, but hundreds of years ago, were the standard for pagan cites, as they symbolized fertility (the penis).

As Christianity spread, the pagan cites were taken over by Christians, but the architecture remained in place. So did other practices, like priests wearing robes, the altar, Christmas and Easter.

My point being, that as time marches on, sometimes like moss on a stone, time will add to and take away from the truth of a concept. We must all be malleable to return to truth.

17:302 Are We to Do Away with the Ego?

No. Getting rid of the ego is akin to "putting away a wife." This is why it is said that divorce is forbidden. It is not human marriage that the scripture eludes to, but rather, this mystical union – and not forbidden. as much as it is impossible. But the metaphor stands as a symbol.

The union of ego (human self) and the Divine is a purposeful union and, once joined, will never separate. "Two walking, one disappears, one is left" is not what we have been told. Jesus was speaking a mystery of the two, inseparable, becoming one. In order for the Divine to navigate through the material, physical worlds, it needs a helpmate that has been fully exercised in discerning between good and evil and is acquainted with the manufacture and distribution of emotions and their currency.

The ego, however, must submit to this mystical marriage. There is no such thing as a forced marriage in the kingdom. The two are joined, and the ego is cleansed of its impurities.

As in the pattern of Queen Esther, she boldly enters the king's chambers under threat of death, but he welcomes her and says, "Ask anything, up to half of my kingdom," because they are EQUAL partners.

Her request?

To spare her people from imminent death at the hands of Haman's gallows.

Who are "her" people?

We are. The human race.

17:303 As We Enter the New Year

I feel the need to send a message to you; yes, *you*.

Please take a good long look at yourself in the mirror after you read this.

Yes, you are lovely in all of your humanness. Look how your eyes give testimony of a life well lived. Even those times that were so hard; see, they have added a subtle beauty to you.

It is time you know the truth of who you are. You are me. Yes, Divinity is what peers out through your eyes to meet the world. I have been wrapped in the wonderment of your body – it is glorious and remarkably perfect. I want you, for one moment, to see how loved you are; the kind of love that is bereft of anything compromising or shallow. Feel, for a moment, the way I feel about you, being inside of you, living life through you. You have not made one false step; yes, everything has had purpose, great purpose, even though this is difficult for you to fathom. No regrets, oh, love of mine! No regrets.

You are experiencing your morning stretch as you awaken from your dream. We are ready to take on this world, to dismantle the norm of judgment and emotions run amok. We will conquer fear and death together – you are highly endowed, unlike any other creation – oh, my human love! Together we will eclipse the age dawning new, as we shed the conscious containment of the past. Only you and I together can do this – for in union, there is power.

See for a moment, will you, what I see in you. Your beauty overcomes me! I love you, my tender dove, and I always will.

17:304 Standing in the ER

I remember standing in the ER waiting room where my son was undergoing amputation of his badly damaged leg. His arm had already been severed at the wreck.

I was somehow transported to a "precipice" and told to LEAP. I remember clearly standing there – internally hysterical, yet outwardly calm. And I did leap. And I heard voices speaking to me many mysteries; things I am still digesting, formulating, and assessing.

I had already departed the institutional church a few years before, but now I understood that I would be forever gone, having leapt out from faith and into knowing. And it was a leap. I flew blindly, having had my dome of consciousness, my "normal" fractured by calamity and tragedy.

I write that, during such times, trauma fractures the dome of our reality, allowing it to seep out like a spy, to view a whole new world. And indeed, I am.

I also understand now that I could not see such things if I had remained in resonance with people and systems from this passing age. That was hard, and still is. I think that, while our internal vibration comes into resonance with the age to come, there must be a severing of emotional ties from what we left behind. It is ultimately a merciful thing. For me at least, I needed to grow stronger, and could not with vibrational variance about me.

The separations were enforced ON me mostly, not through me.

Through the years and through the tears, relationships have been redefined, and some refined.

And it's all good.

17:305 Religion is Like the Womb

Religion is like the womb; necessary to bring life until it is no longer life-giving.

And then there is the whole "narrow way" thing.

A baby pushes itself out from the womb along with the forceful contractions of the mother, and then it passes through the narrow way.

Dark, restrictive, crushing.

You will be okay.

17:306 Understanding Masculine and Feminine Energy

The union of masculine and feminine is at the heart of many stories in the Bible: Adam and Eve, Esther and the king, Jesus and the Bride, Boaz and Ruth, Homer and Haggai, are just a few.

This theme is also at the heart of numerous media themes (too many to list), including *Aquaman*.

Uniting the masculine and feminine is simply this: The human mind is feminine (regardless if you are a man or woman). It is the womb-man of creation.

The spirit is masculine. It gives seed to the womb-man in order to create the worlds of matter. This is the function of the Christ, the God-man, the Emmanuel.

We get to union when the feminine (the human mind) YIELDS to its counterpart, receives the seed, and births the new creation that is both God and man.

Yielding consists of turning from selfishness, self-centeredness, ceasing from judgment and moving into unconditional love (which is a natural byproduct of non-judgment). Also necessary is a willingness to appreciate all circumstances, for in appreciation we raise our personal frequency, thereby contributing to the whole of humanity. We become beacons and resonate a frequency that is above, and not below, the norm. This cannot be contrived, as frequency is a natural byproduct of your state of mind.

So, in short, for union we must YIELD – the Spirit will never force itself upon us.

We must cease from judgment, for in ceasing judgment we will cease to create this present age, with all its dilemmas.

When we cease judgment, we begin to build the "bridge" to the age to come. This is a vibrational bridge and cannot be contrived – it is built with LOVE.

As we yield, we become a vibrational match for the Divine seed which, once conceived, will produce the new creation that is both God and Man – Christ.

SECTION EIGHTEEN

EIGHTEEN

18:307 Christianity May Need a Refresher

Christianity may need a refresher course in what Jesus taught his followers:

Love your enemies. Don't repeat disparaging information about them that may or may not be factual.

Visit those in jail, for as you do this to them, you are doing it to me. He didn't say to cheer that they are being put in jail.

He did say, *"Feed the hungry, clothe the naked and tend to the widows and orphans."* He didn't say, "Do this if they follow all the rules and believe like you do…"

He also didn't say to go out and buy a gun. He said, *"Blessed are the peacemakers, for they shall be called sons of God."*

He did not tell us to protect ourselves. He said, *"Therefore I say unto you, take no thought for your life, what ye shall eat, or what ye shall drink; nor yet for your body, what ye shall put on. Is not the life more than meat, and the body than raiment?"*

A needed reminder:

Blessed are the poor in spirit, for theirs is the kingdom of Heaven.

Blessed are those who mourn, for they shall be comforted.

Blessed are the meek, for they shall inherit the Earth.

Blessed are those who hunger and thirst for righteousness, for they shall be satisfied.

Blessed are the merciful, for they shall receive mercy.

Blessed are the pure in heart, for they shall see God.

Blessed are the peacemakers, for they shall be called sons of God.

Blessed are those who are persecuted for righteousness' sake, for theirs is the kingdom of Heaven.

Blessed are you when others revile you and persecute you and utter all kinds of evil against you falsely on my account.

Rejoice and be glad, for your reward is great in Heaven, for so they persecuted the prophets who were before you.

Matthew 4:1-12

18:308 Jonah and the Whale

We know the story: Jonah is swallowed up inside of a great fish, or whale, as some popular translations state.

In Hebrew, the meaning of the name Jonah is "Dove" and dove is symbolic of Spirit.

The Spirit is swallowed up of the great fish.

The great fish is the Age of Pisces (the FISH), during which consciousness would be plunged into darkness (Roughly from 0 AD to 2000 AD).

The Divine Spirit of all that is, is plunged into darkness within the human frame while the human learns to be obedient to the voice within.

It's all metaphor.

If we continue to take these and other Bible scriptures literally, we will miss the mystery of the story.

Be willing to look at things differently. You will then be discharged from the tutelage of man and enter into the school of the Spirit, which knows no denomination, no sect and no dogma.

18:309 Forerunners

Forerunners often receive, incubate and dispense information that may not (yet) be fit for conscious consumption.

If you are a forerunner, then you are used to being shunned by your peers, funny looks, and whispers behind your back. Don't be upset. This is your path. It is the embodiment of the "new wineskin" that Jesus spoke of. It is almost like your mind wears spandex, while mass consciousness wears a corset.

That which is being revealed to you today will be commonplace teaching and understanding 40 years from now. Keep going. Keep speaking. You are laying seed for tomorrow's mighty oaks.

18:310 Ruffling Feathers

Since 1991, I have talked freely about what I felt was revelatory information concerning spiritual things. I ruffled many feathers, including my own, when I spoke of the things I was learning. The information came to me in many forms: through dreams, visions, visitations, study, and through synchronicities. My excitement and zeal were off the charts.

My tribe and circle of friends (Christian fundamentalists) didn't much care for or understand what I was teaching, which began a lot of rumor-spreading, accusations, and judgments, calling me a false teacher and being deceived by the Devil. It really hurt. The only thing I knew how to do was to keep on going, keep speaking what I had been given, even when it seemed to produce nothing but controversy. I had to be true to myself. I spoke of these foundation-rocking views with frequency, and eventually lost the majority of my friends that had been born and nurtured within Christianity.

Fast forward to 2013. I had an old friend come to visit who is still heavily involved in Christian fundamentalism. She chastised me mildly for no longer believing in the Devil or Hell.

I replied, "These things (the Devil and Hell) will appear externally (outside of you), as long as you need them to. But they are just principles of our largely unseen internal landscape. We learn and perceive them to be outside of us, but in reality, they are all inside.

The Devil is our own adversarial thought life (ego) that resists the truth and reality of our identity as I AM, and Hell is the environment we create while we live in and through this adversarial mind. At some point, we experience a divine "inversion", where we begin to understand that all The Bible stories are internal and archetypical, patterning for us our journey in and through our very human experience. At some point, we are all Adam. We are Job. We are Esther. We are King David. We are Mary. We are Christ. We are all of them, expressing to us our own mysterious and evolutionary journey on Earth."

She looked at me for a while, and finally said, "These things you teach will be commonplace forty years from now."

Amidst the ridicule, accusation and heartache, it has been worth it to see literalism abandoned and the groundswell, grasping the figurative meaning of the Bible, take root. There are so many out there who dare to speak the unspeakable. Keep going!

18:311 Do You Pray?

I was recently asked, "Do you pray?" For so many, this is THE question that is asked from those finding themselves within transition – breaking free of the religious expectations found within fundamentalism.

My answer:

I pray 24/7. My definition of prayer has changed, however.

Prayer is active participation found within the principles of the teachings of Christ. So, when Jesus said, "Do not judge," I try my best to live up to that statement. To me that is prayer.

I try my best to care for those within my sphere of influence, and to show love unconditionally. This is an act of prayer, as it demonstrates that I am trying to walk the talk and, most importantly, creates an atmosphere around me. It is "being the change you wish to see."

18:312 Fact-Check

If someone is a Jehovah's Witness, they should not suggest *The Watchtower* Magazine to fact check.

If someone is a Mormon, they should not suggest *The Book of Mormon* to fact check.

If someone is a Republican, they should not suggest someone watch FOX News to fact check.

If someone is a Democrat, they should not suggest someone watch CNN to fact check.

If someone is a Muslim, they should not suggest someone read the Koran to fact check.

Get it?

18:313 Stepford Lives

I have pretty much adopted a "live and let live" attitude toward Christian fundamentalism, but every now and then, the anger – yes, the anger – pokes its head out from somewhere in me.

You might say that I need to forgive … and I feel that forgiveness has come in layers over time. But then I hear of a story of someone being treated poorly within the Church system, and I feel this anger…

I wonder if this is what happened to Jesus when he observed, from within the Father's house, a variety of abuses occurring, and he begins to overturn tables …

I don't know for sure what is happening to me, but I get … no, *I am* angry.

I am angry that this religious system, at the hands of a few people with power, makes decisions that are not in keeping with the teachings of Jesus.

And they hurt people.

I am angry that innocent people's lives are scarred, hurt and in disrepair.

I am angry that children are manipulated into behavioral patterns that are, for lack of a better word, "Stepford-like", and that their parents reinforce these behaviors with praise and accolades.

Yes, I know that most Christians are kind within their box but threaten the box and see what happens. They will cut you off, they will talk behind your back, and they will disenfranchise you.

It is cult-like, and the worst part about it is, they can't see it. They finger-point and accuse others for abandoning the faith, for being deceived, calling them false prophets, saying that they have turned away from truth to follow myths, when all the while it is them that have marred Christ beyond recognition (Isaiah 52:14) by adopting and morphing sound doctrine into whatever suits their denomination. By the way, Christianity has between 38,000 and 41,000 differing and disagreeing sects.

Religious Trauma Syndrome is a reality, occurring to many who are struggling to break free from the manipulation, programming, and even brainwashing, that fundamentalism employs.

18:314 I Wouldn't Call Myself an Atheist …

While I wouldn't call myself an Atheist, I certainly don't believe in the Christian God that condones violence including rape, murder and genocide. Don't shake your head here – it's in the Bible that Christians follow as the "Word of God."

There comes a time when one must critically look at what western Christianity has done to promote God as a brutal dictator that demands people to submit, or else be sentenced to an eternity in torturous fire. Look, folks, I didn't have the world's best father. I experienced emotional, mental, verbal and sometimes physical abuse, and even with all of that, there is NOTHING I could have done that would have provoked him to torture me forever.

Wake up, Christianity!

18:315 The Chamber Pot

You, each and every one of you, has a chamber, a chamber pot and a chambermaid. The chambermaid is YOU.

The chamber pot is your lowest chakra center, as the totality of your human pain resides there, in the bowl in your pelvic area. It is sheltered and provides the emphasis for all action. It is from here that battles are fought, and victors announced. It is here that the great battles from the Bible are described, as this is not a history book, but a mystery book. These wars are not fought externally, but rather, are descriptive of the savagery that humans are capable of in their emotional targeting of one another.

These battles are waged nation against nation, husbands against wives, brother against brother, and kingdoms against kingdoms. It is here that we must wage the ultimate battle of Armageddon.
We cannot circumnavigate the process of healing.

Once wounded, the soul must journey through pain to find healing.
There may come a time in one's life where wounding is no longer an issue; after all, how do you wound one that is dead?

The life of ego is necessary in order to FEEL our way through duality. Duality is but a village we must visit on our way through humanhood.

The ego navigates the pathway to the cross; that is, the place where the identification with self intersects with one's authentic identity as Divinity.

This is the cross where the life of self, the ego, willingly surrenders to the life of its immortal counterpart, Divinity.

Once crucified, it is buried within the lower realms and is subjected to decay and corruption. It must experience the worm as it consumes the metaphoric life of self.

This is the process of death; death to self, death to offense, death to pain, death to human nature.

This is the process I want to define, as there is NO WAY AROUND this path. One must GO THROUGH it.

Within Christianity, I taught that I must, at all costs, forgive those who caused me pain; physical, emotional and mental wounding. I selflessly forgave. I said the words and thought I meant them. I walked through life, and when the memories provoked tears and pain, I shoved them down, never allowing them to speak, to request vindication, to vibrate out from their resonating chamber.

This pain within the chamber would resound only to itself, but sending out a request, nonetheless, and the request is met with similar frequency, thus creating more of the same circumstances that caused the pain in the first place.

It had been only twelve months, since my mother's passing, that I had opened the door to this chamber and observed this pain. Inside the chamber is a chamber pot, the stench of which is unbearable when uncovered.

With each new offense came a deposit made from the bowels of human pain. Left untended, or simply covered with the veneer of acceptability, can only delay the healing process.

In this battle we fight for our FREEDOM FROM PAIN. It is in this battle that the nature of Christ emerges, as it rides upon the white horse from the Book of Revelation. The very being of Christ in YOU is revealed as victor over your bloody and battered humanity. It is here that you triumph, and your wounds are attended and bound with oil by the Samaritan that is GOOD.

It is here where your healing begins.

Only you can lift the veneer that covers your emotional center. Only you can give voice to the shattered parts of your personality that long to speak. Find a safe place or person that will not only validate but help remove the sludge that sickens your body. This is a worthwhile process, and one that you may discover as you enter the chamber of stillness.

Ask. Seek, Knock. Your path to healing will illuminate and your victimhood will be defeated.

18:316 Is It Just My Imagination?

I heard this internal voice speak to me and it said:

> *"The voice that you think is only your imagination is still part of you and is highly creative. You have many voices that make up your higher self, for we are many."*

18:317 THUMP!

Have you ever been thumped? It is defined as this:

> *One who uses a lot of scripture when they disagree with your statement instead of thoughtfully giving a dissenting reply.*

There is a measure of disdain within some inclusionary religions for fundamentalist Christians. Christianity has earned its intolerable reputation, but we must not throw the baby out with the bathwater, lest we be the same as the fundamentalists.

Non-Christians have a skewed view of the Bible because of those who thump it. It is to our benefit to learn and appreciate the rich metaphorical and allegorical language within it; in particular, the teachings of Jesus.

Most will find appreciation of scripture if it is introduced as metaphor, unconditional love and acceptance, rather than from an historical, literal, exclusionary, and intolerant view.

They will understand that the Bible is a guide to man's journey in consciousness, and what a beautiful story it is.

18:318 Morphing into Christ

If one of my children or grandchildren were threatened or harmed at school, my knee-jerk and very human reaction would be to meet harm with harm, violence with violence, or at the very least, violence with resistance. But I am not all human – I am evolving; morphing into Christ. This universal aspect of me sees from a higher perspective that is not human.

Through this lens, I see and understand the universal principle that what we focus on, we get. What we resist, we create. I believe that there is roughly 10% of the planetary population that will likewise understand this principle and withdraw their focus from the dilemma, and instead focus upon the desired outcome. This 10% is THE tithe.

We have become a nation of fear and have created the mess we are in. Help us refocus by holding America in your heart, over the fires of the altar (your lower chakra centers; the flames of red, orange and yellow) and hear the crackle of the consumed sacrifice of the judgments laid against us (and by us).

America cannot survive without the priesthood that will stand in the gap on our behalf until we become one people, united in peace and love with the rest of our world. The world has much to lend to our process of becoming.

Give us your heart.

18:319 Curious About the Immortal Order of Melchizedek?

Paul said that he so longed to teach them about Melchizedek, but he could not, because they were "babes" used to drinking milk.

The meaty information about Melchizedek required teeth.
Did you know that Abram gave a tenth of everything to Melchizedek?
Did you know Hebrews 7:10 says that Levi, while he was in the loins of his father, paid tithes to Melchizedek?

Did you know Melchizedek is still collecting this tithe?

This tithe is in the form of biology; flesh and blood.

This tithe walks the Earth, in human form, today.

Are you one of them?

Melchizedek priests bridge the vibrational gap that stands between Heaven and Earth (the next dimensional level and Earth).

18:320 We are Divine Beings

"We are Divine beings that have partnered with a fractal of biology
that exists as slowed down frequency, light that has congealed

> *intelligently to produce a partner that will escort us through the*
> *material worlds."*

See below:

Divine inversion. My mentor of the 1990s always spoke this phrase, and I didn't really understand it.

Now, after over 20 years, I think I get it.

Within Christianity all of our beliefs and Bible stories are projected outward from us. From the Garden of Eden to the promised land to the return of the triumphant Christ in the book of Revelation, I projected everything externally.

Now I understand that all of these beautiful stories are written so that by externalizing, seeing these things as historical events that may have occurred in time and space, we are actually learning what is the internal and unseen working of consciousness.

Through story and allegory, the mysteries are revealed.
You are Adam.
You are Eve.
You are the garden.
You are Pharaoh.
You are Moses.
You are Queen Esther.
You are King David.
You are Boaz.
You are Paul and the disciples.
You are the woman with the issue of blood.
You are the blind man.
You are the angel that troubles the water.
You are the cursed fig tree.
You are the Christ.
We are all these things at different stages of our unconscious and conscious evolution.

We are riding a spiral of time that allows for our education within all of these archetypes (and more!).

Again, let this really sink in: We are Divine beings that have partnered with a fractal of biology that exists as slowed down frequency, light that has congealed intelligently to produce a partner that will escort us through the material worlds.

18:321 God Indeed Favors Israel

Do you remember the story of Jacob as he wrestled with the Angel of the Lord and had his name changed to Israel?

Israel is US, a metaphor for ALL of humanity that has wrestled with their Divine Identity that resides WITHIN. We are formerly named Jacob, which means "one who seizes the place of another" – this is the struggle for self-identity, our ego as it dominates our mind. We all struggle with selflessness (the Divine Nature), and we are experiencing that nature (name) changed to IS RA EL (which means "the Divine has prevailed").

This wrestling between Jacob and the angel is metaphoric for an internal struggle within all of us, where the son of perdition (ego) is set down and the nature of Divinity prevails. The ego is seen then as the donkey that bears the creature to death (Jesus riding on a donkey into Jerusalem). The creature willingly submits to the death process which is NECESSARY in order to experience RESURRECTION.

This Divine Nature is wrapped within the swaddle of biology. Metaphor. All of it. We are favored.

18:322 The Rapture is Internal

Speaking of the rapture ... It is an internal event, not occurring outside of you.

The theory of masses of people disappearing off of the face of the Earth was popularized over a century ago and continues today. Within fundamentalism, it is largely substantiated with this scripture:

> *Then there will be two men in the field; one will be taken, and one will be left. Two women [will be] grinding at the mill; one will be taken, and one will be left.*
> Matthew 24:40-41

I remember, at gatherings, we would sing a song over and over with these lyrics:

> *"Two men walking up a hill one disappears and one's left standing still. I wish we'd all been ready. There's no time to change your mind, the Son has come and you've been left behind."*

Isn't it interesting to see this scripture metaphorically – not describing an external event – this "rapture," as it has been termed, occurs internally, within our consciousness, as we experience union between God (the Divine) and man.

Looking internally, rather than externally, we may see that this is describing the marriage between Divinity and the will of man. Looking deeper, the bride is the willful mind of man that is dominated by ego and the groom is Divinity, or Spirit. These two are the two becoming the One that is left.

The one taken is taken in marriage.

The bride taken is the egocentric counterpart, the one that submits to the groom, for the union of the two becoming the One.

The whole of Matthew 24 describes cataclysm, indeed, as we experience the end of duality (life as we know it) and the beginning of the ONE new creation. If we view scripture through the lens of fear and duality, we will be fearful and see fearful things.

I still recall vivid images of people being separated from their loved ones as they were snatched up and away from the Earth, because I interpreted the scriptures using fear. Through the lens of hope, we see a beautiful love story where Divinity "courts" our humanity. We just need to shift out of fear.

And the two will become one flesh.

> *So they are no longer two, but one. Therefore, what God has joined together, let man not separate.*   Mark 10:8-9

1

8:323 I Apologize a Lot, Lately, for Using Scripture

This is my desire – that we begin to see the Bible as a mystery book. With investigation, even the Bible has ripped off stories from other cultures like the Sumerians and Egyptians – the Adam and Eve story, the flood, and others far predate a possible Biblical scholarship.

The Bible, however, has been hijacked by Christianity, claiming it as their own – but it really belongs to all. If we can get past our offenses, we may be able to see the principles and mysteries of creation that are spoken of in other mystical texts (not related to the Bible) and that are hidden in plain sight. There is GREAT CONFLUENCE with other mystical texts and the Bible, if we see the Bible through a lens of MYSTERY!!!

To do this, we must seize the opportunity to move past our judgment and offenses of the Bible and into the school of mystery that it inspires and can also gently lead us into the depths that the ancients used to pen and communicate these truths within it.

I was unable, for YEARS, to read a Bible, because of my knee-jerk reactions and offenses to it, remembering how it tied me in shackles to a fundamentalist religion that was, at best, now considered by me to be insidious.

Once I was able to let go of that programming (this is a hard thing to do), I was able to see the treasure that the Bible is OUTSIDE of Christianity. I could not see that while I was holding it in judgment.

18:324 The Indoctrination Processes

The indoctrination process began when I was just five years old. I heard stories of the rapture and being "left behind;" separated forever from my mommy and daddy, going to burn forever in fire, if I did not accept Jesus into my heart as my personal Lord and Savior.

That is child abuse.

I would stay awake at night in fear as my five-year-old little mind tried to understand these concepts. I am sure, because my parents attended these gatherings and listened to this crap, accepting Jesus into their hearts, that I thought everything the preacher said was true. I trusted my parents – I knew nothing else. So, down the rabbit hole I went.

The pure and unadulterated teachings of Jesus, speaking of love and non-judgment, are the epitome of righteousness. It is all the dogmatic crap that religion mingles with the truth that I find so very abhorrent. I saw love expressed beautifully amidst the manipulation and control.

SECTION**NINETEEN**

NINETEEN

19:325 Letter to a Friend About My Views on Satan

There is so much I would like to say, but I am not sure if you are willing for an open conversation around some foundational Christian beliefs.

I will just mention a few concepts here, to see how you feel about it, and we can go from there. My purpose is not to proselytize, but rather to share my spiritual evolution to spur discussion.

A little history: Born again at age 5 or 6 and within Charismatic Christian Fundamentalism for four decades when I left the church system, in 1999. I was head of the deliverance ministry in our church for the last decade and was involved with the Spiritual Warfare Network and the World Prayer Center.

In reading a little bit of your information, the terminology, it seems, has evolved over the years since I have been gone. We did personal, regional and national deliverance (exorcism) and saw quite dramatic results and many miracles.

Now, I no longer espouse those practices, nor do I entertain even thinking about the demonic.

Here is why:

Jesus said, "Resist not evil" and "If I, by the finger of God cast out demons, then surely the Kingdom is at hand."

This last scripture is what really began my transition. You see, Jesus was alluding to the fact that the Kingdom and Evil do not and cannot co-exist. The Kingdom dimension has a particular frequency that is incongruent with the frequency of evil or the demonic.

The lower frequency of evil cannot manifest in an environment that is higher in frequency. It is almost like its molecular structure is dismantled and reconfigured.

Jesus said, "The Kingdom is at hand" and to "lift our eyes" (our sight or means of perception).

Outside of the Kingdom age, Satan, demons and the demonic do not operate. Jesus was speaking mysteries and told us that we have the "keys." These "keys" are the frequency that is emitted from love, joy, peace, patience, kindness, benevolence and the like.

The world of duality – that is, where good and evil flourish – is established and maintained when human beings eat from the tree that knows and discerns between good and evil. We are told NOT TO EAT OF IT, but we do EVERY DAY THAT WE JUDGE BETWEEN GOOD AND EVIL. This is what creates, maintains and sustains the present dark age.

Do you know how you know if you are eating from the tree of the knowledge of good and evil?

When you see or discern between good and evil.

Over the last two decades of searching, praying, reading and investigating, I now see things quite differently. I now understand that the Father (the highly creative energy that congeals light into form) is inside of me and that GOD IS NOT MOCKED – therefore, whatsoever I sow, I will reap. Where is God? Inside of me. Who is doing the sowing? God is, and is not separate from me, using the human thought system that works within the material world. God is my co-creative partner in the systemic worlds of matter. This system is determined by whatever "tree" (consciousness) we eat from.

If the tree of good and evil, we create a mortal world.

If the tree of life, we create the atmosphere of Divine habitation, where death is swallowed up of life.

The question then begs to be asked, "What tree am I 'eating' from?"

And, "What age am I in?"

And, "Is my wine skin (consciousness) old or new?"

19:326 An Exceptional Year

There is something called "The Great Year" that consists of roughly 24,000 years. It is a really big cycle of time where we may experience high and low culture. For example, there is writings that speak of humans living hundreds of years in the golden age and conversely, very short lives in the dark age where at one point people lived an average of just twenty-three years. Our most recent dark age spanned from 476 – 1453. Little is written about the higher ages that occurred before that, books having been destroyed that spoke of the golden years but also, I suspect the golden ages did not include much writing with communication occurring on a much higher and intuitive level.

I believe that much more will be disclosed about this Great Year containing various ages where the human being is able to learn much through the things experienced. For those wanting more information there is a great book titled, "The Lost Star" by Walter Cruttenden. It is a very good read.

19:327 Sin is Not an Action

Sin is not an action. It is an environment. And you create it every time you judge something and expend emotions toward the thing judged.

Mortality is the stuff of life. Everything dies.

This is called SIN.

Sin is the stuff that is created while we, as humans, live according to selfishness – according to the EGO.

There is no remission of sin without sacrifice. Sacrifice of self. Sacrifice of EGO. This is the shedding of BLOOD – your egocentric life

The EGO is self-protective, and always looks out for NUMBER ONE; it's host – the personality of YOU.

It gets its feelings hurt.

It gets offended.

It gets jealous, seeks revenge, and manipulates circumstances – all in favor of YOU.

This is the stuff of death.

While we remain self-focused, we will live in a mortal world where death and limitation prevails.

We need a SAVIOR, and that SAVIOR is within YOU.

This SAVIOR is our eternal and immortal self. It is courting the EGO to give up its place of authority in favor of unconditional love, the stuff of eternity.

I saw a red-tailed hawk last week. My husband and I were turning into the driveway onto our property, when we saw this beautiful hawk picking at something in the ditch. We stopped, and as I was about to take a video of it, the hawk took off, flying very close to the ground, dragging the carcass of a possum in its talons. Unable to rise higher, the weight of the dead possum proving to be too much, the hawk released the dead thing. The Hawk returned, looking at the lifeless carcass, and took off again; this time, without the weight of death. And it soared. It ascended and came to rest in a tree, able to see from a higher position.

We cannot ascend while we hang on to the stuff of death. The carcass of the old nature – the old man – has to be released.

Drop the dead thing.

Dropping "the thing of death" is fulfilling the commission to "die daily". This is what will produce resurrection!!!

19:328 You Are an Evolutionary Leap in Process

I want to encourage you. You are an evolutionary leap in process. There are chemical and alchemical processes taking place in your body to help advance our species. These processes originate in your etheric bodies and gradually penetrate your biology. Higher dimensional "light" is incoming to our galaxy, solar system and planet, atmosphere, energy body and, ultimately, your physical body.

We have always been evolving; however, at this time, a massive shift is underway to help our physical body adapt to higher dimensional frequencies. You feel it. At times, it IS NOT COMFORTABLE.

The reason for your discomfort is that higher frequencies when incoming are hitting a dissonant chord within your consciousness. Disharmony will result within your framework, and you will feel uneasy. This is a work of GRACE. Discomfort is your prime indicator that there is yet work to do within your consciousness. Carpe Diem! Seize every bit of discomfort and use it! Make it speak to you and tell you about its roots in the soil of your humanity!

It is time to forgive. It is time to structure your thoughts with love, joy and peace. You must not look back, for in looking back, there is wanting for things to be different. There is pain and hurt. Only when looking to NOW is the dissipation of pain. Looking to the now, we may see the beauty that surrounds us and allows us to set our focus there.

In unforgiveness, there is a thorn in our side that anchors us to this passing age. In unforgiveness, we fail to see that all has purpose and that our education in duality is truly necessary and lovely. In forgiveness, we see this.

Forgiveness is like Liquid Wrench that oozes over our stuck places and allows movement.

Listen to your body. What is it telling you?

It speaks!

19:329 Is It All an ILLUSION?

There is teaching out there that teaches all is an illusion, and that to recognize life as such frees us from the confines of it.

There is similar teaching within *A Course in Miracles* (a book/course of study by Helen Schucman), as well. Many are speaking about the concept of everything as an illusion …

Here is my take:

Quantum physics teaches us that, at a quantum level (very small), everything is in a state of flux. Tiny bits of matter are not fixed; they appear to be floating.

I think that our world is continually being shaped BY US. The Law of Attraction teaches this, as well.

I prefer the word TEMPORAL rather than illusion. Illusion, to me, promotes the idea of falsehood or trickery, and our world is anything but …

I see this world as an opportunity to learn about the rapidly advancing "field" of creation. We are learning and awakening to the idea that it is WE who are creating by our focused thought and intention.

This is the role of the EGO. The EGO is the mechanism that can focus thought and emotion. The EGO is not a false self, as some stipulate – it is the force behind creating the temporal worlds of matter.

This world provides the environment for the creature to create and to learn the principles thereof.

It is not an illusion. It is not a mistake. It is a purposeful dalliance by the Divine into the material worlds THROUGH US.

You are Mary. The human race is MARY. We have been overshadowed, penetrated by this mysterious force, and there begins a creative magic within us as we judge between good and evil, providing the emotional currency to back the endeavor.

We are the creature and the creator.

And it is not an illusion.

It is Divine.

It is purposeful.

It is beautiful.

19:330 A Clear Indicator

When we argue about homosexuality, sex, etc., it is a clear indicator of where our consciousness lies:

Because, in the age to come (the Kingdom age) there is "neither male nor female", and we are "neither given nor taken in marriage."

How do you all feel about the part in the scripture that says, "There is neither Jew nor Greek ..." Not only is there no gender identity, there is no national identity, either.

So, if you are arguing about homosexuality or nationalism, then you are not in the kingdom you espouse to be.

19:331 The Ego is a Necessary and Vital Helpmate

For many years I held the view regarding the eviction and death of the ego, but now understand that this view is only a placeholder in consciousness. Such knowledge is necessary to transition out from under egocentricity. But it is vital that we not dismiss the ego, for it is the only mechanism in the worlds of matter that can focus thought and emotion. Without it, there can be no creation. You can no more separate from the ego than you can take electrical charges out of the atmosphere. It is a necessary component of creation.

The ego, while under the materializing influences (fear), is dark and will create worlds that are base and mortal. Ah, but working in tandem with love, we transition into higher fields where we are released from the governor of time. The only way to understand this is to experience it. The understanding you hold is necessary, but don't park there. Keep moving to see the absolute beauty in the design where the helpmate (ego) not only willingly submits to death to self, but then also resurrection as an equal partner to source. This is the pattern, if one can see it.

This mystery is reflected in the parable of the unjust steward, if viewed metaphorically. I encourage you to look further into it. I have it here if you are interested:

> *There was a certain rich man who had a steward, and an accusation*
> *was brought to him that this man was squandering his wealth. So, he*
> *called him and said to him, "what is this I hear about you? Give an*
> *account of your stewardship, for you can no longer be steward."*
> *Then the steward said within himself, "what shall I do? For my*
> *master is taking the stewardship away from me. I cannot dig; I am*
> *ashamed to beg. I have resolved what to do, that when I am put out of*
> *the stewardship, they may receive me into their houses." So, he called*
> *every one of his master's debtors to him, and said to the first, "How*
> *much do you owe my master?" And he said, "A hundred measures of*
> *oil." So, he said to him, "Take your bill, and sit down quickly and*
> *write fifty." Then he said to another, "And how much do you owe?"*
> *So, he said, "A hundred measures of wheat." And he said to him,*
> *"Take your bill, and write eighty." So, the master commended the*
> *unjust steward because he had dealt shrewdly. For the sons of this*
> *world are shrewder in their generation than the sons of light. "And I*
> *say to you, make friends for yourselves by unrighteous mammon, that*
> *when you fail, they may receive you into an everlasting home."*
> 　　　　Luke 16:1-9

If we look at the rich man and the steward as templates/metaphors for the Divine and the ego both dwelling within one body, then we can see the message in this often overlooked and not understood parable from Jesus. The ego is in charge of the master's business and is being chastised and warned that it is squandering wealth and is being called to account. The ego is warned that Divinity will not keep the ego employed as steward of his business. The steward/ego then determines slyly that he must slash the amount of the receivables owed to his employer in order to make friends with those who owe, so that when he is put out of employment as steward of the business and unemployable, he will have a place to stay. Then, in a surprising turn of events the rich man/Divinity returns and praises the steward for reducing the receivables. It is acknowledged that the steward behaved shrewdly in this world and had won for himself friends that will welcome him into their eternal dwellings when he is released from his position. Among other things, this tells me two very important keys: One, the ego will be released from being master of the body and all its workings in consciousness; and two, the ego will be welcomed into eternity.

We see in this mystery that the ego must and will be dismissed as master of "the business," but will also transition into eternity once it has released debt (forgive us our debt, as we forgive our debtors). This is a most profound mystery, and one which is apprehended only when hierarchy is dissolved, and unity is achieved. This understanding is the ultimate redemption.

I understand that is the traditional line of thought (that the ego is a false sense of self) and that it is a leap to think that the ego is a necessary component of creation; however, a lot of puzzle pieces fall into place when it is viewed this way: Master for a time, servant for a time, and then finally partner for eternity. It is misconstrued as a false self, when it should be understood that it is a misplaced master running the show (the son of perdition), until it is removed. Many get stuck in that place and feel it needs to be done away with, and that it is an illusion. Not so. It needs to submit, as a woman to a man, or feminine energy to the masculine, so that in love and partnership, they may create. It is a beautiful love story.

19:332 A Kind Reply from a Fundamentalist

> *"Wow. You have presented some unique concepts that are worth considering."* End of
> reply.

Instead, like many of you likeminded sojourners, we who are challenging the religious systems receive a tongue lashing, threats of Hell, accusations of being the anti-Christ, a deceiver, a Satanist (which is laughable), etc.

Many lose lifelong friends and family. What could be the reason for such sacrifices?

Freedom from the tyrannical Christian God and the departure from fear of separation and eternal damnation.

It took a while for me to be able to process thoughts about a loving creator outside of Christianity because of my lengthy indoctrination (43 years) within the system. I had to redirect my thinking apart and outside from "knee-jerk" reactionary responses that had been ingrained in my delicate psyche as a child, adolescent and adult.

After spending much of my free time within the church walls, listening to adept "fundamentalist speak", playing every CD and reading every book I could get my hands on to learn my craft – "Christianese" – I began to feel deeply dissatisfied and confused. Confused, because I sincerely thought that what I had believed was absolute truth. I had jerked my knee many, many times when I was presented with thinking outside of fundamentalism. But then, I just didn't know anymore.

As I spoke with friends about this growing doubt of fundamentalism, the criticism became severe. Once respected and elevated within fundamentalism, I now was quickly becoming outcast. But I could not stop or even slow down the advancing consciousness that had overtaken me. I could see CLEARLY a loving God that did not judge or condemn me, while his followers still did. I had to run after this God. And run, I did.

So what is it that fuels those who have the passionate need to break free from such institutions (risking family and friends) while others bask in the rigid restrictions that dogmatic rhetoric brings? It was like someone "lit my fuse" and off and out of organized religion I went; searching, seeking the reason for the peace that had now encompassed me.

"Whom the Son (Christ in me) sets free, is FREE, INDEED."

19:333 The Barrier of Brainwashing

So often when we think of brainwashing, we see visions of hypnotism, bright lights and unwilling candidates. But brainwashing takes place every day to young and old, in the workplace, religious institutions, and even at home. No one, under any circumstances, is exempt from the influence of coercive, manipulating people who have an agenda backed by fear. We also see this influence in our governmental structures and in the media.

We have recourse, however, to be led by our Divine and higher self; the voice that whispers in the midst of egocentric dominance. As our intuitive "muscle" builds through use, our intellect begins to wane in the dawn of such a potent source. No longer are we subject to what we see and discern with our five senses; we are seeing and abiding in the secret place of the "Most High." Enthroned deep within the skull lies the pineal gland – surrounded by the twenty-four elders; that is, the twelve paired cranial nerves that feed and nourish this sophisticated piece of equipment, the human brain.

It is from this vantage point that this tyrannist (the human intellect fueled by ego) steps down to relinquish its role as master of the human being. It now finds its place as the servant of mankind.

We are encouraged to meet the Christ (your higher self) in the "upper room;" that is, your elevated consciousness, which is void of the fear from egocentric dominance.

The activated pineal gland is the place where the seventh trumpet sounds (highest frequency) as it leads the transitioning human into the age to come.

19:334 Satan – Not What We Think

We anthropomorphize Satan. Put another way, we ascribe human attributes to Satan, rather than understanding what this "adversary" really is. Sort of like what we do with God when we picture "him" as a male, with a throne and a white beard.

Satan (the adversary) is not a "being" but rather, a physics principle of contraction that holds energy efficiently bound within matter, using the frequency of fear. As such, it stands as an adversary to spiritual expansion.

Love expands. Fear contracts. Fear is used to create dense materialism of all sorts. This world is congealed light and energy slowed down to form matter.

Contraction is, therefore, a servant to the Divine will, and creates at our behest. We are creating 24/7 by our focused thought and emotion. We are protecting this physics principle every time we focus on something and emote towards it.

P.S. We do this unconsciously. The key is to wake up.

19:335 Easter to the Metaphysically minded?

I am not going to go into all of the history of the word "Easter" and, suffice it to say, for those interested in etymology, the word "Easter" is not found in the Bible, and has pagan origins.

The idea of a dying and resurrecting God-man is not a new concept beginning with the Christian Jesus; rather, it is much older and is a part of the fabric of many cultural and mythological stories.

There is a reason for this. This is your story. It is humanity's story told in as many cultures as there are peoples of the Earth. The story of Jesus is the most recent footprint, and should be taken as mystery, not history.

There is great debate on whether or not Jesus was a historical figure, and I am not here to support either argument. The viewpoint that I want to magnify is that Jesus was a PATTERN, and if we fail to discern this pattern or template, if you will, as it applies to our own cross, death and resurrection experience, then we have MISSED the reason for the season.

We are continually exhorted by Christ to "lift our eyes" a phrase common among his parabolic teachings. But where is this Christ? This Christ is within you, wrapped in the swaddle of your humanity.

Are these happenings that are recorded in scripture meant for one man (Jesus) or are we encouraged to "pick up our cross" and to "die daily?"

> *For God so loved the world that he gave his only begotten Son that whosoever should believe (in him, the Christ) will not perish but have life eternal.* John 3:16

Here is the crux of the matter. You may view that this "Son" was one man, or you may understand that this "Son" is the corporeal human race. This corporeal Son has been sent to the Earth plane to live eternally and blissfully (in Eden), then egocentrically as it makes the choice to eat from the tree of the knowledge of good and evil, then to die (to become mortal), and ultimately, to apprehend its immortal state once again. This is resurrection.

Christ has come in the flesh – Yours.

> *This is how you can recognize the Spirit of God: Every Spirit that acknowledges that Jesus Christ has come in the flesh is from God, but every Spirit that does not acknowledge Jesus is not from God. This is the Spirit of the antichrist, which you have heard is coming and even now is already in the world.* 1 John 4:2-3

Jesus is the archetypical awakening Son of Man as it apprehends "Christ" – that is, Christ in you, the Son of God.

You must believe that God inhabits your very being, that you are the symbolic Mary that has been impregnated by something Holy and Divine. That you bear within your frame that pearl of great price, God itself. This knowledge is called Christ.

This is not happening to one man, as Christianity believes; rather, it is occurring in all men as that divine spark comes of age, having grown in the consciousness of man's garden.

What, then, of resurrection?

When you believe, as Jesus did, that God is indwelling YOU, and that your life of self must come to an end, then the last enemy to be conquered is death.

If you don't believe this, you are not sentenced to eternal flames of Hell and separation. You will just remain mortal and ALL THAT IT ENCOMPASSES.

Remember the parable of that landlord or vineyard keeper that went away into a far country, letting out the property to "someone else" that beats the servants of the vineyard – that "someone else" is egocentricity within all men. It is this life of living according to the ego that must be crucified, surrendered and yielded to that eternal portion of Divinity that is cradled within the womb of man. This same egocentric portion within man dies the death of self-surrender and experiences metamorphosis in the grave, ultimately resurrecting as an eternal being called Christ.

This is the reason for the celebration. It is your impending resurrection having been buried within the tomb of the Earth, experiencing death again and again – until you believe in who and what you really are. You are Joshua, clothed in the coat of many colors, races, creeds and religions.

And the stone is rolled away.

19:336 Divinity is Courting You

I have been giving the idea of the ego being "a false sense of self" a good deal of thought, and think we need to see this through the metaphor, or the pattern we have, of physical union or marriage.

Metaphorically speaking, the groom does not seek to join with a false self, or an illusion, for that matter. The groom seeks a wife, a partner, a spouse that it can meld with, become one with. Her duty is then to submit (agree) and OPEN to her groom. They become ONE, even in the mind. Please understand this is not about male and female, but masculine and feminine.

There is a profound truth to this concept of synergy – where the two, together, are worth more than separate components. A synergy is captured by union, and the ONE married is worth more than the two as separate entities.

In the pattern of marriage, the wife is not silenced or called false or "put away."

Remember in the story of Esther and the King, where once it was forbidden to enter the King's chambers, but for Esther, she boldly entered and was told by the King to ask for ANYTHING, up to HALF OF THE KINGDOM. This is because she is an EQUAL partner.

Remember, also, that in the story of Jesus, he did not call himself the Groom, but rather, he called himself the BRIDEGROOM, for the Christ was BOTH masculine and feminine JOINED.

Some teach that they should seek to abandon the egocentric mind, rather than to see the Divine mind and the human mind "wed". I feel this is futility. There is a need to withdraw from our old patterns of thinking, but this means that we much adjust from literalism to figurative understanding; leaving the history for the mystery.

Just like with Esther: She had to leave her family, in order to save them, as she entered into preparations to qualify as Queen. Then, once she was married, she, in turn, went to the King and petitioned for the salvation of her people.

We are her "people" that are under the sentence of mortality. We are the ones who will enter the chambers of the King as an equal partner and will petition the King for our own salvation; that is, transitioning from mortal to immortal. This is not a literal or historical story. This is the mystery of union and the synergy that is captured when the two become one.

The feminine is not to be called false, and it is not an illusion. Rather, it is the womb that incubates the seed of all of creation.

19:337 Who, or What, Are Adam and Eve?

Who, or what, are Adam and Eve?

The timeless story we all know did not originate with the book we call the Bible, but this Genesis (beginning) story is found within older texts.

Genesis Chapter 1:

This is a story about the origin of mankind as it pertains to the unseen workings of energy.

God (for lack of a better term) or Divinity searched for a means to inhabit the material domains. Divinity is love energy, pure and simple. This Divine form has both masculine and feminine energies within and, therefore, it was able to bring forth life again and again in and of itself, seeding into its womb and birthing itself anew continuously.

Adam is FORMED. The masculine principle is.

Eve is within the masculine as the WOMB. She is intrinsically a part of the masculine form.

Adam and Eve in ONE BODY co-exist in a perfect realm – Eden.

But soon, the need for the newly formed Adam to become tangible with another form arises.

Enter *Genesis Chapter 2:*

Adam sleeps and Eve is pulled from him so that the two may, by example, display the delicate interplay of creation in themselves. So, we not only see how humans are created, but we also see another pattern emerge through this process – that is, we see that this masculine principle (the Divine within) of seed-giving requires a form to receive the seed (the human mind or ego).

The material world is made up of congealed love energy that has had its frequency lowered so that it forms matter; trees, dirt, planets, stars, etc.

The feminine principle (mind/ego) begins to succumb to creating via itself instead of receiving the Divine seed from her counterpart. And they are lowered into a mortal environment where their creation is limited to mortal things – their creations are subject to mold, rust and mildew – and, ultimately, the things they create deconstruct, and they return to dust.

This lowering of love energy is called "the fall." It is also called "baptism."

Divine love charted a course to experience the material world, but to do this it needed a bioenergetic form (made from lowered frequency) in which to experience the material worlds THROUGH.

In this way, we see that this dalliance into the material worlds is necessary. The human, mingled with Divinity, is practicing its hand at creating. We create 24/7 this mortal and limited world.

Thus, the need for crucifixion; Death.

The mind needs to recognize that it is not thriving by living via the ego. It is MORTAL and under the restriction of TIME.

The pattern of Jesus emerges.

The dying and resurrecting God-man appears in all of the world's myths and religions, to help show us THE WAY.

This feminine form (the egocentric mind) must die (at the place of the skull). The mind is limited by the five senses and is entrapped by the confines of the skull itself. The Divine mind exists beyond restriction.

The human egocentric form sees the necessity to die and submits willingly to the cross (the place in consciousness where the higher mind intersects with the egocentric mind).

Therefore, it is said that the (only begotten creation) died on the cross, and, on the third day, is raised from the dead. So much important symbolism there.

The Adam and Eve story, the flood, the captivity and the Exodus are all metaphors for our journey here, as mortals. Do you see the pattern emerging when you see from the vantage point of mystery, having forsaken the history?

19:338 Letter to Zach

Zach, within fundamentalism you have been indoctrinated into a belief system. As you grow spiritually, there will come a time when it will no longer make sense to you. I was told from age 5 that I was a sinner, and that I would go to Hell if I did not accept Jesus into my heart. So, I did, and I lived in a constant state of the fear of torture and being left behind. I studied the Bible for over 40 years (and I still study it today), and I know it pretty well – better than most, I would say. I have been where you are.

At church, in Christian fundamentalist systems, love is mingled with fear, and programming – and even brainwashing – begins. We subject ourselves to it, because we still feel "God." God moves in all types of flawed systems. When miracles happen, they tend to validate the flawed system. I saw lots and lots of miracles, and so, down the rabbit hole I went. I surrendered reason for belief and, as we know, belief in various religions is why we abandon reason, and even truth.

Within Christianity, there are between 38,000 and 41,000 differing and disagreeing denominations or sects. Which one has it all right? Yours?

Zach, I have found the "pearl of great price" that Jesus spoke of. It is the indwelling presence of God – within me. I no longer believe as a child, for those childish things must be put away.

I have escaped the religious systems and, someday, you will, too. This is not to say I have escaped God, you see, for NOTHING, no-thing, can separate me from the love of Divinity – God. Not you, or any other believer in fear or tyranny. I am one such person who no longer embraces fear within my spiritual practices. Fears of Hell and separation have no hold on me.

You might want to study the difference between Genesis 1 and 2, for they are different accounts of creation. In the second account, there is a God named Jehovah (the Lord God), and in Chapter 1, there is the Elohim. Each chapter presents some diametrically opposing events. The event in Genesis 2 offers to us a tree from which to eat – the knowledge of Good and Evil; and it is this tree that mankind presently eats from – and we are mortal and die. Eating from this tree, we receive the gift of mortality. It is where human consciousness resides – in the place of knowing between good and evil as our cultural-ism determines. So, when you judge between good and evil, guess which tree you are eating from? This tree allows the ego to flourish. It must continue to feed itself with apples of "rightness".

Jesus came to introduce us to the Father; not a single being with a long white beard that sits up somewhere in the ethers. No, this creative principle, the progenitor, is within you.

At some point, it will become more important to you to become righteous instead of right. As for me, I know the truth and it has, indeed, set me free.

19:339 Conflict is a Choice

Conflict is seductive and addictive. I am a recovering conflict addict.

Conflict is a choice.

The unnecessary output of emotion from perceived conflict is all around us, and we have a CHOICE as to whether or not we join in the fray.

What happens when we "join up" in conflict?

1. We fail to see from above, and instead, we surrender our bird's-eye view for something more granular – in other words, we cannot see the forest through the trees because we are standing in the midst of them.

2. We dispense our valuable emotions and their vibrational equivalent, casting them off and towards the very thing that we do not want – the very thing that enticed us into conflict in the first place – we will ultimately create more of THAT.

3. We surrender our peace, while our EGO plays its games of self will, manipulation and short-sightedness, all in support of this cyclone of "ego-centric" creation. This egocentric domination of the human mind is, and can be, vision-stealing; taking our focus off of what really matters and onto the things that just simply DON'T MATTER.

JUST STOP! Get off of the not so MERRY-GO-ROUND and discover what life actually looks like without the dizzying spell of REPEATING CYCLES.

I declare that there is a divine opportunity to remove yourself from the dominance of the EGO. This is your time to escape. I declare MERCY for you – that there is an end to the conflict that keeps you bound in cycles of self-destruction and futility. I declare that the centrifugal force of the cycle will now let you go and spin you out to the periphery of your conflict and let you out and off of this cycle of SELF-INDUCED PSYCHOLOGICAL PAIN.

Once you are out of this self-imposed torment, you will become naturally buoyant and you will ARISE, and you will see from ABOVE and not be a victim of BELOW. You are meant to THRIVE.

19:340 Human-Centric Ego-Centric Judgment

Alive or in death, when human-centric, ego-centric judgment is dismissed, we become dispassionate observers; then we know how our darkest hours have served us and we see the innate intelligence that chose the experience in the first place.

It is in baptism, under the waters of human consciousness, where Divinity sleeps and the human becomes a lost soul. It is when Divinity is awakened, either in death or life, that resurrects the observer up from the baptism of human conduct and choice. It is then that we see beyond the density that has clouded our perception; we are able to see without the watery filter of ego, and we understand the ritual of immersion.

19:341 Religious Trauma Syndrome

RTS = Religious Trauma Syndrome

There is harm (through fundamentalist Christianity) and it largely goes unrecognized because Christianity is THE cultural religion of America. Its toxic side effects are dismissed or blamed on the victim.

It is real and many people suffer from it.

If you have been indoctrinated into ANY religious grouping, you owe it to yourself to look into this syndrome. Its symptoms are:

> **Cognitive:** Confusion, poor critical thinking ability, negative beliefs about self-ability & self-worth, black & white thinking, perfectionism, difficulty with decision-making

Emotional: Depression, anxiety, anger, grief, loneliness, fear, difficulty with pleasure, loss of meaning

Social: Loss of social network, family rupture, social awkwardness, sexual difficulty, behind schedule on developmental tasks

Cultural: Unfamiliarity with secular world; "fish out of water" feelings, difficulty belonging, information gaps (e.g. evolution, modern art, music)

(List of symptoms from Marlene Winell)

Many suffer with these symptoms, UNAWARE that they have been victims of emotional and mental trauma at the hands of fundamentalism, often beginning from early childhood.

Let's learn to separate God and Jesus from religion, shall we? Christianity can be a monstrous system teeming with those who seek to manipulate and to control the vulnerable mind.

19:342 No One Comes to the Father but By Me

"No one comes to the father but by me."
Christ

Father: Creator, sheer and unlimited power to create located within. Cannot get to this highly creative potential unless we "follow" Christ.

Christ: The yielded human, the ego submitted to Divinity.

Not a sinner's prayer. Not accepting Jesus into your heart. Not walking an aisle.

Acknowledging the I AM within, becoming Christ.

The son of perdition (ego) stepping down, casting its crown before the Divine, yielding its position as master of the body – forsaking it to become the servant of all.

SECTION TWENTY

TWENTY

20:343 What is Righteous Judgment?

What is righteous judgment?

How do we as God-men, create?

Let's look at how Lazarus was raised from the dead by Jesus, with the grief that Christ emoted through his groaning; why did he groan deeply, rather than to simply tell him to arise?

I had this thought come to mind yesterday: What if an art teacher gave you white paint, white canvas, a brush and told you to paint a mountain range as a backdrop for a valley full of wildflowers? Could we do it?

We have experienced grief, sorrow, disillusionment, betrayal, hatred, anger, etc., and we don't like these emotions because we FEEL them and have judged them to be undesirable. And, as a human, THEY ARE. No question.

But in awakening, we must realize that simply judging an event acts as a validator, a propellant, a commander of sorts. When this emotional, and more importantly "vibrational," request is sent out from your body into the field of the possibility of good and evil, we create circumstances of same or similar vibration.

This human judgment gives a directive to create, and it will create – mortally. In other words, our creations have a classroom where they are allowed to manifest. This classroom is called Planet Earth.

Judgment is a forceful "propellant" that directs highly creative emotional current to manifest in our mortal world on Planet Earth.

Within Genesis is profound symbolism when mankind initially "eats" from the tree of the knowledge of good and evil; it is said of them in Genesis Six, "Man is NOW MORTAL therefore his days will be numbered to 120 years." This was the origin of "sin" – that is, creating by the force of EGO rather than spirit. THAT IS WHAT "SIN" IS. Everything the ego creates has an expiration date. Everything. As such, it is an adversary to the potent and creative force that Divinity IS.

Knowing and judging between good and evil brings life limitation and sentences us to mortality. It is in this forceful departure from the immortal and proverbial "Garden of Eden" that we begin the classroom of being MORTALS. *Mortality 101.* It is from this "platform" where the human creates, utilizing roughly 10-11% of its mind through the limitation of ONLY FIVE SENSES.

CONVERSELY, when the EGO relinquishes its role of mortal creation and yields to the Divine element within, this divine element sees in multiple dimensions, and directs and guides its spouse to emote under its Divine impetus of eternity, which is LOVE.

When the ego creates, partnered with Divinity, the timely and focused release of emotional currency is dispensed with LOVE. This coupling, manufacture and distribution of emotion to create has RIGHTEOUS JUDGMENT as its basis. This creation will be eternally focused, as LOVE NEVER FAILS.

Finally, to paint (create) with the full spectrum of "colors," we need those hues and tones to be dispensed or "squeezed" from their containers, so that we may have our unique vibrational signature in the eternal worlds we form. From the iron core of a planet to the flower petal, each emotion dispenses the appropriate color to create a vibrant and texture-filled world and, indeed, a universe.

Bottom line: Within the pattern, Jesus used his emotional currency CONSCIOUSLY to cause Lazarus to arise. Jesus was not moved by his emotions, HE CONSCIOUSLY MOVED THEM to create his desired outcome. Life from the dead.

20:344 "You Don't Say the Name 'Jesus' Enough"

After a meeting, a woman came up to me and said, "You don't say the name 'Jesus' enough. All you seem to talk about is ego and self."

I replied, "That is because Christ is in you, the hope of glory."

She said, "But you don't say the name 'Jesus' enough."

I replied, "Did you know that the letter 'J' was not used until 500 years ago?"

She said, "I don't know about that, but I know you just don't say his name enough."

I replied, "Do you think he is offended?"

She said, "I hope not."

I asked, "Are you offended?"

There was no reply.

Then, later on, she asked why we did not pray during the meeting …?

I replied, "How did Jesus tell us to pray?"

Someone in the audience said, "He said go into your closet so that no one hears you ..."

Another woman asked me, "Why was there no altar call? Why aren't people told about salvation, led through the sinner's prayer to accept Jesus and to ask him into their hearts?"

I asked her if she based those actions on what she had read in the Bible, to which she replied, "Yes, the Bible tells us to do those things." I asked her to tell me where it was, and she said she was not sure, but that she knew it was in there. I knew the verse she was thinking of, and here it is:

> *Matthew 10:32 Everyone who acknowledges me before men, I also will acknowledge before my Father who is in heaven, 33 but whoever denies me before men, I also will deny before my Father who is in heaven.*

Where in the world do we get the ritual of an altar call from this verse? We are told, "the Kingdom of Heaven is within you." If this is so, then where is the Father? Jesus said, "... my father who is in Heaven ..."

Would denying Christ be more like denying Christ is within, or like not loving your neighbor or not walking in meekness, kindness, gentleness, not feeding the poor, clothing the naked and tending to the widows and orphans?

How can we relegate such an important truth to a ritual by raising a hand and walking an aisle and reciting a prayer crafted from another man's words? And how can we consider another person as "lost" or "not saved" because they have not made such a "profession of faith?" How can we judge someone else, considering them less than, for not adopting the same dogma as we do?

It is interesting how we (myself included) have adopted so many habits that are not in keeping with the original instructions given in the scriptures.

We are not told to "pray" in Jesus' name; we are told to "Ask in my name ..." Name means "in the nature of - likeness," which was meek, not self-serving, loving, kind, confident, benevolent and peaceful. In other words, ask while being Christlike, yourself!

Let's examine what we believe and why we believe it. There is so much good information out there, if one is willing to see.

20:345 A Kettle of Hawks

I had the most interesting experience a while back. We had finished a walk around our property, when we came into the back yard and saw something we had never seen before.

There, above the property, we observed dozens of vultures circling very far above. We thought it odd that the parameter of their circle was moving like a tornado across land. Usually, vultures circle above their dead prey and do not move away from it. It was then that we noticed that they weren't buzzards at all, but rather, they were hawks circling in a thermal.

A thermal is an upward current of warm air, used by gliders, balloons, and birds to gain height. Hawks never congregate, as they are solitary raptors; however, when migrating, they will be observed riding thermals. One of the primary ways that hawks find thermals is by observing other hawks circling. This congregation or circling is called a "kettle."

The warm air of the thermal ascends and the kettle of hawks is raised higher up into the atmosphere until they hit a "cold" ceiling. When they come up against this barrier, they have climbed as far as they can and they leave the kettle, utilizing their height to glide, conserving precious energy until they catch the next thermal. This enables them to move efficiently to their destination.

I thought about this occurrence and friendships. We are all solitary beings and we look for our "kettle" so that we may rise above. Sometimes our "kettle" is small and other times it is large. Some of the hawks fly close together, while others are on the periphery. The goal is the same: to ascend. And we help one another find our thermal in the process.

20:346 What If You Went to the Theatre …?

What if you went to the theatre and saw a fictional movie about Christianity, one of the world's foremost religions.

What if in this fictional movie, there is a main character much like David Langdon in Dan Brown's many conspiracy mystery books involving long-held power structures, intrigue and hidden mysteries.

Then, David Langdon's character introduces the concept that the Jesus story was manufactured and fabricated by the Roman Catholic Church for the purposes of controlling the unruly masses during the darkest centuries of our human history. The belief in Heaven and Hell, reward and punishment, were indeed manufactured concepts presented to the darkened minds of that period that had acquiesced, over centuries, into human consciousness.

It introduces to the Christian that everything they believe in is A LIE.

Throughout the movie, fact upon fact is uncovered in the greatest deception ever executed over human minds. Masses of people are disillusioned. Masses of people are in disbelief. Masses of people simply dismiss the evidence in the midst of cognitive dissonance.

(Cognitive Dissonance is the mental discomfort or "psychological stress" experienced by a person who simultaneously holds two or more contradictory beliefs, ideas, or values, and also occurs when confronted with new information that contradicts said beliefs, ideals, and values.)

Now, the movie ends with a disclaimer that it was not a work of fiction at all, but in truth is the history of Christianity and other messiah-like stories and religions. It says that Jesus was a man that walked the Earth at roughly the same time period, but the majority of the stories about him were fabricated (not parallel to his actual teaching) to lead the masses into a submissive and subservient culture.

They knew that fear would be the best motivator, telling the masses that they would burn in never-ending flames forever for non-compliance to the laws set forth by the Roman Catholic Church. It was a carefully devised plan that amassed a literal fortune for the church as it handsomely rewarded artists to record the images of torture and burning flesh in their esteemed works of art.

What will you think?

20:347 You Are Jacob

You are Jacob. What happened to Jacob in all of the Bible's stories beckons you to lift your eyes and see that this is YOUR story.

Jacob lays down and falls asleep with a rock for a pillow. He dreams of angels ascending and descending on a ladder, and when he awakens, he declares, "Surely God is in this place and I did not know it."

Then Jacob wrestled with the angel of God and says, "I will not turn you loose until you bless me." Jacob's name is then changed to "Israel." He comes away from that wrestling with a limp. It is said that the angel touched his hip (symbolically, hips are known as the scales of balance). The divine presence within expands, and he has now become aware of the Divine identity that inhabits him. This wrestling is internal, and the "scales" are tipped!

The story of Jacob did not happen to one man, but to ALL MEN.

Your ego-centric identity "seized the place of another." Jacob means "supplanter" and supplanter means one that seizes the place of another. This is what the ego has done to all of us as our Divinity slumbers beneath the heavy blanket of our humanity.

Jacob wrestles with his Divine nature until he receives the blessing of the knowledge that he IS ISRAEL which means, "May God prevail." And this divine identity does INDEED PREVAIL .... IN YOU!

May the goodness of Divinity bless you as you rest your mind on the rock of revelation today. May you see your Divine nature as it dwells within your spiral staircase, your DNA.

> *"Surely God is in this place and I did not KNOW it."* Genesis 28:16

Now you know it. Christ in you.

20:348 Raising Your Frequency

There is great benefit in raising your frequency and, as a byproduct of raising your frequency, you will be the recipient of information that has been coded into your DNA – this frequency is what accompanies love, non-judgment and appreciation. This frequency is a "key" to the "kingdom" of possibilities that are dormant within you.

Our DNA is waiting for our conscious participation in its evolutionary process. This adaptation is waiting for our command to morph into our next state of being. WE MUST WILL IT TO BEGIN.

Just as a ship does not move out from the harbor into the sea without the command from the captain, you must signal the activation of your DNA. Your DNA will percolate with vibration while releasing mysteries into the well of your consciousness.

We, alone, carry the information for our journey. This map is indelibly written into our intuitive consciousness. It is here that we begin the journey.

20:349 I Must Be Healing

I must be healing.

At any given time, I can sit down at my computer keyboard and, out of my past experiences with the fundamentalist Christian church, I can write for hours. I was so hurt; then angry.

Now, it seems I have moved into neutral. I know that all of my past experiences serve me and, although I still process events from time to time, and miss the interaction with some people, I would not trade where I am today for anything.

The more I forgive, the higher I float. The higher I float, the more I can see. The more I can see, the greater the understanding. The more understanding I gain, the more compassion I feel. The more compassion I feel, the more the miraculous manifests. This is the rising (resurrection) of our being.

If you are familiar with the colors of the seven chakras (the energy centers of the body that are the counterparts to the endocrine system). the lowest is the root chakra that is red, followed by the second chakra which is orange, then yellow, green (heart), next blue at the throat, then purple at the Pineal gland, then Indigo at the crown or top of the head. Hell is typified at the red, orange and yellow chakras, as this is where our emotional pain is fueled.

Throw all of that negative human emotion on the altar just below the green chakra – burn up all of that pain and then come up higher! Yes, come into the bosom of Abraham – into the heart and love-centered life! These are the green pastures that restore the SOUL! This path is the pattern of healing – the Caduceus!

The movement out from "Hell" (the lower three chakras) is what brought healing in the wilderness and is the pattern of the ascended Christ. That's YOU.

20:350 Taking the Bible Literally

Those who take the Bible literally, refusing to see beyond the historical accounts to discover mystical or figurative interpretations, stand in fear, calling them occult. This rigid literalist view is, indeed, a fishbowl of limitation.

The scripture compares itself to "allegory" at least five times. (Ezekiel 17:2, Galatians 4:24, Proverbs 1:6, John 10:6 and John 16:29). So, we must view some (if not most) of scripture as having meaning beyond literalism.

Biblical texts are filled with mystery, with some of the same stories told and recorded in various cultures and myths that far predate Christianity (and even the

Hebrew traditions). These extra-Biblical stories are about various heroes and are referred to by Joseph Campbell in his book, *Hero of a Thousand Faces*. These heroes appear in most of our world's religions, pointing to the same truth as what is offered in the Bible, and most often predating the Christian religion. Jesus has just left the freshest footprint.

We may find Divinity's love story for mankind occultly planted within all of our world's religions, waiting to be uncovered, like the pearl within the tightly closed oyster, a metaphor for the Divine and internal workings of the human being.

Herein lies the conflict within the Christian religion: Christians feel like their Jesus is the only path, not only to salvation (eternal life in Heaven), but also to secret knowledge. There are those outside of the Christian religion who are initiates into the mysteries that understand the depth and breadth of the love story to encompass all into Christ, not just those who accept Jesus into their hearts (a dogmatic practice installed by Christianity but unspoken by Jesus).

The initiate sees CHRIST as the only way or path to the Source of all, the progenitor; not of Hebrew origin, but one who holds the universe, and beyond, in its hands. This way is not Hebrew, or any other worldly culture, because the lineage of Christ is not hemmed in by any historical setting. Jesus said, "Before Abraham was (the founder of the Hebrew traditions) I AM." To claim ownership of universal truth and to try to encapsulate it within any religion is to be the source of all wars and strife.

Christ is the state of consciousness that recognizes the interconnectivity of all men, and that mankind is, indeed, imbued with the Divine. This understanding is not global, but rather, universal. We must lift our eyes beyond the veil of limitation and see that the whole Earth is yielding a crop whose origin is that of the stars and beyond.

This origin is encoded into all myths; myths that will guide us into our heritage as Christ in the Earth. Paramount to this understanding is that Christ is not a man, but ALL MEN that understand that we are a co-partner with the Divine in our baptism into humanhood. This Divine spark is as a seed that planted in the garden (our biology), and we cannot help but become who and what we are: Divinity.

Separation, judgment, elitism and intolerance are not the fruit that comes from Christ, but rather the ego, the serpent found within all of our gardens that lures us into thinking apart from our Divine nature.

Adhering to a historical, rather than mystical, view will keep mankind forever waiting to the return of Christ outside of himself, a place that Jesus told us NOT TO LOOK.

You are the Son that has been sent to save the world. You are a unique amalgamation of the Divine and man. You must believe that you are so much more than a human – you are the revelation of Christ in the Earth, and through your belief and ultimate manifestation, the world will be saved.

Being "saved" is not about escaping the wrath of Hell by raising your hand, walking an aisle and accepting Jesus into your heart. It is believing that the Divine is already, within.

20:351 A Reply to a Gentlemanly Warning

This is a reply to a gentleman who advises me, for safety, to get into the framework of a church system and said, "… like a trampoline, they provide tension and safety, and to not have a framework of belief is dangerous." Here is my reply:

It should be stated that there are between 38,000 and 41,000 differing (and some disagreeing) Christian sects in our world. Which one should I choose for my framework? You see, I have been where you are, fundamentally at the same place of understanding. Disillusionment in 1999 propelled me out from all doctrine and dogma espoused by any organization, forsaking it all for what is written on my heart. Because there is so much disagreement and differing opinions, I choose to seek the source, rather than someone else's interpretation or understanding.

I don't consider the Bible the "Word of God," mainly because of the numerous edits and inconsistencies when viewed historically and literally, and also because of the most recent findings in its source. Frankly, his word is not limited to a book, the framework of which was decided by men predisposed to cultural judgments in the first few hundred years after the advent of Jesus.

Jesus never once directed us to the Bible for salvation, but rather, always pointed within. He saw the foolishness of the rigid adherence to systems that had been pulled past their season of relevance. He was relentlessly hard on the religious.

Frames are for control and, at one time, human consciousness may have needed such rules, regulations and boundaries. But when one comes of age, one must put away those things meant for children. You mention safety and danger – I appreciate the warning and would never give the keys to my car to a five-year-old. But if I hold the keys forever, long after the child becomes a man, then there is dysfunction.

We must begin to think and discern for ourselves – to stretch the intuitive mind and understanding, and to interpret the figurative mysteries resident in scripture. The coming-of-age person must be trusted to discern for themselves, lest we foster a consciousness that remains tethered to the parent.

The present church system does not cultivate healthy adults when the threat of Hell and separation always looms overhead. At some point, LOVE becomes the beacon, and decisions are made based on this "system" that never, ever fails.

20:352 People Don't Change, they Bend

This little phrase has been running across my mind lately. I have heard it every day for a week now and so as usual, I sit down at my computer to write about it and hope that something begins to flow. I think we as Americans are addicted to our microwave society, one that expects rapid change – you know the kind of change that takes place on our one-hour long television dramas. In real life, in real relationships, people don't change, they bend.

We had a juniper tree in our front yard for the seven years where we lived in the city. It was a corner lot on a very busy street. There were always cars buzzing by, but more than that, it was a wide collector street where the westerly winds continually blew. The Juniper grew crooked and always looked as though it was bearing heavy winds. Without the constant influence of the wind it would probably return to growing straight up and down. I think this is analogous to human behavior. With constant pressure people may or may not change direction - most likely they just bend. Then we must ask ourselves, is bending enough?

20:353 Bible Stories Are Metaphors!

Yes, all of these Bible stories, that we try to see literally, are metaphorical mysteries. The axe head that floats, the ark, the animals by two and two, are archetypical by nature, so we can observe and see what is actually internal in me and you.

All has been externalized so the mind can see, by observation, that which is internal and unseen.

All the stories: Rebecca and Leah, King Solomon, Nehemiah and Ezra, and Hosea that married the whore. These stories are you and me and more.

History bends to mystery, and our eyes are opened to see the journey we undertake for thousands upon thousands of years, countless souls in many bodies, experiencing all. Purposeful. Fantastic journey to the center of our Earth – Divinity wrapped in the swaddle of our flesh … and blood … cocooned.

And then tribulation, breaking free. Awakening. Understanding. Striving ends. A new creature emerges. Christ. God + man the one, in one. In all.

From the ark of the covenant to the rock that Moses struck, to Moses and Jacob, Israel, too. All internal. All you.

20:354 We Are All Conditioned

We are all conditioned to know the difference between good and evil and, as a result, we are lowered into time and mortality.

This is an egocentric way of living. It is necessary to live in this world. But we are taught about the age to come, where there is no death, no weeping, etc. We are admonished to "be in the world, but not of the world."

Things are different in the age to come. So how do we get there? By following the instruction of "do not judge lest the judgment with which you judge another fall on your own head." In other words, judgment is circular and highly creative because, whatever the human (imbued with the creator) focuses upon and projects emotion toward, WE CREATE.

So, if you are called to govern in this present age – if you are in law enforcement – then you will judge every day, and your emotions will project out from your body, and it will pull maintenance on whatever it is that you are focusing upon. By pulling maintenance, I mean that whatever it is that you are focusing upon, that same will be reinforced by the compatible vibration that comes from your body. Fear begets more fear. Hatred begets more hatred. "God (the creative force within) in not mocked – whatever you sow so shall you reap."

So, if we are afraid of our border being compromised and we focus upon that circumstance with fear, guess what? We have just created or, at the very least, set into motion more of the same or similar events that will provoke MORE FEAR. We may be informed – we may even judge – but enlisting our emotions is a whole other thing, because thought + emotion is like a car + gas. We create what we focus upon and emote toward.

Lastly, God is not an American. I look very much forward to the day where we are borderless and there is plenty for all of the Earth's inhabitants. How do we get there? We must be the change we wish to see. We must take every thought captive, lift our eyes, and begin to create our beautiful, peaceful Earth of plenty.

The only way of getting out of this frequency of good and evil and fear is by focusing on what we want, instead of focusing upon what we don't want. In this way, a bridge to the next age is established.

20:355 A Lot of Confusion Out There About "Time"

These "no time" teachers have latched on to a fractal of reality; but it is not the totality.

So many are teaching things that do not align with the truth of reality and, therefore, end up with a mess. I have spoken with many people who simply don't understand what these "no time" or "time is an illusion" teachers are saying. I have found an excellent article that may help them understand the portion of our reality that DOES, INDEED, EXIST IN TIME.

Simply put, if we are on a planet that revolves, that also circles the Sun, along with other planets, in a Solar System that curves through space, in a gravitational relationship with another distant star, THEN WE WILL HAVE TIME. Celestial movement creates time, and time SERVES us. This isn't difficult to understand. We have a portion of ourselves that lives in time and utilizes all of the lessons that being physical affords. Being physical is not the totality of who and what we are, but it is a necessary component of being a human on a planet within the construct of time. Saying it does not exist at all is foolishness.

20:356 The Role of the Ego

The ego is THE mechanism that can focus thought and emotion for the human in the material worlds. As such, it is vital, in order for Spirit to have experience and residence while occupying a physical body.

We have been inoculated by Spirit. The virgin soil of humanity (symbolized by Mary being overshadowed) was penetrated, and this eternal bliss entered into limitation, and even death, as it was seeking for a helpmate through which it might navigate and occupy physical worlds. Without the human partner, this was not possible. A biological form was evolved, and when the time came, Spirit pierced our DNA. Eternity is now resident within us.

Ah, but the EGO is given the task to self-protect and, largely, is anything but self-less. This is our journey, then; to surrender willingly to "death" as master of the body, so that we might experience resurrection as a servant to the Divine Nature.

This is the symbolism of marriage – the womb-man yields to Spirit, and a new being is formed within us – Christ.

In the parable of the Unjust Steward, you might remember; it does not make sense. A business owner returns, after an absence, to see to how his business is doing under the jurisdiction of the manager. The manager is chastised for squandering wealth and warned that he will be put out of a job. The owner leaves again, and the manager begins to slash receivables, hoping to make friends from among those that "owe" the business.

When the owner returns, he praises the manager for being "wise in the ways of the world" and making friends that will welcome him into eternal shelters once he is dismissed from his job.

How was he wise?

He forgave DEBT.

Before, he had been squandering the wealth of forgiving debt – forgiveness. This is the key to enter into eternity. The ego must see and understand that it is the mechanism that allows us to move into eternity, where it is welcomed into "eternal shelters." It is a necessary part of the Christ equation.

Queen Esther learns of the plan to annihilate her people, and so boldly enters the King's chambers. She is warned – under threat of death – not to enter into his chambers, but she knows that she must petition for the salvation of her people and does so anyway. Once she is in his chambers, the King tells her to ask for anything, up to half of his kingdom.

The role of the ego has always been to self-protect, but as it evolves, it becomes selfless and recognizes its role as SAVIOR. Queen Esther is an archetype of EGO.

The parallels can go on forever, but you get the idea. Such mystery in the stories within this timeless book! I wish those who have been so disenfranchised by Christians could see that it is not a Christian book, but rather, a mystery book for all.

20:357 Shunning

I so dislike thinking about this particular topic, but – just maybe -- you will share this with a friend, or even with family members that have done this to you.

In her book, *The Bond*, Lynne McTaggart explores the bond between people and groups and touches on the subject of "shunning."

After my departure from Christian fundamentalism, I had many hurtful experiences with many friends, especially those who banded together to ostracize me for speaking about my changing views.

I had friends who would no longer talk to me, or would look the other way in the grocery store; friends who came over to chastise me; friends who blind-sided me at scheduled social outings, withdrawing support from my ministry board under the guise to "help build me up;" friends who came over to my home to visit and announced that they could no longer be my friend, because of what I was now embracing. I had friends who met with my Pastor and told him things that were not true, or that were a skewed version of things. I had a group of friends that I had met together with regularly, to celebrate birthdays, that shunned me, and two of them even left a party where we were casually talking about spiritual things. Most recently, a close friend sent me a text to announce the end of our friendship.

It was a difficult decade – and it continues. The choice to forgive is a daily occurrence and, quite frankly, a challenge. I send them good energy. I pray for them in the way I know how to pray. I pronounce forgiveness and. when my mind wanders to painful experiences, I refocus – go for a walk, pick up a devotional book, turn on the television, call a friend, make jewelry – anything to get my mind off of the wound. But with days like today, nothing works, and so I sit with so many words and not a soul that I would feel right to spill them on. Days like this are few, but they are still there. And so, I write.

My husband, with me through all of this, continually told me to "suck it up" and to "get tougher skin." I had lost even the safe place that he afforded, after a while. I struggled, because it seemed every time I would feel breakthrough and healing, another hit would come. I was growing numb.

While on the way to the post office this morning, I imagined bumping into one of these friends and what I would say to them. I thought it might go something like this: "You have taught me two things; about a God I would never serve and about a person I would never wish to be like."

Then I shake my head, as if I was an observer, and say to myself, "Barbara, you must still be so hurt." And then I wonder if this wound will ever heal.

Foremost in my mind, I thought about the pain I would cause this person with my words, and that brought me a feeling of sorrow. I dismissed these thoughts quickly and, after the post office, I returned home. I am cleaning the house, doing various chores, and this wound is still asking for my attention.

One day, my husband came and stood by my desk, and as I turned to look at him, I noticed Lynne's book in his hands, open. I turned to give him my full attention, and he began to read to me out loud:

"The most fundamental of these needs is a sense of belonging. Humanity is profoundly tribal; we feel most at home in small clusters in which we are a part of the whole. Indeed, so primal is the need to belong that ostracism is one of the most unbearable situations human beings endure.

Robert L. Bear, a former Mennonite, referred to the Amish practice of 'shunning' as a 'living Hell of torture.'

Aborigines reserved the immense life or death power of ostracism for extreme cases, as it often proved fatal. This most primal of human urges – not to stand apart but simply to fit in – particularly with the people who immediately surround us, may well be so necessary to our existence that not satisfying it can be a matter of life and death."
End Quote

It was with a shaky voice and tears that he read that last sentence and I realized then that he was, at last, beginning to understand. What began in 1999 was finally getting validation from the most important person in my life.

Lyle dropped the book on my desk and pulled me to my feet and embraced me long and hard. We both cried.

I experienced months of depression at a time, then weeks, then days, and now, moments. I know that I am healing, and I am thankful for that.

So, I say this to those of you out there that shun, that sever relationships because of spiritual or, more relevantly, because of political views; just love, people. No matter the difference, just love one another and choose to be kind. Choosing to love over judgment is a teaching of Jesus Christ and Christ is a being worthy to emulate. You never know whose soul you may be helping to heal – and that is a BIG thing to do.

20:358 Separate Yourselves?

A friend commented to say that Christians will point out the Bible verses that tell them to separate from those that don't believe as they. My comment:

Yes, it does say that. It is one of many contradictions to the teachings of Jesus, who was, indeed, all-inclusive; EXCEPT, he was sort of hard on the religious folk – you know, that "whitewashed tomb brood of vipers" comment.

20:359 We are Living in the Most Amazing Time

We are living in the most amazing time ever. We have the rare opportunity to experience one of the greatest shifts the planet has felt, thus far, in this present cycle.

You can see it all around you, as you observe the way humans think beginning to change – leaving behind the fear and judgment and refusing to be manipulated by the systems that plague us. We are opening up to love and non-judgment, the two primary factors that will aid in our awakening and evolutionary process.

Yes, you will still see systems that promote division, separation and fear, but those systems are quickly being seen for what they are; a means by which human consciousness may be manipulated.

When you see these systems in action – whether they be by the media, government, politicians or religion – just smile and be thankful that you are awakening. Don't judge the system; but rather, appreciate the womb that has given birth to you.

I am so glad that we are on this journey together. We have plotted our course and set our compass to be here in this moment. Your escalating frequency will heal humanity as the train of the Christ leads captivity captive. Your awakening process will set a tone that will attract others to do the same. Humanity cannot help but experience this morning stretch together.

I am grateful for you. Keep going. Let's help one another stay positive. Let's cheer one another on.

20:360 While We Think We Are Human Only ...

While we think that we are human only, we will experience limitation.

While we think we are Divine only, we will experience incompletion.

Emmanuel is both human and Divine. This is the plan, and the culmination of the ages. The God-man is emergent.

SECTION TWENTY-ONE

TWENTY-ONE

21:361 Terminology

I think there is so much confusion and uncertainty when dealing with terminology.

Soul/spirit/ego/personality/divinity/higher self/oversoul, etc., can be daunting to understand, to say the least; and who can say for sure what exactly each one is?

I know this: that there is a divine spark that knows all and is the progenitor (Father/God) living within me and is growing. How it grows is unknown – I really think it has to do with a culmination of lifetimes, lessons learned, etc.

And, there is the human body with the immaterial intellect/mind/ego. As the human surrenders to that divine mind (love, non-judgment), Christ manifests (Christ is an amalgamation of the divine and the human – they are "wed"

I also know that there will be (if not already) 10% of the population (it is the TITHE) that will forerun this mystical union and will manifest Christ in the Earth.

This manifestation will create the path and pattern for all men to be "saved" and to manifest Christ, as well.

This is likened to "first the blade, then the stalk, then the full ear." The blades are appearing and maturing.

Being "saved" means that we do not perish – body, mind or spirit! The body becomes incorruptible.

21:362 In Times of Conflict

In times of conflict …

> *"Wanting to reform the world without discovering one's true self is like trying to cover the world with leather to avoid the pain of walking on stones and thorns.*
>
> *It is much simpler to wear shoes."*
> Ramana Maharishi

Instead of looking externally at all of the disorder, disfunction, disconnectedness – when we try to fix somebody else, or even world situations, it's much easier to fix how we see things.

In this way we wear "shoes," instead of trying to pad the rough world around us.

21:363 It Is Not About Men and Women

It is not about men and women, nor male or female – it is about energy.

Presently, we are living out a great mystery, a metaphor that is alive by being either male or female. By the patterns in nature, we are to see that the male (masculine) is the seed-giver, but the female incubates and grows the seed, and ultimately gives birth to the creation that is both masculine and feminine.

From this physical example, we are to learn the principles behind masculine and feminine energy.

The masculine provides force, the thrust, the seed which carries dunamis; power; a blueprint.

The feminine provides the egg (potential) to couple with and the form with which to incubate the potential form.

The physical penetration of the male into female and the subsequent deposit, mingling, agreement (yes, the sperm work together, gather into groups of 12-13, form a key circle on the outside of the egg and the egg decides whether or not to allow the penetration of ONE sperm), and adherence and growth of the fetus is a PATTERN.

This is the pattern: Although we are separated into male and female presently, we need to understand that this mystical union that is spoken of is a union of masculine and feminine energy – this will produce a gender-neutral being. "In the kingdom there is neither male nor female ..."

This union will produce a new creation.

Secondly, we can see by this human physical pattern that something else is afoot. When we yield physically (and allow penetration of the sperm into the egg) this, too, is a PATTERN of the yielding of the EGO or human mind to the Divine mind. This yielding produces a God-man – CHRIST. Presently, consciousness is undergoing PENETRATION, and as we allow the Divine impetus of LOVE to permeate and to penetrate, a new creation is being formed within the WOMB OF THE EARTH. This yielding is what is called the HARVEST, as the human mind is no longer subject to or focused on this mortal realm or world. It is ready, like the cocooned caterpillar, to shed the restriction of this passing age and enter into a limitless life. This is the Melchizedek order.

This is Emmanuel that is neither male nor female; but rather, BOTH. This new creation is able to create at will out of its being; not another life, per se (because it continually renews itself and is eternal), but anything it desires, it can create. There is no limitation.

This is your destiny.

Earth is a womb. It has been incubating YOU.

It is the mystery of mysteries, we each, in our own role, are displaying the greatest truth of the universe. We each contain masculine and feminine within one body – both energies highly creative – and when they come into union within, we are truly born again.

21:364 Do You Have It All Right?

It is expanding to accept differing concepts and ideas continually. It is restrictive to think that one has it all "right". There will never be an end to experience. Jesus spoke of the necessity of the new wineskin. The old has stretched as far as it can and cannot contain the volatile expansion that comes with revelation.

The ONE has its place in our origin but is not the goal. How can it be? We are forever individuated, having been replicated and primed for expansion. But, recognizing that we share in union that is making the TWO ONE, is the purpose for the Emmanuel – where God has joined us and we have yielded in union. Now we conceive, again and again bringing forth from our own universal womb what is inherently both God and man. Christ. This is the stuff of genius. That love found a way to explore and inhabit the material planes in and through a helpmate – the human being.

That said, there are those whose ultimate purpose is not to be Emmanuel, and those will return to blend with the ONE. It is our choice. Some purchase land. Some remove the rocks. Some till the soil. Some plant the seed. Some are the bounty. Some reap the harvest. It is not so important for the reaper to convince the tiller to be a reaper. We must appreciate all and recognize we are all, in all fulfilling the purpose for which genius is.

21:365 The Son of Perdition

The "son of perdition" is us (not some devil outside of us). It is the part of us that is controlled and manipulated by the release of emotions via the EGO, as it judges between good and evil via the five senses.

When the son of perdition steps down off the throne; that is, stops judging between good and evil by the five senses, this is called "the great falling away" and is necessary in order for Christ to manifest. Christ judges with the single eye, the eye of union, also called "righteous judgment."

Christ does not look at circumstances and allow his strings to be pulled and manipulated by the bad circumstances of life.

Rather, the Christ only does what he sees and hears his father (the progenitor) do; the father is that creative component inherent within us all.

Christ is the son of that father, although he is experiencing reality as both human and God, and capable of creating material worlds through the use of emotion.

Creating a new world (or at least a bridge into the next age) is accomplished through disengaging judgment after the seeing of our eyes. We must "lift" our eyes and see beyond what is seen with the five senses. We must intuit what the father (the creative potential within all) is showing us (what our intuitive sense shows us). In this way, we focus our emotions on what it is we wish to see.

21:366 History or Mystery

History or Mystery??? Ah the interior life ...

Many are resistant to the Bible being a written account of our interior reality, albeit expressed through exterior stories.

We are beaten down with "belief" in the history and have neglected the mystery. As such, we have wound up with a confused and convoluted religion; one that forsakes, separates and divides itself from those who see beyond the shackles of literalism.

> *"With the Gnostics knowledge was the foundation of their faith; but the historic Christians made faith the basis of knowledge, and the first demand of the new faith was for the convert to believe that all the mythical typology of the past had been made literally true in the present.*
>
> *By faith the fable was crystallized into the dogma of historical fact.*
>
> *The Christ of the Gnostics was a mystical type continued from mythology to portray a spiritual reality of the INTERIOR life."*
>
> Gerald Massey

Speaking of masculine and feminine energies….

> *"The wise woman builds her house,*
> *But the foolish tears it down with her own hands."*
>   Proverbs 14:1

The "wise woman" (feminine energy) is within every single human being. This energy will direct and incubate thoughts and bring them to fruition.

How are you thinking and speaking about your body? Your family? Your planet?

A person who is wise will recognize the power of creation and destruction that is within them.

What are you building?

What are you tearing down?

21:367 Judging Homosexual Behavior

A letter to a friend about judging homosexual behavior:

> *"Please take the time to read Chapter 11 of my book. That will explain a lot.*
>
> *I was, like you, holding the same judgmental thoughts, but my eyes were opened when I began to see things from a metaphysical (beyond physical) view. It is not about men and women, male and female, but rather masculine and feminine, which is inherent within all humans.*
>
> *You can be female and have an abundance of masculine energy, and vice-versa. To create you must have both – in the case of spiritual creation, the feminine (that is the mind, ego, will and womb) must yield to the masculine (the divine force, seed-giver).*
>
> *We judge homosexual behavior because we have deemed it to be evil. The mind/ego is responsible for eating from the tree that knows between good and evil – but we are told not to eat from that tree lest we die – and WE ARE because we participate in JUDGMENT. And JUDGMENT IS CIRCULAR. Jesus said, "Whatever judgment we judge someone with will fall on our own heads." And so it is!*

To stop eating from the tree of the knowledge of good and evil is a prerequisite for eternal life. In Genesis 6 we are told that "man is now mortal" (and the inference is because he ate from the forbidden tree) and we received a limitation of life to 120 years.

So, in order to yield to this divine decree, must cease from our judging between good and evil. There is but a small contingent of humans who have this call – approximately 10% -- this is the tithe that was given to Melchizedek to forge the pathway OUT FROM THE WORLD OF DUALITY or judging between good and evil.

So, when we judge between good and evil, ESPECIALLY when we judge homosexual behavior, it is WE WHO DISPLAY our own SPIRITUAL HOMOSEXUALITY when the feminine (ego) fails to yield to the masculine's decree to cease from judgment – but rather, the ego continues in its dalliance, ego-to-ego.

Science only confirms this reality by our patterns in the natural. But the natural/physical pattern points the way to an eternal, not temporal, principle which has NOTHING to do with men and women but has everything to do with masculine and feminine.

At the end of the day, we must follow Christ – not Paul, or any letter written in the law. The law is now LOVE, which all the law and prophets hang upon. I hope you can see this."

21:368 Intolerance

INTOLERANCE: *Unwillingness to accept views, beliefs, or behavior that differ from one's own.*

Synonyms: Bigotry, narrow-mindedness, small-mindedness, parochialism, provincialism, insularity, fanaticism, dogmatism, illiberality; prejudice, bias, partiality, partisanship, sectarianism, one-sidedness, inequality, unfairness, injustice, discrimination

I think it is time to speak up when someone's intolerance or bigotry is showing. How often have we sat at a dinner table listening to someone who is expressing intolerance? How often have we listened to some malign another person, whether it be a politician, family member or friend, and we just remained silent?

We learn cultural boundaries from one another. We learn through our surroundings, and when we let intolerance go unchecked, we are no better than the one expressing it. Don't be afraid – speak up. Speak truth in love.

You are the iron that sharpens iron.

Practice what you might say to a dear friend when they are intolerant. Practice until it becomes second nature and speak with love AND TOLERANCE.

A Jewish person, Christian, Muslim, Homosexual, Atheist, Democrat, Republican and Buddhist walk into a restaurant – They talk, laugh, drink and deepen their friendship.

It's not a joke. It's what happens when you are not an asshole. I blocked two people this week for hiding behind their religion and promoting intolerance toward gay people. Enough is enough. I spoke with them privately, through Facebook Messenger, and let them know the expectations on my page. Neither one of them budged but continued with their religious rhetoric.

21:369 Repeating Cycles

Okay – So, there are a number of us beginning to recognize repeating cycles/patterns in our lives. This is also a part of the awakening process that provides an expanded view, or maybe a better way of describing it would be a view "from above" the mundane.

It is from this vantage point that we begin to see the things we have set for ourselves to learn and overcome. We no longer see these things as happening to us, but rather, FOR US. These lessons are vital for our progression and ultimate ascension processes. The vibrational currency accrued from these experiences is priceless and USEFUL in the age to come.

We must accrue and gather the full spectrum of emotional experiences in order for us to reap the harvest of currency that comes from the experience. When we understand our cycles of learning and why we set ourselves up for death, time and time again (thank you, Judas), it is only then that the cycle is complete and that "bucket" full to the brim of the specific currency needed for the age to come. This currency varies, just as in the natural. Some are pennies, some nickels, quarters, fifty-cent pieces, dollars, Fives, tens, twenties, fifties, hundreds…

Just as there is fear, hate, jealousy, wrath, vengeance, anger, frustration, complacency, indifference, peace, love, joy, etc. All of these buckets must be filled according to each of our blueprints. As in the natural, a blueprint is written, and the supplies ordered to fulfill the pattern.

It is through these invaluable and challenging times we reap the benefit of experience, and through experience comes currency that is stored in our emotional body. When we come to the place of non-judgment, unconditional love, fearlessness and radical acceptance of the way things are, WE ARE COMPLETE and stand poised to transmute, transform and TRANSFIGURE our physical limited bodies and ready them for our interdimensional habitation.

We must, must begin to inquire of within, as our guidance anxiously awaits our attention and our questioning. This guidance is formatted for your unique and individual learning path and is complete and lacking no-thing that you require for your journey.

You have heard me say that this is a solitary path and, indeed, it is. There are many on the path, but the "way" must be discerned from within. Through this discerning you activate your intuitive Divine mind that awaits your union. It takes a yielded will to know, not to see with the natural eyes, but to find and begin to use your pineal eye. This eye does not see in the natural, which is what your five senses are for. This eye is your guide into the intuited worlds that are not physical. Together, your five senses and your pineal eye will forge a synergy necessary to inhabit the worlds that are both physical and spiritual. This is what your body will be fit for, as well. The bridge is being built into the new world that is being birthed through your conscious habitation, and you are the bridge.

21:370 You Exist in Multiple Dimensions

We exist on multiple dimensions (12 + 1). We each have twelve aspects to our "self"; however, only one is "focused" by vibration and resonance to this physical dimension.

Each of these twelve aspects has its own key or tone/frequency. We are like a keyboard that has twelve notes to this octave – 13, if you count the repeating "C." This "C" is Christ, the basis for each tone and our authentic identity. The twelve disciples surround the Christ in the "upper room" of consciousness.

Our bodies are an instrument that emits frequency. These frequencies come out from our body when we "feel" something or when we have emotions.

This movement is energy in motion.

This energy plays delightfully in the quantum field of probability.

It is in this field where the energy in motion swirls and dances, constructs and deconstructs that which the human god focuses its attention toward.

Emotions play the chord that the spiritual body instrument resonates with. Each tone or key gathers or scatters quantum bits of matter to create circumstances that match the key that is coming from the intender, the human god or God-man (Melchizedek).

If we really and truly understand the emotion/judgment quotient, we would be very MIND-FULL of what we think about and emote, for these are the keys to the quantum field of creation.

Whatever we sow, we will reap.

We really are magnificent. Remember the Morning Star that fell?

21:371 Baptism

Baptism is not ritual, per se; it is a physical act that relays to us something far more mysterious – the journey of the Divine into mortal flesh and blood within humanity. The human body is largely comprised of water, and the Divine takes the plunge into our biology!

Baptism is a metaphor!

Read on ...

The new and the old wineskin is the consciousness in which you perceive reality.

The old wineskin might be your old way of thinking that brings limitation. An old wineskin has stretched as far as it can.

An example of the old wineskin would be seeing the Bible as a historical account of the world.

The new wineskin might be a new way of thinking.

An example would be seeing the Bible as a figurative account of the evolving consciousness of mankind.

An old way of thinking might be that we need to dunk people underwater (or sprinkle) to get them baptized.

A new way of thinking might be that the journey of God within a human being is himself being "baptized" (immersed) into human consciousness. This baptism is done to be "saved".

It is the necessary journey, this divulgence from eternity into human form to redeem for itself a helpmate, a human body from with which to navigate the material realms. Therefore, this "lamb" is slain from before the foundation, when it makes the choice to invest his immortal self into mortality – the infinite into the finite.

Again, baptism is not ritual, per se; it is a physical act that relays to us something far more mysterious – the journey of the Divine into mortal flesh and blood, within humanity.

21:372 His Hands Carefully Caressed the Floor

Years ago, I was getting ready for our Fourth of July party, and I was mopping, thinking about my cousin David, and what he had said about my hardwood floors. I had called him to question my options about refinishing my 130-year-old pine floors.

David traveled over three hours to give me his opinion. On his knees, his hands carefully caressed the floor, stopping to run his fingers over the scars of an era long gone, calling it "beautiful." I watched him, as his eyes twinkled, and his hands touched.

I looked at the scratches and the scars, recalling my kids chasing the dog with his 185-lb frame and long paw nails scraping my floors as he rounded the corners, giving chase. I saw the flaws; but David, a woodworker and craftsman, saw beauty.

That day, David taught me to appreciate the patina, the years, the weathering, and even the scars in the wood. But today, I thought about me. I am learning to appreciate my weathering through the years and to appreciate my scars; physical, emotional and spiritual. We all have patina – each one of us – and to appreciate our journey – the good and the bad – is the beginning of healing and transcendence.

You are flawed and scarred, and you are lovely. You worked hard, played hard and loved even harder to get those scars. The betrayal of a friend, the loss of a loved one, the hurtful wounds of self-loathing. Yes, these are scars that mark our journey, and they may be earned no other way than to truly live.

21:373 You Were in Eden

In Ezekiel 28

> *"You were in Eden, the garden of God. Every precious stone was*
> *your covering: The ruby, the topaz, and the diamond; the beryl, the*
> *onyx, and the jasper; the lapis lazuli, the turquoise, and the emerald;*

and the gold, the workmanship of your settings (timbrels) and sockets (flutes), was in you. On the day that you were created they were prepared."

Here, the Bible alludes to Lucifer (actually it has been mistaken for one solitary being) and how this remarkable being had a marvelous musical instrument of a body, and how this being became prideful and fell (into the 3rd dimension based in fear). The instrument carries the frequency of our emotions as they are "played" and as these frequencies are "played", reality in our mortal dimension is created.

We are that marvelous being that fell. And we will resurrect as we experience re"member"ing, that is, the re-bundling of our multidimensional self.

This is symbolized in the ritual of Baptism (being buried under the waters of very human consciousness) and communion (the "broken bread" descending down the throat, which is called the "grave" in scripture) into the belly of the Earth. We are told to "take this in re-MEMBER-ance of me (CHRIST!)."

The fallen one is the "dark shirt" aspect of US. There was a cosmic war in "Heaven" – and where is Heaven?

IN US. A necessary devolution into futility, for a time.

Our 12-stranded DNA was surrendered for the dualism of TWO, and we lost our multidimensional capabilities.

Now, the parts of us that are light, according to the full spectrum, are being summoned to return to the upper room, as they will reintegrate and surround the CHRIST.

We are light. We are dark. And we are everything in-between.

It is time for union. It is time for re-bundling. It is time for resurrection.

21:374 It's Not About Sex

If read this, you will gain immeasurable understanding about the nature of reality, the universe and the creative potential within you. I wrote this years ago, but in re-reading this morning, I understand that something wrote through me.

Take your time and digest EVERY sentence.

Here goes ....

It's not about sex … The Christian right cites Romans Chapter One as the ultimate indictment against homosexuality. Let's take a closer look:

It is imperative that Romans Chapter One is taken metaphorically, metaphysically, symbolically or figuratively to see the mystery of creation contained within the text. If we take it literally, we are sentenced to see only with our five senses and what they observe in the natural. Romans Chapter One is not about human sex. Rather, it is about the masculine and feminine energies resident within the human being and the ramifications of dysfunctional "relations" within the body.

You will see that these dysfunctional relations produce death and indeed, the human race is mortal and does, indeed … die. Our salvation is not relegated to the time, appointed by some religions, occurring only after death, with entrance to some heaven. No, I say it is apprehended TODAY.

Paul alluded to this mystery when he said, "Wives submit to your husbands and husbands love your wives." He even went further and said, "I speak a mystery [not about husbands and wives] but of Christ and his church." Paul was referring to the mystery of the ages by stating that the teachings about men and women in their respective roles were to be taken figuratively. It should be noted here also that the "church" is not what we think it is. The "church" is the dwelling place of the Divine within the human as well as a dwelling place that is immaterial – in the next dimension, so to speak. It is you, divinely indwelled – and it is the part of you that transcends the material worlds. That is the "church."
We must "lift our eyes" to see these coded mysteries and, if we do, we will see the mechanics of manifesting immortality itself and a world that does not decay. Presently, we have a time limit on our creative outputs. We are sentenced to mortality – *a life that spans no more than 120 years* (Genesis 6). And our world reflects this time limit through aging, disease, rust, mold, mildew and ultimately, disintegration.

For those fixed on schism and finger-pointing; well, they will have a hard time seeing this chapter figuratively. A transition must be made within the mind itself, a shifting of focus much like an eye adjusts to see something near or far. If we are to apprehend the mysteries contained within the scriptural text, then literalism must be surrendered. Please don't misunderstand; the literal translation has a place in time, but keep in mind, the letter kills, but the spiritual (mystical) brings life.

There are many admonitions in the New Testament to "lift our eyes and see" and "let him who has ears to hear, hear." This is absolute instruction to the human being to shift focus, to repent (to see things differently) and to tap into the mechanism (your intuition that connects you with the part of you that does not dwell in the material world) of the body that allows to shift from left brain intellect to right brain intuitive. It requires the ability to see from above the linear and historical accounts presented in the text.

If we perceive Romans Chapter One speaking of human sexuality, we are viewing with a lens that gives a very granular and literal understanding. But if we shift to see that it just may be pointing to something much more mysterious that allows for perception beyond the natural, you will see an overview from above – with an eagle-eye view. If you are able, this is indeed, "where the eagles gather."

We are all male and female, masculine and feminine in one body. This is our state of being as described in Genesis One, before our devolution into duality where we manifest as separate: male and female in respective bodies. It is through this dalliance into duality that the human race beautifully expresses the unseen dynamics and MYSTERIES of creation by literally bringing forth life after its kind.

Literally, we see that the woman is the receptacle (the womb-man). Within the female is the ability to bring forth life. The male deposits seed (through the intimate passage), the child forms, and birth through the narrow way occurs.

Figuratively, the feminine aspect of the human, the womb or the receptacle, is joined with the human will, ego, mind. Ultimately, this dalliance must come to an end. We must willingly submit to the Divine masculine, like the pattern of Jesus in the Garden of Gethsemane, when he willingly faces the cross experience and declares, "Nevertheless not my will, but thy will be done." The pattern of Jesus shows that the human egocentric will must give way or yield to that counterpart within and dwelling in "heaven" that is Divine – the "CHURCH." This is the feminine submitting to the masculine. It is the human will, yielding to the unlimited and immaterial spirit that does not have boundaries, and is not stuck within time and the material worlds. Once this "wedding" takes place, the feminine has access to infinity. Let's take a brief look at this pattern within the story of Esther, as she marries the King. Here is an excerpt from *Escaping Christianity ~ Finding Christ*:

> *"Esther was being prepared to meet the King, to become his Queen,*
> *and as such, she was having her skin anointed with perfumed oil. Oil*
> *is a perfect metaphor for Spirit or Divinity. Once oil is rubbed into*
> *the skin, the oil is irretrievable, as the skin and the oil have become*
> *one. The oil is now animated as it mingles with flesh, and the flesh*
> *becomes supple and beautiful. It is a mutually beneficial relationship.*
> *Metaphorically, we can see that the oil or Divinity (Spirit) and the*
> *flesh (metaphor for baseness) become ONE – like a marriage.*
>
> *The story of Esther is metaphoric for our own process of anointing,*
> *as we are prepared to meet the King. The basis for the word Christ*
> *then, is when Divinity and flesh meet in conscious awareness. Flesh*
> *is anointed as we awaken to the reality that Divinity indwells us.*
> *Divinity is 'pressed into' the mortal framework and there are now*
> *two conscious elements dwelling in one body – and the two become*

ONE. Jesus was called "Emmanuel" or God with man. This meeting is a culmination of a courtship between Divinity and human consciousness that has lasted millennia.

As the story continues, Esther presents herself before the King and plans to ask for the salvation of her people who were under threat of imminent death at the hangman's gallows. We must ask ourselves, are we mortal and subject to imminent death? Are we petitioning for salvation? The King welcomes her into his presence and tells her to ask for anything, anything up to half of his kingdom. Wow – now that is a partnership! Her people were ultimately spared. And that is what comes with the anointing and is what happens to us as this Spark of Divinity expands or grows and becomes one with us. It is like the parable of the mustard seed planted in the Garden. It begins as the smallest of seeds but soon overtakes the 'garden.' It is perfection blossoming in and through us.

This account of Esther and the King is a beautiful metaphor – the Queen (the womb of the egocentric human), once consummation/union takes place, comes boldly to her counterpart, the King (life-giving seed-giver, Spirit/Divinity) and is petitioning for the salvation of her people (the human race). The scriptures are, indeed, a roadmap for us, which if viewed metaphorically, reveal humanity's path through consciousness. And what a journey it is."

This union between the metaphorical King and Queen is when we, the Queen, submit to the King. Once this partnership is consummated, we have access to the riches of the kingdom.

From this elevated view, we understand the necessity to bring our former "single" self, our human mode of egocentric operation; that is, judging between good and evil, into submission. Our pattern son told us, "Do not judge, lest you be judged with the same judgment that you judge another." This is a prerequisite to transition the age.

This admonition is the key to creating, maintaining and sustaining this mortal and limited realm of death that we live in while we "eat from the tree of the knowledge of good and evil." For when we judge between good and evil, we are creating the cycle of death because when Divinity (that is a spark dwelling within the human) decrees a thing, it is so. And so, we create continually, this limited and mortal environment, because we continually judge. And when we judge by saying, "That is evil!" IT IS. We are told that if we eat from this tree, we will "surely die" – and die, we do!

We are called to surrender this act of judging between right and wrong, good and evil. But how can we do this? It is the task of this forerunning brigade to blaze the trail of non-judgment, tolerance, acceptance and LOVE. The world will follow suit when it has had its fill of the hog slop it has been eating; just as the prodigal son returned to his father's house, wrapped in blessing, so will all. In short, human judgment is highly creative. The mortal world is maintained and sustained through human judgment.

What does this have to do with Romans Chapter One? And what of sex?

Please allow me to generalize:

The act of human sex and interplay is a mirror to what occurs in the unseen world of figurative intercourse. In the natural, human sex when executed in a "righteous" manner produces life within the womb (by righteous I mean anatomically correct processes for human conception).

When intercourse is executed figuratively (not necessarily righteously), the spiritual womb becomes a production line and will produce after its own kind. And so, we have the realm of death and decay (Hell – where we presently abide) and will continue to do so when the egocentric seed is deposited in the figurative womb. This means that, whatever the mind of the human incubates, it will create. This is why we are encouraged to take our thoughts captive and to think on things that are pure and lovely. Our thoughts, when mingled with our emotions, are absolutely creative. Human judgment seeds this womb perpetually.

Within all of humanity, this highly creative attribute (figurative intercourse) has the ability to bring forth reality – yes, reality – and everything within this dimension of habitation. So, when the egocentric human copulates within, by seeding the womb with negative and judgmental thoughts and watering these seeds with the corresponding emotional values, it creates. And this creation is mortal and limited.

CONVERSELY – When the egocentric human surrenders its will to that of the Divine (seed-giver/progenitor), something wondrous happens. The awakened human sees that it has been creating a world of limitation, death and decay and SHIFTS out from judgment and into LOVE. When these attributes (masculine/spirit and feminine/human) unite, now with the driving force of LOVE rather than fear (which is what all human creation is centered upon), then Christ is conceived and ultimately birthed. Christ is the God-man, both God and man within the framework of the human being. An immortal being is created by the synergistic and cooperative effort of the human and the Divine. It is called EMMANUEL.

Let's look again:

The Divine (Spirit) is masculine and is the eternal seed-bearer.

The Ego is feminine and is the mortal seed-bearer.

Presently, we are like the pattern of Gomer (Hosea 1), a whore (symbolically copulating with the ego, the snake in the garden within). But the Spirit is consumed with LOVE for this beloved and marries her, redeeming her.

The feminine is the receptacle. It is the human being.

Masculine and feminine energies are the mechanism for creating all that is.

Romans Chapter One (summarized):

> Vs. 19-20 For what may be known of God is manifest in them; His invisible attributes are clearly seen being understood by the things that are made.

Here we see that we manifest the attributes of God and can plainly see them by the things that are MADE/created. WE CREATE because we have these attributes in US.

> Vs. 20-23 His eternal power is seen in us, but we didn't see that we were creating with Divinity's attributes in us! We glorified our own egocentric self and became mortal and limited while retaining the ability to create all that is. We became egocentric beings – fools.

> Vs. 24-28 We dishonored these marvelous mechanisms of creation (our bodies) by exchanging the natural use of the feminine (the womb) for that which is unnatural. We began to copulate with the ego and began our devolution into Hell; that is, mortality. Divine seed was no longer placed in the womb as feminine and Divine masculine did not unite. Womb-man did not have a Divine masculine counterpart. In the same way, masculine ego romped with ego – shameful activities leading to death (mortality).

This is the height of "figurative" sexual immorality. Joining ourselves with ego – the ultimate and despicable fornication.

When the feminine copulates without the Divine masculine, there is no seed to bring forth life.

When the egocentric masculine spills seed outside of the receptacle, there is death to the seed. The mouth/throat is called the grave or sepulcher. The bowels represent Hell. Both allude to death.

When the egocentric masculine and feminine copulate (unrighteous) the resulting creation is corrupted, and we are mortal. Everything dies.

When the feminine "receives" the Divine masculine seed (this is the feminine submitting to the will of the Divine) eternal and immortal life is manifest. This conception is the beginning of birthing the Christ. The Christ is an immortal being endowed with the power to create and maintain immortality.

Now, to those who judge those who commit such things as mentioned in Romans Chapter One:

Romans Chapter Two:

> *Vs. 1 Therefore you are inexcusable, O man, whoever you are who JUDGE, for in whatever you judge another, you CONDEMN yourself; for you who judge PRACTICE THE SAME THINGS.*

This indictment clearly reveals that the sexual immorality referenced in Chapter One is HUMAN JUDGMENT. Sexual immorality is a METAPHOR for the practice of egocentric human JUDGMENT, because judgment reaps mortality and propagates this mortal and limited environment by populating the WOMB with DEATH.

This is why it is said that by partaking of the fruit of the tree of the knowledge of good and evil we will surely DIE.

CHOOSE LIFE.

21:375 Knowing That We Are Creators …

Knowing that we are creators, instead of saying, "I feel bad for (that person)," say, "I feel good for that person, and I am creating a positive outcome for this challenging situation."

In this way, we liberate our emotional body from affecting our physical body in the way of ailment or infirmity. Creators check your language at the positive door!

"Life and death are in the power of the tongue," indeed!

21:376 Pain is a Great Teacher

You have heard it said that pain is your greatest teacher, and why is that?

Being physical affords your spirit (that part of you that is nonphysical) to feel with you both joy and pain and everything in between.

As a physical being endowed with senses, you are able to "feel" the full spectrum of sensations and emotions. Your spirit is in you, feeling right along with you. This is a rare experience. Only if you are human and, in a body, may you experience physical sensations. Physical and emotional experiences teach us how to emote.

The material world allows this. The spiritual or etheric worlds DO NOT.

An environment has been created for the human (endowed with spirit) to experience the full spectrum of emotions as it (your emotional escrow account) becomes the palette to create.

Each emotion carries a corresponding frequency. Each frequency is creative. The human experience affords lavish opportunities from which to learn to emote everything from joy to despair.

Joy carries a frequency. Despair carries a frequency. And everything in between carries a frequency, a vibration.

If one desires to create a painting, should the artist only have one color on the palette?

If the creator wishes to create a world, could it be done with only one color?

The textures in our world – from water to mountains, iron to butterfly wings, flowers to a redwood tree – carries a frequency. If you want to create a splendor-filled material world, and creation comes from thought mingled with emotion, what kind of emotions would you need to experience?

Earth is a school for the fledgling creator to learn, replete with the full spectrum of emotional experiences from which to draw. As a human, we focus on and JUDGE our experiences, unaware that our thought, mingled with our emotion, CREATES. Judgment is the doorkeeper which allows the release of emotional currency to mingle with our thoughts.

And we create according to what we judge, and what we focus upon. The rubber-necking passerby focuses on the accident and judges it, and CREATES more of the same, unbeknownst to it. The thought, mingled with emotion, gestates, and when time is full, the creation is released into the world. "In what form does it appear?" you ask. The same frequency from which it was initially created. If terror is sown, then terror you will reap. It is law.

"God is not mocked. Whatever you sow you shall reap." Galatians 6:7
(Who is the creator here?)

"Weeping may endure for the night (ignorance) but joy cometh in the morning (enlightenment)." Psalm 30:5

21:377 Regarding the Bible and Other Spiritual Texts

Regarding the Bible and other spiritual texts ... there comes a time when no man teaches, and we are free from the tutelage of the written word.

There is a place stirring, percolating deep within man, that does not require the mind's engagement, a place where intellect is suspended and truth drips abundant, like honey from the hive.

I cannot keep up with the written volumes by the hand/mind of man, but there is a deep well of all-knowing available any time I want to suspend, disengage my ego/intellect. We have this treasure in the midst of our earthen vessels, accessible deep waters to swim in, where love is enough.

Where loving is enough.

This love cuts through the dung of human inspiration and allows us untethered to fly, to swim, to lie in the fertile fields of truth incarnate in us, as us.

Let us hypnotize the mind to rest as we drink deeply of the truth found within each as living epistles, knowing chiseled by the hand of Divinity, not written in tablets or ink.

21:378 It Is Finished

I want to clarify the idea of "it is finished." There is, and has been, a lot of discussion regarding the concept of a protracted finish, when we are already complete, or "there." Within Christianity, there is a future promise of perfection or completion, something that has offered little more than deferred hope.

If I may clarify, time exists within the physical, mortal realm. There is no escaping time, as long as we live within an environment that has celestial movement – that is, as long as the sun rises, sets, and as long as we circle the sun, we are within the construct of time, and as such, will experience "process."

With that said, there are aspects of us that are para-dimensional that do not exist within time – we are immortal, celestial and immaterial beings existing eternally, albeit without MATERIAL FORM.

Hence, the purpose for this baptism into time and mortality is to accrue for ourselves a helpmate; that is, the physical and material body that temporarily is experiencing the seemingly endless cycle of life and death.

The intelligence that is the energy of timeless and eternal LOVE found a way to penetrate the physical DNA and, as such, has inoculated the physical form of the human with ITSELF. This inoculation has provided a place for the eternal and immaterial to rest within this manger of humanity while it grows slowly and within time, so as to not blow out the tender circuitry of the human nervous system. It is the mustard seed, the pearl of great price, the treasure hidden within the field. It is what we call GOD within man, or Emmanuel.

Now, once the full measure has been achieved within the construct of time, there is a reaping or harvest, if you will, where there is a separation from the planetary school of "hard knocks." Even though we are eternal beings, we remain incomplete, much like a glass of water that is empty but being poured into a little at a time; this is us as the nature of CHRIST grows within this garden of Eden – your body. This, we are told not to despise – the day of small beginnings.

These mysteries are apprehended as we look to the patterns found within myth, culture and nature. It is the seed growing secretly:

> *Mark 4: 26 He also said, "This is what the kingdom of God is like. A man scatters seed on the ground.27 Night and day, whether he sleeps or gets up, the seed sprouts and grows, though he does not know how. 28 All by itself the soil produces grain – first the stalk, then the head, then the full kernel in the head. 29 As soon as the grain is ripe, he puts the sickle to it, because the harvest has come."*

As a reminder, we exist inside and outside of time. Within time, there is a process of growth taking place that spans millennia. It is difficult to perceive with our presently limited lifetimes, but it is, indeed, there and resident within our DNA.

I hope this is helpful.

Love you all

SECTION TWENTY-TWO

TWENTY-TWO

22:379 Information is Stored Through Frequency

Information is stored through frequency. Continue to raise your own personal frequency and continue to be enlightened.

Raise your frequency by being happy. Find things to smile about, that your JOY MAY BE FULL.

Turn your focus away from controversy, debate, worry and fear. These will keep your frequency LOW.

There is so much opportunity in our world for pain. Seek, instead, buoyancy of heart.

Turn, instead, to love, union, non-judgment, and acceptance. This is the key! For, whatever you set your focus upon, you will have.

We must become a vibrational match for the age to come – the bridge to that age is built with JOY.

22:380 Creating God in Your Image

Religion – ANY religion – has created their God in their image. To let the doctrine that created that image go, is one of the most difficult things I've ever done. However, when you sit in a pew, service after service, hearing things that do not resonate ... things that no longer make sense; when staying becomes more painful than leaving, then you "take up your bed and walk."

Written by my dear friend, Pat Gilder

22:381 Beliefs Forged Within Popular Opinion

I have seen and been through the struggle of having beliefs forged in the furnaces of popular opinion – of religious conditioning – of peer pressure from those within Christianity.

We burn neural pathways into our brain, making straight the path of approval for those who want to be accepted into the "fold".

Human beings need to belong. They are creatures of habit, with few exceptions.

From an early age, people have their beliefs burned within their conscious record, much like a music CD or cinematic DVD is "burned" with a particular song or movie. This is why the following scripture is true:

> Proverbs 22:6, 6 *"Train up a child in the way he should go: and when he is old, he will not depart from it."*

I have seen many people, who are free from their religious indoctrination as young adults, inevitably return to religious indoctrination – because it is familiar to them. Those pathways have been established through repetition, as children. It is sort of like this:

> *Imagine that you are in a strange city, looking for a grocery store, driving along unfamiliar streets (without GPS, of course). It is not a good feeling to be unsure of your surroundings and feeling the frustration that comes from searching. Now, imagine yourself on Autopilot in your own city, not even remembering how you got to the store, because you are so familiar with the route. As you arrive at the store, people cheer, hug and accept you for making it to the store. How would you feel about going there? This is similar to religious indoctrination – it is familiar to us and will strike familiar chords within us. Comfort is found within familiarity, and so, many return. And when they return, they are lovingly accepted back into the fold.*

Indoctrination lasts a lifetime UNLESS … and UNTIL …

There is a seed of RIGHT-eousness planted deep within us that begins to sprout and GROW and eventually it will overtake the "GARDEN" – that is, our consciousness. There is such deep truth that has been a part of us forever, that when it begins to grow, will eclipse those old and familiar pathways – truth that begins to challenge indoctrination.

I remember a story that the reason train tracks are the width they are is because that was the width of horse and buggy carriage wheels. The old always births the new, and the new carries with it the earmarks of the old. The reason why we resort to childhood indoctrination is because that is what we know, not necessarily what is true.

Now, more than ever, people are leaving religious structures because consciousness is much more sophisticated than what we have been force-fed as children – it is no longer that familiar to us, because we, as a civilization, have grown past the point of our programming. No longer do we accept that a loving God would burn people forever – that wasn't God; that was a concept birthed within the "Inquisition" period of time and was adopted as a very effective means to control people.

As I mentioned earlier in this book, a while back, I heard a man named Ian Chellan say this:

> *"For those of you that believe Satan and Lucifer are one and the same, I am here to tell you that they are not. But, don't take my word for it, study FOR YOURSELF."*

I was shocked at the statement, but took his advice to study and, after weeks of reading, do you know what? He was absolutely right!

Too many will just accept what they are told, rather than to become a student and pursuer of truth. I thought to myself, "If I was wrong about Satan and Lucifer being one and the same, then what else do I have wrong???"

That was the beginning of the end of Christian indoctrination for me, and I have not looked back. I became VERY uncomfortable and could simply NOT conform any longer. It became very uncomfortable for me to attend church anywhere that taught similarly; that the reason we have train tracks the width that we do is because that was the width of the horse and buggy carriage wheels. No more.

To break free from those pathways is UNFAMILIAR. Remember, the word familiar is akin to "family." It is a hard thing to leave our parental and religious oversight, but we must if we are to truly grow into the full measure and stature of CHRIST.

22:382 Called to Transition the Age

Those called to transition the age are the ones I am speaking to. (There are those who are called to work with the world's present problems and there are those who are called to something else ... and neither is WRONG). I speak solely to those who feel they are to help transition us out from duality consciousness and into unity.

If you are called to help transition the age, then you must see around corners. When Wayne Gretzky was asked how he was able to become the league's MVP and leading scorer in hockey, he replied this: "I don't play where the puck is; I play where the puck is going to be."

We need to be GLOBALLY minded if we are to transition the age. This means we need to think, emote and practice where consciousness WILL BE. In a globally-minded consciousness, our concern will not be for national interests, but rather, for planetary interests (and beyond – galactic and universal). Right now, we are concerned with national borders (et al) because we have a nationalistic consciousness that is manifesting worldwide. It is us vs. them. Perceived good vs. evil. Right vs. wrong. This is at the heart of duality consciousness.

So, those called to transition the age (and presently, they are in the vast minority!) will need to think in terms of why are people leaving their country in droves and seeking asylum here? The answer to that question is where we need to focus, regardless of what is manifesting in the world.

We must remember that whatever we focus upon and emote toward, we create. The world ahead will vibrate at a different frequency, so those who are called as beacons and resonators must hold a frequency that is compatible with love, peace, joy, benevolence, kindness and hope. In this way, we will establish a highway for consciousness to find and to join us upon.

We are system-busters who came here to forge a path and pattern out from duality consciousness and into unity. Imagine this: An internment camp surrounded by barbed razor wire where everyone is fighting, screaming, yelling and abusing one another. Now, imagine that there is someone hard at work outside of the fray with wire cutters, carefully removing the barbed and razor wire. If the people inside just opened the door, they would see a path created for them to escape. The problem is that the ego gets involved, and would rather fight to be perceived as right, rather than righteous.

I love what Abraham, through Esther Hicks, says:

> *"We simply cannot beat the drum of what is going wrong and allow for what we want to come through."*

And this:

> *"There is no path to peace. Peace is the way."* -- Mahatma Gandhi

22:383 Oh-oh

Consciousness is bulging at the seams – Christianity must evolve and grow like the mustard seed within the garden ... otherwise, it will be known as the woman that birthed the Christ, rather than the Christ it worships ...

Former Evangelical and researcher Christine Wicker says, "When asked to rate eleven groups in terms of respect, non-Christians rated evangelicals tenth. Only prostitutes ranked lower." In an almost comic side note, Wicker wonders how the prostitutes feel about that. Atheists and nonbelievers are looking pretty good.

22:384 Are You Game?

What if I told you that there is a food that is the source of all disease, all wars, all hatred, all discord, all jealousy, all strife? Would you stop eating this food?

It is actually a fruit, and is available and accessible to all humans, and almost all humans eat it.

What if I told you that this fruit is highly volatile and can literally be the catalyst to sustain life on earth? Would you still eat it, even if it caused all of the negative things listed before, if in exchange it gave the Earth life?

The fruit comes from the Tree of the Knowledge of Good and Evil. Eating the fruit opens the eyes to human beings, and they clearly see the difference between good and evil according to their core beliefs and values. Not only does it open eyes but judging between one's perception of good and evil actually gives a great measure of creative power to whatever it is that is being judged. You see, we are gods and as gods, the things we decree ARE. If we look at something and judge it to be evil, then it is EVIL.

Now, regarding the homosexual issue that seems to be the topic of much debate, I say this:

Jesus said that where we are headed there is no male or female and we are neither taken or given in marriage. When we fight amongst ourselves regarding homosexuality and marriage, it is a prime indicator of what age we live in.

This is the age where people eat from the tree of knowing good and evil. Jesus did not judge anyone; only the ego that seeks to be right in everyone was judged. This is the son of perdition that was ultimately crucified, the life of self and selfish agenda. The only thing that will get us where we want to go is LOVE, people. Just love. When we focus on this, nothing else matters. Jesus said, "resist not evil," because he knew that in our resistance there is a strengthening of whatever it is that we resist. Resistance is another prime indicator of duality consciousness or judging between the difference of whatever you discern good and evil to be.

If you discern good from evil, then you are eating from that tree and must submit to the LAW that governs your land. Jesus came to model a way out from the LAW – and that way is LOVE and non-judgment. If we continue to judge between good and evil, then the world as we know it is sustained and the "Kingdom" will not be made manifest within and around us. We are the only ones that can save us – there is no return of an external Savior. This Christ is coming in you but requires a change in diet. Are you game?

22:385 The Garden of Consciousness

Christ is overtaking the "garden of our consciousness," and as such, will not tolerate religions that seek to profit from fear. The tables are being overturned as zeal for the "father's house" (you) is being cleared of dogma.

There comes a time when we must return to love, mainly because ... it never fails.

22:386 Peter is Called "Satan"

In Matthew 16:17, Peter is praised by Jesus because he heard from the voice of the Father within telling him that Jesus was the Christ. Then, in verse 23, Peter is called Satan.

We have within us two wells from which to draw consciousness. From one well comes human reasoning and intellect, and from the other Divinity, or Source consciousness. One from the ego and the other from within our authentic identity – Spirit. Peter drew from the well of Divinity (the Father or source) within and spoke things that were not learned from anyone. And so do we.

Peter also drew from the well of human consciousness, and so do we. Two wells; one Divinity and the other an adversary to Divinity. This adversary is Satan. Just like there is not a little Jesus dwelling inside of us, there is not a Satan in there, either. Satan is what is expressed in us and through us when we drink from the well of our limited humanity called the ego.

This Satan is anthropomorphized by man, as he needs to see an adversary in a form outside of himself. We have given Satan human form outside of ourselves, rather than understanding that it is our own egoist nature within. Satan is the serpent in the tree that is within the sophisticated circuitry of human consciousness.

> *Luke 10:18He replied, "I saw Satan fall like lightning from heaven.
> 19I have given you authority to trample on snakes and scorpions and
> to overcome all the power of the enemy; nothing will harm you.*

Heaven is within you.

From *Escaping Christianity - Finding Christ*

22:387 The Husk of the Shell

Because of the claim of exclusivity on Jesus, Heaven and God, Christianity has earned a level of scorn. In part, Christianity may be a catalyst for Atheism, a label for those who do not believe in the God that has been presented and defined by

Christianity.

Atheism is an ever-growing sector of consciousness that does not support or tolerate the intolerable God of Christianity. Christianity's dogma does not accurately reflect the Bible's pattern and intent for evolving consciousness. The Bible, however, void of the overlay of Christian dogma, does this just fine.

It is time to look beyond the constraints of religion; beyond the husk of the shell, to find the pearls.

22:388 De-Classification

Declassification.

Living in the South, I am often asked where I go to church. This is because we are separated into clumps by what we believe. As a fundamentalist Christian charismatic, I classified people in this way and put people into categories depending on where they went to church. I did this because I knew, by heart, the doctrines within most denominations and religions. I knew who was "saved" and who needed a little adjustment to become just like me. Oh, gawd!

However; now, more than ever, there is an awakening people that are following the example set by Christ. This transitioning and transcendent human group comes from all walks of life. They are Hindu, Buddhist, Jewish, Christian, Wiccan, Pagan and the like, and the best part of all is they are beginning to declassify themselves; for without judgment there are no labels.

Taking it a step further, I long for the day when there are no racial descriptions, no country citizenship, no political identification, no sexual labels (including male and female), for this is truly an earmark of the impending age where "there is neither Jew nor Greek, nor male or female." Galatians 3:28

When we stop judging one another, these aforementioned ideations or categories will be obsolete.

This is globalism, and globalism is not a dirty word unless, of course, you define yourself in a nationalistic way. National consciousness became apparent along the consciousness evolutionary ladder around the year 3113 BC, when the nation of Egypt was incorporated, and we have had nation vs. nation conflict and wars ever since. It has been a part of our learning syllabus; but there comes a time when we must progress. Globalism is next on the horizon, and for those who can receive it, galactic consciousness is next, and after that, universal consciousness.

Consciousness IS ON THE MOVE. It is time to hitch your wagon to a star!

22:389 Opened Eyes

I see parallels within the Christian fundamentalist world and the secular world.

I see just as many miracles outside of Christian fundamentalism as I saw within.

I see the same benevolent power (that I used to believe only worked with believing Christians) working outside of the walls of the church.

I see the same happiness and joy on people's faces outside of any belief system that I used to believe I only saw in Christians.

The main difference that I see, is that Christians still believe that they have exclusive rights to God's blessings because they are focused on what happens within the four walls of their church, and I see how they look, with disparaging eyes, upon those outside of the system.

I see the profiling that they do to me and others – religious profiling, to gage your religious affiliation – and based on that affiliation, they decide whether or not to accept you.

Generally speaking.

And this is … hypocrisy.

Walking an aisle and reciting a prayer that labels me a sinner does not make you more saved than I am. If it is so important, then why didn't Jesus give us instructions to do so?

Wasn't the example that Jesus set just "love?" And acceptance of the "least of these?"

I cannot wait for this mass awakening of Christianity that Christians call for – REVIVAL! RENEWAL! It may not be what they think it is, but it will be AWESOME, as our Christian brothers and sisters find the love and acceptance for all human beings – not just those who look like them and believe like them. That is when they will cease dividing themselves from others – when they see the same God within the eyes of ALL.

22:390 Scaffolding

This is liberating! How many relationships, in how many ways, and how many circumstances, would change on a dime if we acknowledge that there are forerunners, people that are here to challenge us, to wake us up from our dogmatic beliefs? Here to help us step out of our fear, to confront our own insecurities, and to look within to find every need! How much deeper can we feel the connection when we remember, with ancient eyes, the purpose for these divine relationships!

Those who hurt us the most, whose words and actions wound us, those who challenge us to find answers, are our greatest teachers. Our greatest teachers!

Ultimately, we awaken from the self-imposed prison of ego and climb the emotional scaffolding toward release. This scaffolding serves as the platform from which to repair the old waste places in consciousness. It allows us to navigate upward to where we may see the weathering from our participation in resisting the inevitable … a renaissance that requires appreciation of every scar and impediment to our wholeness. Yes, our dark ages SERVE us.

We realize there is a time appointed when we are finished being baptized under the dense waters of human reason and the accompanying egocentric execution, and we arise.

Eckhart Tolle says this:

> *"If I accept the fact that my relationships are here to make me conscious, instead of happy, then my relationships become a wonderful self-mastery tool that keeps realigning me with my higher purpose for living."*

22:391 The Rainbow Wig

We all know the guy with the sign and the rainbow-colored wig at sporting events, holding the sign that says "John 3:16," right?

Here is the scripture:

> *16For God so loved the world that He gave His one and only Son, that everyone who believes in Him shall not perish but have eternal life.*

This scripture, when taken literally, is fraught with problems that have resulted in erroneous doctrines, religions, factions, and wars. Why? Because the literalist must have support, must win converts that believe in his particular doctrine; otherwise, he feels unsafe. To win converts, there must be a threat of some kind, and so, "fear of death" -- reinforced with threats of death – are preached and practiced. Numerous interpretations of this and other scriptures result in very limited human understanding; these texts must not be taken literally if one is to understand the rich mystery that Jesus, Paul and others intimated.

What is the mystery in this scripture?

People must search for themselves, for in the search, the intuitive mind is accessed. If one simply looks to have another teach him, then the limited intellect is activated and a conscious decision is made, either to believe or not, and this belief is always subordinate to the ego, which cannot be wrong.

Let's break it down just a little bit:

For God (more accurately translated "Elohim") so loved the world (more accurately translated, the "cosmos") … and this sounds rather inclusive, does it not? And the word "believes" is actually "trusts." Belief and trust are miles apart in meaning. But, Christianity has translated the word to mean "belief" and this belief is defined by many different doctrines (saying the Sinner's Prayer, raising a hand, walking an aisle, speaking in tongues, etc.)

Trust is an internal action. If I trust that my husband will be my confidant, then I will share. If I trust that he will catch me if I leap, then I will leap. If I trust him to be fair, then I will take chances. If I trust him with my life, then I will live.

If I don't trust him at all, then I am sentenced to a meager, fearful and suspicious life. I have condemned myself to a life of withholding – like a condemned inmate in prison. Furthermore, if you trust, this trust negates judgment.

> *17For God did not send His Son into the world to condemn the world, but to save the world through Him. 18Whoever believes in Him is not condemned, but whoever does not believe has already been condemned, because he has not believed in the name of God's one and only Son.*

If this name is Jesus, how can that be, since the letter "J" was not in use until 1500 AD? No, the trust must be within, for the name we are to trust is I AM. And the I AM has penetrated the human form and has been growing up inside of you, THE ONLY BEGOTTEN, the being that is both celestial and terrestrial (of the cosmos and of the earth) is formed in you. The cosmos is within, in the form of the GREAT

I AM that has been incubating and is, even now, being birthed from within the womb of the human.

Do you trust? Will you live?

Will these dead bones live?

Will death be swallowed up of life?

Will the mortal be clothed with immortality?

22:392 Seeing Around Corners

YOU are seeing around a corner. There is technology that YOU are being exposed to that will be commonplace in a generation or so – and the reason it will be commonplace is because YOU will forge the path for others to follow. YOU see this pattern in the exodus from captivity and into the promised land, where there is no death, and immortality is apprehendable. This is the activation of our multidimensional body as it merges with your physicality. This path is forged by forerunners. YOU see it first, and then make the way straight, for others to follow.

YOU are divinely guided by a force within yourself; YOU have, by following joy, made this intuitive connection strong. YOU bust systems of constraint – YOU break strongholds over the mind, over the collective consciousness, everything that exalts itself over and above the TRUTH of your implicit nature as God-men – capable of everything you set your minds and hearts to. YOU are awakening.

You will bust the systems of thought that have kept humanity in a lock-down position, forever arguing between good and evil. As a human being endowed with the DIVINE, you are awakening to the understanding that your THOUGHTS create. THEREFORE, there must be another exodus from egocentric thought that is focused on granular levels – there must be those who elevate their thinking above the FRAY. YOU must see around corners and into what you perceive as the future. YOU must shape and form this future, for YOU are creators of reality. YOU are encouraged to LIFT YOUR EYES AND SEE – to take up your bed of slumber and constraint, and WALK.

Like the lame and infirm that lay at the poolside awaiting the angels to trouble the waters, remember this troubling of waters is symbolic of having your consciousness MOVED. And when consciousness and expectation match the frequency of compassion, the miraculous occurs. YOU are miracle workers who have chosen to be here at this time. Do the work according to your blueprint, by following JOY. Your own unique path is dappled with footstones that, when you place your sole/soul upon, let you feel the buzz in your body that comes from resonance.

Become resonators. Become beacons. Like a whale that sounds off for its young, others will come to the sound of your arising; and they, too, will find their course.

22:393 Incubating in the Belly of the Earth

It is you. It is me. It is the new creation that has been incubating in the belly of the Earth that is both God and Man – it is Emmanuel, the being that will bridge the gap between Heaven and Earth, between the ages.

It is spirit and matter, celestial and terrestrial, becoming one new man. And the two shall become one ... two men walking, and one disappears; one is left ...

Penetration. Integration. We are the Collective Mary (which means "wished for child") that was overshadowed and who is birthing the Christ.

22:394 Servers of the Divine Plan

It has been 20 years since my departure from the organized church system. I remember a meeting in my home where many were gathered, and I said to them through tears, "I am not satisfied. There has got to be more than this!" The "this" I was referring to was where we were in our spiritual understanding. There were so many people sick and dying within our circle of church, and I and others knew there had to be more – that we were missing something. That night, I launched the rocket of desire to penetrate the veil and move beyond traditional understanding and doctrine.

Looking back, this was a touchstone moment for me. I measured my present comprehension of spiritual truth and discerned that I was found sorely lacking.

Shortly thereafter. I began having more than usual instances of spiritual phenomena. I was heavily involved in the deliverance ministries, helping to set people free from demonic oppression and possession, and during some of these sessions we would see (sense, along with manifestation) the demonic leave through us, the ministry team. We belched and coughed our way through sessions, and the others we were ministering to were set free. This is a thumbnail sketch; however, this happened with dozens upon dozens, if not hundreds, of people.

I didn't understand it, and it was misunderstood by some people within the church and characterized as witchcraft. It was even said that me and my team were calling demons into people – a mischaracterization that hurt me deeply.

I have come to understand this phenomenon a little more, because even though I left the church amidst terrible slander and accusation, it kept on happening to me and to those around me. There are those within many different cultures and religions who are able to remove energetic hindrances from people; energy that sometimes, when leaving, passes through and out of those with the gift. It happens over people, places and even objects that carry with, or within them, attached negative energy.

Horribly misunderstood in the 1990s, I have spent two decades since reading, studying and learning from others who have this same disposition. It is not evil or wicked – it is a gift. And the people who have this gift are increasing upon the planet, to help us as we shed the negative ballast from this passing age. For whatever reason, those who have this gift have many dimensions within their framework (spiritual, etheric, energetic and physical bodies) and are able to, through this ability, remove negative energy off of people, places and things, and it somehow transmutes (changes form) through them. It is almost like these people have a Stargate of sorts within them, where energy may pass through, and even be reconfigured as it passes through. The energy is deposited outside of our physical world through these servers.

People are beginning to rise in their energetic signature by choosing love and non-judgment, and by not becoming embroiled in world situations that can weigh them down. Personal energy signatures rise in frequency as people become more joyful and buoyant. The whole of the planet is experiencing this sort of resurrection and, as a result, energy that does not resonate with this escalation of frequency simply leaves through the "door", no longer able to afflict the world. That "door" is those who have been energetically configured to serve in this capacity. Many of them refer to themselves as empaths – they are sensitive souls who absorb and transmute the negative ballast of our world.

Many empaths have not learned of this process, and instead, act to shield themselves from what they perceive as "spiritual or energetic attack." If they would only work on raising their own vibe, they would find that they can transmute negative energy – mostly with ease.

Case in point: There was a woman within the church who had this gift long before she was a part of the intercessory team. As an empath, she absorbed and transmuted energy, but had become afraid amidst the mischaracterization that was going on. She carried the negative energy in her body – because her frequency became low with the onset of fear – and so, she identified with it, rather than transmuting it. She became compatible with the lower energies that she should have easily transmuted, and became an antagonist to me, slandering and even lying to the pastoral staff. This cemented my departure from the organized church system.

It has been absolutely astounding how many books have been placed in my hands that tell of this very gift. I have been comforted knowing that while I may have been mischaracterized, lied about and slandered, I have performed a service out of love and in service for others.

You may find an on-line book, in PDF form, It is called *Servers of the Divine Plan*. It is out of print and written anonymously.

Here is a great quote from the book:

> *"Awakening servers are by nature energy transmuters, and this function is a very significant part of their overall task upon Earth. However, in identifying their own personality with the character of those energies that they so easily soak up, Servers who have not yet fully restored their higher awareness often allow themselves to lapse into the undesirable conditions that are triggered by local negative influences. In order to remain themselves untainted by deleterious external vibrations, while simultaneously performing their duty of transmutation for the world, Servers must recall their innate ability to sublimate gross energies. Such vital remembrance will be established once again only by awakening their natural and active disposition toward a selfless concern for the well-being of others. LOVE – never fear or selfish orientation – is the key to spiritual success for Servers (as well, of course, as humanity)."*

It should be said that we are all "Servers" of one another. There is none more gifted than another. However, there are those who will awaken before others, and it is their job to serve until others may serve themselves.

As an endnote, this book – it seemed – was illumined on the shelf at the *Half-Price Books* store. I reached for it and felt a nonphysical jolt within. I knew it was important.

I did a little research and found out about the author, who had wished to remain anonymous. The author, his life partner, daughter and best friend literally disappeared. Fearing it to be some kind of doomsday cult, the publisher pulled the book. To this day, their bank accounts have not been touched, and they have not been heard of or seen since.

22:395 Aim High in Steering

I love the term I learned in my high school Driver's Ed class, "Aim high in steering." They had what looked like an old-fashioned video game, where we would have to drive with a steering wheel while looking at a screen in front of us. It continually said to us, "aim high in steering." In other words, we are to look ahead while being mindful of the things around us; but in order to steer our car at any speed, we need to look ahead, rather than what is two inches in front of us. In this way, we will be able to drive our vehicle at speeds beyond what we can take in at an inch-by-inch progression. It is the same way with our spiritual walk.

I loved the Wayne Gretzky quote, "I don't play where the puck is; I play where the puck is going to be," because, much in the same way, this is how we are to live, and that is with vision. It allows us to be present in the moment, while directing our thoughts to what it is that we desire to create. Wayne Gretzky's feet were firmly planted in the ice, but in his mind, he saw where the puck was going, and so he would begin to move preemptively in that direction.

There is this aspect of us that can see around corners, just like Simon, when he declared that Jesus was the Christ. He saw and ascertained information that had not yet been available to the masses. He saw around the bend and declared it. His name was changed to Peter, and Peter is an aspect of our multidimensional self that we develop in order to create what it is that we see in our mind's eye.

22:396 You Are the Cosmic Christ

The cosmic Christ is not held within the confines of any religion. It is not a "being" found outside of yourself. The cosmic Christ is universal in nature, all-encompassing, and is what we are as we yield to the intuitive mind, which is essentially spirit.

Christianity has relegated this cosmic, eternal and universal being to only be found within one particular religion, complete with dogmatic and unscriptural instructions to supposedly obtain it. It is simply not so.

Christ is not a Christian. The term "Christ" was present centuries (if not millennia) before the supposed advent of Jesus. Christ is not an exclusive term to Christianity, nor is it exclusive to Jesus. Jesus was a Christ and sets the pattern for all of humanity to enter into transcendence, not just those who are held within a religion.

Jesus said, "I am the way, the truth and the life and no one comes to the Father but by me."

To understand what this means, we must understand the "way," which is not a recited sinner's prayer, not raising a hand or walking an aisle. It is not getting submersed under the water in a baptismal. This way is LOVE. It is non-judgment. It is inclusion. Jesus did not come to start a religion; he came to help model a path out from RELIGION and religious encumbrances.

This love is the way to the Father – not God. The Father is the PROGENITOR, the creative force behind all things, and with LOVE, is accessible to all who seek, search and knock.

The cosmic Christ embodies the message of LOVE, unconditional and inclusive. That, to me, (generally speaking) is not found within the traditional message of Christianity. Christians, however, may demonstrate this nature in defiance to a fundamentalist approach.

SECTION TWENTY-THREE

TWENTY-THREE

23:397 As a Child, I Experienced Abuse

As a child, I experienced verbal, mental and sometimes physical abuse. I spent a fair amount of time rationalizing that things could have been so much worse, and that I should be grateful for what I had ... and I was. I loved my parents, even though it was at their hands that I suffered most.

I ran across this quote today and thought I might share:

> "A child that is being abused by its parents doesn't stop loving its parents, it stops loving itself."   -- Shahida Arabi

When I read this, my eyes immediately filled with tears. I see now how I have spent a lot of my adult life looking for, searching for approval, and when I don't get it, it is like hearing the words of my father again, "Can't you do anything right?" Or from my mother, "You make me sick."

I learned to stop loving myself. It was not something that happened overnight, but something that was organically innate within us all; the love of self experienced a slow death. I had placed the need for approval outside of myself, so that when I didn't get it, little pieces of my self-respect, the love of self, died. Every careless word, every scornful look, every bit of disapproval went into me like little knives carving away what was once a complete and lovely little girl into a hollow shell that I thought, for sure, no one could ever love. No, not even me.

As a 61-year-old female, I am beginning to love myself and to redeem that little girl whose love of self slipped away. I love what Brene Brown says in her book, *Braving the Wilderness;* that self-worth is non-negotiable. She says this:

> "True belonging and self-worth are not goods; we don't negotiate their value with the world. The truth about who we are lives in our hearts."

I know who I am. I know my value, and no matter what is thrown at me, I will not be defined by another human being. I am retrieving my heart from the depths of self-hate, taking back every little piece, because every piece of me is worthy. I am a worthy being.

Be careful with the hearts of those around you. You have been given the greatest gift of relationship, that must be tended to, like a needful garden. Let your love and approval sprinkle the tender shoots so that they may bloom. And remember to tend to your own garden, so that it may nourish others along the way.

Maybe this is what resurrection is all about.

23:398 Those Who Live in the Interior Worlds

There are those who live in the interior worlds and those who live in the exterior worlds.

Then, there are those who do both, and they live in the overlap.

I began to learn about the overlap in the late 1990s. It is the ability to straddle the dimensions – within this exterior plane, as an Earth walker, and the interior plane of the quantum world, as a God.

> *"Is it not written in your law that you are Gods?"* John 10:34

This Divine force penetrates the worlds of matter and, through us, creates a fifth element among the four of the Earth – that element is a Divine being that occupies biology and creates the material world from thought and focused emotion.

It is a synergy of excellence. It is EMMANUEL. It is you.

23:399 The Three Lower Chakras

The three lower chakras are the fires beneath the "altar" or heart chakra. These chakras are red, orange and yellow, just like flames.

The lower emotions expressed are what create and sustain this world.

Our intent-filled thoughts are propelled by our emotions, and our world is created.

This is the law of attraction.

Our emotional currency is seeded into the quantum world of potential and the quantum world responds in kind, exactly, and according to the demand that we have placed through the propulsion of our emotional output.

We are continually seeding the quantum worlds of possibility by the judgments we make.

When we surrender our right to be hurt, offended, to feel betrayed, to exact revenge, to hate, we are slaying the "beast" of these lower emotions and, thereby, throw them upon the altar instead, to be consumed by unconditional love and non-judgment.

This act slays the beast of our lower emotions and releases the dark and creative emotional potential into the ethers, and renders it dissolved by love.

This, in turn, raises the vibration of the human body, having released the emotional ballast of darkness through non-judgment.

This vibration carries a frequency that is a "key" or "tone" fitting for the next dimensional plane or "kingdom".

Jesus, through his teaching, told us of this mystery of circularity when he stated that, "The judgment with which you judge another will fall on your own head."

The world will self-create through its inhabitants, continually releasing emotional currency into the Earth's atmosphere through judgment.

This is the singular reason why Jesus told us not to judge, for it is in judgment that the quantum worlds are seeded with potential.

If you are in anguish, you seed the quantum field with anguish. Remember that "God is not mocked; what you sow, you shall reap."

The God in you will not be mocked, for you have given the decree through your emotional output and YOU WILL CREATE AND GROW WHAT YOU SOW INTO THE FIELD.

It stands to reason, then, that if negative emotions are no longer seeded into the field, our world will change, will it not?

23:400 Satan is a Principle

Satan is a principle.

It is a principle within the system of creation.

Satan is given directives every moment of every day.

Satan tempts us as we walk in and through egocentricity.

Ego is the directive-giver to this principle, this adversary of Spirit which is eternal.

While we are egocentric, we create a mortal world with a time limit; not only on our lives, but on creation itself.

Therefore, it is an adversary to Spirit.

We anthropomorphize Satan, when it is not a "being," per se, but the principle that binds energy within matter and matter within energy.

Want to defeat this Satan?

Surrender your egocentricity to death so that it may ultimately resurrect, and directive will be issued out from love and compassion, rather than greed and fear.

Just think of what we may create together ...

23:401 Lessons from a Dragonfly

I am still processing this event.

It began with me hearing the phrase, "Lessons from a Dragonfly." I did some reading on what a dragonfly symbolizes, and it is basically this: dragonflies occupy and exist in both water and air, and we need to balance being human with being spirit; mind with intuition; emotions with non-judgment.

Many of us are undergoing tremendous emotional upheaval. Mine reached a pinnacle over one weekend, as I unearthed a deep-seated wound/fear. As I sat on my studio porch, a dragonfly landed nearby and I observed him, hearing that internal voice say, "Lessons from a Dragonfly." I had woken up with a lot of heart flutters; not too unusual, but as the day went on, I found myself on the way to the hospital at 5:00 pm with a heart rate of 189 bpm sustained for an hour and a half.

I stopped after walking out of the house to go back in, to retrieve my cell phone, and miraculously found some metoprolol tablets (a beta blocker to block adrenaline). I took a tablet and reclined on the couch and my pulse rate returned to under 100 in about an hour. The actual racing slowed within 30 seconds of ingesting the pill, so it is my belief that the medicine was not essential for the stabilization of the heart rate. This has happened many times, where the decision to go to the ER is made, and suddenly my heart goes into regular rhythm. I can still feel the effects of excess adrenalin coursing through my veins – I know that this was another kundalini explosion from within my adrenals above my kidneys, and my body has been working ever since to rid the excess via excessive urination. Sorry if this is TMI. Tears come to my eyes every few minutes, as well.

The other night I received a photo via Facebook Messenger of a bridge over a river that was overgrown with grass. The woman who sent it then wrote, "The bridge less traveled."

I know that I energetically link the dimensions and have been bridging the gap for almost three decades. It happens within the etheric bodies and, if there is dissonant energy within me, it will hinder the incremental process. There has been plenty of dissonant energy within me – unable to get a handle on my thinking, hurt feelings and a host of emotional upheaval – mine and/or someone else's. Not sure.

I awakened very aware of the need to balance with dragonfly energy, learning the lessons of being naturally human and supernaturally divine. When there is imbalance, situations arise to correct our trajectory. I feel as though I have been on a month-long bender – my body and my head both aches, but I am learning.

Thank you for all of your kind thoughts and messages. Soon we are off to Iceland - I have felt like this is an important trip, energetically speaking, and it was confirmed with the events of yesterday. I needed a clear slate.

My last trip was to France and London. While in France, I was overcome with its loveliness, repeating over and over, "You are beautiful, France." Less than a week after our departure, the yellow vest protests began, as their consciousness needed purging from their anger. And Notre Dame burned this spring. Consciousness is, indeed, on the move, and we affect change with our presence as our energetic signature assigns itself over regions and territories.

23:402 Suppressing Emotions

I have come to understand that suppressing, hiding or masking our emotions is one of the unhealthiest practices that we do – even the act of "forgiving" before emotions are processed can be very harmful.

We have emotions for a reason, and to ignore them can turn our insides into a volatile and volcano-like environment. Take a look at this most basic definition of how a volcano erupts:

> *Volcanoes erupt when molten rock called magma rises to the surface. Magma is formed when the Earth's mantle melts. ... Runny magma erupts through openings or vents in the Earth's crust before flowing onto its surface as lava. If magma is thick, gas bubbles cannot easily escape, and pressure builds up as the magma rises.*

The Internet says this:

> *"Iceland is home to 32 volcanic systems encompassing around 130 volcanic mountains, 18 of which have erupted since the settlement of Iceland, in around 871 CE. Some volcanoes are considered to be*

> *extinct because they have not erupted for more than 10,000 years and*
> *are not expected to erupt again."*

While visiting Iceland on vacation, we witnessed several "vents" to allow pent up steam or "gas bubbles" to be released from beneath the Earth's surface. They were sulfurous. The Atlantic Ridge and the European Ridge meet in Iceland, and we went to the first parliament site of the world (dated back to 930 CE), where disputes were settled. It is called Althing, and the historical site happens to be situated right between these two tectonic plates – the European and the Atlantic ridges.

I had to marvel at this – I wondered if the people back then realized they had chosen their parliament to be smack dab in the middle of two tectonic plates! It is the best place in the world to view these plates, as here they appear above ground, rising phoenix-like at opposition to one another. What symbolism!

These ancient peoples used to meet here to settle their differences and would literally hold camp in between these hallowed ridges.

There were no laws to enforce the agreements made at this meeting place; the majority ruled over disputes, and the dissenting voices had to give way to the majority. Generally speaking, peace was made in such ways.

So, what about you? How do you settle disputes, disagreements and even emotional disturbances?

We rented a car and drove on the south side of the island for a few days. Iceland has very inexpensive electricity, as they have learned to harness the geothermal heat from the simmering magma below the surface. We saw may "vents" as we drove, where the gas became too voluminous and then was released through these numerous little shacks that had been built over and around a specific system that allowed for the venting to occur.

I read this in the *Power of Now* by Eckart Tolle, that hit me between the eyes:

> *"I have observed that people that carry a lot of anger inside without*
> *being aware of it and without expressing it are more likely to be*
> *attacked, verbally or even physically, by other angry people, and*
> *often for no apparent reason. They have a strong emanation of anger*
> *that certain people pick up on subliminally and that triggers their*
> *own latent anger."*

Hurt people hurt people.

I talked with my husband about the symbolism of the venting shacks. It is a systematic, safe and dynamic way to release pent up energy without doing any real damage to the surroundings. Our emotions churn and burn if we don't have the means to process or release that pent-up energy and then subsequently, like attracts like, and we draw unto ourselves people and situations with similar frequency that resonate with us at our deepest core. Some emotions have been so repressed and unprocessed that we are unaware of what sizzles below the surface.

I have described my repressed anger as a deep scratch in my record, one which seemingly does not allow me to progress as I would like. I have done all the forgiveness moves one can make – counseling, exercises, books, practice, etc., and I must still be angry; and subsequently, I attract undesirable circumstances. And I am really tired of all of this and want desperately to learn the art of "venting" in a healthy and productive way.

23:403 Sometimes Traumatic Events Propel Us

Sometimes traumatic events propel us into unfamiliar territories in consciousness. Something happens and a veil lifts within our psyche, and we are given the opportunity to see things differently. Trauma fractures the dome of our reality, allowing our consciousness to seep out like a spy to see beyond the boundaries of our present perception.

The wound becomes a portal. Trauma causes a split in the fabric of our mind's tapestry, having been woven at the skillful hands of the ego. Trauma breaks the wall of a carefully constructed paradigm, shatters our security and releases us to a borderless world where we see – truly see – the beauty of our unfettered soul. Trauma beckons to us to let go and simply be. Trauma carries us to a precipice from which to launch; fear says, "Turn back;" but love says, "Leap."

As Jacob wrestled with the angelic messenger (your Divine self) he clung to the new and said, "I will not turn loose of you until you bless me," and in this way, the wrestling that is the sweeping undercurrent of change brings about a blessing as our very nature is redefined. Jacob is renamed by this messenger from Jacob (a metaphor for egocentric being) to Israel ("God has prevailed") as the Divine self has now apprehended you.

May we all see our traumatic events as opportunities for insight. Instead of trying to heal the wound, let us travel into it to see the vista of blessings that it offers. Remember the Good Samaritan who found the man lying beaten and bloody and poured oil into his wounds? In the same way, oil – symbolic for the spirit world – saturates us at the wound and elevates us to see ... beyond.

23:404 Praying in Public

I was traveling back from Alaska, sitting in the lounge in the Seattle-Tacoma (Sea-Tac) airport, when I saw two women sit down at a table nearby with their lunch plates. Obviously related as mother and daughter, I saw the daughter reach for the mother's hand, and they bowed their heads in prayer led by the daughter. The mother seemed to squirm, tapping and swinging her foot in what seemed to be discomfort and a protestation of the lengthy prayer.

I thought to myself how I used to do the same. I have to be honest; I prayed to be seen as a spiritual person by others. However, I knew in my heart that Jesus gave this instruction regarding prayer, but I willfully ignored it:

> Matthew 6:5-6 *"And when you pray, do not be like the hypocrites, for they love to pray standing in the synagogues and on the street corners to be seen by others. Truly I tell you, they have received their reward in full. But when you pray, go into your room, close the door and pray to your Father, who is unseen.*

This is a pretty strong rebuke as Jesus called those who pray in public "hypocrites." I was a hypocrite.

I envisioned going up to the mother and daughter and asking how they felt about this instruction given by Jesus about prayer. What would their responses be? It might be that we are told to bless and to give thanks for food, but does that look like a public prayer? I know that Paul said, "Pray without ceasing in the Holy Spirit," but what does that look like? Is it public? What sort of response does it solicit in you to see people pray publicly?

What do you say?

23:405 Jeremiah 29:12

I was at a high school football game and I read this familiar scripture verse on the back of a t-shirt:

> Jeremiah 29:11 *"For I know the plans I have for you,"* declares the Lord, *"plans to prosper you and not to harm you, plans to give you hope and a future."*

and I thought the shirt should have a disclaimer that would represent most within Christian fundamentalism:

"Unless you fail to accept my son as your savior and believe that I killed him for you; well then, no hope, no future. You're screwed. It's the big H. E. double L for you."

Breathing deeply – yep, that was me. I believed that. But now I am so thankful for the relationship I have with a loving creator.

A creator so egoless that it was willing to put itself inside of ALL of us, not just some of us.

A creator so egoless that it reminds me that I was a part of the creative process to bring the universe into being when I was formless, egoless, too …

Please read to the last verse ...

Job 38
4Where were you when I laid the earth's foundation?
Tell me, if you understand.
5Who marked off its dimensions? Surely you know!
Who stretched a measuring line across it?
6On what were its footings set,
or who laid its cornerstone –
7while the morning stars sang together
and all the angels shouted for joy?
8Who shut up the sea behind doors
when it burst forth from the womb,
9when I made the clouds its garment
and wrapped it in thick darkness,
10when I fixed limits for it
and set its doors and bars in place,
11when I said, 'This far you may come and no farther;
here is where your proud waves halt'?
12Have you ever given orders to the morning,
or shown the dawn its place,
13that it might take the earth by the edges
and shake the wicked out of it?
14The earth takes shape like clay under a seal;
its features stand out like those of a garment.
15The wicked are denied their light,
and their upraised arm is broken.
16Have you journeyed to the springs of the sea
or walked in the recesses of the deep?
17Have the gates of death been shown to you?
Have you seen the gates of the deepest darkness?
18Have you comprehended the vast expanses of the earth?

Tell me, if you know all this.
19What is the way to the abode of light?
And where does darkness reside?
20Can you take them to their places?
Do you know the paths to their dwellings?
21Surely you know, for you were already born!

We were born (in the matrix!) of spirit before the foundation of the world. We know all things. We created all things. Christ in you, not a little Jesus but the creative potential of Divinity within us ALL.

Remember.

23:406 Your Sphere of Influence

It is time you begin to understand what makes up your sphere of influence.

As you move into the next sphere of influence (or the next shift in your unfolding process), the vibratory resonance changes. The vibration around you is comprised largely of people and their relationship with you.

As shift occurs, you will see new relationships form and old relationships cease. Shifting is organic and according to your personal blueprint.

As you transition through these spheres of consciousness, you will see that each sphere contains a level of vibration or resonance that you operate within. When spheres of influence overlap, the nature or essence of those overlapping spheres influence you.

These spheres are the blueprints of other people that contain their unique energetic signatures; signatures that will help bring about yours, and their intended purpose. You must define your place within relationships and, most importantly, to discern when you are no longer in resonance with another's blueprint.

You must discern that you all have been set aside for a particular function in this next age and this function will not come to completion if you pull relationships past their season of relevance. You will know when this occurs, as the relationship will turn from harmonic to dissonant.

You have been particularly resistant to free yourself from relationships of this passing age. You have felt the internal conflict and lack of resonance, but you have resisted the move. Because of this resistance and your lack of vision and understanding, steps have been taken to ensure this separation, much like a scissor will cut a pattern out of cloth.

This has not been put upon you, it is your highest self that holds the blade. You don't perceive this because you are caught up in the business of being human. As a puppet dances, your emotions pull your strings.

Seeds of discord have been planted to insure your discomfort. Your highest self knows the consequence of remaining in resonance with this passing sphere of influence and knows the importance of your cooperation.

You must learn to listen to that discord, for it is a dissonant frequency that will propel you to MOVE. Just as JOY draws you in, discord should propel you away.

Singularly, this plays out like a strategic game of chess and it is you alone that moves the pieces while your essence, couched in humanhood, remains unaware.

Your Divine essence knows love at its highest form that you will, in time, come to know, as well. Highest love is void of the fear of loss, including the loss of human relationships. It is imperative that you let go and move forward into the next level of resonance.

Be pliable and flexible and know that all these circumstances work together for the highest possible good. Your subconscious knows what is coming; it is big! So, shed the vibration of this past phase and receive and enter the next sphere. Joy will be your beacon. Find it! Just as a babe must force its way through the birth sac, rupturing it, so must you push through.

You must remain as a pioneer, never settling, staying in tune and step, trendsetting and transitioning, forming a path and pattern for the age to come. Reach back, any time you wish, and remember. You will see the plan coming from the mists of linear thinking, helping you move into circularity and then stepping out of time itself. Remember with ancient eyes.

23:407 A North Korean Mother

I was watching the news – something I rarely do anymore. It was a story of a North Korean mother and daughter who had escaped to China. During their valiant escapade to freedom, they suffered many things. Although they nearly starved to death in North Korea, the dark and turbulent things that they had to do in order to survive in China were horrific.

While in China, they came to realize that what they had been taught in North Korea (about the rest of the world) was complete and utter falsehood. Decades passed, and they went through deprogramming and saw the depth of the brainwashing that had been employed by their former country. Outside of North Korea, they could finally see.

The world did not revolve around North Korea. North Korea was not the favored nation they thought it was. Their leaders were not God-like, nor anything close to the stature they were portrayed to be. Their allegiance had been misplaced – horribly misplaced. The further away this duo strayed from North Korea, the more clearly they saw how manipulated and controlled they had been.

While watching this news report, I could not help but see the similarities between these controlling and abusive governmental systems and how even we, as Americans, fall prey to propaganda. Yes, we do. And it's not just governmental systems (I know we can all think of many circumstances to be politically estranged from one another!), but our religious systems program and brainwash us, as well.

Over the last few years, we have attended a few church services. I often talk of the rhetoric so prevalent within fundamentalism, while my husband, Lyle, says I am too hard on Christianity. The last church service we attended threatened us with Hell, death and separation no less than six times, and Lyle was stunned. He said that he had forgotten what it was like and how before, when we were in the church system, it was normal to listen to threats like these. It had become a part of our consciousness after attending for years and years.

Until we will no longer tolerate such manipulative practices, we will continue to see this sort of thing in America and the world. There comes a time when consciousness must mature; where we call a spade a spade. Fundamentalist Christians threatening a child with torture for noncompliance is child abuse. For that matter, threatening anyone with violence is a crime. You have been duped, and you have given the church system your hard-earned money so that they may continue to do so. Sit in on Sunday school to see how many times your children are threatened with Hell and separation and realize that you are complicit. You think that is love? Concern for their eternal salvation? That is the insidious part of brainwashing.

Wake up people.

23:408 Breaking Through Herd Mentality

Breaking through herd mentality ...

As humans, we are born into the need to conform. We all have, in one way or another, been indoctrinated into our familial expectations, educational expectations, community expectations, religious, workplace, national and global expectations.

We often suppress our intuitive thinking center, abandoning it for the sake of fitting into these aforementioned places. It is a rare person that will think outside of cultural restrictions, and when one does, they more than likely will experience some form of shunning.

I wrote a while back about shunning, and quoted Lynn McTaggart from her book, titled *The Bond*:

> *"The most fundamental of these needs is a sense of belonging. Humanity is profoundly tribal; we feel most at home in small clusters in which we are a part of the whole. Indeed, so primal is the need to belong that ostracism is one of the most unbearable situations human beings endure.*
>
> *Aborigines reserved the immense life or death power of ostracism for extreme cases, as it often proved fatal. This most primal of human urges – not to stand apart but simply to fit in, particularly with the people who immediately surround us – may well be so necessary to our existence that not satisfying it can be a matter of life or death."*

With the advent of social media, it is too easy to act out our aggression against those who want to explore outside of conventional thinking, and the cost can be great to those who do.

I love what Ralph Waldo Emerson said:

> *"Do not follow where the path may lead ~*
> *Go instead where there is no path and leave a trail."*

If you have ostracized someone for their lack of convention, and if you feel it in your heart to do so, take a moment today to reconcile and commit to living a life that sees worth beyond opinion.

23:409 Learn to Discern

A friend told me years ago that "We will not make it in the days ahead unless we learn to discern;" that is, to develop our intuitive minds.

I have the honor to lead an on-line class on Monday evenings, and I have said that the most important thing is to develop the mind that cannot be taught -- the intuitive mind.

We can teach the intellectual mind many things, but in the days ahead, the Bible says that,

> *"There will come a time when no man will teach you." I believe this is because the intuitive mind, the mind that sees beyond the physical world, will be instructing us from a place of KNOWING rather than from belief."*

How do we develop the intuitive mind?

The intuitive mind is not limited to the physical body, as the brain is. The intuitive mind is a field of consciousness that we may tap into using desire and will. This mind is called "The Mind of Christ" and is not limited to human reason.

The Mind of Christ is formed in this way: It is when the human brain (ego/serpent) recognizes its limitations and yields to a place of higher knowing beyond the physical, human plane.

This is the marriage that is spoken of in so many biblical scriptures; but the marriage is not between men and women, but rather between masculine and feminine.

Masculine seeds the form with life, the feminine.

The masculine IS information from the unlimited field of consciousness that the feminine (the human mind/form) yields to. The feminine is within all humans and the masculine courts the feminine as a lover. The masculine NEEDS a WOMB-MAN (or woman) through which to experience and inhabit the material worlds. Once the WOMB-MAN submits and yields to the masculine, a new form is birthed and it is called CHRIST, or EMMANUEL, which means GOD WITHIN MAN.

This is not a CHRISTIAN concept or teaching. This is a universal truth that has been deposited into many religions and cultural expressions. Many have opened this intuitive center and have apprehended this figurative truth that is modeled between the physical man and woman; however, there are those still within literalism that have yet to truly SEE this mystery.

Once this yielding takes place, there are many institutional beliefs that will tumble, and more people that will see beyond the physical limitations of the human mind. The problem remains with the serpent found within the garden of human consciousness, that struggles for survival and to be right. It is in yielding to the metaphorical death of the human mind that we find abundant life.

23:410 Emotional Expressions That Raised the Dead

Emotional expressions are the same across the globe. No one has to teach a baby to have the sides of its mouth curve down and its lips quiver before a cry.

When someone is surprised, the expression is mostly the same worldwide, as is the case with shock, disgust, distrust, joy, pride, curiosity, etc.

Why is this? Is this one huge classroom to learn to have feelings, and does the mastermind behind all this have an agenda? Why are the facial expressions and body language mostly the same, if not exactly the same, around the world? Are we hard-wired for something?

What do these emotions/feelings produce in us? Every emotion causes a release of energy/frequency, of some kind, from our body.

For what purpose?

When we feel something, it provokes our body to respond. A near accident will release adrenalin into our bloodstream, and our pupils dilate. Our pulses quicken. Our bodies sweat and shake. Why? We are hard-wired for survival and to emote according to some invisible, yet common, set of criteria.

Why?

On page 152 of her book, *Bringers of the Dawn*, Barbara Marciniak calls anger and fear "techniques."

Techniques of what?

How to direct the current as it is manufactured and as it leaves your body. Emotions are a propellant of emotional current.

Emotions are manufactured through and because of experience.

Because we judge between good and evil, pain and pleasure, the mind then becomes the dispenser of this valuable current(cy), and it dispenses according to what the mind thinks is good or bad, desirable or not.

The mind thinks all day long, and if it focuses on a painful event, the body cannot distinguish between a memory or the painful event actually happening NOW.

The mind is a masterful puppeteer.

Who or what controls our memory? Is it just the mind, or do we respond to a given stimuli depending on what the puppeteer wants or needs?

Are we, through our emotions, being manipulated to dispense currency at the will of our dark self? Is the will of our dark self-aligned with a collective energy band that wants and needs to keep the world emoting fear and pain?

Can you see then, why it is important that these emotions do not master us?

Remember that in the story of Lazarus dying, Jesus was not moved by the emotions of urgency, fear or sorrow. He waited until he got to the tomb and MOVED his emotions according to a different agenda. You see, human emotions would have mandated a response from Jesus – a knee-jerk response – once he heard that Lazarus lay very ill. Jesus would have JUDGED the situation to be DIRE and to move quickly and with fear.

HOWEVER, when the women confronted him and said, "If you had only been here, he would not have died …"

Jesus said, "I AM THE RESURRECTION." In other words, he could RAISE the level of his emotions upon the spinal column to accomplish what it was that he wanted to accomplish.

As the story tells us, he then wept and told them to roll away the stone. Once the stone was rolled away, auditory emotions ensued. Jesus GROANED and thanked the creative source of all (the Father/progenitor) for HEARING him. This groan was accompanied with the focus to raise the dead to life. And so, it was, and IS. Once we gain conscious control over this magnificent process, we can have whatever we focus upon, because the Father ALWAYS HEARS US – that is, it hears the SOUND from a being that is not consumed with human judgment as it stands as the doorkeeper of the creative processes.

Judgment tethers us to creating the MORTAL WORLD.

Non-judgment untethers us from this mortal world, and the saying that "death is swallowed up of life" manifests.

And remember, in the story of Lazarus, YOU are the Christ (the manifestation of god and man). You are Mary and Martha (the emotional feminine that stands at the grave and weeps) and you are Lazarus (the resurrected one).

23:411 When Judgment Fuels

When judgment fuels, it sentences us to creating in the mortal world of Ego.

When Love rules, it allows us to transcend this mortal "closed system" and to begin to build the vibrational bridge that links the dimensions.

23:412 The Son of Man

The Son of Man is humanity, expressed through slumbering Divinity ~ The Son of God is Divinity, expressed through awakened humanity.

23:413 This Mortal World as a Closed System

I kept thinking of this mortal world as a "closed system." We cannot escape this "closed system" with judgment. Judgment is what strengthens the boundary around us. But LOVE – ah, love – allows us to penetrate the boundary and to fly above and beyond our mortal world!

23:414 Everything is Inside of Us

Here is a conversation I had with an old friend a while back – I was excited to share my evolving views with her …

I said:

> *"Everything is inside of us! Jesus said the kingdom is within you. Hell is not a place but is a state of consciousness and Satan – well, Satan is our EGO! It opposes Christ!*
>
> *It is the creative component within that is an ADVERSARY to our Divinity. As such, it creates and maintains our mortal world. The Old Testament tells of the ego's journey that needed rules, regulations and boundaries, until the time when the Christ seed was deposited into Mary and grew.*
>
> *And, metaphorically, we are Mary! This is the new story or the NEW TESTAMENT! We are the ones that were overshadowed by the Divine and impregnated with Christ! This Christ is being birthed in us, through us, AS US – It is not outside of us, it is inside of us!*
>
> *The manger is within! The Garden of Gethsemane is within! The temptation in the wilderness is within our consciousness as the ego tempts us to follow it! The disciples are the twelve different aspects of our consciousness that surround the Christ! Judas is the aspect of our self that delivers us up to death, time and time again. Luke (the physician) is our healer! Peter is the aspect that can hear the voice of the father (within!). Thomas DOUBTS!*

We are being built into a multidimensional habitation of the Divine, just like it says in the Book of Revelation.

Our multidimensional body is the NEW JERUSALEM that descends out of "Heaven." And Heaven is a higher state of consciousness, just like the "upper room" where we meet CHRIST! It's all INSIDE OF US!!! It is not external! This is the Divine Inversion! Consciously, reality – as I have known it – is inverting!"

I blurted this all out to her in a matter of seconds. She stared blankly at me for a moment or two, and then slowly, deliberately and authoritatively, she said:

"Barbara, you cannot say there is no Hell, for I have been there. You cannot say there is no Devil, for I have stood before him."

My friend had experienced a wide variety of unusual spiritual phenomena, and I did not want to discredit any of it. It was all valid and useful in its time. However, I replied,

"THESE THINGS WILL APPEAR EXTERNALLY, AS LONG AS YOU NEED THEM TO! But they are external archetypes that actually reveal that which is internal and unseen."

SECTION TWENTY-FOUR

TWENTY-FOUR

24:415 Forty Lashes Minus One Lash

When Jesus declared the mysteries of the kingdom, he was flogged with "forty minus one" lashes.

When Paul declared the mysteries of the kingdom he was flogged "five times, with forty minus one" lashes.

What happens when we begin to declare the mysteries of the kingdom; most specifically, equality with God? When we declare, "If you have seen me, you have seen the Father …"?

Or when we declare that Christ is not a noun or a last name for Jesus – a title reserved for one man; but rather, it is a verb and is a reality attainable by ALL men?

Or when we begin to question the concept of Hell; that we are told to love and to forgive our enemies while our loving father tortures his enemies for all of eternity?

Or when we question the idea that there is a Heaven "up there somewhere," when Jesus himself said the kingdom was within?

Or when we begin to see *The Holy Bible* as a book of mysteries; not to be taken literally, but mystically?

When we understand that a book is NOT THE word of God?

Or that people of other religions might be "saved" too?

Or when we begin to question the very concept of being "saved"?

When we understand that the "only way to the Father" is not the recital of a prayer or "accepting Jesus into your heart," but rather, to emulate the behavior of the pattern, and that being the unconditional love and non-judgment of Christ?

What happens when we begin to declare these and other mysteries?

That's right. This is when the "forty minus one lashes" begins. You are lied about; rumors are spread; your integrity and loyalty are questioned; and you are ultimately abandoned, even by those closest to you. Sound familiar?

Yes. These are your "forty minus one lashes", and it is a path that the Christ must endure. Jesus said, "A servant is not greater than his master. If they persecuted me, they will persecute you, also."

This is a mystery. The master is the Christ in you, and the servant is your humanity.

You will receive your "forty minus one lashes" if you are to become Christ to the world. Christ means that you have merged your humanity with Divinity, and you are ONE.

Everything about you will break down (body, mind and spirit), just as the caterpillar becomes a rich nutrient soup as it decomposes within the cocoon – you will do the same.

Christ is an identity that emerges when we receive, in our humanity, the lashes that it takes to ultimately die willingly to the egocentric self, so that the Christ nature may resurrect.

P.S. Your butterfly awaits.

24:416 We Are Undergoing a Measure of Recalibration

In solitude we are undergoing a measure of recalibration necessary for us to maintain our equilibrium in this new field of consciousness.

24:417 Stimulating the Pineal Gland

Let me first say that I don't think there is a set formula for stimulating the Pineal Gland into activation; however, I want to tell you of things that I did that I feel helped me. You are encouraged to seek your own guidance on this subject. I am only sharing my experience:

Some say that the Pineal gland is the third eye, or the single eye, that is referenced in many ancient texts and art. There is bountiful information regarding this, and we know this gland was revered in many cultures and religions.

It is said that this gland is responsible for intuitive "knowing" and that this gland has calcified from non-use, among other chemical reasons (fluoride, etc.).

I became more aware of this gland when I read about it back in 2006, and actually performed an exercise that was said to help stimulate it, vibrate it, shake it loose from its stuck position, during mystery school practices. This exercise consisted of making a very loud toning sound while verbalizing the word "Thoth" (pronounced "toe"). I felt a little silly, there in my bathtub echo chamber, but I did it anyway. It is said that the forcefulness of the air coming up from fully extended lungs through the throat, being expressed through pursed lips, actually causes a vibration at the roof of the palette. I made the very loud tone three times, and at the end of the third tone, I heard a crackling sound shortly thereafter, and what sounded like a radio tuning, and two rather loud tones appeared in the back-left quadrant of my head, near my ear canal. The tones have been there ever since.

Along with the tones has come greatly expanded intuited information, especially regarding the interpretation of parables.

Did this expansion have anything to do with the toning exercise? I don't know for sure.

Next, I read anything I could get my hands on, and especially revisited the parables. I was "seeing" something other than words on a page – suddenly I was seeing patterns and templates emerge. I was seeing what was being expressed behind the written word. I was seeing symbols and archetypes leap off of the page. At times I would shudder and close the Bible, because I felt like I was falling into it. It was like a rose bud that began to bloom, and bloom, and bloom.

Stimulating the Pineal Gland in this way, by looking for the symbolism behind the words, greatly enhanced my ability to understand mysterious texts by Jesus and other mystics. By looking for the intuited information, I was exercising that "muscle." So, it should be noted that rigidly adhering to literalism will not help develop your intuitive faculties. There must be a willingness to learn anew. The ego will try hardest to keep you from advancing, but it must become the servant to the Christ, instead of mastering you.

By exercising your intuition, the Pineal Gland is activated and requires a leaving behind of former understanding, forsaking it not as irrelevant, but rather past its "season of relevance". Historical and literal application has its place, but not in awakening. It has served us as a "tutor," but there comes a time when the student becomes the teacher.

24:418 Before Abraham Was

Now, more than ever, there is an awakening people who are following the example set by Christ. Jesus was not defined by any religious group. In fact, he said, "Before Abraham was ... I AM." Abraham was the founder of Judaism, so, in essence, he was stating that HE WAS PRE-EXISTENT before Judaism was AND he did not call himself a Christian.

This transitioning and transcendent human group comes from all walks of life. They are Hindu, Buddhist, Jewish, Christian, Wiccan, Pagan, and the like, and the best part of all is they are beginning to declassify themselves, for without judgment there are no labels.

24:419 Because I Have Left the Church System

Because I have left the church system does not mean I don't follow Christ.

I have had a conversion experience OUT FROM RELIGION, out from the system that is, in my opinion, egocentric religious idealism based on a limited and literal interpretation of scripture.

My conversion experience included not taking the Bible LITERALLY.

I began to see the scriptures unfold before me; MYSTERIES that far exceed any religious and literal interpretation.

I have nothing against Christians but hold Christianity in contempt of the teachings of Christ.

Many of my Christian friends do not know how to relate, because I question the hypocrisy of the Christian religious structure and culture, including casting aside those who think differently than they do – opposite from the teachings of the one they hold in high esteem.

There is the scripture that says,

> *"I am the way, the truth and the life and no one comes to the Father but by me."*

This scripture is the bedrock of the fundamentalist Christian religious system.

Listen, carefully, to their interpretation, then mine:

> Theirs: The only "way" to get into Heaven is that when an altar call is given, one must accept Jesus into one's heart and say a "sinner's" prayer, which allows one to have a personal relationship with Jesus.

This is, in general, fundamentalist Christianity's idea of a born-again experience (not scriptural, by the way). Usually this opportunity is given along with casual threats of eternal torture in fire, or of being left behind when Jesus comes back to take all those who have accepted him into their hearts and leaves everyone else behind to suffer here on Earth. This scenario is the pre-tribulation rapture understanding. Ugh.

Really? That is the "WAY?"

> What about taking the actual life of Jesus and following THAT
> WAY?! You know, like when he sat with the common folk – the
> lepers, the tax collectors, the bar folk, the prostitutes, the adulteress –
> and DID NOT JUDGE ANY OF THEM! I NEVER saw a command
> from Jesus to recite a sinner's prayer; but rather, he asks us to
> FOLLOW HIM – *AND* – tells us to LOVE, and NOT TO JUDGE.

Non-judgment. Unconditional love (now THERE is a Christ concept!). Put away
your finger-pointing! AND he tells us to BE HARD ON THE RELIGIOUS FOLK!
– the ones who claim to have it all right but are themselves hypocrites to the WAY.

Furthermore, Jesus did not say, "The only way TO HEAVEN is by me." He said,
"THE ONLY WAY TO THE FATHER is by me." And, WHERE DID HE SAY
THE FATHER WAS? That's right – INSIDE OF YOU!

Jesus DID NOT CREATE CHRISTIANITY. Men did that.

Christianity – wake up. Your savior is knocking.

24:420 The Church?

The CHURCH is not what Christianity and the world thinks it is.

In Matthew 16:18, Simon said to Jesus, *"You are the Christ,"* thereby identifying
him for the first time.

Jesus replied, *"You are Peter, and on this rock I will build my church (ekklesia) and
the gates of Hades will not prevail against it."*

Jesus changed Simon's name (which means "to listen") to Peter ("rock," which
symbolizes intuitive knowledge) because the portal of intuition for hearing and
perceiving revelatory information had opened and would no longer be subject to
intellectual or linear methods of discernment.

In the Old Testament account of Exodus 32:22, Moses was put into the cleft of the
rock to see the "hind parts of His robe" (meaning "a time yet to come") as God
passed by Moses, hidden in the cleft.

Moses and Elijah saw the day of the manifestation of the Divine transfiguring
himself from mortal to immortal as they appeared suddenly in the New Testament
records, thousands of years later, as seen in Matthew 17:2. They were apparently

transported through time to see the transfiguration of Jesus on the mount, along with Elijah. Now THAT is revealed knowledge! From within the "rock" we are able to see the un-seeable.

So what is the "church" that is being built? It is not a building with a steeple, nor is it the Christian faith.

Ekklesia, from Ek and Kaleo:

> Ek = From the interior outwards, out from and to
> Kaleo = summoned outward

This simply means that we recognize that we are internally the dwelling place of God. Our journey begins not with letting God in, but rather, in letting him out. Hence the meaning of "Ek" – From the interior outwards, out from and to, and "Kaleo" – summoned outward. Ekklesia – the CHURCH.

If we develop our intuitive sense of hearing, like Simon did, then our name (nature) changes to that of "rock" where we are able to "see" the totality of the I AM that dwells within the human frame. Moses and Elijah saw this occurrence happen before their eyes, as they beheld a time yet to come.

Peter, declaring that Jesus was the Christ, heralded the advent of a new age, where the developing human species would now be able to "intuit" information. This was the coming of the Kingdom within man.

And the "gates of Hades" is internal within man, just as the kingdom of Heaven is within.

In other words, Matthew 16:18 says this, paraphrased:

> Peter says, "You are the Christ. You are that which we have waited for. As Christ, you are a man that is also God."
>
> Jesus replies, "You are hearing and discerning from a place within you that is not intellectually based!"

You are able to intuit, or to hear, the Christ nature that is developing within you!

The pearl within you, this great treasure within "earthen vessels", is forming.

The mustard seed within the garden is beginning to mature! It is coming from within you and expressing itself outward from you!

Divinity is within you and your physical body is a helpmate, utilizing your mind to reason and your tongue for speaking!

At last! The hellish nature of limited mortal man has been eclipsed by the Divine presence that dwells within you!

No more will you be subject to mortality!

Your being, your physical, spiritual and emotional nature, is being established by revealed knowledge as a dwelling place for I AM!

And so, YOU ARE!

24:421 The Pearl of Great Price

Where is this pearl of great price that the master seeks after?

What is within you is precious beyond earthly value.

You house the Christ.

It is intrinsic in your nature, there amongst the salt and fleshy parts of your biology.

It hides.

It waits.

Harvest the pearl.

Let it shine.

24:422 On Revelation

Old Testament thinking:

> God is outside of me and something of a tyrant and to be feared. We carry God in a box on our shoulders.

New Testament thinking:

> God dwells within me in the temple made without hands. The kingdom is within man.

Revelation:

> I am the Divine and am cooperating with the human. The human is
> my helpmate, through which I may create and inhabit the material
> worlds.

This knowledge brings about tribulation and cataclysm, as the mortal surrenders its
mortal habitation, much like a caterpillar surrenders its earthbound structure in favor
of wings.

We are morphing into that new creation. The new creation does not happen without
our consent – we will yield to the process and, in so doing, our DNA recalibrates to a
higher frequency fit for Divine occupation – more than what the initial deposit
required.

The Divine comes SUDDENLY into its temple, and death is swallowed up of life.

the Bible:

> A vivid description of OUR journey and discovery of GOD.

24:423 There Are Two Minds

There are two minds.

The first is the Divine mind. This mind created the Universe and everything within
it.

Then there is the human mind. This mind first appeared in the "garden" and is the
proverbial serpent in the tree.

These two minds give seed to the garden. They are the seed (sperma) givers and are
MASCULINE.

The garden is the womblike environment from which the seed springs to life. The
garden is FEMININE because it provides the STRUCTURE in which the seed
grows. The WOMB-man ... Woman.

Presently, we employ the HUMAN MIND and we have a time limit on life – we are
mortal because we have listened to the SNAKE.

The creations issuing from the snake (human ego mind) are limited to rust, mold,
mildew and disintegration, etc. They will not be eternal.

"Man is now mortal, having eaten from the tree of the knowledge of good and evil – therefore, his lifespan shall be limited to 120 years."
Genesis 6

The mind is masculine.

The form that is penetrated by the seed is FEMININE. We are the form. We incubate all thought, regardless of its origin, and bring it to bear, utilizing emotion as the water and fertilizer for the seed.

The Masculine Divine has approached the human form and has offered "it's hand" in union.

The Feminine human form has yielded, opened for it. In this way, the human form has been penetrated and incubating the holy thing.

The human will birth the Christ.

The Christ is the amalgamation, the offspring of the Divine and the human.

It is Emmanuel – God with man.

We are giving birth to this new creation.

We are birthing our divine selves.

Divinity, within, is orchestrating this divine plan with its helpmate – the human being.

We are the temple.

The creations issuing from the Divine mind are ETERNAL.

24:424 Donkey Rides

The story of Jesus riding on a donkey …

And Osiris-Dionysus riding on a donkey …

This is a cross-cultural story … with a HUGE message:

This is a metaphor for Divinity partnering with the human ego,

Directing the ego's course to the cross to die.

The ego bearing the weight of Divinity,

Going willingly

This is not a story about Jesus or Osiris-Dionysus needing a ride.

24:425 The Ego Manipulates

The ego manipulates memories to best suit itself.

It will remember details to place itself in the most uncompromising position, regardless of the facts.

Its job is to self-protect. And so, conflict is born and history, along with human consciousness, is manipulated.

Has this ever happened to you? Have you listened to an account of a conversation where you were present, and heard the facts repeated completely different than what actually happened?

I have experienced a complete reversal from what was actually talked about. Unfortunately, history is created in this way, and human consciousness actually believes and vibrates to a version that is not reality.

At some level of consciousness, we are aware that we do this to place ourselves in a favorable light.

My question to you is, have you done this?

The answer is "yes." We all do. The key is to become conscious of it.

24:426 The Thing About the Rapture ...

The thing about the rapture is this:

> We are taught, threatened and programmed into believing in the end of the world. If one was so inclined, they might do a study on the word "world" and find that the term more accurately reflects the word "age."

I believe we come to the end of an age again and again. The catastrophes mentioned in the book of Matthew might be taken literally, but more importantly, should be taken figuratively. As belief structures die and new ones are born, we reflect these changes in cataclysm within our own human consciousness.

Look what happened in our own recent history with the civil war. Did we not see the fires burning, violence, death, screaming, families separated and fleeing their homes, dismemberment, etc.? And yet, this war brought the end of an age: Among other things, SLAVERY. This ROCKED our consciousness and brought us into a whole new era.

Jesus spoke often of the age to come, and it is upon us once again.

24:427 You Choose Your Path

After my son, Christian, lost his arm and leg in a tragic motorcycle accident, I heard the words, "He chose this, and so did you ..."

The doctor rushed to my husband and I, and landed on the floor in front of us in a squat. He said, "Christian is in trouble up there. He has lost a lot of blood. His blood pressure is 50/20. We need to take his leg; it is badly damaged and requires a lot of surgery, and Chris does not have time. He is bleeding out." I motioned with my arms as if to push him away and said, "Yes! Go!" I watched as he ran and disappeared back towards the surgical area.

For the first time it hit us; that Chris might not make it through surgery. We stared blankly at one another. Then Christian's wife, Joanna, collapsed onto my lap, on the floor, with a yelp.

An hour or two had passed, and I paced the hallway area and waiting room, wondering how Chris would be able to learn how to walk with a prosthetic leg, if he did not have an arm and a hand to grip a crutch? My thoughts were jumbled and bordered on hysteria; I was projecting way out ahead. I felt nauseated.

Still pacing, thoughts were coming way too fast to process, and I began to feel fuzzy again. Then, I had a feeling of "lifting up". It felt like I floated gently, just a few inches above and to the right of my body, and like I was standing on a pillow.

The floor was not firm beneath my feet. A voice from inside of me spoke in a whisper, saying, *"Barbara, remember, he chose this and so did you."* I stood there, floating, and protesting silently, shaking my head, "No!" Simultaneously, somewhere from behind, yet in me, I heard faintly, *"Yes, I remember."*

24:428 All of the Stuff That We Used to Do in Church

I think about all of the stuff that we used to do in church, the intercession, the warfare and worship.

I just can't see those things as I once saw them. It is almost like I am looking back on someone else's life. I have to confess, if I listen or hear of the way things were (still are), it is almost like hitting a dissonant chord within me. It just does not RESONATE.

I am not "there" anymore.

For those leaving these former concepts behind, most are being led by whether or not something – anything – RESONATES within them. It is like an internal guidance system …

And there are so many using this term. I hear so many people say, "I don't understand everything that is happening nowadays, but it RESONATES within me."

This is where we move out of "knowledge" via the intellect and into "knowing" through our intuitive mind, which is the mind of Christ.

> Isaiah 40:2 … *"Speak kindly to Jerusalem; And call out to her, that her warfare has ended…"*

24:429 On Cognitive Dissonance

I talked to a close friend a few years back. When faced with the possibility that Christianity just may be wrong about a few key beliefs and doctrines, he replied, "I am too old to change the way that I think, and I have no interest in learning anything new."

This is not uncommon for many Christians. They are indoctrinated with fear, and even when the truth, as they know it, is compromised, they resort to cognitive dissonance.

Cognitive dissonance is defined by *Merriam Webster Dictionary* as:

> *Mental conflict that occurs when beliefs or assumptions are contradicted by new information.*

When confronted with challenging new information, most people seek to preserve their current understanding of the world by rejecting, explaining away, or avoiding the new information, or by convincing themselves that no conflict really exists.

Here is a great quote from Franz Fanon regarding Cognitive Dissonance:

> *"Sometimes people hold a core belief that is very strong. When they are presented with evidence that works against that belief, the new evidence cannot be accepted. It would create a feeling that is extremely uncomfortable, called cognitive dissonance. And because it is so important to protect the core belief, they will rationalize, ignore and even deny anything that doesn't fit in with the core belief."*

It takes a lot of fear and programming to hold onto dogma. When challenged, defenses are automatically raised to protect beliefs. When someone feels his or her beliefs are threatened, the brain releases the neurotransmitter norepinephrine. Norepinephrine is the same chemical that is released into the bloodstream to aid in our survival when faced with danger.

The fight or flight mechanism takes over, making it impossible to accept or even to understand new information when it is presented.

While the brain is under the influence of this chemical, it must defend itself. This defensive posturing alienates fundamentalists because of the overarching belief that says they are the only ones that have it all "right".

I recently read this quote and it seems accurate:

> *"Even in the face of indisputable and contrary evidence, 89% of the people will stubbornly hold onto an ingrained belief system, no matter how unsound."*

Friends of Mike Williams and the Gospel Revolution

24:430 Abandoning Fear

If you find yourself abandoning fear and judgment and becoming more and more aware of another presence within you, divinely within, then you are growing into the full stature and measure of CHRIST.

The man known as Jesus modeled "CHRIST" for us. CHRIST is an enlightened human that becomes aware of the indwelling presence of Divinity. Once aware, the human ego/personality of YOU begins to YIELD to this presence. Once yielded, UNION takes place and the human being is CHRISTED. And a new creation is

CONCEIVED and BIRTHED through the WOMB, through MARY (Mary means "wished for child" and is a metaphor for humankind that longs to birth the Christ child). Mary is the human that was penetrated – overshadowed by Divinity and impregnated with the seed of Divinity. Divinity is growing in and through YOU. You carry the wished-for child, the God-man!

As this process takes place, you will find yourself letting go of many things that anchor you to your human core personality. Many habits will give way to authentic intuitive practices. You will eventually stop your "knee-jerk" reactions to things.

While this is happening, you will notice that you are less human. Divinely inspired, you now make more decisions based on intuition, rather than thought.

Intuited information appears more rapidly than intellectual thought. You are being rewired, and much of what you have functioned in will be rerouted. We must learn to rely on intuition, rather than memory. Much of the way we have behaved has been a projection of our pain body. We behave according to pain remembered and projected onto our future path.

Let go of memory. What is necessary will remain. Instead, walk boldly into these rich, intuited landscapes within. You are forming a new blueprint – a blueprint that will help you pioneer into your authentic self.

You are waiting patiently.

24:431 Who Are You?

You are human. You are Divine. There is a powerful symbol of the pearl within the oyster. The pearl is the Divine counterpart that has been invested into you, beginning as a small speck of sand, or like a mustard seed within a garden – it is growing within the husk of your humanity.

Divinity did this on purpose. It found a way to penetrate this virginal human soil, by placing a "code" within our DNA. Slowly, over time, this code would be activated by vibration as humanity evolves out from lower densities and ascends the ladder of consciousness. Such is the symbolism of the serpent on the pole.

Divinity needs a biological framework. It needs to grow, cultivate and ultimately harvest a helpmate. This helpmate will enable Divinity to navigate the material worlds, the material universe; it seeks a willing partner from which to see, hear, taste, touch and speak. Without this human counterpart, it remains energy – unexpressed physically, biologically and individually – in the material universe.

God, Spirit, Divinity – whatever you wish to call it, is immaterial. It has no form. It is highly creative in the physical domains when it has form and force; that is, the womb and the seed. It is in this image that we have been created.

Divinity is both masculine and feminine energy, and as such, created the multiverse on an immeasurable scale. However, to create the details, it needed a mechanism with finer handiwork; much like the difference between a drill bit to tunnel through rock contrasted by a dentist's drill to excavate a tooth. It needs the human part of us, the human brain (as opposed to Divine consciousness), that can focus on the intricacies of creation. That's where we come in.

The human brain – working in conjunction with the mind – can also create. Here in space/time formatting, there is a gap of time between our thought and its eventual manifestation. This is also on purpose. We have limitation; a governor; a speed limit.

Once the human comes to the place of maturity, no longer a child, allowing its emotions to run to and fro (creating a mess, by default!), it is then ready to graduate from the school of Earth, having learned the full spectrum of emotional current; having been subjected to the full spectrum of human suffering and joy.

The Divine courts his helpmate until she (the womb) willingly submits to her partner in creation. Together they will transition the age. This new creation – that is both God and man – is ready to move to its next place of habitation, ready to create and fill worlds without end.
We are learning to take every thought captive, recognizing that our thoughts are the engine (the womb/feminine) and our emotions (the seed/masculine) are the petrol.

As we "park" our judgment, we are ceasing to create the reality we have come to know – Mortality. We are then poised to move into the next age – Immortality.

The present reality is comprised mainly of fear and fear-based frequencies. These are low frequencies that hold captive human thought and focus. As we focus on the lovely things in life, our personal and powerful frequency rises/ascends. Think on things that are pure, lovely and of good report.

This is your destiny. You are awakening. You are the pearl of great price.

24:432 Jumping the Tracks

I can remember that most of the 1990's I spent trying to rationalize what I was thinking, hearing and feeling - the discord within as I attended church and various religious meetings. Something inside me, assuring me of God's unconditional love for me amidst the talks of hell, division, separation and being left behind.

Back in the late 1960's I went on a ski trip with my home church group up to Ontonogan, Michigan where an evangelist from England was going to speak. His name was Harry Brownwood, an anointed speaker and teacher. I used to abandon the kids' group and go sit on the floor where the adults were gathered to hear of Harry's stories of miracles and healings.

Harry was a recovering alcoholic that told of his troubled youth and how God met him in the gutter, a drunk. He spoke with exuberance and played the tambourine. He captivated me, a ten-year-old. He travelled with Andrew and Terry, two young evangelists being mentored by Harry.

Andrew played the piano and sang; Terry spoke with passion to the youth and adults. Terry rode with the youth on the bus trip up and blushed easily and often. The boys on the bus asked him if he wore Burger King underwear and of course he didn't know about the food chain that was taking off like a shot here in America and so he answered, "Why, no. Why would you ask?" The boys just about laughed themselves silly with their retort… "Well then where do you keep your Whopper?"

It was a long bus ride from Milwaukee to the Upper Peninsula of Michigan for Terry. The challenge now was to see him blush, and this coming from a bunch of churched kids!

I sat near the back of the bus in a window seat feeling my throat scratchy and my nose sniffled. By the time we arrived my head was throbbing and my skin itched. My mom had been riding in a car ahead of the bus and I was told to go lay down in my room. No skiing for me. But that day I would hear Harry speak as I snuck down the stairwell to the meeting room in the lodge where we stayed.

After the meeting we headed to the food hall for lunch and I made my way to Harry and asked him to pray for me to be healed. I believed in his ability to heal people and I sure felt awful. Harry laid his big hands on my head and commanded sickness to leave. It did not. Later that evening I returned to the prayer line to have Harry pray for me again and he declined saying that I didn't have enough faith to be healed. I felt so unworthy and embarrassed.

I had a feeling of confusion as I headed back to my room. I was alone and instead of supper I ate some chips and soda. My mom had packed a big bag that we had snacked on during the long bus ride. My throat was so scratchy and the chips when swallowed seemed to scratch the itch there. I awoke the next morning with feet like rockers - so swollen I could barely walk on them. I was in a ten-year old's turmoil - not only was I sickly but I discovered I didn't have enough faith either.

That was a pattern that would set into my young consciousness and belief system of not being good enough for God - belief that would follow me into adulthood. I continually searched for methods and means to please this elusive God. I was a God chaser.

Then in the 1990's at an epitome in my spiritual growth plates I suddenly jumped the tracks of fundamentalism. I can't really say how it happened other than I just got so tired of the same canned responses and knew there was something that we all were missing. No amount of motivated speaking or teaching did it for me any longer. I was jumping the tracks - and by that, I mean that I was departing the deeply etched neural pathways in my brain - I was leaving the programming of my youth, and dependency on a system constructed with fear and deep self-loathing. The Bible says, "Train a child up in the way he should go and when he is old, he will not depart from it." I have come to understand that this is not an exhortation, necessarily, but rather a statement of fact. It is very, very difficult to depart from your childhood conditioning. Many people when their long-standing beliefs are challenged, go through a time of depression and confusion. Thankfully, I jumped the tracks that had been in place from my youth, somehow, and have not looked back.

I know that I am a forerunner of sorts and read in a book the following about people like me (paraphrased): You are systems busters! You put yourself into restrictive systems controlling masses of people using manipulation and fear tactics and YOU BUST OUT OF THE SYSTEM! You are adept at doing this, as this is your strength and gift to the world! The systems that you are busting is in the realm of consciousness and once one person breaks free, it becomes easier for others to break free!

I remember the words about "training a child up" quoted above and I think that this scripture is eluding to childhood patterns that are so very hard to break because we ARE PROGRAMMED BY THE CIRCUMSTANCES OF OUR YOUTH. It takes a lot of effort to depart but depart we must if we are to move forward and out of such restriction.

The bus ride home was hell. I was in full blown hives, now I know that my condition was an allergic reaction to the BBQ flavored chips I had been eating all weekend. I still get hives from Lays BBQ Flavored Potato Chips lol.

Thirty years later I was in Houston at a spirit filled Baptist church listening to a young evangelist from London. He transported me back in time as he spoke with humor and played the tambourine. After the meeting I spoke with him and told him he reminded me of Harry Brownwood and his eyes filled with tears and sparkled. He replied, "Yes! I have been told that I have his mantle!" I told him how special Harry was to me and my family and asked where he was these days… "He replied, "Harry died a drunk.""

I cried all the way home and I am crying now. Harry never jumped the tracks.

A few miles down the road from my home is a large exotic deer ranch where hundreds of deer roam within several hundred acres. This ranch is unusual because it does not have the tall fencing that you usually see but rather the fencing is just a few feet high, a low obstacle that these deer could easily bound over. When asked why they didn't jump the fence the owner said that these deer are born in captivity - they don't know they can.

But I know I can, and you can too.

References

1. Alcott, Louisa May, *Little Women* (1868), Chapter 44.

2. *The Bible* – It should be noted that many translations are used in this book to fit the desired message to be relayed.

3. Brown, Brene, *Braving the Wilderness: The Quest for True Belonging and the courage to Stand Alone* (2017).

4. Brown, Daniel Gerhard, *Angels & Demons* (2000), *The Da Vinci Code* (2003), *The Lost Symbol* (2009), *Inferno* (2013) and *Origin* (2017). Gerhard, born June 22, 1964, is an American author best known for his **thriller novels**, including the **Robert Langdon** novels.

5. Campbell, Joseph (1904 - 1987). Foremost author on the subject of myths, mythology and comparative religion, including his most famous book, "*The Hero With a Thousand Faces*" (1945) in which he discusses his theory of the journey of the archetypal hero shared by world mythologies, the "monomyth".

6. Carey, Ken, *The Third Millennium (1996)*. A timeless and visionary blueprint for conscious living and quantum change as we approach the next century.

7. Chellan, Ian. An Apostle from the World Breakthrough Network, and founder/Sr. Elder of Genesis Centre, a kingdom community based in Dallas, Texas, who claim their Divine Mission to be Christlikeness.

8. Chopra, Deepak, *The Third Jesus (May 2009)*

9. Cohen, Justin, *Twitter (6/15/16)*, Quoted from November 5, 2009 article, "*Five Communication Tools That Saved My Marriage,*" on *Christianity.com* web site, part of Salem Web Network.

10. Crossan, John Dominic and Watts, Richard G., *Who is Jesus? (1996)*,

11. Cruttenden, Walter, *The Lost Star of Myth and Time (2006)*, The book weaves together some of the latest archaeological evidence with cutting-edge astronomy to reveal a history of the world that finally fits with myth, folklore and the archaeological record. While this book explores some of the most interesting aspects of a once advanced civilization that covered the Earth, it is really about what happens to the Earth and consciousness as our solar system moves through space in the mysterious motion known as the "precession of the equinox".

12. Cruttenden, Walter, *The Great Year* (DVD) (2003) Is there some greater celestial cycle, lasting thousands of years, slowly influencing the rise and fall of civilization across the globe? The Great Year investigates and looks back into time seeking answers to questions that still loom over science today.

13. Danna, Joseph, *Reflections of My Higher Self (2017)*. Danna explains how the whole trajectory of our perception, especially of others, begins with how we see ourselves.

14. *Dr. Phil* [television show], 2002 - present, hosted by Dr. Phillip C. McGraw, Clinical Psychologist

15. Duplantis, Jesse - A preacher from the Christian Evangelical Charismatic tradition based in New Orleans, Louisiana, U.S., and the founder of Jesse Duplantis Ministries.

16. Eaton, Mark and Cathy, Hosts of *"No Limits"* newsletter.

17. Emerson, Ralph Waldo (1803 - 1882). American essayist, lecturer, philosopher, and poet who led the transcendentalist movement of the mid-19th century.

18. Fanon, Franz, *Black Skin, White Masks.* Fanon, born in 1925, was a West Indian psychoanalyst and social philosopher known for his theory that some neuroses are socially generated, and for his writings on behalf of the national liberation of colonial peoples. His **critiques** influenced subsequent generations of thinkers and activists.

19. Freke, Timothy and Gandy, Peter, *The Jesus Mysteries (1999)*. Argues that early Christianity originated as a Greco-Roman mystery cult and that Jesus was invented by early Christians based on an alleged pagan cult of a dying and rising "God-man" known as Osiris-Dionysus.

20. *Friends of Mike Williams and the Gospel Revolution*, Facebook group. Mike lives in Houston, Texas and has a weekly program listed to in over 187 countries. His group's ongoing effort is to impact hearts. minds, and societies with the thought that the Creator of the Universe is not about to judge them or the planet because of sin. Because He has already poured out ALL His anger and wrath on Himself 2000 years ago in the form of a Jewish man from the Galilee area named Jesus of Nazareth. They seek to reset religious mindsets that proclaim one leader or individual or group as somehow more righteous or chosen or holy in the sight of God than everyone else.

21. Gandhi, Mahatma (1869 – 1948). Activist, lawyer, politician, and writer born in North West **India.** His upbringing was infused with the Jain pacifist teachings of mutual tolerance, non-injury to living beings and vegetarianism. He was assassinated at age 78.

22. Harpur, Tom, (1929 - 2017). Canadian biblical scholar, columnist, and broadcaster. An ordained Anglican priest, he was a proponent of the Christ myth theory, the idea that Jesus did not exist but is a fictional or mythological figure.

23. Hicks, Esther, American inspirational speaker and author of *The Law of Attraction* series, translated from a group of non-physical entities called Abraham.

24. Hotchkiss, Sandy, *Why is it Always About You?(2003) Explores the dynamics of the narcissistic personality* how such individuals come to have this shortcoming, why **you** get drawn into their perilous orbit, and what **you** can do to break free.

25. Maharishi, Ramana - An Indian Hindu sage and jivanmukta (liberated being) born December 30, 1879. Since the 1930s, his teachings have been popularized in the West, resulting in his worldwide recognition as a enlightened being. He recommended self-enquiry as the principal means to remove ignorance and abide in Self-awareness, together with bhakti (devotion) or surrender to the self.

26. Marciniak, Barbara, *Bringers of the Dawn: Teachings from the Pleiadians*, (1992).

27. Massey, Gerald, (1828 - 1907), English poet and writer on Spiritualism and Ancient Egypt.

28. McTaggart, Lynne, *The Bond: How to Fix Your Falling-Down World, (Atria Books, 2012)*. A new blueprint for living a more harmonious, prosperous, and connected life. I win, you lose, is contrary to our true nature; we have been designed to succeed and prosper when we work as part of a greater whole. We are weak when we compete and thrive only when we cooperate and connect deeply with each other.

29. Melchizedek, Drunvalo, *The Ancient Secret of the Flower of Life, Vol. 1 (1998) & 2 (2000).* Illuminates the mysteries of how we came to be, why the world is the wat it is and the subtle energies that allow our awareness to blossom into its true beauty.

30. Nepo, Mark, *The Book of Awakening: Having the Life You Want by Being Present to the Life You Have* (2000). Nepo wrote this daily guide with quotes and inspiration, after going through cancer a decade before, to help people "meet their days and inhabit their lives."

31. Ober, Sinatra and Zucker, *Earthing: The Most Important Health Discovery Ever? (2014).* How Earthing, also known as Grounding, a method of balancing oneself by reconnecting with the Earth's electrical potential, has the potential to help promote health and healing in the body.

32. Eaton, Mark and Cathy, Hosts *Recovering All* On-Line Magazine

33. Schucman, Dr. Helen, *A Course in Miracles (ACIM)(1976),* A book/spiritual self-study program published by The Foundation for Inner Peace (FIP) and translated into 27 different languages. It includes three sections: the "Text", "Workbook" and "Teaching Manual".

34. *Servers of the Divine Plan,* out of print, and written anonymously. http://library.abundanthope.org/index_htm_files/Servers%20of%20the%20D ivine%20Plan.pdf

35. Seth (via Jane Roberts), *The Nature of Personal Reality* (1974), Chapter 4.

36. Swilley, Jim. An author of 16 books, including popular devotional "*A Year in the Now*", teacher, motivational speaker, Bishop of Now Ministries, Founder/Sr. Pastor of Church in the Now, Founder/Leader of METRON Community.

37. Symons, Barbara, *Escaping Christianity ~ Finding Christ (2014).* Fascinating account of leaving behind fundamentalism and finding and embracing the mystical side of the Bible. Escaping Christianity explores in great detail the metaphorical meaning behind baptism and communion. It is a great encouragement for those spiritual seekers looking for something more than what fear-based religions offer.

38. Tolle, Eckhart, *The Power of Now: A Guide to Spiritual Enlightenment* (1997). Tolle, a German-born resident of Canada, was depressed for much of his life until age 29, when he underwent an "inner transformation". He then spent several years wandering "in a state of deep bliss" before becoming a spiritual leader.

39. *The Truman Show [motion picture] (1998),* Rudin, Niccol, Feldman and Schroeder (producers). Jim Carrey stars as a man adopted and raised by a corporation inside a simulated tv show revolving around his life, until he discovers it and decides to escape. The show has been analyzed as a thesis on Christianity, metaphilosophy, simulated reality, existentialism and reality tv.

40. Wicker, Christine, *Christianity Beyond Belief: Following Jesus for the Sake of Others* (2009)

41. Winell, Dr. Marlene, LEAVING THE FOLD: A GUIDE FOR FORMER FUNDAMENTALISTS AND OTHERS LEAVING THEIR RELIGION. Winell is a human development consultant, educator, and writer in the San Francisco Bay Area whose background includes 28 years of experience in human services, in both community and academic settings. She holds a doctorate in Human Development and Family Studies from Pennsylvania State University, and specializes in communications training for couples

Glossary

Abraham - Abraham (or Abram) is the common patriarch of Christianity, Islam, Judaism and some other religions. He is considered to be a prophet, given direction by God.

Bible – Which version are the quotes in the book from?

Book of the Dead (Egyptian) - A term coined in the nineteenth century CE for a body of texts known to the Ancient Egyptians as the Spells for Going Forth by Day. After the Book of the Dead was first translated by Egyptologists, it gained a place in the popular imagination as the Bible of the Ancient Egyptians.

Bride (feminine) – Not a woman on her wedding day, but the willful mind of man that is dominated by ego, the one that submits to the groom, for the union of the two becoming the One.

Caduceus – A short staff entwined by two serpents, sometimes surmounted by wings. In the U.S., used as a symbol of healthcare organizations and medical practices. Likened to the Nehustan, a bronze serpent on a pole which God told Moses to erect in order to protect the Israelites who saw it from dying from the bites of the fiery serpents which God had sent to punish them for speaking against Him and Moses. The serpent on the pole in this book refers to the ladder of consciousness and the code within our DNA that will be activated by vibration as humanity evolves out from lower densities and ascends.

Cautes and Cautopates - Torchbearers depicted as attending the god Mithras; they hold their torches pointed up and down, respectively, to symbolize sunrise and sunset.

Chakras - The seven main chakras are the main energy centers of the body. When all of our chakras are open, energy can run through them freely, and harmony exists between the physical body, mind, and spirit. Chakra translates to "wheel" in Sanskrit. Chakras run from the base of the spine up to the top of the head and include the Root, Sacral, Solar Plexus, Heart, Throat, Third Eye, and Crown, and are associated with the colors red, orange, yellow, green, light blue/turquoise, dark blue/purple, and violet/white, respectively.

Christ – From the Greek meaning "anointed one". In this book the author explains that Christ is not external, but with, and is the union of God and man within our body/being/consciousness.

Cognitive Dissonance – the state of having inconsistent thoughts, beliefs, or attitudes, especially as relating to behavioral decisions and attitude change.

Council of Nicaea - In 325 A.D., the Roman emperor, Constantine, called a council in the city of Nicaea (modern Iznik, Turkey). The council brought together bishops from all over Christendom in order to resolve some divisive issues and ensure the continued unity of the church.

Divinity – In the Bible, considered the Godhead itself, or God in general. Now, the study of religion and theology, or the state or quality of being divine. The author explains how Divinity is an unexpressed consciousness in materiality (sheer energy) that needed a vessel (us) to occupy space within the material world.

Dogmatism - the tendency to lay down principles as incontrovertibly true, without consideration of evidence or the opinions of others.

Ecclesia (or **Ekklesia**) - In Christian theology means both "a particular body of faithful people" and "the whole body of the faithful."

Ego – Defined as a person's sense of self-esteem or self-importance. In this book the author relates ego to the human brain, the serpent, and intellect.

Elohim - The God of Israel in the Old Testament; A plural of majesty, the term Elohim – though sometimes used for other deities, such as the Moabite god Chemosh, the Sidonian goddess Astarte, and also for other majestic beings such as angels, kings, judges (the Old Testament SHOFEṬIM), and the Messiah – is usually employed in the Old Testament for the one and only God of Israel, whose personal name was revealed to **Moses** as YHWH, or Yahweh.

Emmanuel – (also Immanuel) A Hebrew name in the Book of Isaiah that appears as a sign that "God is with us".

Ephod – Vest worn by priests in the Old Testament that had 12 stones which would light up in response to questions asked by the priests.

Garden of Gethsemane – Garden at the foot of the Mount of Olives in Jerusalem where, according to the four Gospels of the New Testament, Jesus underwent the agony in the garden and was arrested the night before his crucifixion.

God-man – In Christian theology, the union of Christ's humanity and divinity.

Golden, Silver, Bronze, Iron Ages – The four ages of man in a mythological story by Ovid about the creation of the world. In the Golden age, people lived in peace and harmony. In the Silver age, Zeus broke the eternal spring into spring, summer and winter. In the Bronze age, people became warlike and inclined to arms. In the last, Iron age, all things went wrong, great evil prevailed, and people became corrupt and selfish.

Groom (masculine) – Not a man on his wedding day, but Spirit, or Divinity; the seed or idea.

Kryon - A being from "beyond the veil" that author Lee Carroll claims to have channeled and whose communications have been chronicled in 13 of Carroll's books since 1989. Kryon is presented as an entity from the "magnetic service" who is responsible for reconstruction of the magnetic grid of the Earth.

Kundalini – A type of yoga where the techniques of **breath exercises, visualizations, mudras, bandhas, kriyas and mantras are** focused on manipulating the flow of subtle energy through chakras.

Lightworker - Spiritual being in human existence sent to Earth to heal.

Melchizedek (or Melchizedek priest) – Melchizedek (meaning "king of righteousness") was the king of Salem and priest mentioned in the 14th chapter of the Book of Genesis who brings out bread and wine and blesses Abram and El Elyon. In Catholicism, it is priests that offer the same sacrifice of bread and wine daily at mass. Latter Day Saints consider Melchizedek priesthood as the authority of the 12 Apostles and Old Testament prophets, higher than that of the Aaronic authority of John the Baptist and the Levites.

Merkabah (Merkavah) – Compares to the chariot of light that Ezekiel was carried away in. A fully functioning light body (Merkabah) which enabled Jesus and other masters to move from place to place, inter-dimensionally.

Mithraism - Also known as the Mithraic mysteries, was a Roman mystery religion centered on the god Mithras; Predating Roman times, it was the worship of Mithra, the Iranian god of the sun, justice, contract, and war in pre-Zoroastrian Iran.

Ouroboros - The ouroboros is an ancient symbol depicting a serpent or dragon eating its own tail. Originating in Ancient Egyptian iconography, the ouroboros entered western tradition via Greek magical tradition and was adopted as a symbol in Gnosticism and Hermeticism, and most notably in alchemy. Via medieval alchemical tradition, often taken to symbolize introspection, the eternal return or cyclicality, especially in the sense of something constantly re-creating itself. It also represents the infinite cycle of nature's endless creation and destruction, life and death.

Oxbow lake - The bow-shaped pool formed when a river overflows its bank in times of flooding. When the river recedes, the lake remains. However, cut-off from the perpetual flow of life, the waters turn putrid.

Precession of the Equinox – The gradual shift in the orientation of the Earth's axis of rotation where the earth's equinoxes move westward along the ecliptic relative to the fixed stars, opposite to the motion of the Sun along the ecliptic, discovered by Hipparchus in the 100s BC. A cycle of approximately 26,000 years called the Great Year in astrology.

Selah – A Hebrew word used as an interjection in the Bible and found at the ending of verses in Psalms, interpreted as an instruction calling for a break in the singing. It may mean "forever" or "to praise" or "pause and reflect upon what has just been said."

Sheol – In the Hebrew Bible, a place of darkness to which spirits of the dead (the unrighteous) go, based on moral choices made in life. A place of stillness and darkness cut off from life and separated from God.

Space-time continuum - Einstein's theory of special relativity created a fundamental link between space and time. The universe can be viewed as having three "space" dimensions – up/down, left/right, forward/backward – and one "time" dimension. This 4-dimensional space is referred to as the space-time continuum.

Tithe – Generally defined as "one-tenth of annual produce or earnings, formerly taken as a tax for the support of the church and clergy" or "the act of paying or giving as a tithe." The author explains how the tithe is the 10% of the Earth's population that has a greater frequency/sound vibration and has the call to bridge the gap between dimensional boundaries.

Tree of the Knowledge of Good and Evil – One of two specific trees in the story of the Garden of Eden in Genesis 2-3, along with the tree of life. The eating of its fruit represents the beginning of the mixture of good and evil together.

Vesica Pisces – Symbol originally the intersection of two circles, believed by the Pythagoreans to be the first manifestation that gave birth to the entire universe. Later, Christians used it to, in part symbolize the womb of Mary and the coming together of heaven and earth in the body of Jesus (part man, part god) and as a portal between worlds. The symbol is now commonly known as the "Jesus fish".

Yuga – In Hinduism, an epoch or era within a cyclical 4-age life cycle, including Satya, Treta, Dvapara and Kali. The ages are considered to have different stages of evolving and devolving (ascending and descending). The entire cycle takes 24,000 years.

About the Author

I live in College Station, Texas, home of Texas A&M University, with my husband, Lyle. We have been married since 1977, and I am a mother of three sons and grandmother to seven. I have always been a spiritual seeker, and I am a teacher of spiritual mysteries, author and ordained minister. My passion is writing, and for those interested my first book, it is titled, *"Escaping Christianity ~ Finding Christ"* and is available on Amazon and Barnes and Noble online.

Writing is like therapy – I am most comfortable when I can express what it is that percolates within. I love to question doctrines and dogma; especially within the Christian church, because that is my *tribe*. For too long, we have accepted other people's opinions and understandings of spiritual things as fact. My over-arching message is to encourage people to think through things that induce fear and separation, for this was not the message of Christ.

Let's connect!

Barbara

Email: **Barbara@barbarasymons.com**

Facebook: https://www.facebook.com/barbara.symons.3

IG: **https://www.instagram.com/barbarasymons/**

CPSIA information can be obtained
at www.ICGtesting.com
Printed in the USA
LVHW060619030423
743297LV00005B/119

9 780578 664316